# The Gospel of Mark as Model for Action

*A Reader-Response Commentary*

John Paul Heil

PAULIST PRESS
New York/Mahwah, N.J.

Library of Congress Cataloging-in-Publication Data

Heil, John Paul.
    The Gospel of Mark as a model for action: a reader-response commentary/John Paul Heil.
        p.  cm.
    Includes bibliographical references and index.
    ISBN 0-8091-3148-X (pbk.)
    1. Bible.  N. T. Mark—Commentaries.  I. Title.
BS2585.3.H36   1992
226.3'077—dc20                                                              92-17159
                                                                             CIP

Published by Paulist Press
997 Macarthur Boulevard
Mahwah, N.J. 07430

Printed and bound in the United States of America

# Contents

## Chapter VII: Mark 11:1–13:37: On His Way Jesus Brings Forth New Teachings in and about the Temple of Jerusalem ........... 221

## Chapter VIII: Mark 14:1–15:47: Jesus Accomplishes the Way of Suffering and Death .......................................... 273

# Abbreviations

| | |
|---|---|
| AB | Anchor Bible |
| AnBib | Analecta biblica |
| *AusBR* | *Australian Biblical Review* |
| BAGD | W. Bauer, W. F. Arndt, F. W. Gingrich, and F. W. Danker, *Greek-English Lexicon of the NT* |
| *BARev* | *Biblical Archaeology Review* |
| *Bib* | *Biblica* |
| *BN* | *Biblische Notizen* |
| *BT* | *The Bible Translator* |
| *BTB* | *Biblical Theology Bulletin* |
| BWANT | Beiträge zur Wissenschaft vom Alten und Neuen Testament |
| *BZ* | *Biblische Zeitschrift* |
| *CBQ* | *Catholic Biblical Quarterly* |
| ConBNT | Coniectanea biblica, New Testament |
| EKKNT | Evangelisch-katholischer Kommentar zum Neuen Testament |
| *EvT* | *Evangelische Theologie* |
| *ExpTim* | *Expository Times* |
| GNS | Good News Studies |
| *Greg* | *Gregorianum* |
| HNT | Handbuch zum Neuen Testament |
| HTKNT | Herders theologischer Kommentar zum Neuen Testament |
| *HTR* | *Harvard Theological Review* |
| *IBS* | *Irish Biblical Studies* |

| | |
|---|---|
| *IDBSup* | Supplementary volume to *Interpreter's Dictionary of the Bible* |
| *Int* | *Interpretation* |
| *JAAR* | *Journal of the American Academy of Religion* |
| *JBL* | *Journal of Biblical Literature* |
| *JETS* | *Journal of the Evangelical Theological Society* |
| *JR* | *Journal of Religion* |
| *JSNT* | *Journal for the Study of the New Testament* |
| JSNTSup | Journal for the Study of the New Testament—Supplement Series |
| *JTS* | *Journal of Theological Studies* |
| *LB* | *Linguistica biblica* |
| *Neot* | *Neotestamentica* |
| NICNT | New International Commentary on the New Testament |
| *NovT* | *Novum Testamentum* |
| NovTSup | Novum Testamentum, Supplements |
| *NRT* | *La nouvelle revue théologique* |
| *NTS* | *New Testament Studies* |
| QD | Quaestiones disputatae |
| *RB* | Revue biblique |
| *RevExp* | *Review and Expositor* |
| *RevThom* | *Revue thomiste* |
| *RivB* | *Rivista biblica* |
| RNT | Regensburger Neues Testament |
| SBLASP | Society of Biblical Literature Abstracts and Seminar Papers |
| SBLDS | Society of Biblical Literature Dissertation Series |
| SBT | Studies in Biblical Theology |
| *ScEs* | *Science et esprit* |
| *SJT* | *Scottish Journal of Theology* |
| SNTSMS | Society for New Testament Studies Monograph Series |
| Str-B | H. Strack and P. Billerbeck, *Kommentar zum Neuen Testament* |
| SUNT | Studien zur Umwelt des Neuen Testaments |
| *TBei* | *Theologische Beiträge* |

| | |
|---|---|
| *TDNT* | *Theological Dictionary of the New Testament* |
| *TGl* | *Theologie und Glaube* |
| *TTZ* | *Trierer theologische Zeitschrift* |
| *TZ* | *Theologische Zeitschrift* |
| WUNT | Wissenschaftliche Untersuchungen zum Neuen Testament |
| *ZKT* | *Zeitschrift für katholische Theologie* |
| *ZNW* | *Zeitschrift für die neutestamentliche Wissenschaft* |

# I

---

# Introduction

## A. The Gospel of Mark as a Model for Action

The special focus of this commentary will be upon each scene and thus ultimately upon the whole gospel of Mark as a practical "model for action" for its Christian audience. In a sequential, scene-by-scene manner we shall present, explain and interpret Mark's vibrant story of Jesus with emphasis upon the response of the implied reader to each scene. By considering Mark's dramatic narrative as a dynamic process of communication between its author and audience, calling forth definite and active responses applicable to the life of that audience, we hope to illuminate its rich meaning and lasting pragmatic value for Christians of today.

## B. Implied Author and Implied Reader

Before we begin, we need to define some concepts important to our particular approach to Mark's narrative. In our investigation of the Gospel of Mark as a communication process we are concerned with the "implied author," the author discoverable in the text, as distinct from the real author, who, as an historical person (whoever the evangelist "Mark" may have been) has an identity beyond this particular text. The implied author is purely a textual concept, the image of the author as projected by the text. The implied author controls the communication and represents the strategy, values, concerns and objectives of the text. Although a distinction between "implied author" and "narrator," the one who tells the story, is often made, for our purposes the implied author can be considered equivalent to the narrator who tells the story. (In our commentary we will use the name "Mark" both to refer to the gospel itself and to this implied author or narrator of the gospel.)

As the counterpart to the "implied author," who stands at the "giv-

1

ing" end of the communication process, the "implied reader" stands at the "receiving" end of it. Not a real, historical reader, the implied reader is a theoretical construct that represents the responses the implied author intends or assumes on the part of his audience. The implied reader is the reader/hearer/audience that every text presupposes in order to be actualized as an act of communication; it is "the reader" anticipated and created by the text in the process of reading or listening to it.

Our reader-response approach will focus on the responses of this implied reader as determined by the various presuppositions, strategies and indicators within the text. We are concerned with what the text *does* to and how it *affects* its reader, that is, what actions the text calls forth, what mental moves, emotional feelings, anticipations, attitudes, persuasions, realizations, convictions, etc. the text causes its reader to experience in order to produce the meaning latent in the text and thus to bring its act of communication to completion. For Mark's gospel we can consider the implied reader as equivalent to the "narratee," the one to whom the narrator of the gospel tells the story.[1]

Although we employ the terms "implied *reader*" and "*reader-response*," we should not assume that the Gospel of Mark was intended to be read by an individual reader privately and in silence. Scholars have pointed out the importance of keeping in mind the public, rhetorical and oral/aural medium of the gospels, which were meant to be read aloud to a listening audience.[2] But because it has become a generally accepted convention, we will continue to use the term "reader" as synonymous and along with the technically more exact terms of "hearer," "listener" and "audience."

## C. Syntactic, Semantic and Pragmatic Dimensions of the Text

In accord with our method we may distinguish three dimensions for each passage of Mark's gospel. First, the "syntactic" dimension concerns the formal structure of the elements composing the passage, where the unit begins and ends, and how it fits into the context of the narrative. Second, the "semantic" dimension involves what the textual unit actually says or means as determined by analyzing its vocabulary, grammar, rhetoric, context, literary genre, historical-cultural background, narrative function, etc. Third, the "pragmatic" dimension deals with what the passage does to and how it affects its audience, what it calls forth from its reader, what it is intended to accomplish as a process of communication. The individual scenes or units of Mark's gospel narrative can thus be considered "models for action" by their Christian audience. By assuming the posture of the implied reader and making the responses called for by the text, we can experience the vital and enduring value of Mark's powerful story of Jesus for our lives and the lives of all Christians and peoples of the world.

## D. General Presuppositions of Mark's Implied Reader

The communication process operative in Mark's gospel takes place within a distinct historical-cultural context. In order to hear and respond properly to Mark's narrative, we need to consider the general presuppositions shared by the implied author and audience of this gospel. What does the narrator of Mark assume his implied reader already knows as he listens to his story of Jesus?

### 1. THE STORY OF JESUS AND THE STORY OF ISRAEL

A cursory reading of the gospel reveals that Mark presumes his audience is already at least somewhat familiar not only with the basic story of Jesus but also with the story of God's dealings with the people of Israel as recounted in the Jewish scriptures. Mark tells the story of Jesus against the background of and as a continuation of the story of the people of Israel.

Mark's opening verse, "the beginning of the gospel of Jesus Christ, Son of God," indicates the confessional stance or point of view from which his narrative will be told. The author believes and is presenting the "gospel" or "good news" about a certain "Jesus" believed to be the Jewish "Messiah" or "Christ" ("Anointed One") as well as "Son of God." He thus presumes that his audience shares this belief or is at least open to sharing it.

And already in his opening scene Mark begins to tell his story as a correspondence to and fulfillment of a combination of scriptural quotations (Exod 23:20, Mal 3:1 and Isa 40:3 in Mark 1:2–3) relating his story to the story of Israel. The author thus presumes his audience knows about and accepts the authority of the Jewish scriptures.

### 2. SITUATION OF THE IMPLIED READER/AUDIENCE

For the readers or audience, who already possess a fundamental knowledge of the story, the resurrection of Jesus is a past event. The audience, then, is situated between the resurrection and the "parousia" or second coming of Jesus (see Mark 13:24–27). More specifically, while the story of Jesus took place historically within the opening decades of the first century C.E., it is narrated to an implied reader located in the second half of the first century. Many scholars place the writing of Mark in 66–70, some even more precisely in 68–69.[3]

As Mark's story of Jesus is set in Roman dominated Palestine, primarily in the region and environs of Galilee and in Jerusalem and its vicinity, it presupposes that its implied reader has some knowledge of the geography of these areas.[4] But various geographical settings have been proposed for the situation of the intended audience or community of the gospel—Galilee, Syria, Rome.[5] While a Roman setting may be quite possible and even probable, the message of the gospel is general and relevant enough, and its presuppositions basic enough, that it could easily be understood by any Jew and by any Gentile interested, sympathetic and somewhat knowledgeable about Judaism in the first-century Mediterranean regions.

### 3. FIRST-CENTURY JUDAISM

Mark presupposes an implied audience generally familiar with the following:

### a. Institutions

#### 1) Jewish Scriptures

It would be difficult to overstate the extent to which the Jewish scriptures permeate the story of Jesus. First-century Jews lived their lives and understood themselves and their world in terms of their scriptures. As Jews the first Christians used their scriptures to present, interpret and understand the events of the life of Jesus. Mark narrates the story of Jesus not only against the background and within the framework of the Jewish scriptures but with constant reference to them, either explicit or implicit.

For Mark and his first-century audience the scriptures contained the authoritative word or revelation of God. The scriptures and their interpretation provided Jews with directives on how to conduct their everyday lives in accord with God's will as part of the Covenant God had established with his people Israel (*halakah*). For Christians the person and teaching of Jesus brings a new understanding to this dimension of the scriptures.

In addition, the Hebrew scriptures possessed a prophetic or future-oriented character for first-century Jews. While narrating how God's saving will and promises have been accomplished throughout the history of Israel (*haggadah*), the scriptures indicate how God's saving plan, program and promises will come to their prophetic and definitive fulfillment in the future. For Mark and his readers the story of Jesus illustrates how God's plan for salvation has begun to reach its prophetic and final fulfillment in accord with the Jewish scriptures.

## 2) Synagogue

The scrolls of the scriptures were kept in synagogues, the local community centers for teaching and study of the scriptures, for prayer and worship in accord with the scriptures, as well as for other communal affairs and business. Every Jewish town and village had a synagogue. In Mark's gospel much of Jesus' teaching and healing ministry takes place in the various synagogues throughout Galilee (Mark 1:21, 23, 39; 3:1; 6:2).

As the center for scriptural learning and study the institution of the synagogue surely played a major role in the formation of the Jesus traditions and stories. And the various synagogues located not only in Palestine but in the Diaspora of Jews throughout the Mediterranean regions provided an avenue for disseminating knowledge of the scriptures to Gentiles.[6] Not only were Jews concerned with gaining proselytes to Judaism, but there were many Gentiles (the so-called "God-fearers") who were sympathetic toward Judaism and attended the synagogue without actually converting to Judaism.[7] This would account for a basic knowledge and familiarity of the Jewish scriptures among the Gentiles of Mark's audience.

## 3) Sabbath

Closely connected with the synagogue is the joyous celebration of the sabbath, the seventh day of the week. For Jews the sabbath represented sacred time dedicated to God and sharply distinguished from the profane time of the other days of the week. On the sabbath Jews not only refrained from working but participated in a worship ceremony in the synagogue, which consisted of prayers, blessings, scriptural readings and homily.

As one of the elements of the Covenant between God and Israel (Exod 23:12; 34:21), Jews observed the sabbath rest as a commemoration of God's resting after creation (Exod 20:8–11) and of their liberation from Egypt in the Exodus event (Deut 5:15). The holy, joyful and peaceful time of the sabbath rest provided Jews with an anticipation or foretaste of the final rest toward which God had ordered and oriented all of creation (Gen 2:1–3). In Mark Jesus not only teaches and heals on the sabbath but makes authoritative pronouncements about the meaning of the sabbath and his relationship to it (Mark 1:21–28; 2:23–3:6; 6:2).

## 4) Temple

While the synagogue served as the central religious institution for local Jewish communities, the temple functioned as the central and most sacred institution for all Jews. The temple, located in the capital city of Jerusalem, represented God's special election of Jerusalem to be the sacred place of his earthly dwelling among human beings in correspondence to his heavenly dwelling. As the house of God's presence the temple provided the destination and setting for the three annual pilgrimage feasts of the Passover, Pentecost and Tabernacles. The temple was the place where Jews and non-Jews went to pray, worship, listen to teachings and above all to offer sacrifices to God.

Every day in the temple priests offered official animal sacrifices on behalf of the people. In addition, private sacrifices were offered continually on behalf of individuals. Once a year, on the Day of Atonement (*yom kippur*), the high priest entered the Holy of Holies, the special place of divine presence, within the central sanctuary of the temple and performed a sacrifice and ritual for the expiation of the sins of all the people.

In Mark the temple complex as a whole (*hieron*), with all of its precincts and courtyards, plays a role distinct from that of the central and sacred sanctuary (*naos*) within the temple. Jesus manifests his unique authority over the temple complex (*hieron*) by expelling those buying and selling animals for sacrifice (11:15–19), by conducting new and controversial teachings in the temple (11:27–12:44), and by foretelling its ultimate destruction (13:2). Mark refers to the main sanctuary (*naos*) of the temple, on the other hand, only in relation to the passion and death of Jesus. After Jesus is accused (14:58) and taunted (15:29) for intending to destroy the temple sanctuary, at the moment of his death the curtain of this sanctuary is torn in two from top to bottom (15:38).[8]

## 5) Jewish Feasts

Of the various annual feasts (Passover, Pentecost, Tabernacles, Hanukkah, Purim, New Year, Yom Kippur) the pilgrimage feast of the Passover was the most important and the only one mentioned in Mark. In the spring the feast of Passover (*pesach*) or Unleavened Bread (*matzot*) was celebrated by every family or group of pilgrims in a specially prepared room cleansed of anything leavened. It began with the celebration of the Passover meal in which the Passover lamb which was previously slaughtered in the temple was eaten in a ritual commemorating the first Passover and God's salvation of Israel in the Exodus from Egypt (Exod 12). This was followed by the week-long celebration of Unleavened Bread, commemorating the urgent and hasty exit of Israel from Egypt when they could take only unleavened bread. Through this commemoration Jews believed that the original Exodus events were actually made present again for them, so that they relived and participated in these saving deeds of God in a sacramental way, with the hope of participating in the final establishment of God's salvation.

Although the Passover centered on the Exodus, it also celebrated God's other great saving interventions on behalf of his people, such as creation and the sacrifice of Isaac. Passover night was a kind of anniversary of the Covenant, which God had announced beforehand to Abraham in a preparatory night scene (Gen 15). The Passover possessed an eschatological and messianic character, anticipating the coming of the messiah and expectantly looking forward to God's final and definitive salvation. There were Jewish beliefs that the messiah would come during the Passover feast. In Mark the passion and death of Jesus (14:1–2) as well as his final meal with his disciples occur within the context of this Jewish feast of Passover (14:12–26).

## 6) Religious Practices

Several Jewish religious practices, such as prayer, fasting, ritual ablutions and table fellowship play a role in Mark. Jews valued prayer, both communal and personal, as a fundamental response to God's call, placing one in communion with God and in a disposition to do his will. In Mark Jesus himself prays (1:35; 6:46; 14:32–42) and exhorts and teaches his disciples about prayer (9:29; 11:24–25; 13:18; 14:38).

Fasting was an ascetical practice which often accompanied and enhanced prayer. In Mark Jesus suspended this practice for his disciples while he was with them, but indicated the return of fasting after his departure (2:18–20).

Meals, which included prayers of blessing and thanksgiving (6:41; 8:6–8; 14:22–23), had a distinct religious character for Jews. Before eating Jews ritually washed their hands and utensils (7:3–4) to avoid religious defilement before God. After his disciples are reproached for not washing their hands, Jesus brings forth a new teaching on the essence of defilement (7:1–23). And as the sharing of food involved a religious bond or fellowship among the participants, Jesus shocked some Jews by eating with toll collectors and public sinners (2:15–17).

## b. Social Groups

### 1) Scribes

As professional scholars the scribes were trained in the preservation, knowledge and interpretation of the Jewish scriptures and traditions. This learning gave scribes the duty and authority of guiding the people's everyday lives in accord with God's will. Entrusted with such an important task, scribes were highly esteemed by their fellow Jews. As masters and teachers of "Torah," God's revealed Law, they were greeted with respect, wore long robes of distinction, and sat in places of honor (12:38–39).

Scribes came from every walk of life and could belong to other groups, as indicated by Mark 2:16, which refers to "scribes of the Pharisees." With one exception (12:28–34) the scribes, together with the Pharisees, chief priests and/or the elders, function as enemies of Jesus. From the beginning of Mark the authority of the scribes' teaching is contrasted with that of Jesus (1:22), and their staunch opposition to Jesus continues throughout the entire story.[9]

### 2) Pharisees

A religiously elite and primarily lay rather than priestly group, the Pharisees carefully separated themselves from those not as zealously intent upon observing the commandments and traditions of God's Law as they were. The Pharisees were prominent and reputable among the people for their progressive religious dedication. They were proponents not only of the written Torah but of the oral traditions of the elders, and believed in the resurrection of the dead. By their strict religious observances the Pharisees oriented their lives to the coming messianic age, expecting a triumphant Davidic messiah who would gather together the scattered people of Israel, establish God's kingdom and take over political rule.

In a recent study of the social and political roles of Pharisees in Galilee, A. J. Saldarini states:

> Though some Pharisees were part of the governing class, most Pharisees were subordinate officials, bureaucrats, judges, and educators. They are best understood as retainers who were literate servants of the governing class, had a program for Jewish society, and had acquired influence with the people and their patrons. The Pharisees must have worked for either the Temple leadership in so far as it was represented in Galilee, Herod Antipas' government, or landowners.[10]

In Mark the Pharisees function as a significant part of the opposition to Jesus by Jewish authorities. They enter into conflict with him on the issues of proper table fellowship (2:15–17), fasting (2:18–20), sabbath observance (2:23–3:6), ritual ablutions (7:1–23), seeking a sign from heaven (8:11–13), divorce (10:1–11) and paying taxes to Caesar (12:13–17).

### 3) Sadducees

In contrast to the Pharisees the Sadducees were a primarily priestly, aristocratic and conservative party, who accommodated themselves to existing political realities, refused to place oral traditions on the same level as the written Law and did not believe in the resurrection of the dead. In Mark the Sadducees appear in only one scene, when they question Jesus about the resurrection of the dead (12:18–27).[11]

### 4) Herodians

An apparently political rather than religious group, the Herodians presumably were those who supported the rule and policies of Herod Antipas, the ruler of Galilee and one of the sons of Herod the Great. In Mark the Herodians appear only twice: They join the Pharisees both in deliberating how to destroy Jesus (3:6) and in trying to trap Jesus with the question of paying taxes to Caesar (12:13).[12]

### 5) Elders

The elders were probably senior members of prominent families who exercised leadership in the Jewish community.[13] In Mark the elders join the scribes and the chief priests in their rejection and deadly opposition to Jesus (8:31; 11:27; 14:43, 53; 15:1).[14]

### 6) Priests/Chief Priests

Being a member of the prestigious and elite class of priests depended upon one's authentic priestly ancestry. Priests were in charge of temple worship: They performed the various sacrifices, gave blessings, carried out purification rites and officiated questions of ritual purity (e.g. Mark 1:44), administered the collection of tithes and other obligatory temple donations, maintained and policed the temple complex.

Often grouped together with the elders and/or the scribes as principal adversaries to Jesus among the Jewish authorities, the chief priests play a decisive role in Mark, in having Jesus put to death. They are the ones to whom Judas offers to betray Jesus (14:10). They accuse Jesus of many things in his trial before Pilate (15:3). The chief priests are the ones who incite the crowd to demand that Pilate release the imprisoned murderer Barabbas instead of Jesus (15:11) and later they mock him as he dies on the cross (15:31).

### 7) High Priest

It was the privilege and duty of the high priest, the leader of the priests and highest ranking Jew, to enter into the Holy of Holies within the temple sanctuary and perform the sacrifice and ritual of expiation for the sins of himself and all the people on the Day of Atonement. The high priest also functioned as head of the Sanhedrin, the highest judicial council of Jewish authorities. In Mark after the high priest questions Jesus on his claim to be the messiah, he tears his garments and judges the answer of Jesus to be blasphemy, which leads to his condemnation to death (14:53–64).

### 8) Roman Officials

During the ministry of Jesus, Tiberius was the Roman Emperor or "Caesar," Herod Antipas was tetrarch of Galilee and Perea, and Pontius Pilate was the Roman governor of Judea. In Mark the Roman Emperor is mentioned only in the controversy about paying taxes to Caesar (12:13–17). Herod Antipas has John the Baptist beheaded after John rebuked Herod for marrying Herodias, the wife of Herod's brother, Philip (6:14–29); and later Jesus warns his disciples about the "leaven" of the Pharisees and Herod (8:15). After asking Jesus whether he is "King of the Jews" and finding nothing evil done by him, Pilate is nevertheless swayed by the crowd (stirred up by the chief priests) to deliver Jesus to death (15:1–15). Later Pilate grants the dead body of Jesus to Joseph of Arimathea for burial (15:42–46).

After mocking and ridiculing Jesus as "King of the Jews," Roman soldiers carry out his crucifixion (15:16–27). One of them, however, the centurion, after witnessing the death of Jesus, declares him to be truly "Son of God" (15:37–39).

### 9) Toll Collectors and Public Sinners

Toll collectors were those Jews who collected indirect taxes (such as tolls, tariffs, customs) from their fellow Jews on behalf of the Roman occupation. Considered unclean by association with Gentiles, they were despised and rejected by Law-observant Jews, mainly because they used their position for unjust personal gain through fraudulent, dishonest and corrupt tactics. Public sinners included Gentiles, Jews whose occupations brought them into contact with Gentiles (such as toll collectors, prostitutes), and Jews who did not observe Mosaic Law. In Mark Jesus shocks the scribes of the Pharisees by engaging in table fellowship with both toll collectors and sinners (2:15–17).[15]

## 10) Disciples, the Twelve and Peter

In contrast to the scribal disciples, who underwent professional training by being admitted to a circle of students gathered around a prominent teacher, the disciples of Jesus left their occupations attracted by the authoritative call (1:16–20; 2:13–14) and impressively new teaching of Jesus, a teaching with a charismatic authority unlike that of the scribes (1:14–15; 1:21–28). In Mark Jesus calls to himself a special inner circle of disciples, the "Twelve," to be with him and to be sent out as his apostles to preach and exorcise demons (3:13–19; 6:7–13). This group of twelve disciples apparently symbolizes the restoration of the people of Israel, traditionally composed of twelve tribes.

In contrast to the many crowds who follow Jesus, his disciples, especially members of the Twelve, are privileged to receive private and exclusive teachings and revelations of the more profound and secret character of the person and ministry of Jesus. Of the individual disciples Simon Peter plays the most prominent role as leader, spokesman and representative of the disciples.

## 11) Crowds

In addition to the disciples who follow him and the various opposing groups who encounter him, a large crowd drawn from near and far continually surrounds Jesus during his ministry in Mark. This mass of people is attracted from all around Palestine and the Gentile territories beyond—from Galilee, Judea, Jerusalem, Idumea, beyond the Jordan (Perea), and from about Tyre and Sidon (3:7–8). They come to hear Jesus' teaching and to receive his healings and exorcisms (1:32–34; 3:9–10; 6:54–56). They are twice miraculously and overabundantly fed by Jesus (6:30–44; 8:1–10). Although the crowd is favorably disposed toward Jesus throughout his ministry, they are turned against him during his trial. At the instigation of the chief priests they insistently demand that Pilate hand Jesus over to be crucified (15:6–15).

## 12) Women and Children

In first-century Judaism women generally held a sociological status subordinate to that of men. There were, for example, separate places for women in the temple and synagogues. Many of the religious laws, socio-economic customs and practices clearly gave greater prerogatives, authority and responsibility to men.[16] Against this background it is noteworthy that women play a rather significant and exemplary role in Mark: Healed by Jesus, Simon's mother-in-law serves him and the disciples (1:29–31). The hemorrhaging woman (5:24–34) and the Syrophoenician woman (7:24–30) display extraordinary faith in the healing power of Jesus. The poor widow who gives her whole living to the temple treasury (12:41–44) and the woman who anoints Jesus (14:3–9) are held up as praiseworthy figures by Jesus. Although male disciples abandon Jesus when he is arrested (14:50–52), women disciples witness his death and burial (15:40–41, 47) and receive the message of his resurrection (16:1–8).[17]

Although children were highly valued, they had a low sociological status. Dependent and defenseless, children possessed no rights and were not considered full persons. In Mark several children receive healing from Jesus (5:21–43; 7:24–30; 9:14–29). And Jesus surprisingly points to the lowliness and humility of children as qualities necessary for discipleship and entrance into the kingdom of God (9:36–37; 10:13–16).

### 4. APOCALYPTIC-ESCHATOLOGICAL WORLDVIEW

The implied audience and author of Mark's gospel share in a general apocalyptic-eschatological way of thinking and worldview. Familiarity with the basic structure and concepts of Jewish apocalyptic-eschatology is essential for a proper understanding of the overall tone and character of the narrative. We will now consider those elements of first-century apocalyptic-eschatology most relevant for reading Mark.

### a. General Description of Apocalyptic-Eschatology

That the thought world of first-century Judaism and Mark's gospel is "eschatological" means that it involves an intense longing and urgent expectation for the "end"-time or final-age fulfillment of God's promises of salvation for his people. That this eschatology is "apocalyptic" means that it involves the revelation of the long-hidden secrets and mysteries of God's plan for the salvation of his people and the world.

From the experience of extreme distress and oppression by enemies the apocalyptic-eschatological mentality anticipated a worsening of this situation until the present world is utterly destroyed through a cosmic catastrophe. Although pessimistic about the current direction of history and present state of affairs, apocalyptic-eschatology centered upon a trusting faith and confident hope that out of this cataclysmic disaster God would bring forth a new world and creation in which everything that had gone wrong and awry would be finally restored and rectified.

Essentially dualistic in structure, apocalyptic-eschatology involves profound contrasts between this present generation and age as opposed to the age-to-come, the earthly, historical realities as opposed to the heavenly, transcendent realities, the realm of evil versus the realm of good, Satan and his devils against God and his angels, God's wicked enemies versus his chosen, righteous people, etc.

### b. Kingdom of God

In Mark the long awaited eschatological age-to-come is expressed by terms such as "the kingdom of God" (1:15; 4:11, 26, 30; 9:1, 47; 10:14–15, 23–25; 12:34; 14:25; 15:43) and "eternal life" (10:17, 30). There is a sense in which the kingdom of God has finally arrived in and through the teaching, healing, suffering, death and resurrection of Jesus, and it includes the new community of his followers. Yet there is still a future dimension to this kingdom which will not reach its consummation until the return of Jesus at the end of time (13:24–27; 14:61–62). Nevertheless, the eschatological age has already begun and stands in contrast to "this generation" (8:12, 38; 9:19; 13:30) which opposes Jesus and refuses to believe in him.

### c. Sin/Sickness, Demons and Angels

In the apocalyptic-eschatological worldview a largely invisible, spiritual realm stands behind and impinges upon visible, physical reality. This spiritual realm includes a sharp dualism in which God and his angels do battle with Satan and his demons. Angels are heavenly beings who serve as God's messengers or agents appointed for various tasks (1:13; 8:38; 12:25; 13:27, 32). Demons and their leader Satan, often considered to be fallen or rebellious angels, instigate much of the evil in the world. Demons or "unclean spirits" not only tempt people to sin but also cause them to suffer sickness. Sin and sickness, then, were considered to have a common demonic origin (2:1–12).

Although Satan and his demons exercised considerable control over the universe and over human lives, God would ultimately defeat these powers of evil in the eschatological age. The miraculous healing and exorcistic ministry of Jesus represents this definitive breaking in of the kingdom of God in triumph over the kingdom of Satan. Whereas in his various healing miracles Jesus expels the demonic powers causing disease, in his exorcisms he casts out demons who have gained total control over people. In the healings and exorcisms of Jesus people of faith experience in a unique and personal way the salvation of the kingdom of God that has arrived with Jesus.[18]

### d. Revelation of God's Mystery and Secrets

One of the presuppositions of apocalyptic-eschatology is that God can and does intervene into the world, revealing previously hidden aspects of himself and his salvific plan. People look for various "signs" from heaven indicative of God's activity and the approaching end-time (8:11–12; 13:4). In Mark God acts in direct and explicit ways, as when his voice is heard at both the baptism (1:11) and transfiguration of Jesus (9:7), as well as in more implicit ways, such as when the curtain in the temple sanctuary is torn in two from top to bottom at the death of Jesus (15:38).

Jesus, however, functions as God's principal agent of revelation. In Mark Jesus begins his ministry by revealing the "gospel" or "good news" of God, namely, that the kingdom of God has finally arrived (1:14–15). Through his words and deeds Jesus continues to unravel and disclose the mystery of this kingdom. In his authoritative teaching Jesus reveals various dimensions of God's will and plan of salvation. By publicly teaching in parables, for example, he opens up secret aspects of the mystery of God's kingdom in enigmatic and intriguing metaphors. In his healing-exorcistic activity Jesus not only publicly manifests the coming of God's kingdom, but makes it a reality in people's lives. In addition, the disciples are privileged to witness the more private, astounding and profound secrets and insights revealing the mystery of the kingdom of God that has come in and through the person of Jesus.

### e. Eschatological and Messianic Figures

Jewish apocalyptic-eschatological expectations included a rich and varied complex of traditions about eschatological and messianic agents through whom God would establish a new and final era of salvation. The combination of these messianic traditions provides background for interpreting the person and ministry of Jesus. In new, unexpected and unique ways Jesus fulfills, transforms and surpasses many of these traditional messianic expectations.

### 1) Elijah

In the biblical tradition the prophet Elijah (1 Kgs 17–2 Kgs 2) was taken up to heaven without dying (2 Kgs 2:11). There were expectations that Elijah would return to earth as a forerunner to the eschatological age. He would bring about repentance and restore the scattered people of

Israel in preparation for the Day of the Lord (Mal 3:1, 23–24; Sir 48:10; Mark 9:11–12). Although in Mark some think that Jesus represents the returning Elijah (6:15; 8:28), it is actually John the Baptizer who plays the Elijah role (1:2, 6 [see 2 Kgs 1:8]; 9:13). The heavenly Elijah appears together with Moses in the scene of the transfiguration of Jesus (9:2–13). And a popular notion of Elijah as helper in time of need may lie behind the bystanders' misunderstanding of the loud cry of Jesus during his death (15:35–36).

### 2) Prophet

There were expectations of an eschatological prophet (Deut 18:15, 18) and common conceptions about the destiny of an unheeded prophet being that of a martyr's death. In Mark both John the Baptizer (11:32) and Jesus (6:4, 15; 8:28) are referred to as prophets and both suffer the fate of the unheeded prophet.

### 3) Messiah/Christ

The term "Christ," from the Greek *christos,* meaning "anointed one" and equivalent to the Hebrew *mashiach* (messiah), designated in a very general and undifferentiated way the expected final and definitive eschatological agent of God. At the time of Jesus the title "Christ" had no fixed meaning but embraced a variety of messianic expectations, such as that of a kingly, political, Davidic messiah, that of a priestly, Levitical messiah, that of a prophetic, "prophet like Moses" (Deut 18:15, 18) messiah, and others. Although there was ambiguity and fluidity in ideas about the messiah, most included the notion of an exclusively triumphant figure so that the conception of a suffering and dying Christ seems to be new and unique to Jesus.

In Mark the Christ title is combined with and thus modified by such traditional titles and conceptions as "Son of God" (1:1; 14:61), "Son of David" (12:35), "Lord" (12:36–37), "King of Israel" (15:32) and a suffering, dying, rising, exalted and returning "Son of Man" (8:29–31; 14:61–62). The Christ title was so closely linked to Jesus that it became part of or the equivalent to his name (1:1; 9:41). Jesus himself refers to expectations regarding the future coming of "the Christ" (13:21).

### 4) Son of David

Many Jews ardently looked forward to a political, national and earthly messiah descended from King David (2 Sam 7:12–16; Isa 9:1–6; 11:1–9; Jer 23:5–6; 30:9; 33:15, 17, 22; Ezek 34:23–24; 37:24–25; Amos

9:11; *Ps. Sol.* 17:21–25) who, by liberating and restoring them, would initiate the eschatological age of salvation. In Mark Jesus is associated with this expectation by the blind Bartimaeus who cries out to him as "Son of David" (10:47–48), begging for restored health. When Jesus enters Jerusalem on a colt, the Davidic hopes of the crowds are aroused as they exclaim, "Blessed is the kingdom of our father David that is coming!" (11:10). But Jesus relates the common idea that the Christ would be a Son of David to the fact that David himself calls him "my Lord" in Psalm 110:1. Jesus fulfills the longing for a Davidic messiah not as the normally expected political and earthly ruler, but as one who, by suffering, dying, and rising, becomes the heavenly and exalted "Lord" seated at God's right hand over his enemies (12:35–37).

## 5) King

Although very closely related and nearly equivalent to "Son of David," the more general designation "King" allows for other associations and connotations. Aware of earthly kings and having had their own human rulers, the people of Israel, nevertheless, always considered Yahweh as their supreme heavenly King with absolute dominion and sovereignty (e.g. Ps. 47; 96–99). In this vein Jesus announced the arrival of the "kingdom of God" in Mark, which, in accord with apocalyptic dualism, stands in opposition to the evil "kingdom" of Satan (3:23–24). Though not, strictly speaking, accurate, Mark refers to Herod Antipas, who had John the Baptizer put to death, as a "King" (6:14–29). In contrast to such political and mundane kings, Mark presents Jesus as the true messianic King of Israel. Rejected, ridiculed and cruelly mocked as "King of the Jews," Jesus, in ironical and paradoxical contradiction to usual expectations, becomes the enthroned messianic King of Israel precisely by dying on the cross (15:1–32).[19]

## 6) Son of God

As another term for the awaited messianic agent, "Son of God" denoted not physical descent from God but being appointed by God for a special role in his plan of salvation. Extremely rich and complex in its connotations, "Son of God" could designate angels (Gen 6:2, 4; Job 1:6; 2:1; 38:7), the Davidic King (2 Sam 7:14; Ps 2:7; 89:26–27), the people of Israel (Exod 4:22; Jer 3:19; 31:9, 20; Hos 11:1), the suffering righteous man (Wis 2:13, 18) and have other associations such as the Servant of God (Isa 42:1), etc. At the beginning of his gospel Mark refers to Jesus as "Son of God" (1:1). In the baptism (1:11) and transfiguration (9:7) scenes God himself from heaven calls Jesus "my beloved Son." The spiritual realm of demons addresses Jesus as the "Son of God" (3:11; 5:7). In the parable of the wicked tenants Jesus indirectly refers to himself as God's beloved but rejected Son (12:6). At his trial Jesus affirms the high priest's question of whether he is "the Christ, the Son of the Blessed?" (14:61–62). And after witnessing the death of Jesus on the cross, the Roman centurion climactically confesses that "truly this man was Son of God!" (15:39).

## 7) Son of Man

Based upon Daniel 7, the Parables of *1 Enoch,* and 4 Ezra, "Son of Man" designated a heavenly figure with divine honors and powers who functioned as the vindicating leader of God's people and the agent through whom God would establish his kingdom. The "Son of Man" represented a transcendent, apocalyptic messianic figure in contrast to the traditional Davidic, earthly and political messiah.[20]

Jesus used the concept of the Son of Man as a self-designation. Although Daniel's Son of Man is primarily an exalted being, Jesus' understanding of his mission, along with the Semitic view of the representative function of the leader, led him to combine in his person the traits of this exalted Son of Man with those of the suffering people of Israel whom the Son of Man represented, and thus to achieve the synthesis of a suffering and exalted Son of Man. In the teaching of Jesus this Son of Man and the kingdom of God form an indissoluble union. By suffering, dying and rising as Son of Man, Jesus brings about the kingdom and will return as future Judge and King.[21]

As "Son of Man" in Mark, Jesus has divine authority to forgive sins (2:10); is lord of the sabbath (2:28); in accord with God's plan of salvation must suffer, die and rise again (8:31; 9:9, 12, 31; 10:33–34, 45; 14:21, 41); and will return in glory and power at the end of time (8:38; 13:26; 14:62).

## 8) Suffering Servant and Suffering Just One

The figure of the redemptive suffering servant of God as described in the "servant songs" of Isaiah (42:1–4; 49:1–6; 50:4–9; 52:13–53:12) and the suffering righteous or just one who will be vindicated by God, as sketched in several of the Psalms and the book of Wisdom (2:12–20), provide another complex of ideas for interpreting the suffering and death of Jesus. In Mark Jesus' betrayal while eating by one of his own disciples resembles the fate of the faithful yet suffering just one of Psalm 41:9. Jesus' silence at the questions of the high priest (14:60–61) and Pilate (15:4–5) during his trial is reminiscent of the silence of the suffering servant in Isaiah 53:7. Likewise, Jesus' being given wine mixed with myrrh (15:23) and vinegar (15:36) while dying (Ps 69:21), the dividing of and casting lots for his garments (15:24 and Ps 22:18), the mocking and wagging of heads at him (15:29 and Ps 22:7), and the cry expressing his experience of God's abandonment (15:34 and Ps 22:2) portray the dying Jesus as the rejected but obediently suffering just one who will be vindicated for his faithfulness to God.

### f. Resurrection

Resurrection from the realm of the dead was generally considered a prerequisite for God's final judgment and salvation. Although much fluidity and variety of ideas with regard to resurrection flourished, including who exactly would be raised and how it would happen, it was commonly considered a corporate event in which God would raise all the people together at the end of time. Jesus' individual resurrection, by which he is not merely resuscitated or reanimated but transformed into God's heavenly, spiritual realm, thus signals the beginning of the expected end-time resurrection of the dead preliminary to the establishment of the kingdom of God. In Mark Jesus foretells his resurrection (8:31; 9:9, 31; 10:34), teaches about and gives evidence for belief in resurrection (12:18–27), and his resurrection is announced by God's heavenly messenger to the women at the empty tomb (16:1–8).

## E.  Structural Outline of the Gospel of Mark

Before commencing our reading of Mark, we want to provide a structural overview of the entire gospel. One of the major themes spanning Mark's gospel is that of the "Way" of the Lord God being actualized and executed by the "Way" of Jesus.[22] In fact, since this dominant theme provides the scheme and framework for the entire narrative, we have tried to illustrate this in the outline that follows.

# THE GOSPEL OF MARK

I. Mark 1:1–13: Preparation for the Way of the Lord To Be Accomplished by the Way of Jesus.
   A. 1:1–8: John's preaching prepares the Way of the Lord.
   B. 1:9–11: The Spirit descends upon Jesus and God declares him his Son after he is baptized by John.
   C. 1:12–13: Jesus is tested by Satan in the wilderness.
II. Mark 1:14–3:6: Jesus Goes His Way Demonstrating the Arrival of the Kingdom of God by Preaching and Healing, Yet Meets Death-Threatening Opposition.
   A. 1:14–15: Jesus comes to Galilee and preaches the gospel of God's kingdom, calling for conversion and faith.
   B. 1:16–20: Along the Sea of Galilee Jesus calls four fishermen to follow him.
   C. 1:21–28: After they enter Capernaum, Jesus teaches and expels unclean spirits in the synagogue.
   D. 1:29–31: Jesus enters Simon's house and heals his mother-in-law.
   E. 1:32–34: Jesus heals many people and expels many demons at the door of Simon's house.
   F. 1:35–39: After praying in the desert, Jesus goes throughout Galilee preaching and expelling demons.
   G. 1:40–45: Jesus heals a leper, retreats to the desert and attracts people from all around.
   H. 2:1–12: Returning to Capernaum, Jesus forgives and heals a paralytic, causing controversy among some scribes.
   I. 2:13–17: After Levi follows him, Jesus eats with toll collectors and sinners, bringing objections from the scribes.
   J. 2:18–22: With powerful pronouncements Jesus answers the question of why his disciples do not fast.
   K. 2:23–28: As the Pharisees object to his disciples plucking grain, Jesus reveals his lordship over the sabbath.
   L. 3:1–6: After Jesus heals on the sabbath, the Pharisees and Herodians plot to destroy him.
III. Mark 3:7–5:43: The Mystery of the Kingdom of God Is Given to the Followers of the Way of Jesus.
   A. 3:7–12: Jesus heals huge crowds and orders the demons not to make known that he is the Son of God.

B. 3:13–19: On a mountain Jesus selects twelve disciples to be with him and to preach and expel demons.

C. 3:20–30: Jesus addresses the charge that he expels demons by the power of Beelzebul.

D. 3:31–35: Jesus defines the circle of his followers who do the will of God as his true family.

E. 4:1–9: Jesus challenges the crowd with a parable about sowing seed.

F. 4:10–12: Jesus explains about speaking in parables.

G. 4:13–20: To his inner circle Jesus explains the parable about sowing seed.

H. 4:21–25: Jesus continues his teaching with parabolic pronouncements about the lamp and the measure.

I. 4:26–29: Jesus teaches about the kingdom of God through a parable about seed growing steadily until harvest.

J. 4:30–32: Jesus teaches about the kingdom of God through a parable about the amazing growth of a mustard seed.

K. 4:33–34: Jesus speaks in parables to the crowd, but explains everything to his own disciples.

L. 4:35–41: Jesus miraculously stills a storm at sea and rescues his disciples.

M. 5:1–20: Jesus expels an entire legion of demons.

N. 5:21–43: After healing a hemorrhaging woman, Jesus restores life to the daughter of Jairus.

IV. Mark 6:1–8:26: The Followers of the Way of Jesus Do Not Grasp the Mystery of His Person.

A. 6:1–6: Rejected by his home town, Jesus teaches in surrounding villages.

B. 6:7–13: Commissioned by Jesus, the Twelve go out preaching, expelling demons and healing.

C. 6:14–29: Having put John the Baptist to death, king Herod thinks that Jesus is John raised from the dead.

D. 6:30–44: Jesus miraculously provides an overabundant meal for five thousand.

E. 6:45–52: Jesus rescues his disciples by miraculously walking across the stormy sea.

F. 6:53–56: At Gennesaret Jesus is recognized and the sick who touch the fringe of his garment are healed.

G. 7:1–13: Jesus demonstrates that Pharisees and scribes annul God's word with their human traditions.

H. 7:14–23: To the crowd and his disciples Jesus reveals a new teaching about interior uncleanness.

I. 7:24–30: Jesus exorcises the daughter of a Greek Syrophoenician woman with cleverly strong faith.

J. 7:31–37: Jesus' healing of a deaf and mute man is proclaimed despite his command for silence.

K. 8:1–9: Jesus miraculously provides an overabundant meal for four thousand.

L. 8:10–12: Jesus refuses the Pharisees' request for a sign.

M. 8:13–21: Jesus interrogates his disciples about the overabundant feedings.

N. 8:22–26: At Bethsaida Jesus gradually heals a blind man.

V. Mark 8:27–10:52: The Way of Jesus Leads to Suffering, Death and Resurrection.

    A. 8:27–33: After Peter confesses Jesus as the Christ, Jesus teaches the necessity that he suffer, die and rise.

    B. 8:34–9:1: Jesus calls the crowd and his disciples to follow him by denying self and accepting the cross.

    C. 9:2–8: After Jesus is transfigured before three of his disciples, God enjoins them to listen to his Son.

    D. 9:9–13: Jesus teaches his disciples that Elijah has already come.

    E. 9:14–29: By prayer Jesus expels an unclean spirit from a boy whom the disciples could not cure.

    F. 9:30–32: Jesus teaches his disciples the necessity of his death and resurrection, but they do not understand.

    G. 9:33–50: Jesus teaches his disciples about service, acceptance, and respect for others.

    H. 10:1–12: Jesus teaches the crowds, Pharisees and disciples about divorce.

    I. 10:13–16: Jesus blesses children and teaches his disciples to be child-like to enter God's kingdom.

    J. 10:17–31: On his way Jesus teaches his disciples about the difficulty of giving up riches for God's kingdom.

    K. 10:32–34: On the way to Jerusalem Jesus tells the Twelve that he will suffer, die and rise.

    L. 10:35–45: Jesus teaches the disciples the need for humble service of others in imitation of himself.

    M. 10:46–52: Leaving Jericho Jesus heals the blind beggar Bartimaeus who then follows him on the way.

VI. Mark 11:1–13:37: On His Way Jesus Brings Forth New Teachings in and about the Temple of Jerusalem.

    A. 11:1–11: Jesus triumphantly enters Jerusalem and returns to Bethany with the Twelve.

B. 11:12–14: Coming from Bethany with his disciples Jesus curses a fig tree for not bearing fruit.
C. 11:15–19: After Jesus teaches that the temple is for all peoples, the Jewish leaders seek to destroy him.
D. 11:20–25: Passing by the withered fig tree, Jesus teaches his disciples about faith, prayer and forgiveness.
E. 11:27–33: The authority of Jesus in the temple is questioned by the chief priests, scribes and elders.
F. 12:1–12: Jesus' parable about wicked tenants causes the Jewish leaders trying to arrest him to leave.
G. 12:13–17: Jesus amazes the Pharisees and Herodians sent to trap him with the issue of paying taxes to Caesar.
H. 12:18–27: Jesus teaches the Sadducees that God will raise the dead to life.
I. 12:28–34: After Jesus answers a scribe's question about the greatest commandment, no one dares to question him.
J. 12:35–37: The great crowd gladly hears Jesus question the scribes' assertion that the Christ is the Son of David.
K. 12:38–40: Jesus warns against and denounces the hypocrisy of the scribes.
L. 12:41–44: To his disciples Jesus praises a poor widow's donation to the temple treasury.
M. 13:1–2: Leaving the temple Jesus foretells its destruction to one of his disciples.
N. 13:3–8: To four disciples on the Mount of Olives Jesus foretells events commencing the end of the age.
O. 13:9–13: Jesus warns about future persecution and the need for the gospel to be preached to all.
P. 13:14–23: Jesus prepares his disciples for the great tribulations prior to the end of the age.
Q. 13:24–27: Jesus describes the end and the coming of the Son of Man to gather his elect.
R. 13:28–31: Jesus teaches about the nearness of these events and the enduring value of his words.
S. 13:32–37: Since they do not know the time of the Son of Man's coming Jesus exhorts all to be watchful.
VII. Mark 14:1–15:47: Jesus Accomplishes the Way of Suffering and Death.
A. 14:1–2: Two days before Passover the chief priests and scribes seek to kill Jesus without a tumult.
B. 14:3–9: At Bethany a woman anoints Jesus for burial.
C. 14:10–11: Judas Iscariot, one of the Twelve, seeks to betray Jesus to the chief priests.

D. 14:12–16: The disciples prepare for Jesus to eat the Passover meal with them.

E. 14:17–21: While eating with the Twelve, Jesus foretells his betrayal by one of them.

F. 14:22–25: Jesus interprets the meal as symbolic of his death for all and as an anticipation of God's kingdom.

G. 14:26–31: Jesus predicts abandonment by his disciples and Peter's denial of him.

H. 14:32–42: Through prayer at Gethsemane Jesus accepts his death while the disciples are overcome with sleep.

I. 14:43–52: After Judas betrays him, Jesus is arrested and abandoned by his disciples.

J. 14:53–65: After Jesus admits his true identity, he is condemned to death.

K. 14:66–72: After Peter denies Jesus three times, he remembers Jesus' prediction and weeps.

L. 15:1–5: The Jewish leaders deliver Jesus to Pilate who asks about his kingship and wonders at his silence.

M. 15:6–15: Pilate releases Barabbas instead of Jesus whom he scourges and delivers to be crucified.

N. 15:16–20: After mocking Jesus as King of the Jews, the soldiers lead him out to crucify him.

O. 15:21–32: Jesus is crucified and mocked by passers-by, chief priests, scribes and those crucified with him.

P. 15:33–41: As Jesus dies, the centurion confesses him to be Son of God while women from Galilee look on.

Q. 15:42–47: Pilate grants Jesus' body to Joseph of Arimathea who buries it in a rock-hewn tomb.

VIII. Mark 16:1–8: The Resurrection of Jesus and the Way of the Lord.

A. 16:1–8: Upon hearing that Jesus is risen and is going to Galilee, the women flee from the tomb in fear.

IX. Appendix: Mark 16:9–20: The "Longer Ending" of Mark. (It represents early Christian tradition, but is not part of the original Gospel of Mark.)

A. 16:9–20: The risen Jesus commissions and empowers the Eleven disciples to preach the Gospel to all.

(The "Shorter Ending" of Mark: "But they reported briefly to Peter and those with him all that they had been told. And after this Jesus himself sent out by means of them, from east to west, the sacred and imperishable proclamation of eternal salvation.")

# Notes

1. For more discussion of the "implied author," "implied reader" and "reader-response" criticism, see B. C. Lategan, "Reference: Reception, Redescription and Reality," *Text and Reality: Aspects of Reference in Biblical Texts* (ed. B. C. Lategan and W. S. Vorster; Atlanta: Scholars, 1985) 70–71; T. J. Keegan, *Interpreting the Bible: A Popular Introduction to Biblical Hermeneutics* (New York/Mahwah: Paulist, 1985) 73–108; R. A. Culpepper, *Anatomy of the Fourth Gospel: A Study in Literary Design* (Philadelphia: Fortress, 1983) 205–11; J. L. Staley, *The Print's First Kiss: A Rhetorical Investigation of the Implied Reader in the Fourth Gospel* (SBLDS 82; Atlanta: Scholars, 1988) 21–49; J. L. Resseguie, "Reader-Response Criticism and the Synoptic Gospels," *JAAR* 52 (1984) 307–24; R. M. Fowler, "Who is 'the Reader' in Reader Response Criticism?," *Reader Response Approaches to Biblical and Secular Texts* (Semeia 31; ed. R. Detweiler; Decatur: Scholars, 1985, 5–23; E. V. McKnight, *Post-Modern Use of the Bible: The Emergence of Reader-Oriented Criticism* (Nashville: Abingdon, 1988).

2. See, for example, T. E. Boomershine, "Peter's Denial as Polemic or Confession: The Implications of Media Criticism for Biblical Hermeneutics," *Orality, Aurality and Biblical Narrative* (Semeia 39; ed. L. Silberman; Decatur: Scholars, 1987, 47–68; G. L. Bartholomew, "Feed My Lambs: John 21:15–19 as Oral Gospel," *Orality,* 69–96; J. Dewey, "Oral Methods of Structuring Narrative in Mark," *Int* 43 (1989) 32–44.

3. M. Hengel, *Studies in the Gospel of Mark* (Philadelphia: Fortress, 1985) 28–30; D. Senior, " 'With Swords and Clubs . . .'—The Setting of Mark's Community and His Critique of Abusive Power," *BTB* 17 (1987) 10–20.

4. For a full discussion of the role of Galilee in Mark, see S. Freyne, *Galilee, Jesus and the Gospels: Literary Approaches and Historical Investigations* (Philadelphia: Fortress, 1988) 33–68.

5. F. J. Matera, *What Are They Saying About Mark?* (Mahwah: Paulist, 1987) 7–17.

6. In recent years several ancient synagogues have been discovered and excavated both within Israel and the Diaspora. See L. I. Levine (ed.), *Ancient Synagogues Revealed* (Jerusalem: Israel Exploration Society, 1981); *The Synagogue in Late Antiquity* (Philadelphia: American Schools of Oriental Research, 1987); J. Gutmann (ed.), *Ancient Synagogues: The State of Research* (Brown Judaic Studies 22; Chico: Scholars, 1981).

7. Although the existence of such Gentile sympathizers or "God-fearers" is sometimes disputed, see J. A. Overman, "The God-Fearers: Some Neglected Features," *JSNT* 32 (1988) 17–26.

8. G. Biguzzi, *"Io distruggerò questo tempio": Il tempio e il giudaismo nel vangelo di Marco* (Rome: Pontificia Università Urbaniana, 1987) 109–13.

9. D. Lührmann, "Die Pharisäer und die Schriftgelehrten im Markusevangelium," *ZNW* 78 (1987) 169–85.

10. A. J. Saldarini, "Political and Social Roles of the Pharisees and Scribes in Galilee," SBLASP 27 (1988) 205.

11. On the Pharisees, Scribes and Sadducees in Mark, see A. J. Saldarini, *Pharisees, Scribes and Sadducees in Palestinian Society: A Sociological Approach* (Wilmington: Glazier, 1988) 146–57.

12. For the suggestion that the "Herodians" are a literary invention of Mark to enhance Jesus' relationship with John the Baptist who was killed by Herod (Mark 6:14–29), see W. J. Bennett, "The Herodians of Mark's Gospel," *NovT* 17 (1975) 9–14. But most likely the "Herodians" were an actual, historical group allied in some way with Herod. See H. H. Rowley, "The Herodians in the Gospels," *JTS* 41 (1940) 14–27.

13. Saldarini, *Pharisees,* 154.

14. The term "elders" (*presbyteroi*) in Mark also refers to the past generations of Jewish leaders and forefathers, as in "the tradition of the elders" (7:3,5).

15. J. A. Fitzmyer, *The Gospel According to Luke I–IX* (AB 28; Garden City, NY: Doubleday, 1981) 469–70.

16. See T. S. Frymer-Kensky, "Women," *Harper's Bible Dictionary* (Ed. P. J. Achtemeier; San Francisco: Harper & Row, 1985) 1138–41.

17. A. Gill, "Women Ministers in the Gospel of Mark," *AusBR* 35 (1987) 14–21; M. A. Beavis, "Women as Models of Faith in Mark," *BTB* 18 (1988) 3–9; E. S. Fiorenza, *In Memory of Her: A Feminist Theological Reconstruction of Christian Origins* (New York: Crossroad, 1983); J. A. Grassi, "The Secret Heroine of Mark's Drama," *BTB* 18 (1988) 10–15; *The Hidden Heroes of the Gospels: Feminine Counterparts of Jesus* (Collegeville, MN: Liturgical Press, 1989) 12–44; E. S. Malbon, "Fallible Followers: Women and Men in the Gospel of Mark," *The Bible and Feminist Hermeneutics* (Semeia 28; ed. M. A. Tolbert; Chico: Scholars, 1983), 29–48; W. Munro, "Women Disciples in Mark?," *CBQ* 44 (1982) 225–41; L. Schottroff, "Maria Magdalena und die Frauen am Grabe Jesu," *EvT* 42 (1982) 3–25; M. J. Selvidge, " 'And Those Who Followed Feared' (Mark 10:32)," *CBQ* 45 (1983) 396–400.

18. See J. P. Heil, "Miracles," *Harper's Bible Dictionary,* 639–41.

19. See F. J. Matera, *The Kingship of Jesus: Composition and Theology in Mark 15* (SBLDS 66; Chico: Scholars, 1982).

20. Some scholars hold that the "Son of Man" was merely an Aramaic idiom used as a substitute for the personal pronoun, and thus a "circum-

locutional" way for Jesus to refer to himself simply as a human being. This theory has been recently reexamined and rejected by C. C. Caragounis, *The Son of Man: Vision and Interpretation* (WUNT 38; Tübingen: Mohr, 1986).

21. See Caragounis, *Son of Man,* esp. 81, 250.

22. E. Manicardi, *Il cammino di Gesù nel Vangelo di Marco: Schema narrativo e tema cristologico* (AnBib 96; Rome: Biblical Institute, 1981).

# II

# Mark 1:1–13

*Preparation for the Way of the Lord To
Be Accomplished by the Way of Jesus.*

## A. Mark 1:1–8: John's Preaching Prepares the Way of the Lord

¹The beginning of the gospel of Jesus Christ, Son of God.
²As it is written in Isaiah the prophet,
"Behold, I send my messenger before you,
who will prepare your way (Exod 23:20; Mal 3:1).
³The voice of one crying in the wilderness:
'Make ready the way of the Lord,
make straight his paths!' " (Isa 40:3)—
⁴John the Baptizer appeared in the wilderness, proclaiming a baptism of repentance for the forgiveness of sins. ⁵And all the country of Judea and all the inhabitants of Jerusalem were going out to him and were being baptized by him in the Jordan river, acknowledging their sins.

⁶Now John was clothed in camel's hair with a leather belt around his waist, and ate locusts and wild honey. ⁷And he was proclaiming: "One stronger than I is coming after me, the thong of whose sandals I am not worthy to stoop and loosen. ⁸I have baptized you with water; but he will baptize you with the Holy Spirit."

### 1. MEANING OF MARK 1:1–8

**a. *1:1* Superscription introducing and summarizing the narrative.**

*1:1* The Gospel

With a vigorous opening thrust our author succinctly summarizes the entire narrative to follow as the beginning of the powerful public proclamation of the exciting good news about Jesus who is both the Christ and Son of God. What is to follow is "gospel," not yet in the sense of a title for the written documents we know as "gospels," but in the sense of a public proclaiming of God's good news or glad tidings. This "gospel" boldly announces the fulfillment of prophetic promises for God's decisive and definitive end-time of salvation (Isa 40:9; 52:7–10; 61:1–2). As the powerful word of God himself the very proclamation of the "gospel" initiates and makes present for its audience the salvific action that it announces. This heralding of joyful news has its "beginning," its basis or foundation, with what is to follow—not only the appearance of John the Baptist but the entire story of Jesus.

### *1:1* Jesus Christ, Son of God

This good news is about one named "Jesus Christ." The superscription thus serves as a confessional proclamation acknowledging that Jesus of Nazareth has so uniquely and completely fulfilled what is expressed by the term "Christ," namely God's "anointed one" or expected "messiah" who would bring about the end-time of God's salvation, that it has become part of his proper name.[1] The confessional messianic title "Son of God" further designates Jesus Christ as the special and unique agent of God's salvation.[2] The reader expects the narrative to demonstrate how these titles apply to Jesus.

**b. *1:2–5* In accord with scripture John appears in the wilderness as the messenger of "the Way of the Lord" who proclaims repentance and baptizes people who acknowledge their sins.**

### *1:2–3* The Way of Jesus

Through the double occurrence of the key term "way":

> *1:2* . . . who will prepare your *way* (*hodon*)
> *1:3* Make ready the *way* (*hodon*) of the Lord,

the first quotation (1:2), a combination of Exodus 23:20 and Malachi 3:1, is linked to the second quotation (1:3) of Isaiah 40:3, so that both parts of this composite scriptural citation can be subsumed under the heading of what is "written in Isaiah the prophet." [3] This prepares the reader for the cardinal concept of "the way" to serve as the distinctive theme and dynamic framework for the narrative that follows.

"Your way" refers to the "way" of Jesus. The one whom the superscription (1:1) designates "Jesus Christ, Son of God" is now addressed by

God himself, the speaker of the combined quotation from Exodus 23:20 and Malachi 3:1:

*Exodus 23:20:* Behold, I send a messenger before you, to guard you on the way and to bring you to the place I have prepared.

*Malachi 3:1a:* Behold, I send my messenger to prepare the way before me, and the Lord whom you seek will suddenly come to his temple.

*Mark 1:2:* Behold, I send my messenger before you, who will prepare your way.

In Exodus 23:20 the "way" refers to the "exodus" event of the people of Israel, the movement or "way" of salvation through which God's angel delivered them from slavery in Egypt and brought them through the wilderness into the promised land. In Malachi 3:1 the "way" alludes to the salvific coming of God himself into the temple to purify the priests (Mal 3:3). Mark 1:2 thus inserts "your way," the dynamic "way" of the constant and continual movement of Jesus to be illustrated in the narrative to follow, into the biblical tradition of God's "way" of salvation, the dynamic process by which God acts for the salvation of his people.

## 1:3 The Way of the Lord

In the quotation of Isaiah 40:3 in Mark 1:3 an anonymous "voice" crying in the wilderness urgently enjoins the people of Israel to prepare for a new "exodus," a new "way" of salvation, the "way" by which the Lord God himself will lead his people from exile in Babylon through the wilderness and back to their homeland. The "way" and "paths" of the Lord express the dynamic process and movement by which God himself saves his people. This heralding voice thus sets the stage for the Marcan narrative to demonstrate how the salvific Way of the Lord God (1:3) will be accomplished by the Way of Jesus (1:2).

Based on its rich biblical tradition, the important concept of the "way" or "ways" of the Lord embraces two distinct but complementary dimensions. The "way" of the Lord, first of all, as seen above, expresses the dynamic "way" that God himself goes before and with his people to bring them to salvation.[4] Secondly, the "way" of the Lord designates the human behavior through which the salvific will or plan of God is realized.[5] This significance is exemplified in Mark 12:14, when the Herodians acknowledge that Jesus truly teaches "the way of God," that is, the moral doctrine that conforms to the will of God and that people are to follow in order to enable God to effect his plan of salvation. In Mark both of these dimensions of "the way of the Lord" are included in the "way" of Jesus: In Jesus God is made present and walks among people for their salvation; and by following the "way" that Jesus goes and teaches, people can complete the "way" of the Lord (see 10:17–21) and thus realize the salvific presence of God among them.[6]

### 1:4 John the Baptist as Messenger-Elijah

"My messenger" whom God sends before Jesus to prepare his way (1:2) refers to John the Baptist, who appears in 1:4. This allusion to John as God's "messenger" of Malachi 3:1 begins Mark's presentation of John as the prophetic Elijah figure of the last days (1:6; 9:11–13). The close connection between Malachi 3:1 and 3:23 indicates how the "messenger" is identified with Elijah:

> *Malachi 3:1:* Behold, I send *my messenger* to prepare the way before me.
>
> *Malachi 3:23:* Behold, I will send you *Elijah* the prophet before the great and terrible day of the Lord comes.

According to Jewish eschatological expectations, the prophet Elijah, who had been taken by God to heaven (2 Kgs 2:11), would return to earth as a forerunner to God's final, messianic age. One of his main tasks was to bring the people to repentance in preparation for God's coming.

The task of this Elijah-messenger to prepare the "way" of Jesus (1:2) is continued by "the voice of one crying in the wilderness" (1:3). The exciting appeal of this heralding voice for the people to "prepare the way of the Lord, make straight his paths!" begins the messenger's preparation for the "way" of Jesus.

### 1:4 The Wilderness

In accord ("as [*kathōs*] it is written," 1:2) with the scriptural citation John the Baptist appears "in the wilderness." This appearance of John "in the wilderness" links him to the "voice" which cries out "in the wilderness" (1:3). With its related biblical background the "wilderness" setting adds to the theme of preparing the salvific "way of the Lord." Although "wilderness" represented a deserted and hostile area with such obstacles as lack of food and water and dangerous wild beasts, for Israel it served ultimately as a special place of encounter with God and of the experience of his salvation (Deut 8:14–16). It was through the terrible wilderness that God led Israel out of slavery in Egypt and into the promised land in the original Exodus event; and it was through the dreaded wilderness that

God brought Israel out of Babylonian exile and back to its homeland in a second Exodus. The appearance of John as the "voice" crying out "in the wilderness" signifies the necessity for the people to return to the wilderness as the appropriate place of repentance in preparation for the endtime experience of God's salvation.[7]

## 1:4 A Baptism of Repentance

John's proclamation of "a baptism of repentance for the forgiveness of sins" further specifies the heralding voice's urgent invitation to "prepare the way of the Lord" (1:3). People can prepare for the new, decisive and definitive "way" of God's salvation by returning to the wilderness to be baptized by John as a symbolic gesture of their sincere repentance, which leads to God's forgiveness of their sins.

As a ritual immersion and cleansing in water, John's "baptism" represented an external gesture symbolic of an inner willingness to turn away from sinfulness and back to God (Isa 1:16; Jer 4:14; Ezek 36:24–25). The genuine conversion indicated by this baptism leads to God's forgiveness of sins and thus serves as an appropriate preparation for the eschatological "way of the Lord" to be accomplished (Isa 40:1–11; 55:6–11).

## 1:5 The People's Response to the Preaching of John

The preaching of John the Baptist enjoys an amazing success. Indeed, not only "all" of the surrounding region of Judea but also "all" the inhabitants of Jerusalem, the religious and social center of the Jewish people, are attracted to John. The truly sincere conversion of these people is described in a threefold manner: First, by "going out to him" they exhibit the willingness to return to the "wilderness" (1:3–4) as the place for a new beginning with God. Second, they undergo the ritual of baptism in the waters of the Jordan river as the sign demonstrating their inner repentance. And third, they publicly confess their sins, thus actualizing and confirming their conversion which opens them to God's pardon as necessary preparation for the salvific "way of the Lord" to be realized among them.

## c. 1:6–8 Characterized by his clothing and food, John proclaims the coming of a stronger one who will baptize with the Holy Spirit.

## 1:6 John Clothed as the Prophet Elijah

Like the prophet Elijah in 2 Kings 1:8 John is clothed with a leather belt and the hairy garment of a prophet (Zech 13:4). This continues the allusion to John as the God-sent messenger-Elijah who will prepare the "way" of Jesus (1:2) and thus enhances Mark's portrayal of John as the expected Elijah figure, the prophetic forerunner introducing the eschatological age of God's salvation.

John's food of "locusts and wild honey" underlines his ascetical existence as a nomadic dweller of the wilderness. John not only proclaims a return to the wilderness for a baptism of repentance, but he himself lives in the wilderness and thus serves as a living symbol of the authentic conversion he preaches.

### 1:7–8 The Stronger One to Come

John plays his prophetic Elijah role of introducing the eschatological age by proclaiming the coming of a "stronger one." That this "stronger one" will come *after* him corresponds with John's task of preceding and preparing the "way" of Jesus:

1:2  I send my messenger *before you,* who will prepare your way.
1:7  One stronger than I is coming *after me.*

Whereas John first appeared "proclaiming" (1:4) a baptism of repentance leading to the forgiveness of sins, a baptism presently received by the people (1:5), he now is "proclaiming" (1:7) a message with a future orientation. The content of his prophetic message forms a carefully arranged chiasm:

*a* One stronger than I is coming after me,
*b* the thong of whose sandals I am not worthy to stoop and loosen.
*b* I have baptized you with water,
*a* but he will baptize you with the Holy Spirit.

This chiastic structure of John's message, in which statements about John (b) are enveloped within prophecies about the "stronger one" (a), aptly expresses both the close continuity and the great contrast between John and Jesus, the "stronger one."

The close continuity between John and Jesus is illustrated by John's role of preceding and preparing the "way" of Jesus (1:2) as the stronger one coming after him. But the great contrast between them is expressed by the extreme unworthiness of John to perform even the most menial task of loosening the sandals of the one "stronger" than he. Jesus will be even mightier than the prophet John.

### 1:8 Baptism with the Holy Spirit

That Jesus will "baptize" as John has "baptized" indicates their close relationship. But whereas John's preliminary baptism with "water" has already brought about repentance and pardon of sins (1:4–5), the future "baptism" of Jesus will be even greater. Those baptized with John's baptism of repentance can now look forward to being "baptized," that is, completely "immersed" by the "stronger one" with the cherished gift of the "Holy Spirit," the special salvific presence and power of God. A generous outpouring of God's "Spirit" was expected in the eschatological age (Joel 3:1–2; Isa 32:15; 44:3). And in the biblical tradition the powerful "Spirit" of God accompanies and guides the people of Israel along the salvific "way" of the Lord (Isa 63:11–14; Ezek 36:24–27).

By prophetically foretelling their future immersion with the Holy Spirit, John the Baptist has completed his role as the returned Elijah who has prepared the people for the "way of the Lord" (1:3) to be accomplished by the "way" of Jesus (1:2). John's preaching and activity indicate how the "way of the Lord," as the dynamic process by which God effects salvation, includes repentance, forgiveness of sins (1:4–5) and immersion with the Spirit (1:8). After John led the people to conversion and the pardon of their sins, he has awakened them to an expectation of being immersed with God's Spirit by "the stronger one" to come.

## 2. MARK 1:1–8 AS MODEL FOR ACTION

Through the opening superscription (1:1) the implied author invites the implied reader/audience to listen to his proclamation of the "good news" and thus be moved to share his belief in Jesus as "Christ" and "Son of God." That what is to follow is only a "beginning" of this public proclamation implies its eventual continuation and completion by the convinced audience.

The remarkable response of "all" the people of Judea and Jerusalem to the exuberant and urgent preaching of a baptism of repentance by John (1:4–5) attracts us as Mark's readers to a similar response. With a willingness to acknowledge our sinfulness and undergo conversion we can vicariously enter the "wilderness" for a new beginning with God and ready ourselves to participate in the salvific activity of the "way of the Lord" to be actualized by the "way" of Jesus (1:2–3). A readiness to repent and receive God's pardon prepares us for future immersion with God's Holy Spirit by Jesus as the "stronger one" to come (1:7–8). Conversion, forgiveness and the expectation of "baptism" with the Holy Spirit enable us to follow the "way" that Jesus will go and teach in Mark, and thus experience and accomplish in our lives the dynamic process of salvation known as the "way of the Lord" together with him.

As a "wilderness" dweller and thus a living symbol of the conversion he proclaims (1:6), John provides a model for Christian preaching. His "proclaiming" (1:4, 7) as God's "messenger" (1:2) and "voice crying out in the wilderness" (1:3) commences the public proclamation of the gospel announced by the superscription (1:1). In order for Christian readers to effectively continue and complete this "beginning" of the proclamation of good news to others, they are called to imitate the ascetical and repentant lifestyle of the Baptist, who, aware of his unworthiness, humbly prepares others for the coming of the "stronger one" (1:7–8).

## B. Mark 1:9–11: The Spirit Descends upon Jesus and God Declares Him His Son after He Is Baptized by John

> [9]And it happened in those days that Jesus came from Nazareth of Galilee and was baptized in the Jordan by John. [10]And immediately, upon coming up out of the water, he saw the heavens being torn open and the Spirit, like a dove, descending upon him. [11]And a voice came from the heavens, "You are my beloved Son; with you I am well pleased!"

### 1. MEANING OF MARK 1:9–11

**a. *1:9* Jesus comes from Galilee and is baptized by John.**

It was "in those days," when the end-time fulfillment of God's plan of salvation was beginning (1:2–3) and people were coming to receive John's baptism of repentance (1:4–5), that Jesus also came to John in the wilderness and was likewise baptized. The inclusion of Jesus in this movement of repentance and awareness of sinfulness as preparation for God's coming salvific activity is indicated by the structural similarity between 1:5 and 1:9:

> *1:5* And there were going out to him
> all the country of Judea and all the inhabitants of Jerusalem
> and they were being baptized by him in the Jordan river,
> acknowledging their sins.
> *1:9* . . . and there came
> Jesus from Nazareth of Galilee
> and he was baptized in the Jordan by John.

Jesus thus stands in continuity with John and in solidarity with the people's situation of sinfulness and conversion in expectation of a new and decisive saving intervention by God. But Jesus is also different: He confesses no personal sinfulness and he comes not from the sacred and central city of Jerusalem or its surrounding region but from the more obscure village of Nazareth in the less sacred region of Galilee.

### b. *1:10* Jesus has a vision of the Spirit descending on him.

Once Jesus has been baptized by John and comes up out of the water of the Jordan, he experiences an "interpretive vision" of God's Spirit descending upon him. The background for understanding this "interpretive vision" of Jesus is found in Jewish exegetical tradition: The young Isaac has a comparable "interpretive vision" in which he "sees" the angels in heaven at the very moment when his father Abraham is ready to sacrifice him (Gen 22:10). As part of this vision a heavenly voice points out or "interprets" the salvation-historical importance of both these figures. Similarly, Jacob has an "interpretive vision" in the dream in which he sees a ladder set up between heaven and earth with angels ascending and descending on it (Gen 28:12). The heavenly voice of the angels interprets his significance at this moment of God's salvific plan.[8] Likewise, the "interpretive vision" of Jesus indicates his unique significance at this new moment of God's end-time plan of salvation.

As a motif in this distinctive Jewish literary genre of "interpretive vision," the "tearing open" or "splitting" of the heavens not only enables Jesus to have this vision into heaven and hear the voice "from the heavens" (1:11) but also indicates the heavenly origin of the Spirit's descent. Jesus "sees" the interpretive event of the "Spirit," God's special divine power, descending upon him and thus equipping him as a unique agent of God. The interpretive event points out Jesus as one who has been uniquely endowed with God's Spirit at the moment that he has associated himself with the repentant and sinful situation of his people by undergoing John's baptism of repentance.

"Like a dove" not only portrays in a vivid and visible way the descent of the invisible Spirit, but may also serve as a symbol of Israel (Pss 55:7; 68:13; 74:19; Hos 7:11; 11:11), thus underlining Jesus' mission to his people.

### c. *1:11* God proclaims Jesus as his beloved Son.

Within this "interpretive vision" the voice of God from the heavens accompanies and interprets the descent of the Spirit upon Jesus. In contrast to John and the people baptized by him (1:5) Jesus alone is addressed by God: "*You* (not John or any other) are my beloved Son; in *you* I am well pleased!" God himself declares that Jesus is his unique agent, his "beloved Son," with whom he is "well pleased" to grant his Spirit for the salvation of his people.

This striking declaration of Jesus as "my beloved Son" by God's voice from heaven serves as a summarizing title combining two lines of Jewish tradition. First, "Son of God," originally referring to the people of Israel (Exod 4:22; Jer 3:19; 31:9, 20; Hos 11:1), came to designate the long awaited Davidic messiah-king who would save his people Israel (2 Sam 7:14; Pss 2:7; 89:4, 26–27). Second, the identification of Jesus as the Spirit-equipped agent of God shows strong allusions to the chosen and favored "Servant of God" mentioned in Isaiah 42:1:

"Here is my servant whom I uphold,
my chosen one with whom I am pleased;
I have put my Spirit upon him,
he will bring forth justice to the nations."

Thus, God has appointed Jesus as his specially chosen "beloved Son" in the sense of his Spirit-equipped "Servant" sent to his people Israel to initiate a new and decisive situation of salvation.[9]

### 2. MARK 1:9–11 AS MODEL FOR ACTION

Having been called to an attitude of conversion (1:4–5) and given the expectation of a marvelous immersion with God's Holy Spirit (1:7–8), the audience now focuses upon Jesus as the one who, now that he himself has been endowed with God's Spirit (1:10), is enabled to bestow upon them the help and power of the Holy Spirit. The reader realizes that Jesus, who has closely aligned himself with the sinful and repentant situation of his people (1:9), has been uniquely empowered by God to address and alleviate our human condition. Through the heavenly voice of God himself, declaring Jesus to be his "beloved Son" (1:11), the narrator persuades his listeners to share his confession of Jesus as the messianic "Son of God" (1:1) and invites us to orient our lives toward the Spirit-gifted Jesus as the "stronger one" (1:8) who can guide and lead us on God's new and decisive "way" of salvation (1:2–3). As readers of Mark we are being attracted to want to follow the "way" of Jesus that Mark will narrate for us.

## C. Mark 1:12–13: Jesus Is Tested by Satan in the Wilderness

[12]At once the Spirit drove him out into the wilderness. [13]He was in the wilderness forty days, tested by Satan; and he was with the wild beasts; but the angels ministered to him.

### 1. MEANING OF MARK 1:12–13

**a. *1:12* The Spirit drives Jesus into the wilderness.**

The Spirit that had just descended upon Jesus (1:10) now vigorously leads him deeper into the "wilderness." Just as God had once led his people Israel out of Egypt and into the "wilderness" to "test" their fidelity to his covenant and discipline them as his chosen people (Deut 8:2–18), so he now sends his "beloved Son" into the hostile "wilderness" to allow him to be likewise "tested," so that he can be found worthy and approved for his task of leading the new "way" of salvation as God's chosen Son.

**b. *1:13a* For forty days Jesus is tested by Satan.**

"Forty days," a biblically fixed time and round number of symbolic significance, recalls not only the forty-day ordeals of such chosen figures as Moses, who spent forty days on Mount Sinai (Exod 24:18; 34:28), and Elijah, who wandered through the wilderness for forty days to Mount Horeb (1 Kgs 19:4–8), but also alludes to the forty years of Israel's sojourn and testing in the wilderness (Deut 8:2). Similar to Israel who was tested for forty years, Jesus is tested by Satan for the symbolically significant duration of "forty days."

Whereas Israel was tested in the wilderness by God himself, Jesus is tested by "Satan," the personification of all evil who, together with his host of demons, stands in fierce opposition to God and his angels in accord with Jewish apocalyptic-eschatological thought. Through his on-going "testing" or "tempting" for forty days, Satan is permitted to try to thwart the salvific "way" that Jesus is to accomplish as the Spirit-gifted "beloved Son" of God from its very beginnings in the wilderness.

**c. *1:13b* Jesus is with wild beasts.**

In accord with the wilderness setting, that Jesus was "with the wild beasts" continues to describe his testing ordeal. In the biblical tradition wild animals are often associated with the wilderness, contributing to its dangerous and hostile character (Isa 34:9–15; Jer 10:22; Zeph 2:14; Ezek 34:5, 25). As Israel of old encountered terrifying wild beasts during its testing while wandering through the wilderness (Num 21:6–9; Deut 8:15), Jesus likewise confronts the horror of "wild beasts" while tested by Satan in the wilderness.

**d. *1:13c* But angels minister to Jesus.**

Although Jesus is harassed by the temptations of Satan and threatened by the terror of the wild beasts, "the angels" of God "minister" or "serve" him.[10] As an angel of God provided nourishment for Elijah during his sojourn in the barren wilderness (1 Kgs 19:4–8) and God sent an angel to guide and protect Israel wandering through the wilderness (Exod 14:19; 23:20, 23; 32:34; 33:2), so God's angels sustain and guard his "beloved Son" against the temptations of Satan in the wilderness. The Spirit-equipped Son of God is thus helped by God to withstand and prevail over the evil designs of Satan.

The testing of Jesus by Satan in the wilderness continues to demonstrate that Jesus is the favored "Son" of God, who is not only equipped with God's Spirit but granted the divine protection of angels to overcome the evil obstacles that may prevent him from completing the "way" of God's salvation. Having already been afforded divine assistance in his encounter with the demonic power of Satan, Jesus is prepared for his healing and exorcistic ministry, in which he will prevail over the demons responsible for sin and sickness. Before he begins his ministry, then, Jesus is shown to possess the attributes necessary to master the demonic powers of evil and thus actualize the salvific "way of the Lord."

### 2. MARK 1:12–13 AS MODEL FOR ACTION

God's protection of Jesus during his testing by Satan assures Mark's audience that Jesus is uniquely qualified to assist them in their own struggles with the powers of evil that threaten to control all human lives. As readers we are further persuaded to orient our lives toward and place our faith in this Jesus who, equipped with God's Spirit (1:10) and guarded by God's angels against the menace of evil (1:13), can effectively lead us on the "way" (1:2–3) of God's salvation. We are now prepared to follow the "way" of Jesus to be narrated by Mark and thus to join Jesus in realizing the salvific "way of the Lord" in our often misdirected and disoriented lives.

### Notes

1. For more on the "Christ" title, see Chapter I.
2. For more on the "Son of God" title, see Chapter I.
3. This accords with a quite common Jewish method of scriptural interpretation, *gezerah shawah,* the second exegetical rule of Rabbi Hillel. It consists of the mutual interpretation of scriptural passages, which can be associated with one another through a term they have in common.
4. In addition to the above references to Exod 23:20, Mal 3:1 and Isa

40:3, see Exod 13:21; 15:13; 33:12–17; Isa 35:8; 40:9–11; 55:8–9; Pss 77:20–21; 103:6–7.

5. See Deut 10:12; Hos 14:10; Pss 24:4–5; 27:11; 86:11.

6. See Manicardi, *Il cammino,* 148–57.

7. U. W. Mauser, *Christ in the Wilderness: The Wilderness Theme in the Second Gospel and its Basis in the Biblical Tradition* (SBT 39; Naperville, IL: Allenson, 1963).

8. These "interpretive visions" occur in the Aramaic "targums," the often elaborative Aramaic translations of the Hebrew scriptures, which were orally transmitted to the community in the synagogue worship. For a full explanation see F. Lentzen-Deis, *Die Taufe Jesu nach den Synoptikern: Literarkritische und gattungsgeschichtliche Untersuchungen* (Frankfurter Theologische Studien 4; Frankfurt: Knecht, 1970).

9. Lentzen-Deis, *Taufe,* 277–79.

10. For more on the significance of "angels" in the Jewish apocalyptic-eschatological milieu, see "Sin/Sickness, Demons and Angels" in Chapter I.

# III

# Mark 1:14–3:6

*Jesus Goes His Way Demonstrating the Arrival of the Kingdom of God by Preaching and Healing, Yet Meets Death-Threatening Opposition.*

## A. Mark 1:14–15: Jesus Comes to Galilee and Preaches the Gospel of God's Kingdom, Calling for Conversion and Faith

[14]After John had been arrested, Jesus came to Galilee, proclaiming the gospel of God, [15]and saying, "The time is fulfilled and the kingdom of God is at hand! Repent, and believe in the gospel!"

### 1. MEANING OF MARK 1:14–15

**a. *1:14* After John's arrest Jesus comes to Galilee proclaiming God's good news.**

*1:14* John's Arrest

That John had been "arrested" or "handed over" inserts an ominous note. Despite the very favorable response to his preaching (1:5), John apparently encountered an as yet unexplained opposition. John's "arrest" hints at the possibility of a similar fate for Jesus and his followers. But as a "divine" or "theological" passive verb, the "arrest" of John is subsumed within God's overall plan of salvation.[1]

"After" (*meta*) John had been arrested the stage is set for the appearance of Jesus as the "stronger one" who, as John himself had foretold, would come "after" (*opisō*) him (1:7).

40

*1:14* The Way of Jesus Begins in Galilee

Fulfilling John's prediction that a stronger one would "come" after him (1:7), Jesus "came" into Galilee. This "coming" of Jesus initiates his "way" prepared by the messenger John (1:2), which will actualize the "way of the Lord" (1:3), God's dynamic process of salvation for his people.

In contrast to the region of Judea and the principal and sacred city of Jerusalem as the realm of John's successful preaching (1:5), Jesus, who had come from Nazareth in Galilee to be baptized by John (1:9), begins his "way" in the region of "Galilee."

*1:14* Jesus Proclaims the Gospel of God

Whereas John appeared publicly "proclaiming" a baptism of repentance for the forgiveness of sins (1:4) as a preparation for the "way of the Lord" (1:3), Jesus inaugurates this salvific "way" by publicly "proclaiming" the "gospel of God." The "gospel" or "good news" (*euaggelion*) that comes from God (see Isa 52:7–10; 61:1–2) and that Jesus proclaims will eventually become the "gospel" about himself as the Christ and Son of God (1:1).[2]

**b. *1:15* Jesus urges conversion and faith in the good news that God's kingdom has arrived.**

*1:15* The Fulfillment of Time

The powerful and authoritative content of Jesus' proclamation of the gospel of God begins with his exciting announcement that the "time is fulfilled!" The long period of hopeful waiting for God's decisive and definitive "end-time" of salvation has finally been completed. In accord with God's plan the appropriate "time," as determined by God, has passed so that *now* is the time for his salvific intervention on behalf of his people.

*1:15* The Kingdom of God at Hand

In close correspondence to his announcement that the time is now ripe for God's salvific intervention, Jesus indicates the arrival and beginning of that decisive and long-awaited salvific action of God as he boldly exclaims that "the kingdom of God is at hand!" As an apocalyptic-eschatological concept rooted in the OT (Mic 4:7–8; Pss 103:19; 145:11–13; Wis 6:4; 10:10, etc.) "kingdom of God" refers to the dynamic "kingship," "sovereignty," "royal rule" or "reign" of God which stands in sharp opposition to the "kingship" or powerful realm of Satan and his host of demons responsible for all that has gone wrong and awry in the world.[3] That Jesus was proclaimed as God's "beloved Son" by God himself (1:9–11) and enjoyed the protection of God's angels during his testing by Satan in the wilderness (1:12–13) arouses the expectation that the arrival of God's kingdom is intimately connected with the person and activity of Jesus himself.

### *1:15* Appeal for Conversion and Faith

That the time is *now* fulfilled and that the kingdom of God is *now* at hand arouses an anticipation for the manifestation of this good news and adds to the urgency of the accompanying commands of Jesus: "Repent and believe in the gospel!" As John the Baptist proclaimed a baptism of "repentance" as preparation for the "way of the Lord" (1:2–4), so Jesus indicates that the proper response to his stirring announcement of the arrival of God's kingdom is "repentance" or "conversion," that is, a radical turning away from one's past ways and a reorientation of one's life to this new salvific activity of God. Coupled with this conversion is the call for "belief" or "faith" in the sense of acknowledging, accepting, submitting and entrusting oneself to the new salvific activity now present in the gospel of God proclaimed by Jesus.

### 2. MARK 1:14–15 AS MODEL FOR ACTION

John's arrest subtly yet ominously alerts the reader to the danger and risk that can result from opposition to preaching the "way of the Lord." This prepares us as Mark's readers to reckon with the possibility of similar opposition to Jesus and to ourselves as followers of the way of Jesus.

Jesus' authoritative and exuberant proclamation that God's kingship is presently at hand creates excitement and anticipation in us as readers, further attracting us to follow the way of Jesus that is beginning in Galilee and leading us to look for the full revelation and demonstration by Jesus of his stunning message.

The urgent command of Jesus to "repent and believe in the gospel!" reinforces and intensifies John's prior call for conversion (1:4). Captivated by the thrilling and delightful "good news" of God exclaimed by Jesus, we are further induced to convert our lives, to turn away from our past and open ourselves anew to God's salvific and sovereign "kingship" newly arrived in the person and preaching of Jesus and to entrust ourselves totally in faith to this gospel of God as powerfully proclaimed by Jesus.

## B. Mark 1:16–20: Along the Sea of Galilee Jesus Calls Four Fishermen to Follow Him

[16]And passing along the Sea of Galilee, he saw Simon and Andrew the brother of Simon casting a net in the sea; for they were fishermen. [17]And Jesus said to them, "Come after me and I will make you become fishers of people!" [18]Immediately leaving their nets, they followed him. [19]And going on a little farther he saw James the son of Zebedee and John his brother, who also were in a boat mending their nets. [20]Immediately he called them, and leaving their father Zebedee in the boat with the hired men, they went after him.

### 1. MEANING OF MARK 1:16–20

a. *1:16–18* **The fishermen Simon and his brother Andrew promptly accept the authoritative and intriguing summons to follow Jesus.**

*1:16* Simon and His Brother Andrew

Jesus continues his dynamic and salvific "way" by "passing along" the Sea of Galilee. He sees two brothers named Simon and Andrew. Simon is indicated as the more prominent of the two, since his name is mentioned twice, with Andrew being defined in relation to him ("the brother of Simon"). Jesus encounters them while they are engaged in their work as fishermen.

*1:17* The Powerful Call of Jesus to Become "Fishers of People"

Reminiscent of the manner in which the prophet Elijah suddenly and authoritatively called Elisha away from his work to be his follower (1 Kgs 19:19–21), Jesus issues a forceful and captivating command to Simon and Andrew in the midst of their labor as fishermen. With compelling abruptness he bluntly bids them to follow him on his "way" by "coming after" him. But his bold beckoning includes an alluring promise to transform their lives: "I will make you become fishers of people!"

The enticing metaphor "fishers of people" has some biblical background. For example, in Habakkuk 1:14 God makes people "like the fish of the sea." And in Jeremiah 16:14–16 God will send out "fishers" to gather the people of Israel from all the lands to which they were scattered and bring them back to their own land.

But what it means to become a "fisher of people" is strikingly illustrated by Jesus himself in this scene. Like a clever fisherman he masterfully lures these two brothers into his following. He attempts to capture these fishermen by inviting them to no longer catch mere fish but to gather people as they are being gathered by him. Like fishermen collecting fish they will be enabled by Jesus to bring people into the kingdom of God whose arrival Jesus has just excitingly heralded (1:15).

### 1:18 The Immediate Response to Follow Jesus

Without deliberation or the slightest hesitation Simon and Andrew "immediately" leave behind their "nets," symbolizing their past work and lives, and become disciples by "following" the "way" of Jesus. These brothers thus illustrate the kind of conversion and faith that Jesus' proclamation of the arrival of the kingdom of God is evoking (1:15).

### b. *1:19–20* The fishermen James and his brother John abandon their work and their father to follow Jesus.

### 1:19 James and His Brother John

Continuing his dynamic "way" by "going on a little farther," Jesus sees another pair of fishermen brothers, James and John. The mention of their father Zebedee enhances the theme of familial relationship. Jesus encounters them, like Simon and Andrew, busy with their everyday work as fishermen mending their nets in the boat.

### 1:20 The Sudden and Powerful Call of Jesus

Jesus "immediately calls" James and John with the same powerful authority and abruptness with which he beckoned Simon and Andrew.

### 1:20 The Commitment to Follow Jesus

With the same amazing promptness demonstrated by Simon and Andrew, James and John become disciples of Jesus by "going after him" on his "way" without delay or debate. They further exemplify the type of conversion from the past and faith in the gospel of God that Jesus urges (1:15) as they willingly "leave behind" not only their life's work and support as fishermen "in the boat with the hired men" but also their family relationship with their father Zebedee.

### 2. MARK 1:16–20 AS MODEL FOR ACTION

The overwhelming authority and striking charismatic power demonstrated by Jesus in this scene further draws us to adhere to Jesus and follow him as he continues his salvific "way." As we identify with Simon and Andrew, we are invited to become fascinated and intrigued at the prospect of Jesus empowering us, called to be followers like them, to become "fishers of people" and thus to bring others into the kingdom of God. The remarkably quick and ready response of conversion and faith displayed by Simon and Andrew leads us to imitate them by likewise leaving behind our past lives and old work, allowing Jesus to transform, renew and reorient us and our work, so that we may cling more closely to his "way." The extraordinary example of James and John further induces us to deepen our conversion and faith by likewise abandoning our former livelihood, security and family relationships in order to become more completely committed disciples of Jesus.

## C. Mark 1:21–28: After They Enter Capernaum, Jesus Teaches and Expels Unclean Spirits in the Synagogue

[21]Then they went into Capernaum, and immediately entering the synagogue on the sabbath, he was teaching. [22]And they were astounded at his teaching, for he was teaching them as one having authority and not as the scribes. [23]And immediately a man with an unclean spirit was in their synagogue, and he cried out, [24]"What have you to do with us, Jesus of Nazareth? Have you come to destroy us? I know who you are—the Holy One of God!" [25]But Jesus rebuked him, "Be quiet and come out of him!" [26]Then convulsing him and uttering a loud cry, the unclean spirit came out of him. [27]And all were amazed so that they asked among themselves, "What is this? A new teaching with authority! He commands even the unclean spirits and they obey him!" [28]And his fame immediately went out everywhere into the whole surrounding region of Galilee.

## 1. MEANING OF MARK 1:21-28

**a. *1:21-22* Those in the synagogue at Capernaum are astounded by the authoritative teaching of Jesus.**

*1:21* Teaching in the Synagogue at Capernaum on the Sabbath

Continuing to actualize the salvific and dynamic "way of the Lord" (1:2-3), Jesus, accompanied by the four fishermen he had just called to follow him (1:16-20), "went" into a village on the northwestern shore of the Sea of Galilee known as "Capernaum."[4] On the "sabbath," the day when Jews assembled in their local "synagogue" or place of assembly for their weekly worship service which centered on scriptural readings and homily, Jesus entered the synagogue at Capernaum and began his "teaching."[5]

*1:22* The Authoritative Teaching of Jesus

The people in the synagogue were "astounded" at the teaching of Jesus, for, as the narrator relates, he was teaching them as one who had "authority" and not like the "scribes." The amazing "authority" Jesus possesses refers to his direct authority from God as God's "beloved Son" (1:11), which he demonstrated by his powerful, authoritative proclamation of the "good news" that the kingdom of God has arrived and his authoritative command for conversion and faith in this gospel of God (1:14-15). That Jesus teaches with such authority and "not like the scribes" not only establishes the superiority of Jesus' teaching to that of the Jewish scribes, who lack this direct divine authority and must depend upon the indirect handing down of past traditions and teachings, but also arouses suspense with the implication of a contrast and conflict between the teaching of Jesus and that of the "scribes" as the professional and official teachers of the Jews.[6]

**b. *1:23-24* A man with an unclean spirit encounters Jesus.**

*1:23* A Man with an Unclean Spirit in the Synagogue

While Jesus was teaching in their synagogue a man possessed by a demon or "unclean spirit" was present.[7] This signals the beginning of a miraculous exorcism or healing story. The essential characteristics of this literary genre are: 1) The presence of a person (or representative of that person) in need of healing or exorcism; 2) the powerful words or actions of the healer which effect the healing or exorcism; and 3) the fact or confirmation of the miraculously sudden healing or exorcism.[8] With the presence of this man possessed by an unclean spirit the stage is set for a battle between Jesus with his divine authority and the demonic power of evil.

### *1:24* The Unclean Spirit Addresses Jesus

As is the case in exorcisms, this man is so totally controlled and suppressed by the unclean spirit that it replaces his personality and speaks through him. In its taunting query the unclean spirit speaks as a representative of the entire host of invisible demons that torment the world: "What have you to do with *us,*[9] Jesus of Nazareth?" The implication is that Jesus has no concern with or power over the demonic realm of evil. But this question functions as an ironic understatement for the reader, who knows that Jesus, as God's Son (1:11) who has already overcome the testing of Satan through divine protection (1:12–13), is indeed very much involved with combating the demonic powers of evil.

The unclean spirit's mocking challenge, "have you come to destroy us?," functions as another ironic understatement, since Jesus has powerfully proclaimed the advent of God's kingship (1:15), which stands in diametrical opposition to the demonic kingship of Satan. With its use of the verb "come" the unclean spirit's question refers not only to this particular "coming" of Jesus into the synagogue at Capernaum but also to his fundamental "coming," that is, his salvific "way" (1:2–3). Indeed, Jesus has "come" as part of the "way of the Lord" to destroy the evil powers of the demonic sphere and usher in the kingdom of God.

In an attempt to defend itself from destruction and ward off the exorcising power of Jesus through its superior knowledge as part of the spiritual realm, the unclean spirit audaciously asserts: "I know who you are—the Holy One of God!" The unclean spirit reveals for the reader its knowledge of the more profound identity of Jesus of Nazareth as God's "Holy One," that is, one who has been specially separated from others and consecrated for God's salvific purposes. As God's "Holy One" Jesus thus stands in stark antithesis to this unholy, unclean spirit.

### c. *1:25–26* Jesus expels the unclean spirit.

### *1:25* The Powerful Words of Jesus' Rebuke

Jesus' forceful "rebuke" of the unclean spirit serves as the second essential characteristic of the literary genre of exorcism; namely, the powerful words or action of the healer. With the same mighty word of "rebuke" with which Yahweh in the OT "rebuked" opposing forces (Pss

106:9; 119:21; Zech 3:2; Job 26:11; 2 Sam 22:16), Jesus "rebuked" the unclean spirit.

With the content of this potent rebuke, "be quiet and come out of him!," Jesus silences not only the unclean spirit's vain struggle to avoid the exorcising power of Jesus but also the inappropriate revelation by the unclean spirit of Jesus' more profound identity as the Holy One of God. Jesus vigorously compels the unclean spirit to free the man from the grisly grip of demonic power by "coming out" of him.

### 1:26 The Unclean Spirit Leaves the Man

With visible ("convulsing him") and audible ("uttering a loud cry") confirmation the unclean spirit dramatically and decisively "came out" of the man in exact correspondence to the forceful and authoritative rebuke of Jesus to "come out" of him. This functions as the third essential element of the literary genre of exorcism; namely, the fact or confirmation of the sudden and miraculous healing. Freed from demonic possession the man personally experiences the salvation Jesus has come to actualize as part of the arrival of the kingdom of God.

**d. *1:27–28* All are amazed and Jesus' fame spreads throughout Galilee.**

### 1:27 Amazement at the New Teaching of Jesus

This impressive exorcism of Jesus reinforces and increases the previous astonishment of the people at his authoritative teaching (1:22), so that now "all" are "amazed" and question the meaning of this extraordinary event. That "even" the unclean spirits obey his command demonstrates the powerful "authority" of his "new teaching" that the "kingdom of God is at hand!" (1:15).

### 1:28 The Fame of Jesus Extends to All of Galilee

So great and exciting is the wonderful news of the new and authoritative teaching of Jesus that God's kingship has arrived and of its convincing illustration by this startling exorcism, that the "fame" of Jesus "went out" beyond the synagogue at Capernaum and permeated the entire surrounding region of Galilee.

### 2. MARK 1:21–28 AS MODEL FOR ACTION

This remarkable exorcism by Jesus of a man overcome by an unclean spirit represents a personal experience of the salvation Jesus brings. This man personally experiences in his own life what the divine exorcising power of Jesus means for the lives of human beings tormented by the mysterious power of evil. By vicariously identifying with this man and with the people who witness his exorcism, we realize that Jesus as the "Holy One of God" possesses the divine power to liberate our personal lives also from the inextricable grasp of the evil powers that can totally control and overwhelm us.

That Jesus teaches with a direct divine authority, as displayed by the exorcism, and not like the scribes, the official Jewish teachers, not only awakens and attracts us as readers to heed this wonderfully new teaching about the arrival of God's kingdom but also alerts us to a possible impending opposition between the teaching of Jesus and that of the Jewish scribes.

The people in the synagogue at Capernaum present us with a model for spreading the gospel. As we identify with their excited astonishment and amazement at this dramatic evidence that God's kingship over evil is breaking into the world in the person of Jesus, we are led likewise to extend this good news to others, realizing that the deliverance from demonic power that Jesus offers is not limited to selected individuals or groups but applies to all human beings.

## D. Mark 1:29–31: Jesus Enters Simon's House and Heals His Mother-in-Law

<sup></sup>

29And immediately going out of the synagogue, they went into the house of Simon and Andrew with James and John. 30Simon's mother-in-law was lying sick with a fever, and immediately they spoke to him about her. 31And approaching he raised her up, grasping her hand. Then the fever left her and she served them.

### 1. MEANING OF MARK 1:29–31

#### a. *1:29* Jesus enters the house of Simon and Andrew with James and John.

Jesus, accompanied by the four fishermen he previously called to be his first followers (1:16–20), continues the vibrant movement of his salvific "way" as they "go out" of the synagogue at Capernaum and "go into" the house of Simon and Andrew. This "going out" and "going into" serves as a transition changing the focus from the public setting of the "synagogue" to the private and familial setting of the "house." The mention of "Simon and Andrew with James and John" reminds the reader of their presence as witnesses to the previous scene of exorcism (1:21–28) and establishes them as participants and witnesses to what will now happen.

**b. *1:30* They inform Jesus that Simon's mother-in-law has a fever.**

The prominence of Simon among the four is again indicated (1:16) as it is his mother-in-law who "was lying sick with a fever." This functions as the first element of the literary genre of a miraculous healing story—the presence of a person in need of healing. That the person is Simon's "mother-in-law" enhances the familial character of the scene, indicating how the illness of a family member affects the harmony and well-being of the entire familial community, the "house." With faith in Jesus' healing power, which they have just witnessed in the previous exorcism, the four disciples show their concern and involvement in the sickness of this member of the family and household as they inform Jesus about her, thus interceding on her behalf.

**c. *1:31* Jesus miraculously heals Simon's mother-in-law and she serves them.**

With his compassion aroused Jesus continues his salvific "way" as he "approaches" Simon's mother-in-law and enacts the second element of a miraculous healing story—the powerful words or action of the healer. Instead of the mighty words he pronounced in the previous exorcism, here Jesus performs an emphatic healing gesture as he "grasped her hand" and "raised her up." By "grasping her hand" Jesus now takes control of her who had been controlled by a demonic fever. And by "raising her up" he reverses her disabling position of "lying down."

Overpowered by Jesus, who has now taken control of the woman, the demon causing the fever "leaves" her and she is able to fulfill her familial task of hospitality as she "serves" them. This represents the third element of a miracle story of healing—the fact or confirmation of the sudden healing. As the demonic fever "leaves" her, Simon's mother-in-law is freed from her debilitating ailment and personally experiences the salvation Jesus brings in the form of healing. And that she now "serves" them illustrates how Jesus has restored her to her important position within her family and has enabled her to reinstate the harmony and well-being of the household.

## 2. MARK 1:29-31 AS MODEL FOR ACTION

We continue to be attracted to follow the salvific "way" of Jesus, as he demonstrates his power and compassion to heal. That Jesus is willing and able to heal even a woman, a person of low social status, and thus to restore harmony to the familial household of his first followers gives us, his later followers, the hope that Jesus can extend his healing power to all of us and our family members, who continue to suffer the disharmony of demonic diseases that disrupt our personal and familial lives.

The four disciples in this scene serve as a model of faith and intercessory prayer. We are called to imitate their faith in following Jesus and their faith in Jesus' power to heal. As they compassionately interceded on behalf of Simon's mother-in-law by informing Jesus of her illness, we are urged likewise to intercede for those who are sick by praying to Jesus on their behalf.

Healed and restored by Jesus, Simon's mother-in-law offers us an appealing model of ideal discipleship. Her humble "service" of hospitality to the guests of her household points to the humble service toward others that Jesus demands of us as his followers (9:33–35; 10:35–45).[10]

## E. Mark 1:32–34: Jesus Heals Many People and Expels Many Demons at the Door of Simon's House

> [32]When evening came, after sunset, they kept bringing to him all those who were ill and those possessed by demons. [33]And the whole city was gathered at the door. [34]Then he healed the many who were ill with various diseases and expelled the many demons, but he did not allow the demons to speak because they knew him.

### 1. MEANING OF MARK 1:32-34

#### a. *1:32* The people bring to Jesus all who are ill and possessed.

That it is "after sunset" on the "evening" of the sabbath (1:21) means that the day of sabbath has passed (the Jewish day was reckoned from sunset to sunset), so that the people of Capernaum may do the work of bringing the sick and possessed to Jesus without violating the sabbath rest. After Jesus has exorcised one of their men (1:21–28) and healed one of their women (1:29–31), the people of Capernaum, in their compassion for the sick, "kept bringing" to him "all" the ill and those possessed by de-mons in the hope that he can also heal large groups of people.

### b. *1:33* All Capernaum is gathered at the door of Simon's house.

That the "whole city" of Capernaum "was gathered at the door" of Simon's house indicates not only how Jesus' fame (1:28) and the people's attraction toward him as a healer have increased, but also how serious and widespread is their need for healing. The whole city was gathered at the door of the house where Jesus has just healed Simon's mother-in-law, in hopeful anticipation that he can and will continue to exercise his wonder-ful healing power.

### c. *1:34* Jesus heals and exorcises them but forbids the demons to reveal his identity.

The anticipation is fulfilled as Jesus healed all of "the many" who were sick and expelled all of "the many" demons.[11] His miraculous heal-ing and exorcistic power is enhanced as he demonstrates that he can heal and exorcise not only individuals but great numbers "with various diseases."

That Jesus "did not allow the demons to speak because they knew him" develops 1:24–25, where the unclean spirit exclaimed that "I know who you are—the Holy One of God!" and Jesus countered with "be quiet and come out of him!" There is apparently something inappropriate about the demons revealing to people the more profound identity of the person of Jesus. This creates suspense for the reader, who now questions and looks for the reason Jesus forbids demons to reveal him.

### 2. MARK 1:32–34 AS MODEL FOR ACTION

The amplification of healing and exorcistic power that Jesus displays in this scene further induces us to follow his salvific "way." His great power to heal and exorcise further convinces us that God's kingship has arrived with him. Our hope is aroused in what Jesus can do for our human condition of suffering, since he possesses the marvelous power and com-passion to heal and exorcise not just isolated cases but large numbers with various ailments.

The people of Capernaum who compassionately bring their sick to Jesus serve as a model calling us likewise to have concern and compassion for the sick by enabling them to encounter the healing power of Jesus.

Jesus' forbidding of the expelled demons to reveal his more profound identity causes us to question the reason for this and thus to probe whether there is more to Jesus and the kingdom of God than has so far been revealed by his power to heal and exorcise.

## F. Mark 1:35–39: After Praying in the Desert, Jesus Goes throughout Galilee Preaching and Expelling Demons

[35]Then rising very early before dawn, he came out and went on to a deserted place and was praying there. [36]Then Simon and those with him pursued him, [37]and found him and said to him, "All are seeking you!" [38]But he said to them, "Let us go on to the next towns that I may preach there also, for that is why I have come out." [39]So he went throughout all Galilee, preaching in their synagogues and expelling demons.

### 1. MEANING OF MARK 1:35–39

#### a. *1:35* Jesus leaves Capernaum and goes to the desert to pray.

The temporal notice of Jesus "rising very early before dawn" not only facilitates his departure from the crowds seeking him (1:37) but also provides a fitting time (Pss 5:4; 88:14) for his prayer.

That Jesus "came out" of Capernaum and "went on" to a deserted place emphasizes the continuous movement of his "way" of salvation. As a place of critical encounter with God reminiscent of the place of Jesus' baptismal consecration with God's Spirit (1:3–4, 9–11) and of his experience of divine protection during his testing by Satan in the wilderness (1:12–13), the "deserted place" provides an appropriate environment for Jesus to "pray," that is, for the "beloved Son of God" (1:11) to discern and place himself in union with the salvific will of his Father. This "praying" of Jesus in a "deserted place" thus signals a critical turning point in his salvific "way."

#### b. *1:36–37* Simon and his fellow disciples find Jesus.

That only "Simon" is specifically named again indicates his preeminence among the first followers of Jesus. Simon and "those with him," that is, Andrew, James and John (1:29), "pursue" and "find" Jesus praying alone in a deserted place. Speaking on behalf of the people of Capernaum whom Jesus has abandoned, they exclaim with perplexed alarm, "All are seeking you!" They thus express the surprising incongruity of Jesus seemingly forsaking all of the people he has been attracting and healing.

### c. *1:38* Jesus summons his disciples on to the nearby towns.

Jesus' response to the bewildered Simon and those with him proceeds from his having prayed to God, that is, having discerned the will of God at this turning point in his "way." He is, in effect, telling them that it is not God's will for him at this time to return and remain with the people of Capernaum. Instead, his Father wants him to extend his preaching beyond Capernaum to the "next towns" and the disciples are invited to follow him.

"For that is why I have come out" explains not only why Jesus has "come out" (1:35) of Capernaum, but also why he has "come out" in a more fundamental and absolute sense: He has "come out" in accord with God's plan in order to continue the movement of the salvific "way of the Lord" (1:2–3).

### d. *1:39* Jesus preaches and expels demons throughout Galilee.

Following God's will as discerned in his praying, Jesus continues his salvific "way" as he "went" throughout the region of "all Galilee," the region to which his fame has already spread (1:28). He was preaching in their "synagogues," the normal Jewish gathering places for hearing and responding to the word of God in worship. The message he was "preaching" was the good news that the kingship of God is now at hand, calling for repentance and faith (1:14–15). And he was "expelling demons," thus mercifully alleviating the evil afflictions of the people of Galilee and thereby demonstrating the arrival of God's kingdom.

### 2. MARK 1:35–39 AS MODEL FOR ACTION

The praying of Jesus at this critical turning point in his "way" of salvation provides us with a model for prayer. We are advised to imitate Jesus by likewise praying to discern God's will for us at critical moments in our lives as we attempt to follow the "way" of Jesus.

The exchange between Jesus and his pursuing disciples who are alarmed at his apparent abandonment of the people he just attracted and healed teaches us two important points. First, we learn that the preaching and healing ministry of Jesus has a universal dimension. It is not limited to the people of Capernaum but extends to all of Galilee. Secondly, we realize that the "way" of Jesus can contradict our normal, human way of thinking because it accords with God's will. This challenges us to a deeper faith and trust in following the "way" of Jesus as the "way of the Lord" and not as our own way.

## G. Mark 1:40–45: Jesus Heals a Leper, Retreats to the Desert and Attracts People from All Around

⁴⁰Then a leper came to him begging him, and kneeling said to him, "If you will, you can make me clean!" ⁴¹Moved with pity and stretching out his hand, he touched him and said to him, "I will, be clean!" ⁴²And immediately the leprosy left him, and he was made clean. ⁴³Then sternly warning him, he dismissed him at once, ⁴⁴and said to him, "See that you tell no one anything, but go, show yourself to the priest and offer for your cleansing what Moses prescribed, as proof for them." ⁴⁵But going out he began to proclaim everywhere and to spread abroad the word, so that he (Jesus) could no longer openly enter a town, but was out in deserted places; yet they were coming to him from everywhere.

### 1. MEANING OF MARK 1:40–45

#### a. *1:40* A leper approaches Jesus and begs for healing.

That a person with the highly contagious and dreaded skin disease of leprosy dares to approach Jesus initiates the suspense of this healing story.[12] Against its Jewish apocalyptic background leprosy was considered demonic in origin and the result of human sinfulness.[13] The scourge of leprosy was not only physically painful, but it rendered a person "unclean" and thus banished him from society. A leper could be restored to the community only after verification of his healing by a priest and the offering of sacrifice (Lev 13–14).[14] In Jewish thought lepers were in the same "unclean" category as the dead (Num 12:12). According to the OT story of the prophet Elisha curing Naaman the Syrian of his leprosy (2 Kgs 5:1–14), to cure a leper was thought to be as difficult as raising a dead person and possible only by the power of God (2 Kgs 5:7).

As the first element of the healing genre the leper beseeches Jesus with a posture of prayerful ("begging") homage ("kneeling"). The leper exhibits his bold faith in Jesus' uniquely divine power to cure him as he exclaims, "If you will, you can make me clean!"

#### b. *1:41* With compassion Jesus touches the leper and commands the healing.

The powerful action and words of Jesus in response to the leper's prayerful request serve as the second element of the healing genre. Jesus is "moved with pity" at the excruciating distress and urgent plea of the leper. With the dramatic gesture of "stretching out his hand," reminiscent of the way that divine wonder-working and saving power was transmitted through God and Moses in the Exodus event (Exod 4:4; 7:19; 8:1; 9:22; 14:16, 21, 26–27), Jesus, without the slightest fear of contamination, "touched" the leper, thus transmitting the divine power to expel the demonic infection and cure him. In precise correspondence to the words of the leper's trusting supplication, the concise command of Jesus indicates that indeed he has both the compassionate willingness and the unique divine power to cure the leper: "I will, be clean!"

### c. *1:42* The leprosy suddenly leaves and the man is cleansed.

The instant effectiveness of Jesus' command functions as the final essential element of the healing genre, the fact or confirmation of the sudden healing. In the manner of an expelled demon the leprosy "immediately left" the man so that he is now wonderfully "cleansed." This completes the concise "catchword" connection of the healing encounter:

> *1:40* If you *will,* you can make me *clean!*
> *1:41* I *will,* be *clean!*
> *1:42* Immediately the leprosy left him, and he was made *clean.*

The leper's daringly confident faith in Jesus' power to heal even leprosy is rewarded by the immediate and miraculous cleansing.

### d. *1:43–44* Jesus warns the man to say nothing and sends him to the priest.

In order to complete the total healing of the leper by restoring him fully to the community, his cleansing must be officially confirmed by a priest in accord with Mosaic law (Lev 13–14). On behalf of the leper the priest makes a sacrificial offering of atonement to God before the leper can be reinstated as an active member of society (Lev 14:1–20). Accordingly Jesus "dismissed him at once," after "sternly warning" the man to remain completely silent about his miraculous cure, so that without delay he can show himself to the priest for official verification of his cure and offer for his cleansing "what Moses prescribed." The leper's execution of this command of Jesus will serve as "proof for them," that is, the formal and legal evidence of the cure that "they," the rest of Jewish society, need to accept the man back into the community. And so Jesus not only liberates this individual from the demonic disease of leprosy, but enables him to be restored to his full, legal status in society. The healing is thus a personal experience of the salvation Jesus offers and a further demonstration of the arrival of God's kingship.

### e. *1:45* As the man talks freely, Jesus retreats to the desert yet people keep coming to him.

This cure of leprosy is so magnificent and marvelous and its display of special divine power so significant for others, that the cured leper simply cannot contain the news of it within himself. Instead of obeying Jesus' command by remaining silent and promptly going to the priest, the man goes out and begins "to proclaim everywhere and to spread abroad the word" about this splendid demonstration of God's compassionate healing power at work in Jesus. As a result of the leper's broadcasting the news of his cure, Jesus becomes so popular and so much in demand that he can no longer enter a town publicly, and so he withdraws to "deserted places" outside. But even this does not prevent the people from "coming to him from everywhere." And so, while the reader is favorably impressed by the remarkable enhancement of Jesus' power and popularity in this scene, there remains a note of suspenseful tension, created by the leper's disobedience of Jesus' stern command for silence and Jesus' unsuccessful attempt to withdraw from the many people streaming to him.

### 2. MARK 1:40–45 AS MODEL FOR ACTION

This phenomenal exposition that Jesus possesses the unique divine power to cure even the demonic disease of leprosy further demonstrates the arrival of God's kingship with the person of Jesus and further leads us to follow the salvific "way" of Jesus by converting our lives and placing our faith in the gospel he proclaims (1:14–15).

The daringly bold and prayerful faith in Jesus' will and ability to heal portrayed by the leper serves as a model for our imitation. By empathizing with the leper's personal experience of total healing in the form of liberation from a dreaded demonic disease and restoration to the community, we are persuaded to hope that Jesus can and will extend his unique divine power to heal us, who often suffer similar pain and alienation from our fellow human beings because of the power of evil and sinfulness.

As one who "proclaimed everywhere" and "spread abroad the word," the cured leper presents us with a model for effective evangelization. We are called to be likewise so excited by the good news of Jesus and its significance for our human condition that we cannot contain it within ourselves but must joyously share it with everyone.

The suspense aroused by the leper's disobedience of Jesus' order for silence and Jesus' futile endeavor to avoid the crowds of people coming to him provokes our curiosity and continues to caution us that there is more to Jesus and following his "way" than has been illustrated even by this extraordinary cure of leprosy.

## H. Mark 2:1–12: Returning to Capernaum, Jesus Forgives and Heals a Paralytic, Causing Controversy among Some Scribes

[1]When he returned to Capernaum after some days, it became known that he was at home. [2]Then many gathered together so that there was no longer room, not even around the door, and he was speaking the word to them. [3]Then they came bringing to him a paralytic carried by four men. [4]But unable to get near him because of the crowd, they removed the roof above him, and having made an opening, they lowered the pallet on which the paralytic was lying. [5]Then seeing their faith, Jesus said to the paralytic, "Child, your sins are forgiven!" [6]Now some of the scribes were sitting there, questioning in their hearts, [7]"Why does this man speak thus? He blasphemes! Who can forgive sins but God alone?" [8]But immediately perceiving in his mind that they thus questioned within themselves, Jesus said to them, "Why do you question these things in your hearts? [9]Which is easier, to say to the paralytic, 'Your sins are forgiven,' or to say, 'Rise, take up your pallet and walk'? [10]But that you may know that the Son of Man has authority to forgive sins on earth"—he said to the paralytic—[11]"I say to you, rise, take up your pallet and go to your home!" [12]Then he rose and immediately taking up his pallet, he went out in front of all, so that they were all amazed and glorified God, saying, "We have never seen anything like this!"

### 1. MEANING OF MARK 2:1–12

**a.** *2:1–2* **Returning to the house in Capernaum, Jesus preaches to the many people gathered around the door.**

Having earlier departed from the house of Simon and Andrew in Capernaum in order to preach and heal throughout Galilee (1:29–39) and having been forced to leave the cities for deserted places (1:45), Jesus now continues his salvific "way" as he "returns" to Capernaum after some days. When it becomes known that he has returned to the house of Simon and Andrew, he attracts so many people that even the doorway is filled. That "he was speaking the word to them" means that he was continuing to proclaim the arrival of God's kingdom, calling for repentance and faith (1:14–15).

### b. *2:3–4* Four men lower a paralytic to Jesus through the roof.

As four men bring a paralytic to Jesus, the reader is alerted to the beginning of a healing story. That the paralytic is "carried by four men" not only underlines the crippling effects of his inability to walk alone and thus his dependence on others, but also indicates the communal or interpersonal dimension of the sickness, which involves not only the afflicted individual but also evokes the care and concern of those around him.

Undaunted by the crowd blocking the normal passage to Jesus through the doorway, the four men are so intent upon bringing the paralytic to Jesus for healing that they perform the unusual but clever action of removing the roof and making an opening so that they can lower the paralytic directly to Jesus.[15]

### c. *2:5* Seeing their faith, Jesus forgives the paralytic's sins.

Jesus sees the lowering of the paralytic through the roof as a demonstration of the faith that these four men and the paralytic have in his healing power. But instead of healing the man's paralysis as anticipated by the reader, he rather unexpectedly but emphatically pronounces the forgiveness of his sins: "Child, your sins are forgiven!" Although surprising, this declaration of forgiveness is quite relevant here in view of the apocalyptic-eschatological idea that sickness and sinfulness were interrelated with both having a common demonic origin.[16]

### d. *2:6–7* Some scribes inwardly question whether Jesus can forgive sins.

The presence of "some of the scribes," the official teachers and interpreters of Jewish law and traditions, begins to develop the hint of conflict between Jesus and the scribes, which was introduced for the reader in 1:22 when the people were astounded at the teaching of Jesus "for he was teaching them as one having authority and not as the scribes." The scribes' opposition to Jesus begins privately with a "questioning in their hearts." They belittle Jesus as only "this man" and question why he "speaks thus," that is, why he dares to pronounce divine forgiveness of the paralytic's sins. They think that Jesus "blasphemes," a serious charge of irreverent violation or mockery of God's authority, in this case, by usurping God's unique prerogative to forgive sins. For the scribes this alleged blasphemy of Jesus amounts to a denial of God's sovereign unity: "Who can forgive sins but God alone?"[17]

The scribes' objection to Jesus' declaration of forgiveness of sins here serves as the first trait of the literary genre of a controversy or pronouncement story. This type of story includes three basic elements: 1) Opponents question or object to something said or done by Jesus and/or his followers as being contrary to the law or will of God; 2) Jesus counters the question or objection with superior questioning or argumentation; and 3) the final result or climax is a powerful pronouncement revealing a new teaching about God's will and/or a new aspect of Jesus' character and relationship to God.[18] In this instance a pronouncement story is combined with a miraculous healing story into a narrative unity.

### e. *2:8–9* Jesus counters the scribes' questioning of his power.

Jesus' ability to "immediately perceive in his mind" what the scribes are thinking to themselves already begins to illustrate his superiority. He forces their private objections of his authority to forgive sins into the open as he begins his counter-questioning, the second feature of the pronouncement story: "Why do you question these things in your hearts?" Jesus then proposes a provocative rhetorical question, "Which is easier, to say to the paralytic, 'Your sins are forgiven,' or to say, 'Rise, take up your pallet and walk'?" With this perplexing question Jesus induces his listeners to ponder and realize that the anticipated pronouncement of his healing power is equivalent to his unexpected pronouncement of forgiveness. Both healing and forgiveness require the authoritative power of God (Pss 41:5; 103:3), now operative in Jesus. The point is that Jesus could just as easily have pronounced the paralytic's healing, because he has effected the equivalent by pronouncing his forgiveness.

### f. *2:10–11* Jesus reveals that he is the Son of Man who has the authority to forgive sins as he commands the paralytic's healing.

Jesus then explains why he pronounced the paralytic's forgiveness rather than healing. It was to make his audience "know" that he is not just "this man," as the scribes contemptuously suppose, but the "Son of Man" who "has authority to forgive sins on earth." This represents the third element of the pronouncement story, the climactic pronouncement revealing a new aspect about Jesus' character. Here Jesus reveals himself to be the heavenly, messianic agent of God which Jewish tradition knew as the apocalyptic "Son of Man" (Dan 7; 4 Ezra).[19] As this transcendent "Son of Man" figure sent to them by God, Jesus now has God's unique "authority to forgive sins" not just in the heavenly realm but even in their midst "on earth."

Jesus delayed his powerful pronouncement of the paralytic's healing in order that it might visibly demonstrate his divine authority as "Son of Man" to forgive sins on earth. And so now he commands the paralytic to "rise, take up your pallet and go to your home!" This functions as the second element of the miraculous healing story, the powerful words or action of the healer. No longer dependent upon the four men to carry him, the paralytic may now "rise" by himself and "take up" the pallet he was forced by his illness to lie upon. He may now walk and in accord with the communal or interpersonal dimension of the healing, Jesus sends the paralytic "home," thus restoring him to his family.

With Jesus' mighty words of healing the narrator climactically concludes his emphasis in this scene upon the divine authoritative power of the words or speech of Jesus:

2:2 . . . he was *speaking* the *word* to them.

2:5 Jesus *said* to the paralytic, "Child, your sins are forgiven!"

2:7 (Scribes): "Why does this man *speak* thus?"

2:9 (Jesus): "Which is easier, to *say* to the paralytic, 'Your sins are forgiven,' or to *say*, 'Rise, take up your pallet and walk'?"

2:10 . . . he *said* to the paralytic—

2:11 "I *say* to you, rise, take up your pallet and go to your home!"

### g. *2:12* The paralytic is healed and all glorify God.

By "rising" and "immediately taking up his pallet," the paralytic is enabled to do exactly what Jesus commanded. As he "went out in front of all," he demonstrates his miraculous healing, which indicates that his sins have been forgiven and now proves that Jesus as "Son of Man" has the authoritative divine power to forgive sins on earth (2:10). This serves as the third element of the healing story, the fact or confirmation of the sudden healing.

The scene closes on an exuberant note as "all" who see the paralytic, now healed and forgiven, walk "in front of" them are "all" astounded and "glorify God" for what they have just experienced, acknowledging that "we have never seen anything like this!" In other words, they have never witnessed such a display of divine authoritative power as Jesus has just performed with his mighty pronouncements of the paralytic's healing and forgiveness.

That "all glorified God" represents the proper interpretation and response to Jesus' pronouncement of divine forgiveness and healing. It overshadows the scribes' charge that Jesus "blasphemes" against God by irreverently claiming for himself the unique divine prerogative to forgive sins (2:7) as a wrong interpretation. By "glorifying God" all acknowledge that God's unique authority both to forgive sins and heal is now marvelously operative in Jesus.

## 2. MARK 2:1–12 AS MODEL FOR ACTION

As this story moves us forward on the salvific "way" of Jesus, we are invited to imitate the exemplary faith of the paralytic and the four men who carry him so that our faith can be deepened and our experience of Jesus broadened. By empathizing with the paralytic, we vicariously experience Jesus' divine authoritative power not only to heal the physical disease that is a consequence of sinfulness but to eradicate the underlying cause of disease by forgiving sins. We are thereby given a new insight into Jesus' more profound identity; namely, that he is the heavenly "Son of Man" now authorized by God to forgive sins on earth. The healing of the paralytic, then, stimulates in us the hope that we can likewise experience a total healing from Jesus, a healing that includes not only the alleviation of our physical suffering and restoration to our place in the community but also the forgiveness of our sinfulness and restoration of our relationship to God.

The crowds of people in this scene present us with a model of eagerness to listen to the authoritative teaching of Jesus (2:2) and of the proper interpretation and response to the power of Jesus to heal and forgive sins (2:12). We are thus called to join them in eagerly heeding the teaching of Jesus and in glorifying God for bestowing upon Jesus the divine power to liberate us from the demonic sickness and sinfulness that afflict our lives.

The scribes serve as negative examples for Mark's audience. The exhilarating amazement of "all" the people who glorify God leads us to reject the scribes' vile charge of blasphemy against Jesus. But the conflict that is developing between Jesus and the scribes alerts us to the possibility of further misinterpretation and opposition as we follow the "way" of Jesus.

# I. Mark 2:13–17: After Levi Follows Him, Jesus Eats with Toll Collectors and Sinners, Bringing Objections from the Scribes

<sup>13</sup>Then he went out again along the sea, and all the crowd came to him and he taught them. <sup>14</sup>Then passing on, he saw Levi the son of Alphaeus sitting at the customs office, and he said to him, "Follow me!" And he got up and followed him. <sup>15</sup>Then he reclined at table in his house, and many toll collectors and sinners were reclining with Jesus and his disciples; for there were many who followed him. <sup>16</sup>But the scribes of the Pharisees, seeing that he was eating with sinners and toll collectors, said to his disciples, "Why does he eat with toll collectors and sinners?" <sup>17</sup>Then hearing this, Jesus said to them, "Those who are well do not need a physician, but those who are sick do; I have not come to call the righteous but sinners!"

### 1. MEANING OF MARK 2:13–17

**a. *2:13* Jesus goes along the sea and teaches all the crowd.**

Jesus advances the movement of his salvific "way," as "he went out again along the sea." This recalls for the reader the earlier scene of Jesus' calling of his first followers, which began with his "passing along the Sea of Galilee" (1:16–20). That "all the crowd came to him" extends the motif of the persistent attraction of great numbers of people to Jesus wherever he goes on his "way" (1:32–34, 37, 45; 2:2). He continues to "teach them" with his superior authority (1:21–28, 38–39; 2:2), inviting conversion and faith in the good news of the arrival of God's kingship (1:14–15).

**b. *2:14* Levi the toll collector answers the call to follow Jesus.**

"Passing on" his "way," Jesus "saw" a Jewish man named "Levi the son of Alphaeus" engaged in the occupation of collecting indirect taxes (tolls, tariffs, customs) from the people, as he was "sitting at the customs office." Suspense is aroused for the reader by the fact that this man clearly has a Jewish name ("Levi") and is from a Jewish family ("son of Alphaeus") yet is a toll collector, a profession many Jews considered disreputable and sinful because of its association with Gentiles in the often dishonest collection of revenue from Jews on behalf of the foreign Roman government.<sup>20</sup> With the abrupt authoritative command to "follow me!," Jesus summons this Jewish toll collector to conversion by leaving behind his questionable profession. Without the slightest hesitation Levi surprisingly obeys Jesus' powerful command as he "got up" from his work of sitting at the customs office and promptly "followed him." Just as Simon, Andrew, James and John had earlier left behind their families and professions as fishermen at the dynamic directive of Jesus (1:16–20), so Levi admirably abandons his shameful profession as a toll collector to "follow" Jesus on the "way" of God's salvation.

### c. *2:15* Jesus and his disciples recline at table with many toll collectors and sinners.

Having called the Jewish toll collector Levi to be his follower, Jesus then "reclined at table in his house." For Jews "reclining at table" in the social and religious festivity of a meal signified the establishment of a close interpersonal bond among the participants, known as "table fellowship."[21] That "many toll collectors and sinners were reclining with Jesus and his disciples" creates the outrageous situation of Jesus establishing table fellowship with despicable "toll collectors" and public "sinners," that is, Gentiles and/or Jews who clearly and publicly live contrary to Mosaic law. This first mention of "his disciples" as the group of various people Jesus has called to follow him (1:16–20; 2:14) draws them into this scandalous celebration of table fellowship. The added note that "there were many (toll collectors and sinners) who followed him" not only enhances the charismatic capability of Jesus to attract many such followers but magnifies the offensiveness of the incident.

### d. *2:16* The scribes of the Pharisees object to Jesus' eating with toll collectors and sinners.

When "the scribes of the Pharisees" witness this shocking celebration of table fellowship that Jesus and his disciples conduct with detestable sinners and toll collectors, they question his disciples: "Why does he eat with toll collectors and sinners?" This functions as the first element of the "pronouncement story" genre, the objection by opponents of Jesus to behavior they consider to be contrary to their sacred traditions and the will of God. With the mention of "the scribes of the Pharisees" the opponents of Jesus now include not merely "the scribes" in general (1:22; 2:6) but the scribes of "the Pharisees," a religiously elite group of Jews who strictly observed not only the written Torah but the oral traditions of the elders. Since the Pharisees carefully separated themselves from those not as zealously concerned to follow the commandments and traditions of God's law as they were, Jesus' table fellowship with toll collectors and public sinners is especially offensive to them.[22] That the scribes of the Pharisees question "his disciples" draws them into the dispute by their association with Jesus. Although still indirect, the opposition to Jesus has become more overt, progressing from the scribes' questioning within themselves (2:6–7) to their questioning of his disciples.

### e. *2:17* Jesus proclaims that he has not come to call the righteous but sinners.

When Jesus hears the scribes of the Pharisees challenge his disciples about his table fellowship with toll collectors and sinners, he overwhelms them with the provocative, climactic pronouncement: "Those who are well do not need a physician, but those who are sick do; I have not come to call the righteous but sinners!" This serves as both the second and third elements of the pronouncement story, the superior counter-argumentation and the powerful pronouncement revealing a new aspect of Jesus' character and relationship to God.

With the proverb-like saying that it is the sick rather than the healthy who need a physician, Jesus justifies and explains his table fellowship with toll collectors and public sinners by revealing himself to be the "physician" equipped with God's authoritative power to "heal" the "sick" in need of God's mercy, the toll collectors and sinners, by forgiving their sins after they have converted, as illustrated by the call of Levi (2:14). This resonates with the point of the previous pronouncement story, that Jesus is the Son of Man who has divine authority both to heal and to forgive sins (2:1–12).

In the final thrust of his powerful pronouncement Jesus reveals a new and revolutionary aspect about the purpose of his "coming," his salvific "way of the Lord," as he proclaims that he has not "come" to call "the righteous," those who observe the Jewish law and traditions like the scribes of the Pharisees, but "sinners," the "sick" in need of God's healing forgiveness like the toll collectors and public sinners with whom Jesus is eating. Jesus' stunning pronouncement not only justifies and reveals his table fellowship as a joyous celebration of the divine healing and forgiveness that Jesus extends to "sinners" who answer his call to conversion (1:15), but ironically indicts the scribes of the Pharisees as the "well" and the "righteous" who fail to convert to the "way" of Jesus by not realizing their own need for God's healing and forgiveness now present in Jesus.

The opponents of Jesus in this scene sadly fail to realize what the reader sees as a new and astounding revelation of the salvific "way" of Jesus: That this is no ordinary meal with an ordinary Jewish teacher and his followers, but an anticipation of the eschatological "messianic banquet" (Isa 55:1–7; 25:6–8) of the coming kingdom of God (1:15) in which sinners who have answered Jesus' urgent call to conversion experience the marvelous table fellowship of divine healing, forgiveness and reconciliation offered by the one who is the messianic "Son of Man" with God's authority to heal and forgive sins on earth (2:10).[23]

## 2. MARK 2:13-17 AS MODEL FOR ACTION

The toll collector Levi and the group of toll collectors and public sinners who recline at table with Jesus present us with a model of conversion. We are persuaded to imitate them by radically turning away from our past lives of sinfulness to experience the fellowship of divine healing forgiveness and merciful reconciliation now available for those who answer the call of Jesus to conversion and follow his "way."

As the "righteous" who refuse Jesus' call to conversion and the "well" who do not need the healing forgiveness of the "physician," the scribes of the Pharisees provide us with an intriguing counter-model of conversion. They teach us not to become so complacently convinced of our own presuppositions about God's saving will and plan that we close ourselves to the innovative salvific "way" now revealed by Jesus, as he shockingly eats with despised sinners. They caution us constantly to reexamine our lives and our relationship with God for areas where we need conversion lest we become presumptuous and fail to realize our need for God's healing forgiveness and reconciliation now offered by Jesus.

Jesus and his disciples, who share table fellowship with Levi, the toll collectors and public sinners who answer Jesus' call to conversion and follow him, offer us a model of evangelizing reconciliation. The call to conversion and reconciliation demonstrated by Jesus and his disciples empowers us to eliminate the barriers that separate us from those we consider public sinners by calling them to conversion and thus inviting them to experience and celebrate along with us the fellowship of reconciliation and the divine forgiveness granted by Jesus, the "physician" and messianic "Son of Man."

## J. Mark 2:18-22: With Powerful Pronouncements Jesus Answers the Question of Why His Disciples Do Not Fast

[18]Now the disciples of John and the Pharisees were fasting. And (people) came and said to him, "Why do the disciples of John and the disciples of the Pharisees fast, but your disciples do not fast?" [19]But Jesus said to them, "Can the wedding guests fast while the bridegroom is with them? As long as they have the

bridegroom with them they cannot fast. [20]But the days will come when the bridegroom is taken away from them, and then they will fast on that day. [21]No one sews a patch of unshrunk cloth on an old cloak. If he does, the patch tears away from it, the new from the old, and a worse tear is made. [22]And no one puts new wine into old wineskins. If he does, the wine will burst the skins, and both the wine and the skins are ruined. Rather, (put) new wine into fresh wineskins!"

### 1. MEANING OF MARK 2:18–22

#### a. *2:18* Some question Jesus as to why his disciples do not fast.

Still within the context of Jesus and his disciples "eating" with toll collectors and public sinners (2:13–17), the narrator introduces the contrasting topic of "fasting" as he states that it was the custom of "the disciples of John" and of "the Pharisees" to "fast," that is, to abstain from food for certain periods of time as an ascetical religious practice.[24] The fasting of "the disciples of John" represents a fitting response to the Baptist's call for conversion and preparation for God's coming salvation (1:2–8) and accords with their master's own ascetical lifestyle (1:6). They are fasting, then, in mournful and earnest anticipation for the coming eschatological intervention of God announced by John. That the "Pharisees" also fast not only adds to the number and variety of religiously observant Jews who are fasting but also resumes the note of conflict from the previous scene, where it was the "scribes of the Pharisees" who objected to the eating of Jesus and his disciples with toll collectors and sinners.

The disapproving query raised by those who came to Jesus, "Why do the disciples of John and the disciples of the Pharisees fast, but your disciples do not fast?," serves as the first element of a pronouncement story, the objection to the behavior of Jesus and his disciples as contrary to the law or will of God. This reproachful question implies the denigration of the authority of Jesus' teaching as inferior to that of both John the Baptist and the Pharisees, since those who follow their teaching observe the revered practice of fasting, which the disciples of Jesus ignore.

#### b. *2:19* Jesus proclaims that the "wedding guests" cannot fast while the "bridegroom" is with them.

Jesus' counter-question functions as the second element of the pronouncement story, the superior questioning or argumentation. With the rich imagery of a wedding feast, which symbolized the joyous festivity of the eschatological age of God's salvation (Isa 61:10; 62:4–5), Jesus characterizes himself as the "bridegroom" of the eschatological marriage feast which is already present and his disciples as the "wedding guests," as he asks, "Can the wedding guests fast while the bridegroom is with them?"[25] Jesus promptly answers his own question, which vindicates himself and his disciples from the charge of not fasting during this time of great joy by emphatically affirming the fact that the "bridegroom" of the long awaited eschatological wedding feast is already with them: "As long as they have the bridegroom with them they cannot fast."

### c. *2:20* But when the "bridegroom" is taken away, they will fast.

Continuing his explanation, Jesus inserts a sadly ominous note, subtly alerting the reader to his future death, as he predicts that there will be a time when he as the bridegroom "will be taken away" from his disciples, the wedding guests. "On that day," as joy turns to sorrow, it will be most appropriate for the followers of Jesus to fast out of mourning at the great loss and absence of their "bridegroom." But for now the disciples of Jesus must suspend the practice of fasting in order to celebrate with proper festivity "as long as they have the bridegroom with them."

### d. *2:21* No one sews a patch of unshrunk cloth on an old cloak.

The third element of this pronouncement story, the climactic and dominant pronouncement which reveals a new aspect about Jesus and his relation with God, consists of two proverbial statements which metaphorically express the incompatibility of the radically new situation of God's salvific intervention that has now arrived with the person of Jesus and the old situation advocated by the opponents of Jesus. These two parabolic sayings apply to the whole new circumstance of the breaking in of God's kingdom in and through Jesus, as illustrated not only by his disciples who do not fast, but also by his authoritative declaration of God's healing forgiveness (2:1–12) and his table fellowship with public sinners (2:13–17).

In the first maxim Jesus employs the image of "unshrunk cloth" to portray the new authoritative teaching (1:27) about God's "way" that has now appeared with his person and the image of an "old cloak" to depict what has now become the old teaching and way of responding to God's salvific plan, as represented by Jesus' adversaries. Just as no one would sew new "unshrunk cloth," with its tendency still to shrink, as a patch to repair an "old cloak" lest a worse tear results when the "new" tears away from the "old," so the teaching and person of Jesus are so drastically new and different that they cannot be compatibly joined to the old Jewish teaching about how God acts and how people are to respond to him. Like "unshrunk cloth" the aggressive newness of Jesus' person and teaching about God tends to "tear away" from the "old cloak" of the past.

### e. *2:22* No one puts new wine into old wineskins.

With this second proverbial assertion Jesus not only reinforces the point of the first saying about the incompatibility of the new situation of Jesus with the old situation of his opponents, but also emphasizes the superiority of the new way over the old way. Here Jesus uses the image of "new wine" to represent the new situation and the image of "old wine-skins" to characterize the old situation.[26] Just as no one would place "new wine," with its inclination to ferment and churn, into "old wineskins" lest they "burst" asunder and both wine and skins are irretrievably lost, so the exciting and provocative newness of the teaching and person of Jesus cannot be contained by the stiff oldness of past ways of thinking and acting about God's salvation. Like "new wine" the agitating newness of Jesus and his teaching would "burst" the "old wineskins" of the past.

With a final flourish, which accentuates the arrival of the "new wine" and thus underlines the preference and supremacy of the new situation over the old, Jesus exclaims, "Rather, put new wine into fresh wineskins!" In other words, the revolutionary newness of the "new wine" requires a corresponding newness of "fresh wineskins," that is, a fresh attitude and behavior toward the salvific activity of God now operative in the person and teaching of Jesus.

### 2. MARK 2:18–22 AS MODEL FOR ACTION

We are invited to join the disciples of Jesus who do not fast by like-wise recognizing and appropriately celebrating the salvific presence of the eschatological "bridegroom" so that we can experience the exhilarating joy and happiness that following the new authoritative teaching of Jesus, the "bridegroom," offers us.

The opposition to Jesus and the alarming notice that "the bride-groom will be taken away from them" alerts us to the dark side of the good news about Jesus. As we follow the "way" of Jesus we can expect not only joy and happiness but sorrow and sadness. The tragic obstinacy which deprives us of the presence of Jesus calls us to mournful fasting.

Jesus' rousing climactic pronouncements urge us to continual con-version. The revelation of the stirring newness of God's salvific activity now present in Jesus and his teaching, as the aggressive "unshrunk cloth" which tears away from the "old cloak" and the agitating "new wine" which cannot be contained in "old wineskins," warns us to modify our old attitudes, categories and behavior so that we can recognize, appreciate and experience this radically new saving action of God available to us in and through Jesus.

## K. Mark 2:23–28: As the Pharisees Object to His Disciples Plucking Grain, Jesus Reveals His Lordship over the Sabbath

[23]Then he passed through the grainfields on the sabbath, and his disciples began to make a way, plucking the heads of grain. [24]Then the Pharisees said to him, "Look, why are they doing what is not permitted on the Sabbath?" [25]But he said to them, "Have you never read what David did when he was in need and was hungry, he and those who were with him: [26]How he went into the house of God when Abiathar was high priest and ate the loaves of presentation, which it is not permitted for any except the priests to eat, and gave them also to those who were with him?" [27]Then he said to them, "The Sabbath was made for people, not people for the Sabbath! [28]Thus the Son of Man is lord even of the sabbath!"

### 1. MEANING OF MARK 2:23–28

#### a. *2:23* The disciples follow Jesus through the grainfields, plucking the heads of grain.

Jesus advances the movement of his salvific "way of the Lord" (1:2–3) as he "passed through" some grainfields on the Jewish sacred day of rest, "the sabbath."[27] That the disciples are followers of this "way" (*hodon*) of Jesus is underscored as they "began to make a way (*hodon*)." Their accompanying activity of "plucking the heads of grain" already arouses suspense as it clashes with the prescription of rest from work on the sabbath.

#### b. *2:24* The Pharisees accuse the disciples of violating the sabbath.

The complaint of the Pharisees introduces the first element of a controversy or pronouncement story: Opponents object to the behavior of Jesus and/or his disciples as being against the law of God. Here the Phari-

sees accuse Jesus' disciples of doing on the sabbath "what is not permitted" by the Mosaic law (Exod 20:8–11; 23:12; 34:21; Deut 5:12–15),
namely the work of plucking grain.[28] The adversaries of Jesus have pro-
gressed from "the scribes" (2:6) to "the scribes of the Pharisees" (2:16) to a
general "they" with reference to "the disciples of the Pharisees" (2:18) and
now to "the Pharisees" themselves. They bring their accusation directly to
Jesus as the master responsible for his disciples, and thus make it a question of the "new teaching" and "authority" (1:22, 27) of the "way"
of Jesus.

### c. *2:25–26* Jesus refers to the case of David and those with him, who ate the sacred loaves of presentation reserved for priests.

The reply of Jesus functions as the second element of the pronouncement story, the superior counter-questioning and argumentation. To vindicate his disciples and further illustrate the authority of his new teaching,
Jesus resorts to scriptural argumentation. With perhaps a tinge of sarcasm
("have you never read") he turns the attention of his Pharisaic antago-
nists, who as zealous proponents of God's will were presumably well-
versed in scripture, to an illustration of how God's salvific will was accomplished in an incident from the story of the great Jewish hero, David. With
reference to 1 Samuel 21:2–7 Jesus recalls what not only David himself
but "those who were with him" did when they were "in need" and
"hungry": They entered the sacred "house of God" and with the permission of the eminent "Abiathar," the official "high priest" of God who
recognized the importance of David, they were allowed to satisfy their
urgent need by eating the holy "loaves of presentation," which only consecrated "priests" could lawfully eat (Lev 24:5–9).[29]

By focusing on the "need" and "hunger" of David and his companions, Jesus indicates that the reason his disciples are doing the work of
plucking grain on the sabbath is to satisfy their physical need of hunger by
eating the grain. There is at least the implication that David and those
with him likewise ate on the sabbath. For, as the incident concludes in 1
Samuel 21:7: "So the priest gave him (David) the holy bread; for there was
no bread there but the bread of the Presence, which is removed from
before the Lord, to be replaced by hot bread on the day it is taken away."
According to Leviticus 24:8–9, the day on which the bread of Presence
was replaced and eaten by the priests was the sabbath: "Every sabbath day
Aaron shall set it in order before the Lord continually on behalf of the
people of Israel as a covenant for ever. And it is for Aaron and his sons,
and they shall eat it in a holy place . . ."

The point of this scriptural example is that David's eating of the sacred bread of the Presence which was otherwise forbidden did not violate God's will but actually furthered past salvation history. That the important presence of David allows "those who were with him" likewise to eat is emphasized through repetition:

> *2:25* David . . . in need and hungry, he and those who were with
> him.
> *2:26* . . . and gave them (loaves) also to those who were with him.

This facilitates the application to the disciples, who are allowed to eat on the sabbath because they are with Jesus. The argument proceeds in a traditional Jewish *qal wahomer* (from the "light" to the "heavy") manner, which is an *a fortiori* type of logical assertion—if A is true, then all the more does B follow.[30] In other words, if David and those who were with him did not transgress God's will but actually advanced salvation history by eating the sacred bread of the Presence, then all the more are the disciples who are with Jesus on his "way" of actualizing the new eschatological age of God's kingship (1:15; 2:21–22) surely not contradicting God's will but actually fulfilling it by eating on the sabbath.

### d. *2:27* Jesus asserts that the sabbath was made for people.

Continuing his counter-argumentation, Jesus keenly and concisely explains to the Pharisees: "The sabbath was made for people, not people for the sabbath!" Here Jesus reverts to the original meaning and position of the sabbath in God's plan of creation. God intended the sabbath for the benefit of human beings—to give them rest, relaxation and refreshment, in imitation of himself who rested on the seventh day of creation (Gen 2:1–3; Exod 16:22–30; 31:16–17). The sabbath, then, was meant to be a humanizing principle to give people a regular period of refreshment. Jesus would thus rescue and restore the original role of the sabbath as subordinate to proper human living from the Pharisees' attempt to make human beings slavishly subservient to an absolute and unreasonable observance of the sabbath. By allowing his disciples to satisfy their human need for food and thus be refreshed on the sabbath, Jesus actually accomplishes God's original purpose for the sabbath rest.

### e. *2:28* Jesus proclaims that the Son of Man is lord even of the sabbath.

As the climactic pronouncement of the entire controversy and the new revelation about Jesus and his relation to God, which serves as the final element of the pronouncement story, Jesus exuberantly exclaims:

"Thus the Son of Man is lord even of the sabbath!" This advances Jesus' previous revelation of himself as the transcendent, messianic "Son of Man" with heavenly authority now on earth:

> *2:10* ... the Son of Man has authority to forgive sins on earth
> *2:28* Thus the Son of Man is lord even of the sabbath.

The "Son of Man" was normally considered to be an apocalyptic-eschatological agent with divine power in the heavenly realm, but now Jesus reveals that as the Son of Man he has God's power not only to forgive sins "on earth" but to be "lord" with God's authority "even" over the sabbath. The presence of Jesus as the Son of Man allows the disciples to satisfy their human need, hunger, and thus to fulfill God's will for their refreshment by doing, even on the sabbath, the work necessary for them to eat. That Jesus is "lord" of the sabbath, then, means not that he ignores or abrogates the sabbath observance, but that he has God's authority to enable the sabbath to accomplish the human refreshment that God originally intended for it. By revealing that Jesus is the Son of Man who has lordship even over the sabbath, this final pronouncement powerfully vindicates the "new teaching" and "authority" (1:22, 27) of the "way" of Jesus against the accusation of the Pharisees.

### 2. MARK 2:23–28 AS MODEL FOR ACTION

Identifying with the disciples and thus continuing on the salvific "way" of Jesus, we discover a new dimension to the authoritative teaching of Jesus. That Jesus allowed his disciples to experience God's original purpose for the sabbath by satisfying their human need for food and thus being refreshed teaches us that following the "way" of Jesus brings with it the fulfillment of our basic needs as human beings. By following the "way" of Jesus, we can achieve the full, God-intended potential of our humanity.

The Pharisees, who charge the followers of Jesus with breaking God's law by doing the work necessary to satisfy their hunger on the sabbath, warn us of the danger of making God-given institutions like the sabbath so absolute that they fail to accomplish the benefits that God originally intended for our human lives. We are urged to follow the lead demonstrated by Jesus as the Son of Man who has lordship even over the sabbath, so that we can liberate ourselves and others from the inhumanity that unreasonable and rigid observance of religious institutions and practices can perpetrate.

## L. Mark 3:1–6: After Jesus Heals on the Sabbath, the Pharisees and Herodians Plot To Destroy Him

[1]Then he again went into the synagogue, and there was a man there who had a withered hand. [2]And they watched him closely (to see) if he would heal him on the sabbath, so that they might accuse him. [3]Then he said to the man who had the withered hand, "Come up into the middle!" [4]And he said to them, "Is it lawful to do good on the sabbath rather than to do evil, to save life rather than to kill?" But they remained silent. [5]Looking around at them with anger and deeply grieved at their hardness of heart, he said to the man, "Stretch out your hand!" He stretched it out and his hand was restored. [6]Then the Pharisees went out and immediately took counsel with the Herodians on how to destroy him.

### 1. MEANING OF MARK 3:1–6

#### a. *3:1* Jesus enters the synagogue where there is a man with a withered hand.

Resuming the movement of his salvific "way," Jesus "went into" the synagogue "again." This is the synagogue at Capernaum, where Jesus had earlier demonstrated his new teaching and authority by expelling unclean spirits from a possessed man (1:21–28). The presence there of a man "who had a withered hand" arouses the expectation of a miraculous healing.

#### b. *3:2* They watch to see if they can accuse Jesus of healing on the sabbath.

Tension is sparked as "they," that is, the Pharisees who opposed Jesus in the previous scene (2:23–28), scrutinize Jesus to see whether he will heal this man on the sabbath. The issue of healing "on the sabbath" continues the sabbath theme of the previous incident. According to Jewish tradition a person in immediate danger of death could be healed on the sabbath, but since this man only has a withered hand, his healing ignites controversy.

"So that they might accuse him" represents the most explicit and direct expression of the opposition against Jesus thus far in the narrative. No longer do the enemies of Jesus merely question in their hearts (2:6–7) or indirectly confront Jesus through his disciples (2:16, 18, 23–24). Now they are intent upon producing an official accusation directly against Jesus himself.

**c. *3:3* Jesus calls the man into the middle of the synagogue.**

With his superior knowledge of the thoughts of his adversaries (2:8) Jesus is aware of this attempt against him. But rather than withdrawing from the conflict, he provokes it by taking the initiative and calling the man into the middle of the synagogue. The suspense increases as the eyes of all are focused on the man with the withered hand. Jesus forces the issue into a public demonstration for all in the synagogue.

**d. *3:4* They refuse to answer Jesus' question whether it is lawful to do good and save life on the sabbath.**

With a powerful rhetorical question Jesus justifies his anticipated healing and provokes his Pharisaic opponents: "Is it lawful to do good on the sabbath rather than evil, to save life rather than kill?" The only possible answer is that of course it is "lawful," that is, God's will to do good and save life on the sabbath. Jesus thus elevates the case of healing this man with a withered hand into a matter of actually saving his life. The point is that it would certainly be in accord with God's original purpose for the sabbath, which was made for the benefit of people (2:27), to heal and thus save the life of this man.

Suspense is heightened as the Pharisees refuse to acknowledge the obvious answer that Jesus has masterfully evoked. For them to reply would deprive them of the accusation they are intent on bringing against Jesus. But by obstinately "remaining silent," they sadly resist the lordship that Jesus as the divinely empowered Son of Man has over the sabbath (2:28).

**e. *3:5* Angered and grieved at them, Jesus heals the man.**

Jesus responds with the strong emotions of "anger" and "deep grief," underlining the lamentable tragedy of the Pharisees' refusal to answer. Their stubborn silence reveals their "hardness of heart," a traditional biblical expression of obstinate unbelief and blinding by God characteristic of Pharaoh and the people of Israel, who continually, inexplicably and tragically refused to accept the saving plan of God.[31]

Not allowing the Pharisees' resistance to deprive the man of healing on the sabbath, Jesus boldly enacts the second step of the healing story, the efficacious words of the healer, "Stretch out your hand!" The sudden and miraculous healing is completed with the confirmation that "he stretched it out and it was restored." This "restoration" by God's power of the man's hand to its originally intended shape corresponds well with the sabbath's basic purpose of bringing about rest and refreshment to human lives. By executing this saving and restoring activity of God on the sabbath, Jesus further demonstrates how as the "Son of Man" he is "lord even of the sabbath" (2:28).

### f. *3:6* The Pharisees and Herodians plot to kill Jesus.

Jesus' public display of the marvelous and merciful saving power of God on the sabbath does not sway his enemies from their evil design. On the contrary, now that they have the evidence they seek for an accusation against him, they leave the synagogue and immediately take counsel with the "Herodians," supporters of the Roman government and political policies of Herod Antipas, the ruler of Galilee.[32] The purpose of their counsel is to plan "how to destroy him," which rings ironic for the reader in view of the Pharisees' refusal to acknowledge the "doing of evil" and "killing" that is against God's will for the sabbath (3:4). The opposition against Jesus is thus broadened to include not only the Jewish religious authorities of scribes and Pharisees but also the political group known as the Herodians. Their joint conspiracy "to destroy him" intensifies the attack against Jesus and marks the climax not only of this particular controversy but of the entire opposition that has been building against Jesus throughout the narrative (2:1–3:6). This develops Jesus' earlier foreboding hint that "the days will come when the bridegroom is taken away from them" (2:20), and thus awakens an ominous anticipation of the execution of this sinister plot. The ominous note of John's arrest (1:14) has thus evolved into the ominous note of a death plot against Jesus.

### 2. MARK 3:1–6 AS MODEL FOR ACTION

Continuing on the salvific "way" of Jesus, we further experience what it means that Jesus is the Son of Man with lordship even over the sabbath (2:28). Jesus' controversial healing of the man with the withered hand on the sabbath gives us the hope that he can and will likewise restore and save our lives, so that we can achieve our full potential as human beings in accord with God's original purpose that the sabbath effect rest and refreshment for the benefit of our humanity.

The Pharisees' obstinate opposition and "hardness of heart" serve as a negative example warning us to heed the authoritative teaching of Jesus and thus allow him to transform our old and hardened categories for God's will and action into an openness for the new and marvelous ways that God acts for our benefit as human beings in and through Jesus.

The plotting of the Pharisees and Herodians to destroy Jesus alerts us to the tragic consequences of refusal to convert and believe in Jesus.

Their evil intent induces us to realize and reckon with the danger of death-threatening opposition that stands in the way of following Jesus.

## Notes

1. When a passive verb is unaccompanied by an explicit agent, God is often to be understood as the implicit "divine" or "theological" agent, depending upon the context. See M. Zerwick, *Biblical Greek* (Rome: Biblical Institute, 1963) #236, p. 76.

2. See "The Gospel" in Chapter II.

3. See "Kingdom of God," "Sin/Sickness, Demons and Angels" and "King" in Chapter I.

4. For a discussion of what might have been the house of Peter and of the first-century synagogue beneath the presently standing one of a later date, see S. Loffreda, *A Visit to Capharnaum* (2d ed.; Jerusalem: Franciscan Printing, 1980); J. F. Strange and H. Shanks, "Has the House Where Jesus Stayed in Capernaum Been Found?" *BARev* 8/6 (1982) 26–37; "Synagogue Where Jesus Preached Found at Capernaum," *BARev* 9/6 (1983) 24–31.

5. For more on "Synagogue" and "Sabbath," see Chapter I.

6. For more on the "Scribes," see Chapter I.

7. On the apocalyptic-eschatological background of "demons" or "unclean spirits," see "Sin/Sickness, Demons and Angels" in Chapter I.

8. See Heil, "Miracles," 639–41.

9. For OT background to this question, which often occurs in a context of combat, see Judg 11:12; 2 Sam 16:10; 19:22; 1 Kgs 17:18; 2 Kgs 3:13, etc.

10. See "Women and Children" in Chapter I.

11. "The many" here represents the Semitic inclusive or universal "many" which is equivalent to "all"; it expresses "all" but with the connotation of a great number. See J. Jeremias, *"polloi," TDNT* 6.536–45.

12. I. H. Marshall (*The Gospel of Luke* [Grand Rapids: Eerdmans, 1978] 208) points out that "the term leprosy in the Bible does not mean the disease commonly so-called today (Hansen's bacillus) but covered a wide variety of skin diseases, including some which were obviously regarded as highly contagious and incurable, while others were capable of cure."

13. In Num 12:1–16, for example, God punishes Miriam with leprosy because of her sin of speaking against Moses. And on the demonic nature of diseases such as leprosy, see O. Böcher, *Christus Exorcista:*

*Dämonismus und Taufe in Neuen Testament* (BWANT 96; Stuttgart: Kohlhammer, 1972) 72.

14. With regard to the cultic uncleanness of leprosy, M. Noth (*Leviticus* [Philadelphia: Westminster, 1965] 104–5) says: "The inflicted man was no longer whole, and therefore no longer cultically competent: his outward appearance was deformed. Fundamentally, every disease, as far as it was visible in the body, excluded a man from cultic community for as long as it was present."

15. The removing of the roof here becomes more understandable when we consider that Jewish Palestinian houses often had flat roofs composed of mud, leaves and tree branches. Thus, removing them or making an opening in them was not extremely difficult, but still unusual.

16. See "Sin/Sickness, Demons and Angels" in Chapter I.

17. A more literal translation would be: "Who can forgive sins but the one God (*heis ho theos*)?"

18. R. C. Tannehill, "Introduction: The Pronouncement Story and its Types," *Pronouncement Stories* (Semeia 20; ed. R. C. Tannehill; Chico: Scholars, 1981, 1–13; "Varieties of Synoptic Pronouncement Stories," *Pronouncement Stories,* 101–19; "Attitudinal Shift in Synoptic Pronouncement Stories," *Orientation by Disorientation: Studies in Literary Criticism and Biblical Literary Criticism* (ed. R. A. Spencer; Pittsburgh: Pickwick, 1980) 183–97.

19. See "Son of Man" in Chapter I.

20. See "Toll Collectors and Public Sinners" in Chapter I.

21. S. K. Williams, "Meals," *Harper's Bible Dictionary,* 616–17: "In describing meals that Jesus participated in, the Gospels state that he reclined (at table). This expression indicates that in the Palestine of Jesus' day the Greco-Roman custom of reclining at formal meals had become widespread. . . . On couches placed around a large table (or three tables placed to form an open-ended rectangle), guests and host reclined on the left elbow and ate with the right hand, body diagonal to the couch and feet extending off the back. Usually three persons reclined on one couch."

22. See "Pharisees" in Chapter I.

23. J. F. Priest, "Messianic Banquet," *IDBSup,* 591–92.

24. See "Religious Practices" in Chapter I.

25. In the OT the relationship between Israel and her God is often depicted as a marital union with Israel as the "bride" and Yahweh as the divine "bridegroom." According to Isa 62:5, ". . . as the bridegroom rejoices over the bride, so shall your God rejoice over you."

26. Animal skins were utilized as containers for wine.

27. See "Sabbath" in Chapter I. And on the significance of the sabbath for Jews, E. Lohse ("*sabbaton*," *TDNT* 7.8) states: "The weekly Sab-

bath is for Judaism a sign of divine election, for no people apart from Israel has sanctified God in keeping the Sabbath, Jub. 2:19, 31; 50:9f. The day of the rest which the patriarchs celebrated grants a foretaste already of eternal glory, which will be an unending Sabbath. The wonderful power of the Sabbath is so great that on the seventh day even the ungodly in Gehenna may rest from their torment. For this reason the Sabbath commandment is as urgent as all the other commandments of the Torah put together."

28. It is the circumstance of the sabbath which makes the disciples' plucking or reaping of grain here a transgression of the Jewish Torah. For, as stated in Deut 23:25: "When you go into your neighbor's standing grain, you may pluck the ears with your hand, but you shall not put a sickle to your neighbor's standing grain." Thus, since the fruits of the land were God's gift to the entire people of Israel, an individual Israelite could satisfy his hunger from another's grainfield, but he could not abuse this right by taking more than needed.

29. According to the biblical account it was actually Ahimelech, the father of Abiathar, who encountered David. Perhaps Abiathar is mentioned instead because of his greater prominence and association with David (1 Sam 22:20–23; 23:6–11; 2 Sam 20:25).

30. The *qal wahomer* type of conclusion exemplifies the first exegetical rule of Rabbi Hillel; see Str-B, 3.223–26.

31. Exod 4:21; 7:3; 9:12; 10:20; 11:10; 14:4,17; Deut 29:18; Pss 81:13; 95:8–11; Jer 3:17; 7:24; 9:13; 13:10; 16:12; 18:12; 23:17.

32. See "Herodians" in Chapter I.

# IV

# Mark 3:7–5:43

*The Mystery of the Kingdom of God Is Given to the Followers of the Way of Jesus.*

## A. Mark 3:7–12: Jesus Heals Huge Crowds and Orders the Demons Not To Make Known That He Is the Son of God

⁷Then Jesus withdrew with his disciples toward the sea, and a great multitude from Galilee followed. Also from Judea ⁸and from Jerusalem and from Idumea and beyond the Jordan and from around Tyre and Sidon a great multitude, hearing all he was doing, came to him. ⁹He told his disciples that a small boat should be ready for him because of the crowd, lest they crush him. ¹⁰For he had healed many, so that all who had diseases were pressing upon him to touch him. ¹¹And the unclean spirits, whenever they saw him, were falling down before him and crying out, "You are the Son of God!" ¹²But he sternly ordered them not to make him manifest.

### 1. MEANING OF MARK 3:7–12

#### a. *3:7–8* Withdrawing to the sea with his disciples, Jesus attracts a great multitude from various areas.

After the notice of the death plot against him (3:6) Jesus continues his salvific "way" as he "withdrew" with his disciples, who have been involved with him in the previous controversies with Pharisaic opponents. They retreat "toward the sea" of Galilee, the place along which Jesus had called his first disciples (1:16–20) and later taught all the crowd who had come to him there (2:13).

The ongoing theme of Jesus attracting great crowds (1:32–34, 37, 45; 2:2, 13) bursts into a rich blossoming here. A "great multitude," drawn by all that they heard Jesus was doing, namely, his miraculous healings and exorcisms as well as his authoritative teaching, follows Jesus and his disciples to the sea. The great following that Jesus arouses significantly surpasses that of John the Baptist. A great multitude comes to Jesus not only from the surrounding local region of Galilee, but also from the principal and sacred Jewish city of Jerusalem and its surrounding region of Judea, precisely the areas from which people came to John (1:5). But Jesus' attraction extends beyond this in all possible directions, as people amazingly come from as far as Idumea south of Judea and Jerusalem, from "beyond," that is, east of the Jordan river where John baptized (1:5) and from around Tyre and Sidon north of Galilee. This stunningly large and varied following indicates not only how widespread and universal is the appeal of Jesus but also how great is the human need he is addressing.

**b. *3:9* Jesus tells his disciples to prepare a boat lest the crowd crush him.**

That Jesus tells his disciples to prepare a boat for him intensifies the motif of the huge crowds being attracted to Jesus. So great are the masses of people coming to him that there is the danger they might "crush" him. The disciples' preparation of a small boat provides Jesus a vehicle of escape from the thronging crowds and gives the hint of a possible continuation of the "way" of Jesus on the sea.

**c. *3:10* Because Jesus had healed many, those with diseases are pressing to touch him.**

The reason why the huge crowds are thronging around Jesus is his wonderful power to heal those afflicted with diseases. That he has already "healed many" induces all others with diseases to strive to touch him. This massive and tumultuous commotion to "touch" Jesus emphasizes not only the deep need of these people for healing but also the availability of divine healing power present in Jesus.

**d. *3:11* The unclean spirits proclaim Jesus to be the Son of God.**

Whenever the "unclean spirits," the demonic powers which are holding these people in the grip of disease, saw Jesus, they were falling down in defeat and homage to his superior power and publicly acknowledging his more profound identity by crying out, "You are the Son of God!" Their proclamation echoes and reinforces the true and deeper character of Jesus already proclaimed by the heavenly voice of God himself after the baptism of Jesus: "You are my beloved Son; with you I am well pleased!" (1:11).

**e. *3:12* Jesus sternly orders the unclean spirits not to make him known.**

But Jesus sternly "orders" or "rebukes" these unclean spirits not to proclaim openly or publicly his more profound identity as the Son of God. In accord with Jesus' earlier "rebuke" and silencing of the unclean spirit who knew that he was "the Holy One of God" (1:24–25) and his not permitting the demons who knew him to speak (1:34), his rebuke and silencing of the unclean spirits here continues to indicate the inappropriateness for his deeper character to be revealed by the evil realm of demonic powers. But at this point it remains bewildering as to exactly why it is so inappropriate or untimely for the demons to make publicly manifest that Jesus is the Son of God.

### 2. MARK 3:7–12 AS MODEL FOR ACTION

The streaming of great multitudes to Jesus from all surrounding directions leads us, as we take the position of Mark's implied reader and identify with the common human plight of these people, to realize the global dimension of Jesus' power to heal and expel demonic powers. We are attracted to Jesus as one who possesses unlimited divine power to heal us and all people by freeing us from the grip of demonic diseases and thus restoring us to our God-willed human wholeness.

Identifying with the disciples who continue to follow Jesus after the initiation of a death plot against him (3:6) and whom Jesus tells to prepare a boat for his possible escape from the thronging crowds, cautions us to be ready for dangerous obstacles as we strive to be disciples who continue to follow the salvific "way" of Jesus.

Jesus' stern rebuke to prevent the unclean spirits from publicizing his more profound identity as the Son of God warns us to avoid such inappropriate, premature and incomplete proclamations of Jesus' true and deeper character so that we can be open to Jesus' own further, more complete and authentic revelation of himself as the Son of God.

## B. Mark 3:13–19: On a Mountain Jesus Selects Twelve Disciples To Be with Him and To Preach and Expel Demons

<sup></sup>¹³Then he went up toward the mountain and summoned those whom he wanted and they came to him. ¹⁴He appointed twelve

(whom he also named apostles)[1] that they might be with him and that he might send them out to preach [15]and to have authority to expel demons. [16]So he appointed the twelve: Simon whom he named Peter; [17]James, the son of Zebedee, and John the brother of James, whom he named Boanerges, that is, "Sons of Thunder"; [18]and Andrew, Philip, Bartholomew, Matthew, Thomas, James the son of Alphaeus; Thaddeus, Simon the Cananean, [19]and Judas Iscariot who betrayed him.

### 1. MEANING OF MARK 3:13-19

**a. *3:13* Jesus ascends a mountain and selects those whom he wants.**

Rather than escaping the thronging crowds in the boat prepared for him by the disciples (3:9), Jesus proceeds on his salvific "way" by going up toward the mountain or hills around the Sea of Galilee. His ascent toward the mountain elevates him above the people so that he can, with impressive authority, selectively "summon" to him "those whom he wanted" from out of and in the presence of the people. Those whom he sovereignly selects promptly answer his summons as "they came to him."

That this scene takes place on a "mountain" evokes the OT tradition of the mountain as a place of special encounters with God. For example, Moses ascends the mountain for unique encounters with God in Exodus 19:3; 24:9–11. It is appropriately on the "mountain" as the traditional place of nearness to God that Jesus acts with majestic divine authority to choose those whom he wants from the people.

**b. *3:14-15* Jesus appoints twelve to be with him and to be sent out to preach and exorcise.**

That those whom Jesus sovereignly selects out of the people number "twelve" points toward their relationship to the people of Israel as a whole, since "twelve" designated the traditional number of tribes composing Israel. There are instances in the OT (Num 1:1–19, 44; 13:1–16; Deut 1:19–28) where twelve men are chosen to be symbolic representatives for the entire twelve tribes of Israel and endowed with special tasks oriented toward the people as a whole. The "twelve" Jesus appoints, however, are oriented not only to the whole of Israel but to all the people who have come to him from all directions, even beyond the borders of Israel (3:7–8).[2]

Jesus assigns his selected twelve the privilege and task first of all of "being with him" on his "way" of salvation. Their "being with him" places the twelve, in distinction to both the people and the demons (3:7–

12), in a special position to experience fully the person of Jesus so as to grasp his more profound character. Since Jesus has just forbidden the unclean spirits to make his true identity openly known before the people (3:11–12; 1:24–25, 34), the twelve, by "being with him," will be able to rectify for the people such inappropriate proclamations of Jesus' deeper identity by the demonic realm.

In addition to "being with him" the twelve have been chosen so that Jesus might "send them out to preach," that is, to continue and extend his own mission of urging people to repent and believe in the gospel announcing the definitive arrival of the kingdom of God (1:14–15, 38–39). Jesus will also grant them a share in his own wonderful and powerful divine "authority" (1:22, 27; 2:10) "to expel demons" and thus to actualize the arrival of God's kingship by eradicating the evil power that overwhelms people's lives. Jesus thus empowers the twelve to assist him as coworkers in alleviating the deep and widespread need for people to be healed (3:7–10). It will be through the twelve's experience of "being with him" that the preaching of the "gospel of God" proclaiming the arrival of God's kingdom (1:14–15) can begin to become the preaching of the "gospel of Jesus Christ, Son of God" (1:1).

### c. *3:16* Simon whom Jesus named Peter is listed first among the Twelve.

The unspecified "twelve" Jesus appointed (3:14) are here designated as "*the* twelve" Jesus appointed. "The Twelve" thus refers to that precisely defined and specially selected group whom Jesus has authoritatively assigned to be with him and to continue his preaching and healing ministry to the people.

At the head of the list of the Twelve is Simon whom Jesus named "Peter" ("rock" in Greek). With his extraordinary authority Jesus bestows upon Simon the new name of Peter, thus indicating a new, public and distinctive role for Peter at the head of the Twelve. This develops the prominence Peter has already displayed: Jesus called him together with his brother Andrew to be his first followers (1:16–18); Jesus healed his mother-in-law (1:29–31); he led others in pursuit of Jesus when he left Capernaum (1:35–37).

### d. *3:17* Jesus named James and John "Sons of Thunder."

Jesus had earlier called "James the son of Zebedee and John his brother" to be among his first four followers (1:19–20, 29). Here they are included as the second and third members of the list of the Twelve, upon whom Jesus also bestowed the name "Boanerges" which means "Sons of

Thunder."[3] That Jesus gave them, like Peter, a new name associates them with Peter and hints at a possible special role for these three among the Twelve. But whereas the new name Jesus gives James and John is only a surname for them as a pair of brothers and not as individuals, Peter receives an actual new name as an individual, which thus indicates his preeminent position among the Twelve. The epithet "Sons of Thunder" suggests that there is something distinctive about the character or role of this pair of brothers.

### e. *3:18–19* Judas Iscariot who betrayed Jesus is listed last among the Twelve.

Andrew, the brother of Peter (1:16, 29), is listed as the fourth member of the Twelve. The rest of the list includes a James, designated the son of Alphaeus, to distinguish him from James the son of Zebedee, and a Simon designated the Cananean to distinguish him from Simon Peter.

The final member of the Twelve is "Judas Iscariot who betrayed him."[4] His distinctive position at the end of the list contrasts starkly with Peter's preeminence at the beginning. The notice that Judas "betrayed" Jesus suggests his association with the Pharisees and Herodians who are plotting to destroy him (3:6) and inserts an ominous anticipation of a disgraceful deliverance of Jesus into the hands of his enemies. Judas' betrayal sadly indicates that the vile power of evil can reach even one of the selected Twelve. But that Jesus himself has authoritatively chosen Judas as one of the Twelve paradoxically places his betrayal within the wider horizon of the divine plan of salvation.

### 2. MARK 3:13–19 AS MODEL FOR ACTION

We are drawn to Jesus as one who has exercised divine authority to choose and empower a special group of followers to fully experience his person and to extend his preaching and healing to all people. We are assured and encouraged that Jesus has both the intent and the means of meeting the global need for us and all human beings to hear the gospel which calls us to submit our lives to God's kingship and be healed of the evil powers and influences that afflict us all.

The Twelve, chosen and commissioned by Jesus for the benefit of all the people, present us with a model of authentic discipleship. That Jesus appointed the Twelve to "be with him" indicates our need to "be with him" by following him on his entire "way" of salvation, so that we can fully experience his person and thus come to a proper understanding of his profound character. Our "being with him" will enable us to preach and communicate to others the gospel which is about Jesus Christ, Son of God (1:1). The Twelve's task to preach and expel demons makes us aware of the responsibility and power we have as followers of Jesus to extend his gospel to all people and to alleviate human suffering.

Jesus' establishment of the special group of the Twelve, of Peter's position of preeminence at the head of the Twelve, and of the association of Peter, James and John as a distinctive group within the Twelve calls us to be open to the mutual benefit we can experience through the different roles we followers of Jesus have in the task of learning and communicating the authentic understanding of the profound character of Jesus and extending his preaching and healing ministry to all people. The sad note that Judas Iscariot, one of the Twelve, betrayed Jesus alerts us to the mystery of evil operative on the "way" of Jesus and warns us of the possibility of evil opposition to Jesus even among his closest followers.

## C. Mark 3:20–30: Jesus Addresses the Charge That He Expels Demons by the Power of Beelzebul

> [20]Then he came home and again the crowd gathered, so that they could not even eat a meal. [21]When his relatives heard this they set out to seize him, for they said, "He is out of his mind." [22]And the scribes who had come down from Jerusalem said, "He is possessed by Beelzebul," and "by the prince of demons he expels demons."
> [23]Then summoning them, he said to them in parables, "How can Satan expel Satan?
> [24]If a kingdom is divided against itself,
>     that kingdom cannot stand.
> [25]And if a household is divided against itself,
>     that household will not be able to stand.
> [26]And if Satan has risen up against himself and is divided,
>     he cannot stand but is coming to an end.
> [27]But no one can enter a strong man's household to plunder his goods, unless he first binds the strong man, and then he can plunder his household.
> [28]Amen, I say to you, all sins and whatever blasphemies people utter will be forgiven them. [29]But whoever blasphemes against the Holy Spirit will never have forgiveness, but is guilty

of an everlasting sin!" [30]For they had said, "He has an unclean spirit."

### 1. MEANING OF MARK 3:20–30

#### a. *3:20* Jesus and his disciples cannot eat because of the crowd.

Continuing his salvific "way," Jesus "came home." He thus returns to the "home" of Simon in Capernaum where he healed his mother-in-law and all the sick of the city (1:29–34) and the "home" where "many gathered together so that there was no longer room, not even around the door, and he was speaking the word to them" (2:1–2). Here "again" so great a "crowd" gathers that "they," that is, Jesus and his disciples (3:13–19), "cannot even eat a meal." This reinforces the impression that Jesus is continually attracting large crowds who want to hear him and be healed (1:32–34, 45; 2:2; 3:7–12).

#### b. *3:21* The relatives of Jesus think he is out of his mind.

When his "relatives" hear that Jesus is so preoccupied with the crowd that he cannot even eat a meal, they want to "seize" him from the crowd. They would thus deter Jesus from accomplishing his "way" of salvation. These "relatives" of Jesus, literally "those from him" (*hoi par' autou*), with their false assessment that "he is out of his mind" stand in contrast to the Twelve Jesus has just chosen "to be with him" (*hina ōsin met' autou*) in order to grasp his proper and profound identity (3:14). That even his own relatives misunderstand him adds to the tension created by the mounting opposition against Jesus.

#### c. *3:22* Jerusalem scribes accuse Jesus of expelling demons by Beelzebul.

That "scribes have come down from Jerusalem" extends and intensifies the opposition of scribes against Jesus. Whereas earlier "some of the scribes" (2:6) and "the scribes of the Pharisees" (2:16) had clashed with Jesus, now scribes have come from as far as Jerusalem, the sacred center of Jewish authority. Introducing the first element of a controversy or pronouncement story, these Jerusalem scribes raise a twofold accusation against Jesus: First, they viciously attack his person as being demon possessed—"he is possessed by Beelzebul (another name for Satan, chief of all demons)."[5] Then they maliciously attribute his exorcistic activity to this demon possession—"by the prince of demons (Beelzebul, Satan) he expels demons." This implies that the exorcisms of Jesus, as the evil work of Satan, will ultimately bring harm rather than healing to the people. Tension has heightened with this most serious and direct assault on the person of Jesus aimed at discrediting his healing ministry before the people.

**d. *3:23–27* Jesus counters their charge with parables about Satan.**

*3:23* How Can Satan Expel Satan?

After summoning "them," not only the scribes but also the crowd (see 7:14), Jesus begins to actualize the second element of the pronouncement story, the superior counter-questioning and argumentation, by speaking to them in "parables," that is, in comparisons or metaphors. C. H. Dodd offers a useful general definition of the literary genre of the NT parable: ". . . the parable is a metaphor or simile drawn from nature or common life, arresting the hearer by its vividness or strangeness, and leaving the mind in sufficient doubt about its precise application to tease it into active thought."[6]

Jesus introduces his parabolic counter-argumentation as he takes up the scribes' charge that he expels demons by the prince of demons (Satan) in the rhetorical question, "How can Satan expel Satan?" This challenging query raises the questionability of the scribes' accusation and suggests that it is contradictory and absurd.

*3:24–26* Satan Is Coming to an End

Jesus then cleverly transforms his opponents' charge into the premise of a rhetorically powerful argument composed of three conditional sentences logically leading to the unavoidable conclusion that the power of Satan is in fact coming to an end. The first conditional sentence, "If a kingdom is divided against itself, that kingdom cannot stand" (3:24) appeals to common knowledge about the consequences of civil war and rebellion to assert the impossibility ("cannot") for a divided "kingdom" to stand. The second sentence, "If a household is divided against itself, that household will not be able to stand" (3:25) calls upon general experience about the outcome of family strife and dissension to insist upon the inevitable ("will not be able") downfall of a divided family.

Building upon this logical pattern, the third sentence, "If Satan has risen up against himself and is divided, he cannot stand but is coming to an end" (3:26), achieves a climactic conclusion:[7] "Kingdom" and "household" become "Satan," quite appropriately in light of the apocalyptic-eschatological conception of Satan as the leader of a well-organized group of demons. The premise elaborates the idea of rebellious division with a double verbal expression: "If Satan has risen up against himself and is divided." And the potent assertion emphasizes not only the impossibility ("cannot") for Satan to stand but also the inevitability and present reality of his downfall—"but is coming to an end!"

By audaciously accepting as a premise his opponents' accusation that he expels demons by the power of Satan, Jesus has masterfully presented them with a dilemma forcing them to reexamine their convictions about his person and his exorcisms. On the premise that in Jesus' exorcisms Satan has in fact risen up against himself and is divided, the scribal opponents must either admit that Jesus is actually bringing about the decisive downfall of Satan's kingdom or abandon the premise. Acceptance of the conclusion invites them to realize that the kingdom of God has arrived with the person and activity of Jesus (1:14–15, 21–28). Abandoning the premise opens for them the question of how it is that Jesus expels demons if not by Satan's power.

But Jesus' argument also induces the gathered crowd (3:20) to probe the real significance of the exorcisms Jesus performs for them. While they are inclined to gladly accept the convincing conclusion that with the exorcisms of Jesus the demonic power of Satan is coming to an end, the provocative premise of Jesus acting in collusion with Satan agitates them to likewise ponder how it is that Jesus can expel demons.[8]

### 3:27 The Stronger One

With another potent parabolic assertion Jesus answers the question of how he can exorcise, for both the scribes and the crowd, by overriding and correcting the premise that he expels demons by the power of Satan. He is not in collusion with Satan. Rather, through the parable, in which the "strong man's household" aptly portrays Satan's demonic realm or "household" (see also 3:25) of demons, Jesus reveals himself as "the stronger one" who has already bound "the strong man" (Satan) so that he can now "enter" and "plunder his goods" and "his household" by expelling demons and thus bringing about Satan's definitive downfall (3:26). John the Baptist has already pointed to Jesus as "the stronger one" to come, who will baptize with the Holy Spirit (1:7–8). And Jesus as God's Son endowed with God's Spirit (1:9–11) has already fundamentally overcome the testing by Satan in the wilderness (1:12–13). This has enabled him to "bind the strong man" (Satan) and expel demons not by Satan but by the Holy Spirit of God.

Through his parabolic counter-argumentation (3:24–27), which pushes his listeners to ponder and probe, Jesus has offered both his scribal opponents and the crowd that follows him the chance for a new and deeper understanding of the true significance of his exorcisms; namely, that they point to the final collapse of Satan's power and thus the arrival of God's kingdom in and through the person of Jesus as "the stronger one" equipped with God's Spirit.

### e. *3:28–29* Jesus warns that blasphemy against the Holy Spirit will never be forgiven.

With the words, "Amen (or 'truly'), I say to you," Jesus introduces a solemn warning, which represents this controversy story's climactic pronouncement revealing a new aspect of Jesus' character and relationship to God. After declaring the general assurance that "all sins and whatever blasphemies people utter will be forgiven them" by God, Jesus turns to the case at hand. Referring to his scribal opponents who have just accused him of exorcising by the power of Satan rather than by the Holy Spirit, Jesus warns them that "whoever blasphemes against the Holy Spirit," that is, irreverently mocks and directly denies the activity of God's Spirit, "will never have forgiveness, but is guilty of an everlasting sin!" Those who blaspheme against the Holy Spirit by denying that it is God's Spirit rather than Satan that enables Jesus to expel demons cannot be forgiven by God because they are in effect denying the very power of God to forgive. Jesus has already illustrated how the divine power to heal demonic disease is equivalent to the divine power to forgive sins (2:1–12). If the scribes deny that the power of God's Spirit is operative in the exorcisms of Jesus, they are also denying themselves God's forgiveness and thus bringing upon themselves the guilt of an everlasting sin. Through this serious warning Jesus has revealed to both the scribes and the crowd that it is by God's Holy Spirit that he expels demons and to deny that he has God's Spirit is to deny oneself God's forgiveness.

### f. *3:30* For they had charged him with having an unclean spirit.

The narrator concludes by summing up and reinforcing the previous charges against the person of Jesus by both his relatives ("He is out of his mind," 3:21) and the scribes from Jerusalem ("He is possessed by Beelzebul," 3:22) as he reports that "they" had said, "He has an unclean spirit." This repetition of the accusation in terms of Jesus having an "unclean *spirit*" directly contrasts and ironically underlines how Jesus has just revealed that he has the "Holy *Spirit*." That Jesus, "the stronger one to come" (1:7), exorcises and heals people by the power of the Holy Spirit begins to fulfill the Baptist's promise that "he will baptize you with the Holy Spirit" (1:8).

## 2. MARK 3:20–30 AS MODEL FOR ACTION

As we listen to the exchange between Jesus and his scribal adversaries, we are granted further insight into the true significance of the person and ministry of Jesus. The provocative and forceful argumentation of Jesus invites us to believe that his exorcistic activity is not a temporary demonic delusion but actually effects the ultimate and definitive downfall of the demonic power of evil in the world, thus indicating the arrival of God's kingship for our lives in and through the person of Jesus. We are called to understand that Jesus can expel demonic power from our lives because he possesses God's Holy Spirit. And we are warned that if we fail to recognize and accept the salvific activity of the Spirit in Jesus, we thereby deprive ourselves of God's merciful forgiveness.

Jesus' argumentation induced the crowd who came to have him expel the demons from their lives to understand the deeper and broader significance of his exorcistic activity. By identifying with the crowd, we are persuaded not only to realize the salvific effect of Jesus' exorcisms for our own lives but to perceive that his exorcisms are bringing about the final collapse of the power of evil for the whole world.

The serious opposition that Jesus encounters not only from the Jerusalem scribes but even from his own relatives alerts us, who are called to continue the ministry of Jesus (3:14–15), to the possibility of similar opposition. The impressive way that Jesus counters this opposition provides us a model. As Jesus provocatively forced his adversaries to reexamine their false convictions and imaginatively transformed their accusations into a new offer of the gospel message, so we are challenged to win over our opposition with new and creative invitations for them to grasp the true significance of the person and activity of Jesus. As Jesus solemnly warned his opponents to recognize that God's Spirit is operative in him for their healing and forgiveness, so we have the responsibility of leading others to the divine healing and forgiveness offered by Jesus.

## D. Mark 3:31–35: Jesus Defines the Circle of His Followers Who Do the Will of God as His True Family

³¹Then his mother and his brothers came, and standing outside they sent to him and called him. ³²A crowd was sitting around him, and they said to him, "Your mother and your brothers

(and your sisters)[9] are outside seeking you." [33]Then answering them he said, "Who are my mother and my brothers?" [34]And looking around at those seated around him in a circle he said, "Here are my mother and my brothers! [35]For whoever does the will of God is my brother and sister and mother!"

### 1. MEANING OF MARK 3:31–35

**a. *3:31–32* The crowd around Jesus informs him that his mother and brothers are seeking him.**

In 3:20–21 after so great a crowd gathered around Jesus in the house at Capernaum that he could not even eat a meal, his relatives declared him to be out of his mind and came to seize him away from the crowd. Now his mother and brothers are standing outside the house and calling for him to come to them. Their position of "standing outside" despite their close familial relationship to Jesus sharply contrasts that of the crowd "sitting around him." The crowd, positioned between Jesus and his family, inform him that they are "outside" seeking him. Suspense is aroused as Jesus is presented with the choice of going "outside" to join his family or remaining in the house with the crowd.

**b. *3:33* Jesus asks who are his mother and brothers.**

With a surprising rhetorical question Jesus answers the crowd: "Who are my mother and my brothers?" Thus distancing himself further from his family "standing outside," Jesus raises a thought-provoking query as to who it is that stands in the proper familial relationship to him.

**c. *3:34–35* Those who do God's will comprise the family of Jesus.**

As he "looks around" at the crowd who have surrounded him, Jesus astonishingly declares that "those seated around him in a circle" constitute his true mother and brothers rather than those "standing outside." Jesus thus defines his true family and indicates where his true familial allegiance lies. He then explains the criterion for the establishment of this new family, which also functions as a stirring appeal for more members of it: "Whoever does the will of God is my brother and sister and mother!" The circle of those who have come to Jesus to follow his "way" are doing the "will of God" and achieving a close personal relationship with Jesus as they associate themselves with his true family. This new familial relationship is offered to anyone who wishes to do God's will by following the "way" of Jesus.

## 2. MARK 3:31–35 AS MODEL OF ACTION

Appealing directly to Mark's audience, Jesus invites new members into his new family association composed of those who do the will of God by gathering themselves around him. As we continue on the "way" of Jesus, we are called to accomplish God's will by aligning ourselves ever closer to the person of Jesus, so that we can experience this new familial relationship not only with him but with fellow followers of him.

Jesus' preference for the circle of his followers rather than for his own family serves as a model for us. We are advised of possible opposition or distraction from close associates as we try to follow the "way" of Jesus. Realizing the priority of doing God's will by drawing close to Jesus, we must disassociate ourselves from those personal relationships and allegiances which would hinder us and associate with the new family of those who seek to follow Jesus.

## E. Mark 4:1–9: Jesus Challenges the Crowd with a Parable about Sowing Seed

> [1]Again he began to teach by the sea. And a very large crowd gathered about him, so that he got into a boat and sat in it on the sea. And all the crowd was beside the sea on the land. [2]Then he taught them at length in parables, and he said to them in his teaching:
>
> [3]"Hear this! A sower went out to sow. [4]And as he was sowing, some seed fell along the way, and the birds came and devoured it. [5]Other seed fell on rocky ground where it did not have much soil, and immediately it sprang up because it did not have depth of soil. [6]And when the sun rose it was scorched, and because it had no root it withered. [7]Other seed fell among thorns, and the thorns grew up and choked it, and it did not produce fruit. [8]But others fell into the good soil and produced fruit, growing up and increasing, and it yielded thirtyfold and sixtyfold and a hundredfold."
>
> [9]Then he said, "Whoever has ears to hear, let that person hear!"

### 1. MEANING OF MARK 4:1–9

#### a. *4:1–2* From a boat Jesus teaches the crowd in parables.

Continuing his "way," Jesus "again" began to teach the crowd publicly and openly "by the sea." This recalls the previous scenes of Jesus attracting people by the sea, especially 2:13: "Then he went out again along the sea, and all the crowd came to him and he taught them" (see also 1:16; 3:7). But with the notice that "a very large crowd" now gathers about Jesus, the theme of the steady and progressive accumulation of more and more people around Jesus reaches a certain climax:

1:33    The *whole city* was gathered at the door.

2:2     *Many* gathered so that there was no room even around the door.

2:13    *All the crowd* came to him.

3:7–8   A *great multitude* from Galilee followed and also from Judea and from Jerusalem and from Idumea and beyond the Jordan and from around Tyre and Sidon a *great multitude.*

3:20    Again *the crowd* gathered so that they could not even eat.

4:1     A *very large crowd* gathered about him . . . and *all the crowd* was beside the sea on the land.

So "very large" or "huge" (*pleistos*) has the crowd become that Jesus now enters the boat as anticipated when he alerted the disciples to prepare a boat lest the crowd crush him (3:9). This separation of Jesus from the crowd prepares him to confront them as the authoritative teacher rather than be mobbed by them as the powerful healer (3:10–12).

For the first time Jesus is actually *on* the sea not merely *beside* it. That Jesus is "sitting" places him in the normal magisterial posture for teaching.[10] Jesus' position of sitting in the boat *on the sea* sharply contrasts the position of "all the crowd" who was beside the sea *on the land.* By assuming this sitting position on the sea, Jesus has placed himself in direct confrontation with the massive crowd on the land and positioned them for the hearing of his authoritative teaching.

Whereas Jesus previously addressed the charge of the Jerusalem scribes "in parables" (3:23), he now teaches this huge crowd "at length (or "many things" [*polla*]) in parables."[11] This parabolic "teaching" of Jesus is emphatically introduced: "He began to *teach*" (4:1); "he *taught* them" and "he said to them in his *teaching*" (4:2). And so this rather elaborate and solemn introduction to the public and open teaching of Jesus to a huge crowd of global proportions and significance (3:7–8) underlines the great importance of this particular teaching and creates considerable anticipation for hearing these parables of Jesus.

**b. *4:3–8* Jesus teaches a parable about sowing seed.**

*4:3* A Sower Went Out to Sow

Like the traditional Jewish "Shema" ("Hear, O Israel . . . ," Deuteronomy 6:4–9; Mark 12:29–30) which calls upon the people of Israel to pay serious and close attention to an undivided and wholehearted devotion to their one Lord God, Jesus' command to "hear!" his parable exhorts his audience not only to listen closely in order to understand but to probe the deeper significance and apply the parable to themselves.

The beginning of the parable, "a sower went out to sow," suggests an agricultural theme about the planting and growing of seed. According to Jewish scriptural tradition, behind the natural process of seed growing and producing lies the creative activity of God (Gen 1:11–12). In addition this creative process of agricultural growth and production serves as an appropriate comparison for the effectiveness and productivity of the word of God in Isaiah 55:10–11:

> [10]For just as from the heavens
>     the rain and snow come down
> And do not return there
>     till they have watered the earth,
>     making it bring forth and sprout,
> Giving seed to the sower
>     and bread to the eater,
> [11]So shall my word be
>     that goes forth from my mouth;
> It shall not return to me empty,
>     but shall do my will,
>     achieving the end for which I sent it.

A parable about a sower who went out to sow, then, involves the creative action of God and is open to a possible comparison with the dynamic and effective word of God.

That a sower "went out" to sow leads Mark's audience to identify the "sower" with Jesus because of the previous references to his activity of "going out" to preach and teach:

> *1:35* . . . he *came out* (*exēlthen*) and went on to a deserted place
>     and was praying there.

*1:38* Let us go on to the next towns that I may *preach* there also, for that is why I have *come out* (*exēlthon*).

*2:13* Then he *went out* (*exēlthen*) again along the sea, and all the crowd came to him and he *taught* them.

*4:3* A sower *went out* (*exēlthen*) to sow.

The parable of a sower who went out to sow, then, would seem to characterize Jesus in his ministry of preaching and teaching.

### 4:4–7 Various Failures of the Seed to Produce

As the parable focuses upon the seed that is sown, it imparts to its listeners an experience of a threefold, progressive failure of the seed to produce: On a first level of failure is the seed which falls along the way or path of the sower and is devoured by birds (4:4). Here there is not even a question of growth; the seed disappears before it has a chance to grow and produce. On a second level of failure is the seed which falls on rocky ground and actually begins to sprout. But it grows prematurely with no depth of soil and is scorched and withered by the sun because it has no root (4:5–6). On a third level of failure is the seed that falls among thorns. Although this seed grows, so do the thorns, which out-grow it and choke it so that, alas, it does not produce fruit (4:7). This tragic failure to produce fruit serves as the climactic point which sums up this threefold, progressive failure of seed that is sown by the sower.[12]

### 4:8 Extraordinary Success of the Seed Falling into Good Soil

After bringing its audience through an experience of the protracted and tragic failure of seed to grow and produce, the parable now confers a contrasting experience of surprising and extraordinary success. Some seed does fall into the good soil and produces fruit. Indeed, as the parable pointedly emphasizes, by "growing up and increasing" this seed produces an abundant and progressive yield of "thirtyfold and sixtyfold and a hundredfold," which far surpasses the previous and progressive threefold failure. As a vivid agricultural metaphor this parable allows its audience to share the sower's experience of the inevitable, progressive and overwhelming success of the seed that falls on good soil despite the repeated and steady failure of the seed that does not fall on good soil.

**c. *4:9* Jesus emphatically appeals for a true hearing of the parable.**

Having told the crowd the parable, Jesus emphatically challenges and exhorts them to "hear" its true significance: "Whoever has ears to hear, let that person hear!" Together with the initial summons to "hear!" (4:3), this closing invitation envelopes the parable within a framework of urgent appeals to really "hear" and understand it. By challenging the individuals of his audience to "have ears to hear," Jesus invites them to allow God to uncover and open their ears so that they can truly hear, understand and take to heart the message of the parable, and at the same time warns them not to allow his word to cover and close their ears like the prophetic word of God often did to the people of Israel (Isa 6:9–10). Only one who hears this parable with an openness to God's gift of "ears to hear" can really "hear" and understand it.

For the Marcan audience the parable portrays what has thus far happened in the narrative with regard to the preaching and teaching of Jesus. The sower who went out to sow seed, whose growth and productivity characterizes the effectiveness of God's word, represents Jesus who went out to preach and teach the gospel of God (1:14–15). The various and unfortunate yet inevitable failures of some of the seed correspond to the failures of the scribes (2:6, 16; 3:22), the Pharisees (2:16, 24; 3:6) and his own family (3:21, 31–35) to accept the gospel of Jesus. The inevitable and magnificent success of the seed which fell "into the good soil" (*eis tēn gēn tēn kalēn*) and produced an abundant and progressive yield by "growing up and increasing" corresponds to the crowds of people attracted by Jesus, who have gradually and steadily "grown up and increased" from the first four followers (1:16–20) to the "very large" (*pleistos*) crowd that now stands "on the land/soil" (*epi tēs gēs*) before Jesus.

In fact there are three important scenes of opposition to Jesus in the narrative that are immediately followed by references to the crowd that is still following Jesus despite this opposition: After the first controversy in which the scribes question Jesus' power to forgive the sins of the paralytic (2:1–12), "all the crowd" came to Jesus by the sea (2:13); after the decision of the Pharisees to plan with the Herodians how to destroy Jesus (3:1–6), great multitudes come to Jesus from every direction (3:7–12); and after the opposition of scribes and relatives to Jesus in the Beelzebul controversy (3:20–35), "a very large crowd" gathered around him at the sea (4:1). The huge crowd itself, then, not only embodies the extraordinary success already produced by the preaching and teaching of Jesus as the sower, but stands as living evidence of the inevitable growth and progress of this success in the future.

Through his parable about sowing seed Jesus invites the crowd and the Marcan audience to share a new and deeper understanding and experience of their following the "way" of Jesus. Through the parable Jesus assures, encourages and gives his audience hope in a double way: First, the parable assures them that the current rejections of Jesus by some are to be expected, just as the failure of some seed is expected and foreseen by the sower. But along with, yet despite these various failures, they may now share in the confident encouragement of Jesus, the sower, by realizing that they themselves, as the "very large crowd" of people who are now following Jesus, represent the steady growth and extraordinary success which far surpasses present failures to follow Jesus. Secondly, the parable warns and prepares them for future rejections and opposition as they follow the "way" of Jesus, which are as inevitable as the failure of some seed, but encourages them, nevertheless, to have the hope for continual and overabundant success in the future, which is as assured as the growing and increasing success of the sower.

### 2. MARK 4:1-9 AS MODEL FOR ACTION

When we identify with the "very large crowd" and allow ourselves to have "ears to hear" what Jesus is teaching with the parable of a sower who went out to sow, we are persuaded not to be distraught, discouraged or deterred from following the "way" of Jesus when we experience the inevitable rejections and expected opposition to it, but to share the confident assurance, encouragement and hope of Jesus that, despite the failures of some to follow him, God will ultimately uphold the "way" of Jesus and bring about an abundant increase of followers, just as he has led us to follow Jesus and just as he brings the sower a growing and increasing yield.

Jesus' teaching of this parable serves as a model for our own teaching and preaching of the gospel, empowering us to challenge others by exhibiting and extending to them the same bold confidence, encouragement and hope that Jesus the sower has in God's power to bring his salvific "way" to an extraordinary and ever-increasing success despite inevitable opposition to it. Furthermore, the universal and global dimension of the very huge crowd of people (3:7-8, 20; 4:1) whom Jesus challenges with this parable propels us to teach and preach the "way" of Jesus to all peoples and cultures of the world.

## F. Mark 4:10-12: Jesus Explains about Speaking in Parables

[10]And when he was alone, those around him with the Twelve asked him about the parables. [11]Then he said to them, "To you has been given the mystery of the kingdom of God, but to those outside everything happens in parables, [12]so that
      'looking they may look but not see,

and hearing they may hear but not understand,
lest they convert and it be forgiven them' (Isa 6:9–10)."

### 1. MEANING OF MARK 4:10–12

**a. *4:10* The circle of Jesus' followers ask about the parables.**

The words, "when he was alone," change the narrative focus from the open and public scene of Jesus teaching a huge crowd to one of the secluded privacy of Jesus with an inner circle of his followers. Those "around him" (*peri auton*) refers to the crowd which was previously sitting "around him" (*peri auton*, 3:32, 34) in a circle and whom Jesus defined as his new family who do the will of God in contrast to his actual mother and brothers standing "outside" (3:31–35). Included with them are "the Twelve," that special group of disciples whom Jesus earlier granted the privilege "to be with him" and to be sent out to preach and exorcise (3:13–19). This inner crowd or circle of followers along with the Twelve now question Jesus about the "parables" they have heard him speaking not only to the Jerusalem scribes (3:23) but also and especially to the very large crowd (4:2).[13] The implication is that these disciples do not understand the significance of Jesus' parables and apparently do not "have ears to hear" (4:9) the real meaning of the previous parable about sowing seed (4:3–8).

**b. *4:11a* To the disciples is given the mystery of God's kingdom.**

In answer to this inner circle of disciples Jesus first replies that "to you has been given the mystery of the kingdom of God." In other words, in the parables, and especially in the parable of the sower (4:3–8), these disciples "have been given" by God (divine passive) the "mystery," that which in accord with apocalyptic-eschatological thought has long been a hidden secret but is now revealed to privileged witnesses, about the coming of "the kingdom of God" whose imminent arrival Jesus has begun to proclaim (1:14–15) and demonstrate. And as the parable of the sower indicates, this "mystery," that which is secretly and paradoxically mysterious about the coming of God's kingdom, includes the extraordinary success it achieves in and through the person of Jesus, as the sower, despite and along with the inevitable opposition to it.

**c. *4:11b–12* To those outside everything happens in parables.**

Jesus continues with a contrasting parallel statement:

*4:11a* To you the mystery of the kingdom of God has been given
*4:11b* To those outside everything happens in parables

Those "outside" (*exō*) include not only the relatives of Jesus who stood "outside" (*exō,* 3:31, 32) seeking to remove Jesus from his inner crowd (3:31–35) and the opposing Jerusalem scribes who have demonstrated that they too are on the "outside" as Jesus addresses them in "parables" (3:20–30), but also the rest of the very large crowd whom Jesus has just taught in "parables" (4:1–2) but who now stand on the "outside" of this private conversation between Jesus and his inner circle of disciples. For these outsiders "everything," that is, according to the parallelism, everything concerning the mystery of the kingdom of God, "happens" or "takes place" in parables. Whereas the inner circle "is given" the mystery of God's kingdom, for "those outside" this mystery remains hidden in the puzzlement and enigma of the parables.

And the reason everything happens in parables for those outside is "so that" (*hina*), in accord with God's plan as recorded in Isaiah 6:9–10, they may continually "look" but not really "see" and continually "hear" but not really "understand" lest they "convert" and "it be forgiven them" by God. In other words, the parables are purposely meant to blind those outside from "seeing" the mystery of God's kingdom that is now revealed in the miraculous healings and exorcisms of Jesus (3:20–30) and to deafen them from "hearing" with "understanding" (4:9) this mystery present in the parables of Jesus (4:2–8), so that they may fulfill the tragic role within God's mysterious salvific plan of those who fail to "convert" and "be forgiven" (1:4; 2:10; 3:28) now that God's kingdom is arriving with the person and ministry of Jesus (1:14–15). By thus blinding and deafening "those outside," the parables ironically bring about the reality of the expected and inevitable failure expressed in the parable of the sower, which is, however, ultimately surpassed by overwhelming success.

### 2. MARK 4:10–12 AS MODEL FOR ACTION

As we identify with the inner circle of disciples, the realization that God gives us the "mystery of the kingdom of God," the mystery of the ultimate triumph and success of Jesus in bringing about God's kingship despite failure and opposition, gives us the encouragement and responsibility to persevere on the "way" of Jesus despite the inevitable and expected failure of others to see, hear and understand this mystery. But "those outside" function as a negative example cautioning us against complacency as "insiders" and warning us of the possible danger of becoming "outsiders," so that we must constantly be open to Jesus' revelation of the paradoxical mystery of how God's kingdom is realized in our lives.

## G. Mark 4:13–20: To His Inner Circle Jesus Explains the Parable about Sowing Seed

¹³And he said to them, "Do you not understand this parable? Then how will you understand any of the parables? ¹⁴The sower sows the word. ¹⁵These are the ones along the way where the word is sown. As soon as they hear, immediately Satan comes and takes away the word sown in them. ¹⁶And these are the ones sown on rocky ground who, when they hear the word, immediately receive it with joy. ¹⁷Yet they have no root in themselves but are temporary. Then when tribulation or persecution because of the word arises, they immediately fall away. ¹⁸And others are those sown among thorns. They are the ones who hear the word, ¹⁹but worldly anxiety, the lure of wealth and the craving for other things intrude and choke the word, and it becomes unfruitful. ²⁰But those sown on the good soil are the ones who hear the word and accept it and bear fruit thirtyfold and sixtyfold and a hundredfold!"

### 1. MEANING OF MARK 4:13–20

#### a. *4:13* Jesus indicates that the disciples do not understand the parable.

Although the inner circle of disciples have been given the mystery of the kingdom of God (4:10–12) in the parable about sowing seed (4:3–9), Jesus' question, "do you not understand this parable?.," indicates that they do not yet grasp the meaning and thus the "mystery" that is expressed through the parable. They need Jesus to explain it for them and thus to illustrate and confirm that they indeed have been "given" the mystery of God's kingdom. His additional question, "then how will you understand any of the parables?.," designates "this parable" about the sower who sows seed as the master parable which holds the key to understanding all the other parables of Jesus.

#### b. *4:14–20* Jesus explains the parable about sowing seed.

*4:14* The Sower Sows the Word

Jesus explains the parable about sowing seed with an allegorical interpretation of it, which itself functions as another parable. He begins by merely making explicit what was already implicit in the original parable, namely, that the "seed" represents the "word" of God, the "gospel of God" about the imminent arrival of God's kingdom that Jesus has been preaching and teaching (1:14–15, 21, 38–39; 2:2, 13). The "sower," then, represents first of all Jesus but also the disciples whom he has commissioned to continue his preaching (3:14).

### *4:15* Failure of Those Along the Way

As Jesus allegorizes the threefold, progressive failure of the seed to produce fruit, it becomes evident that the "seed" represents not only the "word" but also the "people" who hear the word. The seed sown along the path represents those people whom "Satan," corresponding to the "birds" who devour the seed in the original parable (4:4) and the supreme leader of the demonic realm of evil according to the apocalyptic-eschatological worldview, robs of the word as soon as they hear it, so that they fail to really receive the word. This characterizes the scribes (2:6, 16; 3:22), Pharisees (2:16, 24; 3:6) and relatives of Jesus (3:21, 31–35) and explains why they have not responded favorably to the preaching and teaching of Jesus. It also alerts and prepares the disciples for this kind of failure in their own future preaching.

### *4:16–17* Failure of Those on Rocky Ground

The seed sown on rocky ground represents those people who receive the word with joy when they first hear it, but because they last only temporarily and "have no root in themselves" (corresponding to no depth of soil and no root in 4:5–6), whenever they meet tribulation or persecution (corresponding to the scorching sun in 4:6) on account of the word of the gospel, they quickly "fall away" (corresponding to "withered" in 4:6). The failure of this group to persevere after hearing and receiving the word with joy not only prepares the disciples to expect this kind of response to their own future preaching, but serves as a negative model against which they can assess their own perseverance in the light of the tribulation and persecution they encounter as disciples.

### *4:18–19* Failure of Those Among Thorns

The seed sown among thorns represents those people who actually hear the word of the gospel, but before it can produce fruit the "thorns" (4:7), that is, the various preoccupations and anxieties of this world, the lure and deceitfulness of wealth and the craving for other things "intrude and choke the word." The failure of the word to produce fruit in and for this group not only readies the disciples to reckon with this sort of failure in their own future preaching, but warns them of the various external dangers that can destroy the word's productivity in their own lives as disciples of Jesus.

### 4:20 Abundant and Ongoing Success of Those on the Good Soil

But, in remarkable and encouraging contrast to all of the failures, the seed sown on the good soil represents those people who "hear" the word and "accept" it and "bear fruit" in a surprisingly abundant and ongoing manner—"thirtyfold and sixtyfold and a hundredfold!" These are the kind of people who repent and believe in the gospel of Jesus (1:15), who answer his call to become followers of his "way" (1:16–20; 2:14), who are chosen to be with Jesus and to be sent out to preach and exorcise (3:13–15) and who form the new family of Jesus by doing the will of God (3:31–35). This amazing success of the word to produce fruit not only encourages and assures the disciples of overwhelming success despite failures in their own future preaching, but affirms and strengthens their own discipleship with the hopeful confidence that the teaching and preaching of Jesus will ultimately enjoy a magnificent triumph over opposition and rejection. With this parable Jesus has thus explained to his inner circle of disciples the "mystery of the kingdom of God," that is, the secret, mysterious and paradoxical way that the gospel of God's kingship achieves astonishing and continual success despite and along with inevitable failures.

### 2. MARK 4:13–20 AS MODEL FOR ACTION

This allegorical interpretation of the parable about sowing seed imparts to us, as we identify with the disciples, a more explicit expression of the mystery of the kingdom of God (4:11) as the key to understanding all the parables of Jesus, the mystery of the ultimate and overwhelming success of the preaching of the gospel despite inevitable failures of people to respond favorably and adequately to it. This explanatory parable, then, stimulates and encourages us both as disciples who follow the "way" of Jesus and as preachers and teachers of Jesus' gospel of God's kingship:

1) We are urged not to become disheartened at the failure of those who do not even hear the word of the gospel when it is preached. This is due to the influential power of evil at work in the world, which robs people of the word as soon as they hear it (4:15), and illustrates the inevitable and expected failure that is part of the paradoxical mystery of the kingdom of God.

2) When we preach and teach the gospel, we can expect some people to respond with an initial enthusiasm which does not endure because of

their unwillingness or inability to withstand the tribulations and persecutions that come with the word of the gospel (4:16–17). At the same time we are cautioned to evaluate our own perseverance and endurance to the afflictions and opposition we encounter as disciples.

3) In our evangelizing we will encounter the failure of those who actually hear the word of the gospel, but because of such preoccupations as worldly cares and anxieties, the concern for gaining riches and cravings for various other things, the word never really achieves its fruition in or for them (4:18–19). But we are warned not to succumb to the preoccupations that can undermine and destroy the word's productivity in our own lives as disciples.

4) Despite and along with all the various and inevitable failures of response to the word we preach, we are encouraged to have the joyful assurance of an overwhelming and ongoing success of the word of the gospel. And we are confirmed in our own lives as disciples, confidently assured of the ultimate success and triumph of the "way" of Jesus despite repeated rejection and opposition (4:20).

## H. Mark 4:21–25: Jesus Continues His Teaching with Parabolic Pronouncements about the Lamp and the Measure

> [21] Then he said to them, "Does the lamp come to be placed under the bushel basket or under the couch? Is it not to be placed on the lampstand? [22] For there is nothing hidden except to be manifested; nor did anything become secret except to come to be manifest. [23] If anyone has ears to hear, let that person hear!"
>
> [24] And he said to them, "Watch what you hear! With the measure you measure, it will be measured to you and still more will be added to you. [25] For the one who has, will be given more; but the one who does not have, even what that one has will be taken away!"

### 1. MEANING OF MARK 4:21–25

#### a. *4:21–22* Jesus proclaims that what is hidden and secret is to become manifested.

Jesus continues his private instruction to his inner circle of disciples with parabolic pronouncements appropriately utilizing the indoor, domestic images of the oil burning "lamp" and the grain "measure" as opposed to the outdoor, agricultural images employed in the seed parables

(4:3–8, 26–29, 30–32) of his public teaching directed to the wider group of both his disciples and the crowd "outside."

*4:21* The Lamp That Comes To Be Manifested

His initial questions—the first must be answered negatively and the second positively—cause his disciples to realize the absurdity of "the lamp" to be hidden from view under a "bushel basket" or under a "bed" or "couch" (probably a dining couch) rather than displayed on "the lamp-stand" and thus openly visible to all. The "lamp" in the noteworthy formulation, "does *the* lamp *come*," symbolically alludes to both the profound identity of the person of Jesus as well as his teaching ("word") about the kingdom of God, since Jesus has often been portrayed as the one who "*comes*" on his "way" preaching, teaching and healing throughout the narrative.[14] Just as "the lamp comes" to be displayed before all, so is the previously hidden identity of Jesus (1:24–25, 34; 3:11–12) and the "mystery of the kingdom of God" (1:14–15; 4:11) to be openly manifested.

*4:22* What Is Hidden and Secret Is To Be Manifested

With explanatory pronouncements Jesus promises a future and further "manifestation" of what is "hidden" and what became "secret," namely, his profound identity and the mystery of God's kingdom. Nothing is now hidden except "so that" (*hina*), in accord with God's purpose (see also 4:12), it might become manifested, just as in the past nothing became secret except "so that" (*hina*), in accord with God's plan, it might "come" (as the lamp "comes" in 4:21) to be manifest. In other words, God will eventually make openly manifest that which became secret but is now still hidden about Jesus' profound identity and the mystery of the kingdom of God. Jesus' hidden and secret identity as the "Son of God," which he forbade the expelled demons to make "manifest" (3:12), will eventually, as that which is now still "hidden," be "manifested" and, as that which became "secret," will come to be "manifest" by God. And although the mystery of the kingdom of God (that which became "secret") has been given to the disciples (4:12), there is still more to be "manifested" about it by God (that which is still "hidden"). Jesus thus alerts his disciples to expect further revelation of his person and the mystery of God's kingdom.

**b. *4:23* Jesus emphatically appeals for true hearing.**

As Jesus had emphatically challenged the crowd to a true and attentive "hearing" which leads to understanding the parable about sowing seed (4:3–8) with the appeal, "whoever has ears to hear, let that person hear!" (4:9), so he similarly summons the disciples to really "hear" and understand both his explanation of the parable of the sower (4:13–20) and his further parabolic pronouncements (4:21–22) with the solemn challenge: "If anyone has ears to hear, let that person hear!"[15] Jesus thus urges his disciples to allow God to give each of them "ears to hear" (see on 4:9), so that they can really "hear" and understand the significance of his private instruction to them, lest they become like the "outsiders" who continually "hear" but do not "understand" (4:11–12).

**c. *4:24–25* Jesus proclaims that those who have will be given even more.**

*4:24* Hearing/Understanding and Measuring

Jesus advances his private instruction to the disciples ("and he said to them") with a yet more explicit warning about the object of hearing, "watch *what* you hear!," thus exhorting them to truly understand *what* they have heard and will hear, the manifestation of what is still hidden and secret (4:21–22). Employing the process of "measuring" as a metaphor for hearing and understanding Jesus, with a proverb-like pronouncement, promises his disciples that "with the measure you measure," that is, as they hear and understand the revelation God has made and will make manifest, "it will be measured to you and still more will be added to you," that is, God (divine passives) will grant them even more hearing and understanding of his revelation (see Prov 1:5; 9:9).[16]

*4:25* More Given to the One Who Already Has

As Jesus further explains and promises, "the one who has" hearing and understanding of what God has revealed and will reveal (4:21–22) about the mystery of Jesus and God's kingdom, that person "will be given more" hearing and understanding by God (divine passive). The disciples to whom the mystery of the kingdom of God "has been given" (*dedotai,* 4:11) "will be given" (*dothēsetai*) even more insight into the mystery by God. "But the one who does not have" true hearing and understanding of God's revelation, will have even one's superficial perception "taken away" by God. Thus, the disciples as "those who have" (4:11) will be given even more insight into God's manifestation of the mystery of Jesus and the kingdom, while "those outside" as "those who do not have" (4:11–12) will be given even less understanding. With these promises Jesus not only encourages his disciples to intensify their hearing and understanding of what God has made and will make manifest to them, but also warns them that the non-understanding of the "outsiders" will even further deteriorate.

### 2. MARK 4:21–25 AS MODEL FOR ACTION

As we identify with the disciples, Jesus alerts us to allow God to intensify our hearing and understanding, so that we may not only further probe and penetrate the meaning of what he has already manifested about the mystery of Jesus and the kingdom of God, but also remain ready and open to hear and understand God's future and further revelation of Jesus and the kingdom (4:21–23). We are thus called to look for more revelation and to continually deepen our insight into Jesus and God's kingdom. And we are assured that, according to the grace and purpose of God, he will continue to increase and intensify our hearing and understanding of what Jesus manifests to us about the mystery of his person and the kingdom of God. But we are advised that those who do not understand Jesus and God's kingdom will continue not to understand in accord with God's plan (4:24–25). We are thus warned to expect continued misunderstanding, opposition and rejection by some of the "way" of Jesus.

These parabolic pronouncements of Jesus to his disciples provide us a model for preaching and teaching. We are invited to make manifest the revelation of Jesus to all peoples and cultures, challenging them to allow God to grant them a deeper and deeper insight into the mystery of the person of Jesus and the kingdom of God, and preparing them to reckon with a continued and deeper misunderstanding of Jesus and the kingdom by some in accord with God's purpose. And so we are warned and must warn others of our need to progress as disciples to an ever deeper insight of Jesus and God's kingdom, lest we become like "those outside" who continually digress and understand even less.

## I. Mark 4:26–29: Jesus Teaches about the Kingdom of God through a Parable about Seed Growing Steadily until Harvest

> [26]Then he said, "This is how it is with the kingdom of God; it is as if a man should scatter seed on the land [27]and should sleep and rise night and day, and the seed should sprout and grow, he himself does not know how. [28]By itself the land bears fruit, first a blade, then an ear, then full grain in the ear. [29]But when the fruit is ripe, immediately he sends out the sickle, for the harvest has come."

## 1. MEANING OF MARK 4:26-29

### a. *4:26* The kingdom of God is like the situation of a man who scatters seed.

With the words, "then he said," Jesus resumes his public teaching in parables to both the crowd "outside" (4:1–2, 11) as well as his inner circle of disciples (4:10).[17] In contrast to the first parable about sowing seed (4:3–9), which is the key to understanding the other parables (4:13), Jesus explicitly indicates that the metaphorical experience expressed in the parable to follow is to be compared with the kingdom of God: "This is how it is with the kingdom of God." And so Jesus draws his listeners into an experience of how the kingdom of God operates as he narrates the story of a "man" who "scatters seed on the land." As already illustrated in the parable of the sower, the "seed" represents the "word" (4:14) of God and the "man" or sower who sows the seed represents Jesus in his preaching and teaching of the "word" or gospel about the kingdom of God (1:14–15) to people "on the land/soil" (*epi tēs gēs,* 4:1, 8, 20, 26).

### b. *4:27* The seed grows, but the man does not know how.

While the "man" proceeds with the normal and common rhythm of human living, "sleeping and rising, night and day," the "seed" proceeds to "sprout and grow," but the man himself does not know precisely "how" the seed grows. This accords with the biblical background of the parable, according to which agricultural growth happens through the creative power and activity of God (Gen 1:11–12; 1 Cor 3:6–7), but the activities and "ways" of God are essentially beyond human comprehension (Isa 55:8–11). Not even Jesus as the "man" who scatters the seed/word knows exactly how it is that God brings about the growth in the crowds (1:16–20, 33; 2:2, 13–15; 3:7–8, 20; 4:1) "on the land" (4:1) who receive the word/seed through Jesus' preaching and teaching of the gospel of God's kingdom.

### c. *4:28* The land produces fruit gradually of its own accord.

That the land bears fruit "by itself," that is, "of its own accord" or "automatically" apart from human activity, underlines how the land produces in an inevitable way, completely and radically through the creative power of God.[18] God causes the land to produce not only in an automatic and inevitable but also in a gradual and steady fashion—"first a blade, then an ear, then full grain in the ear." This gradual and steady growth of the seed/word not only characterizes the gradual and steady growth of the word of God that the audience has seen Jesus experience thus far in the narrative in terms of the steady growth of more and more crowds who follow him, but also points to an inevitable and steady growth of the "word" through God's creative power in terms of more and more people responding to the future preaching and teaching of the gospel. The growth to a very large and "full" crowd now attracted to Jesus corresponds to the growth to "full" grain in the ear within the parable:

3:7 ... a great multitude (*polu plēthos*) from Galilee followed.

3:8 Also from Judea and from Jerusalem and from Idumea and beyond the Jordan and from around Tyre and Sidon a great multitude (*plēthos polu*), hearing all he was doing, came to him.

4:1 And a very large (*pleistos*) crowd gathered about him ...

4:28 ... first a blade, then an ear, then full (*plērēs*) grain in the ear.

### d. *4:29* When the fruit is ripe, the harvest comes!

Once the gradual and inevitable growth reaches the point when "the fruit is ripe," the man "immediately sends out the sickle" to cut the ripened fruit and begin the process of gathering in the crop, for finally and quite wondrously "the harvest has come!" This last line of the parable imparts to its listeners an experience of the excitement and joy of the "man," who, as soon as the fruit is ripe, reaps the harvest. While the man scattered the seed, it was God who caused its inevitable and steady growth until it became ripened fruit, so that the man can rejoice in the yield of his labor through the wondrous activity of God. Through the parable Jesus (as the "man" who sows the seed/word) encourages his audience to share his own joyous assurance and hopeful confidence that the kingdom of God will eventually, inevitably and surely come about as God himself effects the gradual and steady growth of more and more people into an ultimate "harvest" of those who hear and accept the word of God through the preaching and teaching of the gospel by Jesus and his disciples.[19]

### 2. MARK 4:26–29 AS MODEL FOR ACTION

We are encouraged to continue Jesus' preaching and teaching of the word/seed of the gospel, propelled by the joyous assurance and hopeful confidence of Jesus himself that God will effect a steady and inevitable growth of people who hear and accept the gospel so that they ultimately grow into a harvest of people who live under the kingship of God. We can be heartened that God, in a hidden manner that we human beings cannot even comprehend (4:27), will bring about this harvest of people despite those who reject and do not understand the gospel (4:11–12). It is our responsibility to spread the word of the gospel of Jesus about God's kingdom, so that God can cause its marvelous and steady growth in more and more people, and then we can joyfully share with Jesus in the ultimate harvesting of people for the kingdom of God.

## J. Mark 4:30–32: Jesus Teaches about the Kingdom of God through a Parable about the Amazing Growth of a Mustard Seed

> [30]And he said, "How shall we compare the kingdom of God, or in what parable shall we put it? [31]It is like a mustard seed which, when it is sown upon the earth, is the smallest of all the seeds upon the earth. [32]But when it is sown, it grows up and becomes the greatest of all the shrubs and puts forth large branches, so that under its shade the birds of heaven are able to dwell."

### 1. MEANING OF MARK 4:30–32

#### a. *4:30* By what parable shall we compare the kingdom of God?

Jesus continues his public teaching to the larger crowd along with his disciples by introducing this final and climactic seed parable with a double question: "How shall we compare the kingdom of God, or in what parable shall we put it?" By explicitly bringing together the terms "kingdom of God" and "parable" this question recalls for Mark's readers that the mystery of the kingdom of God is given to the disciples in the parables, while these same parables cause the crowd "outside" not to understand (4:11–12). It can be expected, then, that the following parable will continue to blind and deafen the crowd to the mystery of God's kingdom, but will grant the disciples and thus Mark's readers further insight into it. With his use of the inclusive "we" ("How shall *we* compare . . . shall *we* put it?") Jesus challenges his listeners to join him in expressing and communicating yet another imaginative experience of God's kingdom by means of a parable.

#### b. *4:31* God's kingdom is like the case of a small mustard seed.

The kingdom of God can be compared to the phenomenal growth of the proverbially tiny mustard seed by the wondrous creative power of

God. When a mustard seed is sown "upon the earth" (*epi tēs gēs*), it is the smallest of all the seeds "upon the earth" (*epi tēs gēs*). The words "all" and "upon the earth" place the growth of the mustard seed into a universal and global context. The focus moves from a mustard seed sown upon the earth/soil to a mustard seed which is the tiniest of "all" other seeds on the entire earth/world.

c. *4:32* **Once sown, a mustard seed grows up so that the birds can dwell in the shade of its branches.**

Although the mustard seed is the tiniest of all seeds, the repetition of "when it is sown" (4:31, 32) begins to emphasize the process of the automatic and inevitable growth (4:28) of the tiny mustard seed merely because it is sown. Although small, "once it is sown," the mustard seed inevitably "grows up" through the creative power of God and "becomes the greatest of all the shrubs." The universal and global focus continues with a striking contrast between the mustard seed as the smallest of "all" the seeds "upon the earth" and the full grown mustard shrub as the greatest of "all" the shrubs. That the grown mustard shrub "put forth large branches, so that under its shade the birds of heaven are able to dwell" brings the parable's worldwide and universal focus to a climax: So great is this greatest of "all" the shrubs from the smallest of "all" seeds upon the entire "earth" that the birds of "heaven" can safely dwell under the shade of its "large" branches.

The global and universal significance of the full grown mustard plant is confirmed by its allusion to several OT passages in which a great tree symbolizes a kingdom which provides protection for *all* the birds, *all* the beasts and *all* the peoples of the world. In Ezekiel 17:23 the restored kingdom of David is compared to a tree which has become so "great" that "under its shade" (see 4:32) "every bird" will rest. In Ezekiel 31:6 the kingdom of Pharaoh is likened to a tree which has become so great that in its boughs "all the birds of heaven" nested, under its "long branches" (Ezek 31:5) "all the beasts" bred, and in its "shade" lived "all the multitude of nations." And in Daniel 4:10–12, 20–21 the kingdom of Nebuchadnezzar is symbolized by a great tree of global significance whose "top reached to heaven, and it was visible to the end of the whole earth" (Dan 4:10–11, 20), and "under" which and in whose "branches" the beasts and "the birds of heaven dwelt," and "all people" were fed from it (Dan 4:12, 21). With their parallelism between birds, beasts and people these texts indicate how the mustard shrub, the greatest of all shrubs on earth, has a worldwide and universal significance as a place where all the "birds of heaven" and thus symbolically all the peoples of the world can live in safety and security.

The growth of the mustard seed, symbol of the word of God (4:14), from its insignificant beginnings through inevitable growth to its full stature as the greatest of all shrubs with worldwide proportions for all people characterizes how the word sown by Jesus eventually grew into a great multitude of people with a universal and global dimension, coming from beyond Israel from every possible direction: ". . . a great multitude from Galilee followed. Also from Judea and from Jerusalem and from Idumea and beyond the Jordan and from around Tyre and Sidon a great multitude, hearing all he was doing, came to him" (3:7–8). This crowd anticipates and foreshadows the universal and global dimension toward which the kingdom of God is moving through the inevitable growth effected by God's creative power, despite modest beginnings. Through this parable, then, Jesus invites his listeners to share his confident assurance that, like the mustard seed, the kingdom of God whose word/seed has already been sown by Jesus will eventually and surely become the greatest of all kingdoms, embracing all the peoples of the world and empowering them to live under its protection and security.

### 2. MARK 4:30–32 AS MODEL FOR ACTION

Through the experience of the parable of the mustard seed we are encouraged to continue Jesus' preaching and teaching of the word/seed of the gospel about God's kingdom, because once the word/seed has been sown, we can share the confident conviction of Jesus that God will cause its inevitable growth into a kingdom of worldwide and universal significance offering all the peoples of the world a haven for secure living under the kingship of God. Once we have sown the mustard seed/word of God's kingdom, no matter how insignificant its beginnings, we can be absolutely assured that God will cause his word to grow into his ultimate, global kingdom embracing all the peoples of the world. We are called, then, to spread the mustard seed/word of Jesus' gospel of the kingdom of God to all nations, cultures and peoples of the world and to raise the consciousness of others to realize that God's kingdom is meant for and will eventually embrace all of creation.

## K. Mark 4:33–34: Jesus Spoke in Parables to the Crowd, but Explained Everything to His Own Disciples

[33]And with many such parables he continued to speak to them the word, as they were able to hear. [34]Without a parable he did

not speak to them, but privately to his own disciples he continued to explain everything.

### 1. MEANING OF MARK 4:33–34

#### a. *4:33* In many such parables Jesus spoke the word to the crowd.

The scene of Jesus teaching in parables (4:1–34) comes to a conclusion with the summarizing notice that the preceding parables were only an exemplary selection of the "many such parables" Jesus continued to speak to the crowd. By means of these parables Jesus spoke to them the "word," that is, the word of the gospel about the kingdom of God (1:14–15; 2:2), which was represented by the "seed" (4:14) in the parables. Jesus spoke the word publicly to the crowd "outside" in parables (4:3–9, 26–32) "as they were able to hear," which means without understanding the "word" about the mystery of God's kingdom, as already indicated by 4:11–12: "to those outside everything happens in parables, so that . . . hearing they may hear but not understand."

#### b. *4:34* To his own disciples Jesus explained everything.

As emphasized by the use of a double negative expression, Jesus spoke the word to the crowd "outside" exclusively in parables: "Without a parable he did not speak to them." But in contrast to this public teaching exclusively in parables, Jesus privately continued to explain to his own disciples "everything," that is, "everything" concerning the mystery of the kingdom of God which has been given to the disciples in the parables (4:11). And so this conclusion to Jesus' parable discourse reiterates and thus reinforces the distinction between his continual public teaching of the crowds (with the disciples) in puzzling parables so that they will not understand in accord with God's purpose (4:11b–12) and his special private instruction to his inner circle of disciples, in which he explains "everything" so that they can understand the mystery of the kingdom of God that has been given them in the parables (4:11a).

### 2. MARK 4:33–34 AS MODEL FOR ACTION

As we identify with the disciples on the "way" of following Jesus, we are called to keep our eyes continually fixed on the person of Jesus as the one who will bring us to a more profound understanding of the mystery of the kingdom of God, portrayed in perplexing parables but unable to be fully understood without Jesus' further instruction. Since some will never understand the parables, it is our responsibility to allow Jesus to further instruct us to understand more fully the mystery of the kingdom of God, so that, in accord with the message of the parables, God can work through us to bring about his kingdom for all peoples.

## L. Mark 4:35–41: Jesus Miraculously Stills a Storm at Sea and Rescues His Disciples

[35]On that day, when evening had come, he said to them, "Let us cross to the other side." [36]And leaving the crowd, they took him with them, as he was in the boat, and other boats were with him. [37]Then a great storm of wind came up and the waves were beating into the boat, so that the boat was already filling. [38]But he was in the stern, asleep on a cushion. Then they woke him and said to him, "Teacher, do you not care that we are perishing?" [39]Then he awoke, rebuked the wind, and said to the sea, "Quiet! Be still!" Then the wind ceased and there was great calm. [40]And he said to them, "Why are you afraid? Do you not yet have faith?" [41]Then they were filled with great awe and said to one another, "Who then is this that even the wind and the sea obey him?"

### 1. MEANING OF MARK 4:35–41

#### a. *4:35–36* Jesus and his disciples begin to cross the sea.

This scene is closely connected to the preceding (4:1–34) as it takes place on the "evening" of "that day" on which Jesus has been teaching the large crowd in parables (4:1–2) the "mystery of the kingdom of God" (4:11). As a direct continuation of the notice that Jesus was "explaining everything" privately to his disciples (4:34), he now "says to them": "Let us cross to the other side!" This exhortation, reminiscent of Jesus' earlier mission-expanding exhortation, "Let us go on to the next towns that I may preach there also, for that is why I have come out" (1:38), followed by the report that he went throughout all Galilee preaching and healing (1:39), creates an anticipation of a new expansion of the "way" of Jesus by preaching and healing across the Sea of Galilee in places he has not yet been.

As they leave the crowd Jesus has been teaching on the shore, the disciples take Jesus with them "as he was in the boat," that is, the "boat" which the disciples had earlier prepared for him lest he be crushed by the thronging crowd (3:9) and the "boat" in which he has just been teaching the crowd (4:1). This fulfills the expectation of Jesus' movement away from the crowd by way of a sea journey in the boat and establishes another private situation of Jesus with his disciples, open to a further explanation or revelation of the mystery of God's kingdom by Jesus (4:10–11, 21–25, 34). That "other boats were with him" not only indicates the continual attraction of people to Jesus, but also serves to contrast with the "boat" that contains Jesus with his disciples: Although other boats were with him, only the disciples are privileged to have Jesus in their boat.

**b. *4:37* A great storm endangers the boat.**

Suspense is aroused by the acutely dangerous and distressful situation of the boat containing Jesus and his disciples already being filled with the beating waves stirred up by a great storm of wind. This signals the beginning of a miraculous, sea-rescue epiphany. The literary genre of "epiphany" can be defined as the narration of:

> a sudden and unexpected manifestation of a divine or heavenly being experienced by certain selected persons, in which the divine being reveals a divine attribute, action or message. The essential characteristic of an epiphany is that it reveals some aspect of God's salvific dealings with his people. An epiphany thus presents or offers a particular revelation to certain people, who are then free to accept or reject it.[20]

In a sea-rescue epiphany the epiphanic action takes the form of a sudden manifestation of God's unique, creative power over stormy waters, representative of the waters of chaos exceeding the order and limits God placed upon them when he created the world. The life-threatening distress of the boat of disciples in the stormy waters, evoking feelings of utter helplessness and desperation, recalls similar situations in Jewish tradition of extreme danger from chaotic waters, in which only God, through his unique power over the waters of chaos, can help and save his people (Exod 14:10–30; Jonah 1:4–16; Ps 107:23–32; *T. Naph.* 6:1–10; 1 QH 3:6, 12–18; 6:22–25; 7:4–5).[21]

**c. *4:38* The terrified disciples awaken the sleeping Jesus.**

That Jesus was in the stern of the boat "asleep on a cushion" not only alludes to the sea-rescue story of the prophet Jonah, who was likewise incongruously asleep in the boat during a raging sea storm (Jonah 1:5), but also establishes the pre-epiphany absence of Jesus from the plight of his disciples. In their consternation the disciples awaken Jesus with a question indicating the inappropriateness of his sleeping while they are in danger of losing their lives: "Teacher, do you not care that we are perishing?"

**d. *4:39* Jesus powerfully stills the wind and sea.**

Then occurs the sudden epiphanic action as Jesus awakens and unexpectedly exercises the uniquely divine power of "rebuking" the wind and commanding the sea to silence (Pss 107:29; 89:10–11; 65:8; Job 26:11–12). He treats the chaotic elements of "wind" and "sea" as personified entities possessed by demons and thus exorcises them with a powerful and authoritative command as he had earlier exorcised a man with an unclean spirit in the synagogue at Capernaum:

> *1:25* But Jesus rebuked him, "Be quiet and come out of him!"
> *4:39* He rebuked the wind and said to the sea, "Quiet! Be still!"

The epiphanic action effecting the sea rescue is completed as the "wind ceased" and there was "great calm" (*galēnē megalē*) in contrast to the previous "great storm" (*lailaps megalē*). The uniquely divine power to control the chaotic wind and waters of the sea indicates an absolute power to save. In Wisdom 14:1–4, for example, God's power to bring a boat safely through the raging waves shows that he "can save from every danger." Jesus has thus manifested to his disciples his uniquely divine and absolute power to save his people from any danger.

**e. *4:40* Jesus questions the disciples' fear and lack of faith.**

Jesus' questions to the disciples, "Why are you afraid? Do you not yet have faith?," begin the response portion of this sea-rescue epiphany, in which Jesus, the epiphanic being, directs the epiphanic action of the divine power to still a sea storm to those privileged to witness and experience it, and evokes from them a response to it. These "chastising" questions of Jesus are actually designed to call the disciples to a new confidence and a new and greater faith in Jesus, a faith based upon this new revelation of his uniquely divine and absolute power to save his people. This is the "faith" they "do not yet have," but are now invited to have.

**f. *4:41* The disciples question the profound identity of Jesus.**

The disciples respond to the sea-rescue epiphany by being "filled with great awe" at this manifestation of unique divine power and by asking one another about the profound character of Jesus: "Who then is this that even the wind and the sea obey him?" This response of the disciples to Jesus' epiphany goes beyond that of those who witnessed Jesus' exorcism of the man with the unclean spirit in the synagogue at Capernaum:

> *1:27a* And all were amazed . . .
> *4:41a* Then they were filled with great awe . . .
> *1:27b* so that they asked among themselves, "What is this? A new teaching with authority! He commands even the unclean spirits and they obey him (*hypakouousin autǭ*)!"
> *4:41b* and said to one another, "Who then is this that even the wind and the sea obey him (*hypakouei autǭ*)?"

Not only do unclean spirits obey Jesus (1:21–28) but *"even"* the wind and the sea obey him. The question of who Jesus is because he has stilled the storm goes above and beyond the question of his identity and significance as a healer-exorcist. As the absolute and divine power to save, Jesus' power to still the wind and sea surpasses even his marvelous power to heal and exorcise. The disciples are so overwhelmed by the epiphany that they can only raise the provocative question of Jesus' deeper significance and more profound character based on this amazing new revelation of his divine power to rescue people by stilling the chaotic elements of wind and sea.

### 2. MARK 4:35–41 AS MODEL FOR ACTION

By identifying with the disciples, we vicariously share in their privileged experience of being rescued from possible death by a new and wonderful display of Jesus' uniquely divine power to save people by controlling the elements of chaos, symbolic of the most extreme forms of distress and danger. The prodding question of Jesus (4:40) and the provocative final question of the disciples (4:41) invite us, who already know Jesus' identity as "Son" (1:1,11; 3:11) and "Holy One" (1:24) of God, to increase our confidence and faith in Jesus as the one who possesses not only the divine power and authority to heal and expel demons but also the absolute divine power to save people from any and every life-threatening danger. As the disciples' experience of the epiphany of Jesus leads us, so we are called to lead others to consider the deeper significance and more profound character of Jesus based on the manifestation of his absolute power to save.

## M. Mark 5:1–20: Jesus Expels an Entire Legion of Demons

> [1]Then they came to the other side of the sea, to the territory of the Gerasenes. [2]When he came out of the boat, immediately there met him a man from the tombs with an unclean spirit,

³who had his dwelling among the tombs, and no one could bind him any longer, even with a chain. ⁴For he had often been bound with shackles and chains, but the chains had been pulled apart by him and the shackles broken, and no one was strong enough to subdue him. ⁵Night and day among the tombs and on the hillsides he was always crying out and bruising himself with stones.

⁶When he saw Jesus from afar, he ran up and prostrated himself before him, ⁷and crying out in a loud voice, he said, "What have you to do with me, Jesus, Son of the Most High God? I adjure you by God, do not torment me!" ⁸For he had been saying to him, "Unclean spirit, come out of the man!" ⁹Then he asked him, "What is your name?" And he said to him, "Legion is my name, for we are many." ¹⁰And he begged him earnestly not to send them out of the territory.

¹¹Now a large herd of swine was feeding there on the hillside. ¹²And they begged him, "Send us into the swine, let us enter them." ¹³So he let them, and the unclean spirits came out and entered the swine. Then the herd of about two thousand rushed down the cliff into the sea, and were drowned in the sea.

¹⁴The herdsmen fled and told it in the city and in the countryside, and people came to see what had happened. ¹⁵And they came to Jesus and saw the demoniac sitting there clothed and in his right mind, the one who had had the legion, and they were afraid. ¹⁶And those who had seen it told them what had happened to the demoniac and to the swine. ¹⁷Then they began to beg him to leave their district.

¹⁸As he entered the boat, the man who had been possessed begged him that he might remain with him. ¹⁹But he did not permit him, rather he said to him, "Go back to your home and to your family and announce to them how much the Lord has done for you and how he has had mercy on you." ²⁰Then he left and began to proclaim in the Decapolis how much Jesus had done for him; and all were amazed.

### 1. MEANING OF MARK 5:1-20

#### a. *5:1-5* **A horribly possessed man meets Jesus in the land of the Gerasenes.**

Jesus and his disciples continue the salvific "way of the Lord" (1:2–3) as they "came to the other side (*peran*) of the sea" of Galilee, the mission-expanding goal that Jesus had announced at the start of this sea journey (4:35): "Let us cross to the other side (*peran*)." This "other" or eastern side of the Sea of Galilee is further specified as "the territory of the Gerasenes," that is, the land of the people of the city of Gerasa, one of the federation of ten hellenistic cities known as the "Decapolis."[22] Whereas crowds had earlier streamed to Jesus in Galilee from all surrounding directions (3:7–8), Jesus now goes to people beyond the region of Galilee (1:14, 39).

As Jesus comes out of the private setting with his disciples in the boat and enters the public domain, he is immediately encountered by a man coming from the tombs with an unclean spirit, thus signalling the beginning of an exorcism story (see 1:21–28, 34, 39; 3:11–12, 20–30). The particularly gruesome, inhuman and desperate condition of the man who is completely overcome by demonic possession is dramatically described. He no longer has a home or "dwelling" among the living, human community but must reside "among the tombs" (5:2, 3, 5), the unclean realm of the dead and appropriate place for one with an unclean spirit. Not only is he cut off from human society, but no human being has been able to alleviate his plight despite past attempts to bind him with chains and shackles. Jesus is presented with an extremely difficult, humanly insuperable case of demonic possession as "no one" could bind him any longer and "no one" was strong enough to subdue him (5:3–4). This is a well known, public case of demonic possession with relevance for the entire region of the Gerasenes as the man was continually, "night and day," and openly "crying out" not only among the tombs but on the surrounding hillsides. He is so totally overwhelmed by the destructive demonic force that he is pathetically wounding himself with stones (5:5). The dreadful condition of the man thus arouses in the audience feelings of horror, frustration and sympathy.

### b. *5:6–10* The demoniac recognizes the superiority of Jesus.

Already recognizing his superiority "from afar," the demoniac runs up and prostrates himself in homage to Jesus (5:6). Continuing the public nature of the encounter, the man cries out "in a loud voice" so that all bystanders can hear. The unclean spirit's taunting question, "What have you to do with me?," gives expression to the absolute otherness of Jesus who stands in diametrical opposition to the demonic realm. His identification of Jesus as "Son of the Most High God" not only underlines Jesus' divine power and vast superiority as it extends the previous demonic identifications of him as "the Holy One of God" (1:24) and "the Son of God" (3:11), but provides an answer to the disciples' previous question:

"Who then is this that even the wind and the sea obey him?" (4:41). Desperately trying to avoid being exorcised, the unclean spirit rather incongruously and vainly adjures Jesus "by God" not to torment him (5:7). For, as the narrator explains, Jesus had already begun to pronounce the powerful words of exorcism, demanding the unclean spirit to come out of the man (5:8).

Through his overwhelming superiority as Son of the Most High God, Jesus orders the demon to surrender his name and thus his control over the possessed man. Forced to comply, the demon explains that "legion is my name, for we are many." Jesus thus discloses the real intensity and seriousness of the case: The man is overcome by not just one demon but a "legion," a whole military regiment of "many" demons (5:9)![23] Realizing that Jesus is about to expel them from the man, the demonic legion earnestly requests to remain in the territory of the Gerasenes, thus creating the suspense of a potential threat to the rest of the populace (5:10).

### c. *5:11–13* Jesus allows the demons to enter a herd of swine and they are drowned in the sea.

The repulsiveness of the situation increases with the notice that a large herd of "swine," animals which are particularly "unclean" for Jews (Lev 11:7–8; Deut 14:8; 1 Macc 1:47), was feeding there on the hillside (5:11). The many demons make their request to remain in the territory more specific as they beg Jesus to send them into the "unclean" swine, an appropriate place for the "unclean" spirits, as their next dwelling place in the land (5:12). Jesus surprisingly seems to grant their wish as he permits the unclean spirits to come out of the man and enter into the swine, thus illustrating the reality of the exorcism in a visible way. But the attempt of the legion of unclean spirits to remain in the territory is thwarted as the herd of some two thousand swine suddenly rush down the cliff into the sea and plunge to their total annihilation as they are drowned quite appropriately in the chaotic abyss of the "sea," whose destructive and demonic nature was just demonstrated in the previous scene (4:35–41). Jesus has thus powerfully purged the land of the Gerasenes not only of a threatening legion of unclean spirits but of a herd of unclean swine (5:13).

### d. *5:14–17* The people beg Jesus to leave their region.

Those who were tending the herd of swine serve as witnesses who intensify the public nature of this particularly astounding exorcism as they excitedly broadcast it not only to the urban populace "in the city" but also to the rural populace "in the countryside." As a result people from the whole area come to see for themselves what has happened (5:14).

They confirm the reality of this mighty exorcism as they come to Jesus, the powerful exorcist, and see the one who has been exorcised now restored to the human community as one who is no longer running about and crying out among the tombs and on the hillsides (5:5), but is now peacefully "sitting there clothed and in his right mind." This is the one whom the entire region knew to be horribly possessed by a "legion" of demons whom no human being among them had the power to subdue. Like the disciples who had witnessed the special divine power of Jesus to exorcise and still the sea storm (4:41), these people are overcome by "fear" at this remarkable display of superhuman power by Jesus (5:15).

After the witnessing herdsmen relate to the people how Jesus has expelled the legion of demons from the possessed man and destroyed their herd of swine (5:16), the people beg Jesus to leave their district (5:17). Ironically, they "beg" Jesus, who has eradicated a legion of unclean spirits who had "begged" him to remain as a menace to the territory, to likewise leave their region. Despite what Jesus has done for the terribly possessed man and for the people of the whole territory, they want nothing to do with him and his demonstration of mighty, divine power.

**e. *5:18–20* The exorcised man proclaims what Jesus has done for him.**

As Jesus again entered the boat to leave the area, the man who had been possessed, in sharp contrast to the people of the region who have "begged" Jesus to leave them, "begs" Jesus "that he might remain with him" (5:18). But as "being with" Jesus is a special privilege reserved for the Twelve (3:14), Jesus does not grant the man's request. Rather, he commissions him to return to his "home" and his "family" and to "announce" to them how much "the Lord" has done for him and how much he has had "mercy" on him through this wonderful exorcism. Thus Jesus not only completes the man's personal experience of salvation by restoring him, who had been so alienated from human society that his "home" was in the tombs (5:3), to his proper "home" and "family" within the human community, but also empowers the man to "announce" to them the significance of the exorcism as a demonstration of the end-time salvific "mercy" now coming from "the Lord" God through Jesus (5:19).

But the good news of this spectacular exorcism demonstrating the saving mercy of God's coming kingdom through Jesus is so great that it cannot be limited to the man's home and family. He becomes a preacher of Jesus' gospel of God (1:14) as he begins to publicly "proclaim" not only throughout the territory of the Gerasenes but throughout the entire "Decapolis," the wide ten-city region to the east and south of the Sea of Galilee, how much "Jesus has done for him." His public proclamation thus indicates how the exorcism is to be attributed to the power of the "Lord" God now operative in the person of the "Lord" Jesus:

> *5:19* How much the *Lord* has done for you . . .
> *5:20* How much *Jesus* had done for him.

As a result of the man's proclamation of his personal experience of salvation through the divine mercy and power at work in Jesus, "all were amazed." And so, although Jesus himself has been asked to leave the region, through the evangelization of the healed man the gospel of Jesus and the marvelous, salvific effect of his person and power has, nevertheless, been heard and felt throughout the broader area as "all" are left astounded (5:20).

## 2. MARK 5:1–20 AS MODEL FOR ACTION

Through this Gerasene demoniac's personal experience of salvation we gain a deeper appreciation of the might of the divine saving power available and operative in Jesus. After feeling the horror of how gruesome and destructive the power of evil can become in an individual's life, the frustration at human powerlessness to liberate a person from total domination by demonic power, and the empathy for the desperate plight of a fellow human being, we are relieved and uplifted by Jesus' display of a divine saving power that is vastly superior to the most intense and extreme forms of evil power that can take complete control of a person's life with menacing ramifications for the lives of other human beings. We are assured that Jesus has the divine power and compassionate mercy to free us and all human beings from any and all evil powers and influences which prevent us from living full and authentic human lives.

The herdsmen who witness the exorcism and the people they bring to Jesus serve as negative models for Mark's audience. They have become so content and comfortable with the threat of unclean spirits and presence of unclean animals in their midst that they are alarmed when Jesus mightily destroys the evils to which they have accustomed themselves. Fearfully and tragically rejecting Jesus, they sadly choose the complacency of old and dehumanizing ways of living rather than the risk of new and more human possibilities that the liberating power of Jesus offers.

The exorcised demoniac, however, provides us with an ideal model of evangelization. Having personally experienced how Jesus has freed him from an inhuman existence, he was sent by Jesus to recount to his own people how he was restored to human living through God's liberating power and mercy. Overjoyed by his new life and freedom from evil power, he publicly proclaims the good news of what Jesus has done for him so that all who hear him are astonished by the mighty divine power at work in Jesus. His example inspires and empowers us to likewise share our own personal experience of the divine liberating and humanizing power of Jesus as Son of the Most High God with all our fellow human beings.

## N. Mark 5:21–43: After Healing a Hemorrhaging Woman, Jesus Restores Life to the Daughter of Jairus

[21]When Jesus had crossed again in the boat to the other side, a large crowd gathered about him, and he was beside the sea. [22]Then came one of the synagogue officials, Jairus by name, and seeing him he fell at his feet, [23]and begged him earnestly, saying, "My little daughter is at the point of death. Come lay your hands on her so that she may be saved and live!" [24]Then he went off with him, and a large crowd followed him and pressed upon him.

[25]And there was a woman who had had a hemorrhage for twelve years. [26]She had suffered greatly at the hands of many doctors and had spent all that she had, yet was not helped but rather grew worse. [27]Having heard about Jesus, she came up behind him in the crowd and touched his cloak. [28]For she had been saying, "If I just touch his clothes, I shall be saved!" [29]And immediately her flow of blood dried up and she felt in her body that she was healed of the affliction. [30]And immediately Jesus, aware in himself that power had gone out from him, turned around in the crowd and said, "Who touched my clothes?" [31]But his disciples said to him, "You see the crowd pressing upon you, yet you say, "Who touched me?" [32]And he looked around to see who had done it. [33]But the woman, afraid and trembling, having realized what had happened to her, came and fell down before him and told him the whole truth. [34]He said to her, "Daughter, your faith has saved you! Go in peace and be healed of your affliction!"

[35]While he was still speaking, people came from the synagogue official's house and said, "Your daughter has died. Why trouble the teacher any longer?" [36]Overhearing what was said, Jesus said to the synagogue official, "Do not be afraid; just have faith!" [37]And he did not allow anyone to accompany him except

Peter, James and John the brother of James. [38]When they came to the house of the synagogue official, he saw a commotion, people weeping and wailing loudly. [39]As he entered, he said to them, "Why are you making a commotion and weeping? The child is not dead but sleeping." [40]And they ridiculed him. But putting them all out, he took along the father and mother of the child and those with him and went in where the child was. [41]And taking the hand of the child, he said to her, "*Talitha koum,*" which means, "Little girl, I say to you, arise!" [42]And immediately the little girl arose and walked around; she was twelve years old. At that they were astounded with utter amazement. [43]But he strictly ordered them that no one should know this, and said that she should be given something to eat.

### 1. MEANING OF MARK 5:21–43

#### a. *5:21–24* Jairus begs Jesus to save his daughter's life.

After Jesus has left the territory of the Gerasenes in the boat with his disciples, he crosses back to the "other" (western) side of the Sea of Galilee, returning to the place from which he began the journey. A "large crowd" gathers about him as he is "beside the sea" (5:21). This motif of the continual attraction of crowds to Jesus along the sea establishes the public character of the scene in reminiscence of his public teaching of the huge crowd in parables at the sea (4:1–2) and of his public healing of crowds at the sea (3:7–12).

An individual by the name of Jairus, who was a synagogue official and thus a prominent public figure in the community, initiates a healing story as he falls at the feet of Jesus and earnestly begs on behalf of his little daughter who is "at the point of death." That it is a situation involving a father and his "little daughter" underlines the communal, familial dimension of the story. Her sickness not only involves herself but has ramifications for her family and community. Acting as a representative for his deathly sick daughter, Jairus, with an intensely impassioned plea, expresses his faith that Jesus has the power to cure her, as he entreats him to come and lay his hands on her so that she may be "saved" from death and "live" (5:22–23). In quick response to this urgent, life and death crisis Jesus promptly goes off with Jairus. The large crowd follows and presses upon Jesus, reinforcing the public nature of the scene and arousing the suspense of a possible hindrance to the haste of the healer (5:24).

**b.** *5:25-29* **A hemorrhaging woman is healed by secretly touching the clothing of Jesus.**

The story of Jairus' daughter is interrupted by another healing story introduced by the presence of "a woman who had had a hemorrhage for twelve years" (5:25). Sympathy is evoked by the length and frustration of her predicament. Having experienced the powerlessness of the many doctors at whose hands she has suffered greatly and to whom she has unfortunately given all her money, she has only grown worse (5:26). In addition, there is a communal dimension to her affliction, which involves the discharge of blood, thus rendering her ritually "unclean" and excommunicated from the worshipping community (Lev 15:25-30). The lowly social status of this woman as a nameless female whose financial resources have been depleted and who has no position in the community sharply contrasts the status of the named male, Jairus, who holds a prominent place in society as a synagogue official. Having heard of the wonderful healing power of Jesus, she secretly comes up behind him in the crowd and touches his cloak with the hopeful faith that his healing power is so extraordinary that she must merely "touch his clothes" to finally be "saved" from her agonizing affliction, which no doctor could cure (5:27-28). The secret, indirect way that she approaches Jesus from behind contrasts with the public, direct way that Jairus encountered him. Her bold faith is rewarded by the sudden and miraculous healing which takes place as her flow of blood immediately dries up and she feels within her body the healing of her terrible affliction (5:29).

**c.** *5:30-32* **Jesus looks for whoever touched him and received his healing power.**

Jesus will not permit the woman's healing to remain secret and unnoticed. Dramatic tension builds as Jesus perceives that healing power has gone out from him and demands to know who in the crowd touched his clothes (5:30). The disciples' exasperated reply indicating the impossibility of their knowing who touched Jesus because of the pressing crowd underlines the hidden uniqueness of this particular woman's "touching" of Jesus (5:31). The suspense continues as Jesus searches for the healed woman (5:32).

**d.** *5:33-34* **Jesus confirms the faith and healing of the woman.**

In fear and trembling at the realization of her miraculous healing, the woman comes forward and humbly falls down before Jesus, publicly acknowledging the "whole truth" of being suddenly cured of her painfully persistent malady after merely touching Jesus' cloak (5:33). In response Jesus congratulates her as a true and restored "daughter" of Israel and points out that it was her remarkable faith in the greatness of the divine healing power available in him that gained this personal experience of "salvation" from her illness: "Your faith has saved you!" He then publicly pronounces her definitive healing, bidding her to go in "peace," properly restored to a full and harmonious relationship with God and her people, and, after twelve years of pain and frustration, to be finally and completely "healed of your affliction!" (5:34).

### e. *5:35-37* Hearing of the death of Jairus' daughter, Jesus encourages faith.

While Jesus was still addressing the "daughter" of Israel whose faith in the greatness of his power won her healing, people come from the synagogue official's home and inform him that "your daughter has died." Their added question, "Why trouble the teacher any longer?," implies that Jesus is powerless now that the child has died (5:35). Jesus, however, encourages Jairus not to be afraid at this report of death but to "just have faith!" (5:36). Although the "daughter" of Jairus has died while Jesus was detained by the healing of a "daughter" of Israel, the praiseworthy faith of this daughter in the greatness of Jesus' saving power now serves as a model for Jairus. This prominent synagogue official is urged to "just have faith" in the extraordinary power of Jesus like the nameless and lowly hemorrhaging woman whose notable "faith" saved her.

That Jesus allows no one to accompany him to the dead girl except Peter, James and John the brother of James limits the witnesses to the event and prepares for the more private nature of what will take place (5:37). This special sub-group of the Twelve is composed of three of the first four followers called by Jesus (1:16-20). Their privilege of accompanying Jesus here develops and intensifies the unique prerogative of the Twelve to "be with him" (3:14) for the special, private revelations of the more profound character of his person and power. It also further exemplifies how the "mystery of the kingdom of God" is given privately to the special circle of Jesus' disciples in contrast to "those outside" (4:10-11).

### f. *5:38-43* Jesus miraculously restores the girl's life.

As Jesus approaches the synagogue official's home, he observes that the commotion of the death-mourning ceremony has already begun with "people weeping and wailing loudly" (5:38). This further illustrates the public and communal dimension of the event. Entering the house, Jesus reproaches them for already having initiated the funeral commotion and weeping. Supremely confident of his power over death he audaciously announces that "the child is not dead but sleeping" (5:39). His treatment of death as if it were no more than sleep enhances the power of Jesus and prepares for him to majestically raise the girl from death as if awakening her from slumber. Certain that the child is really dead they react with chiding "ridicule," disclosing their lack of the faith Jesus has just encouraged. Jesus then transforms the public scene into a private one as he sends them all out of the house. He then goes to the dead child with only her parents and "those with him," Peter, James and John as the special group of three disciples privileged to witness what he will reveal (5:40). After performing the powerful healing gesture by "taking the hand of the child," Jesus pronounces the powerful healing words by commanding the little girl to arise. The double reporting of these words in both the native Aramaic language, *"Talitha koum,"* and their translation, "Little girl, I say to you, arise!," not only inserts a note of realism but intensifies and reinforces the miraculous power of Jesus' healing command (5:41).

The miraculous healing takes place as the little girl immediately arises and walks around, demonstrating her restoration to life. The mention that she was "twelve years" old not only indicates that she was old enough to walk but links her personal experience of the salvation Jesus brings her after a period of "twelve years" to the hemorrhaging woman's experience of the saving power of Jesus after a "twelve year" period of affliction (5:25). After witnessing this special revelation of Jesus' mighty power to raise one who has died back to life, those present, the parents and the privileged group of three disciples, are "astounded with utter amazement" (5:42). These disciples along with Mark's audience have now witnessed a staggering progression of revelations of Jesus' more profound character and mighty power: They have experienced the demonstration of Jesus' absolute saving power in the stilling of the chaotic wind and sea (4:35–41), of his mighty power to exorcise an entire legion of demons from a man whom no human being could subdue (5:1–20), of his miraculous power to heal the hemorrhaging woman who merely touched his clothing (5:25–34), and of his astonishing power to even raise the dead back to life (5:35–43).

Although impossible to be kept because of the public knowledge of the girl's death, Jesus' stern orders that "no one should know this" continue to underline the special, private nature of what Jesus has revealed about himself to privileged witnesses. His orders for secrecy here develop his previous attempts to prevent knowledge about his more profound character to be made public (1:24–25, 34, 44–45; 3:11–12) and thus create for the Marcan audience an aura of curious wonderment and suspense.

Jesus' final directive that the girl should be given something to eat completes the healing by illustrating the reality of her restoration to the realm of the living (5:43).

## 2. MARK 5:21–43 AS MODEL FOR ACTION

The hidden and humble hemorrhaging woman serves as an unlikely but ideal model for faith in the greatness of Jesus' divine power to heal. Through imitation of her bold and daring faith in Jesus we can personally experience the salvific power of Jesus to heal the deeply annoying and frustrating afflictions we suffer in the course of human living and to restore through faith our often broken lives to the wholeness of a peaceful, harmonious relationship with God and our fellow human beings.

The exemplary faith of the hemorrhaging woman in the magnificent power of Jesus provides the impetus for us to fulfill the reassuring command of Jesus not to be afraid but "just have faith" when we learn of the death of a relative or friend. Jesus' astounding power to raise Jairus' little daughter from death to life encourages us not to fear death and assures us of God's ultimate triumph of life over death through our faith in the divine power of Jesus.

As we identify with the disciples who have been privileged to witness this revelation of the more profound character of Jesus as demonstrated by his most extraordinary power to raise the dead to life, and as we are puzzled by Jesus' stern orders that this should be kept secret, we are alerted to remain ever open to new and further revelations of the significance of Jesus as we follow his "way," so that we can understand the reason for such secrecy and thus come to a deeper realization of the mystery of the kingdom of God as brought about in and through the person of Jesus.

## Notes

1. The clause "whom he also named apostles," while having some good manuscript support, is somewhat awkward grammatically and seems to be an interpolation from Luke 6:13. The designation "apostles" (literally, "those sent") in Mark 6:30 appears to be a natural consequence of the function of the Twelve to be "sent out" (3:14; 6:7) and so does not necessarily require this clause.

2. For this and many other pertinent points on Mark 3:13–19, see K. Stock, *Boten aus dem Mit-Ihm-Sein: Das Verhältnis zwischen Jesus und den Zwölf nach Markus* (AnBib 70; Rome: Biblical Institute, 1975) 7–53.

3. There are philological difficulties with the Aramaic "Boanerges"; see BAGD, 144.

4. The meaning of "Iscariot" remains obscure; perhaps it refers to the origin of Judas from Kerioth; see BAGD, 380–81.

5. On the origin and meaning of the name "Beelzebul," see BAGD, 139; J. M. Efird, "Baal-zebub" and "Satan," *Harper's Bible Dictionary,* 86 and 908–09.

6. C. H. Dodd, *The Parables of the Kingdom* (New York: Charles Scribner's Sons, 1961) 5. For an elaboration of this definition, see J. R. Donahue, *The Gospel in Parable: Metaphor, Narrative, and Theology in the Synoptic Gospels* (Philadelphia: Fortress, 1988) 6–20.

7. Grammatically this is a "real" (*ei* with indicative) conditional sentence referring to a concrete case ("If really, as you say . . .") as opposed to the "eventual" (*ean* with subjunctive) conditional sentences in 3:24–25, which refer to a generality. See Zerwick, *Biblical Greek,* #306, 320.

8. For a helpful discussion of Mark 3:22–26, see R. C. Tannehill, *The Sword of His Mouth* (Philadelphia: Fortress, 1975) 177–85.

9. These words are lacking in some manuscripts.

10. C. Schneider, *"kathēmai," TDNT* 3.443.

11. For the definition of a "parable," see above on Mark 3:23.

12. It seems to have been normal agricultural practice in Palestine to freely scatter seed before plowing it under the soil. See J. Jeremias, *The Parables of Jesus* (New York: Charles Scribner's Sons, 1963) 11–12.

13. Both this inner "crowd" and the Twelve were present for the "parables" of Jesus in the Beelzebul controversy in 3:20–30: The inner "crowd" (3:32, 34) is either equivalent to or included within the "crowd" who gathered around Jesus in 3:20; and the Twelve who had just been called in 3:13–19 are included with Jesus as the "they" who could not even eat a meal because of the crowd in 3:20.

14. For previous references to the "coming" and "going" of Jesus on his "way," see Mark 1:7, 14, 21, 29, 35, 38–39; 2:1, 13, 23; 3:1, 7, 20; 4:3. In Sirach 48:1 the person of the prophet Elijah is compared to a fire and his words to a burning torch.

15. The progression from the relative construction ("whoever," in 4:9) to the conditional construction ("if anyone," in 4:23) perhaps intensifies the "challenge" aspect of the appeal.

16. For possible background to the image of "measuring" as a metaphor for "hearing/understanding," see J. Marcus, *The Mystery of the Kingdom of God* (SBLDS 90; Atlanta: Scholars, 1986) 153–56.

17. Note the stylistic change from "he said *to them*" as the introduction to the parabolic pronouncements of the private instruction to the disciples (4:21, 24) to merely "he said" as the introduction to the public

teaching in parables (4:26). There is also a thematic change from the indoor, domestic imagery (lamp, bushel basket, bed, lampstand, measure, 4:21–25) of the private instruction to the outdoor, agricultural imagery (sower, seed, soil, growth, harvest, 4:3–8, 26–32) of the public parables.

18. In Lev 25:5, 11 what grows "of itself" grows apart from human activity and thus solely by God's creative action.

19. In Jewish tradition the image of the "harvest" in itself often refers to the gathering of crowds of people, whether for judgment (Joel 4:13: "Put in the sickle, for the harvest [of people, see 4:9, 11–12, 14] is ripe"; Isa 27:12) or missionary activity (Matt 9:36–38; Luke 10:1–2; John 4:30, 35, 39–41).

20. J. P. Heil, *Jesus Walking on the Sea: Meaning and Gospel Functions of Matt 14:22–33, Mark 6:45–52 and John 6:15b–21* (AnBib 87; Rome: Biblical Institute, 1981) 8.

21. For a full discussion and comparison, see Heil, *Jesus Walking on the Sea,* 17–30.

22. Gerasa was actually located thirty-three miles to the southeast of the Sea of Galilee.

23. In Jewish apocalyptic literature the demonic realm is often portrayed as a vast army under the leadership of Satan. In the words of D. S. Russell (*The Method and Message of Jewish Apocalyptic* [Philadelphia: Westminster, 1964] 257): "we have the picture of a great angelic host and an innumerable company of evil spirits and demons of every kind marshalled under the leadership of a demon prince. They have taken control not only of man's nature but also of the world in which man lives. They are arrayed like a great army . . ."

# V

---

# Mark 6:1–8:26

*The Followers of the Way of Jesus Do Not Grasp the Mystery of His Person.*

## A. Mark 6:1–6: Rejected by His Home Town, Jesus Teaches in Surrounding Villages

[1]Then he went away from there and came to his home town, and his disciples followed him. [2]And when the sabbath came he began to teach in the synagogue, and many who heard him were astonished, saying, "From where does this man get these things? What kind of wisdom has been given this man? What mighty deeds are done by his hands! [3]Is not this man the carpenter, the son of Mary and brother of James and Joses and Judas and Simon? Are not his sisters here with us?" And they took offense at him. [4]But Jesus said to them, "A prophet is not without honor except in his home town and among his own relatives and in his own house!" [5]So he was not able to do any mighty deed there, apart from curing a few sick people by laying his hands on them. [6]But he was amazed at their lack of faith and went about the surrounding villages teaching.[1]

### 1. MEANING OF MARK 6:1–6

#### a. *6:1* With his disciples Jesus goes to his home town.

Continuing the persistent movement of "the way of the Lord" (1:2–3), Jesus "went away" from there, the place where he astoundingly raised the daughter of Jairus from the dead (5:21–43), and "came" to his home town, Nazareth in Galilee (1:9, 24). His disciples, who have just witnessed an amazing succession of mighty miraculous deeds as Jesus stilled a sea

131

storm (4:35–41), exorcised the Gerasene demoniac (5:1–20), healed the hemorrhaging woman and restored Jairus' daughter to life (5:21–43), continue to actualize their discipleship as they "follow" Jesus to witness what will happen as he brings his salvific "way" to the people of his home town.

**b. *6:2–3* The townspeople take offense at Jesus.**

As he had done earlier in Capernaum (1:21–28; 3:1–6), so now in his home town of Nazareth Jesus brings his new and divinely authoritative teaching about the arrival of God's kingdom (1:14–15) to their sabbath service in the synagogue. As the people in the Capernaum synagogue were "astonished" (1:22), so people in the Nazareth synagogue are now "astonished" at the teaching of Jesus. In their astonishment, however, they raise a series of contemptuous questions about the person of Jesus which functions as the rhetorical device of dramatic irony for the Marcan audience. As a specific rhetorical device "irony" refers to the presence of two contradictory or conflicting levels of meaning in one expression in which some degree of unawareness is expressed or implied. Irony requires the audience to hold the two contrasting levels of meaning together in tension to arrive at what the author intends to communicate. In "dramatic irony" the audience shares with the author knowledge of which the characters in the scene are ignorant, thus establishing them as the unsuspecting "victims" of the irony.[2]

Underlining their incredulous contempt with repeated scornful references to Jesus as merely *"this man,"* the people of Nazareth express the incongruity of such extraordinary and lofty "things"—such "wisdom" and "mighty deeds"—coming from such an ordinary and lowly individual. But this ignorant disdain for Jesus contradicts what the reader knows about him, namely that he is not merely *"this man"* but the chosen "Son of God" (1:1, 11, 24; 3:11) and that "these things"—the "wisdom" he teaches and the "mighty deeds" he performs—come from God. The irony is that the same incongruity which leads the townspeople to spurn Jesus because they know him as an ordinary human being calls the audience to realize that Jesus is indeed that ordinary human being whom God has chosen as his Son who now offers divine wisdom and performs miraculous deeds (6:2).

The irony continues as the people of Jesus' home town express their condescending knowledge of *"this man"* as simply a "carpenter" whose origins and family they know. They can name his mother and brothers and know that his sisters reside in their midst. But the reader knows more than this. The reader knows that Jesus is not simply a "carpenter" and "son of Mary" but the chosen "Son of God" and that his true family, his true mother and brothers and sisters are those who "do the will of God" by following the "way" of Jesus (3:20–21, 31–35). The townspeople, as "victims" of the irony, do not know the more profound identity of Jesus and can not properly relate to him as part of his true family since they know only his family at Nazareth. Consequently, "they took offense at him," that is, they were scandalized by and stumbled over him because his words and actions seemed to exceed what they previously knew and expected of him. But the irony enables the audience to overcome this shocking rejection of Jesus by his ignorant fellow citizens through superior knowledge of the true identity and true family of Jesus. The irony calls the reader to look beyond the ordinary, human background and origins of Jesus to see his extraordinary, divine character in order to relate to him as part of his true family who gather around him and do God's will (6:3).

### c. *6:4* Jesus reproaches them for dishonoring him as a prophet.

Ironically illustrating the "wisdom" attributed to him (6:2), Jesus interprets his rejection by the people of Nazareth as something to be expected in accord with the proverbial and ironical statement that a prophet is honored by everyone except his home town, relatives and family. In contrast to their designation of him as only a "carpenter" Jesus reveals himself to be a "prophet," one inspired and sent by God to speak the word of God. By announcing that his fate as a prophet is to be rejected by his own people, Jesus not only enables his disciples (6:1) and thus the audience to understand and surmount his present rejection, but also prepares them to expect similar rejections of themselves as his followers. With a rhetorically potent progression Jesus intensifies his rejection as a prophet: He has been dishonored not only by his "home town" but also by his own "relatives" and even by his own "house" (family), as already illustrated when his relatives came to seize him, thinking he was out of his mind (3:20–21), and when his mother and brothers came to call him away from his true family (3:31–35).

### d. *6:5–6* After curing a few sick people, Jesus teaches in other villages.

In ironic contrast to the earlier attribution of "mighty deeds" to him (6:2) Jesus can perform no "mighty deed" there because of their faithless repudiation of him. But not even their rude rejection of him can totally block the divine and compassionate power at work in him, as he does miraculously cure a few sick people by laying his hands upon them (6:5). But Jesus is so amazed by their lack of faith in him that he abandons his home town, relatives and family and goes to the surrounding villages teaching. Their appalling faithlessness cannot deter him from teaching and thus continuing the salvific "way" of the Lord (6:6).

### 2. MARK 6:1–6 AS MODEL FOR ACTION

The dramatic irony of this scene enables us to understand and overcome the scornful rejection of Jesus by his home town. Through the irony we can see and experience in the denigrated carpenter of Nazareth and lowly son of Mary the dishonored prophet and hidden Son of God who offers people of faith the divine wisdom of the gospel and the mighty deeds of God's salvation. The irony of Jesus' repudiation requires us to hold together in paradoxical tension both the ordinary, human and the extraordinary, divine dimensions of Jesus. In ironic contrast to the faithlessness and dishonor of Jesus' own relatives and family, our faith in the rejected Jesus allows us to become part of his true family who accomplish the saving will of God.

Jesus, who despite unbelief and rejection continues to heal a few and to teach elsewhere, serves as a model of perseverance, encouraging us to likewise persist in our preaching and teaching of the gospel and in our healing and helping of others. We are not to be deterred by lack of faith and acceptance, which we, like Jesus, the dishonored prophet, can expect even by those closest to us, but to carry forward the salvific "way" of the Lord by taking our message and ministry to new places.

## B. Mark 6:7–13: Commissioned by Jesus, the Twelve Go Out Preaching, Expelling Demons and Healing

[7]He summoned the Twelve and began to send them out two by two and gave them authority over unclean spirits. [8]He instructed them to take nothing for the journey except a walking stick only —no bread, no bag, no money in their belts, [9]but to wear sandals and not put on two tunics. [10]And he said to them, "Wherever you enter a house, stay there until you leave from there. [11]Whatever place does not welcome you or listen to you, leave there and shake the dust off your feet in testimony against them." [12]So they went out and preached in order that people repent, [13]and

they expelled many demons and anointed with oil many sick people and cured them.

### 1. MEANING OF MARK 6:7-13

**a. *6:7* Jesus sends out the Twelve with authority over demons.**

Jesus once again authoritatively "summons" to himself the special group of Twelve disciples whom he earlier summoned "to be with him" and to have the authority to preach and expel demons (3:13–19). Now that the Twelve have been privileged to be given the mystery of the kingdom of God in the parables Jesus taught (4:1–34) and to be with him as witnesses of his mighty miraculous deeds (4:35–5:43), Jesus officially "sends them out" as his apostles. In sending them out not individually but "two by two" Jesus strengthens the reliability of their testimony to his message and ministry (Deut 19:15). As he "gives them authority over unclean spirits," Jesus empowers the Twelve to share not only in his personal superiority over the demonic realm of evil (1:12–13) but in his ability to actualize the kingdom of God by expelling demons from the lives of others.

**b. *6:8-9* Jesus instructs the Twelve to travel lightly.**

Jesus instructs the Twelve to take with them only what is absolutely necessary for traveling—a walking stick, sandals and only one tunic as clothing. They are not to encumber themselves by carrying "bread" or food, a "bag" for provisions, or money in their belts. These strict instructions indicate both the extreme urgency of their mission and the greatness of the power they have been given. They are to dedicate themselves solely and completely to their ministry and to rely for their livelihood totally upon the divine authority Jesus has granted them.

**c. *6:10-11* Jesus tells them when to stay and when to leave.**

Continuing his instructions, Jesus explicitly tells the Twelve to remain in whatever house receives their message and provides for them, not to move from house to house, until they have completed their mission in that village or area (6:10). If any place refuses to welcome them or listen to their proclamation of God's gospel (as happened to Jesus in his home town, 6:1–6), the Twelve are to "shake the dust off their feet" as a solemn and serious gesture of decisive separation, serving as a "testimony against them," and thus leaving them to the judgment of God if they continue to reject his gracious offer for their salvation (6:11).

**d. *6:12-13* The Twelve preach, expel demons and heal.**

Empowered and instructed by Jesus, the Twelve extend his ministry as they "go out and preach" so that people "repent" or "convert," turning away from past sinfulness and back to God (6:12). They thus continue Jesus' preaching of the gospel of God announcing the arrival of God's kingship and calling for people to convert their lives and believe in the gospel (1:14-15). With their "authority over unclean spirits" given them by Jesus (6:7), the Twelve also continue to extend the exorcising and healing ministry of Jesus, as they "expelled many demons and anointed with oil many sick people and cured them," thus liberating human lives from the horrible grip of evil power and further manifesting the arrival of God's kingdom. In sharp contrast to the faithless rejection of Jesus himself by his home town where he could cure only a "few sick people" (6:5), the Twelve receive a more favorable response of faith indicated by their curing of "many sick people" (6:13).

### 2. MARK 6:7-13 AS MODEL FOR ACTION

The Twelve present us with a model of the empowerment and responsibility Jesus gives us as disciples of his "way." Like the Twelve we are authorized with the divine power of Jesus himself to extend his mission and ministry by calling people to conversion and faith in God's gospel and alleviating the diseases and suffering that afflict human lives. As disciples of Jesus we possess the power to heal and free people from the grip of demonic power (6:7). It is our responsibility to "travel lightly" like the Twelve, not worrying about our own needs but dedicating ourselves completely to our urgent mission and relying totally on the divine power granted us (6:8-9). We are to accept and depend upon the assistance of those who welcome us, but leave to God's judgment those who reject the gospel (6:10-11). We can be encouraged, however, that we will encounter much faith and be enabled to help and heal many (6:12-13).

## C. Mark 6:14-29: Having Put John the Baptist to Death, King Herod Thinks That Jesus Is John Raised from the Dead

[14]King Herod heard about it, for his name had become manifest, and people were saying, "John the Baptizer has been raised from the dead and that is why mighty powers are at work in him." [15]But others were saying, "He is Elijah." Still others were saying, "He is a prophet like any of the prophets." [16]When Herod heard

about it, he was saying, "It is John whom I beheaded; he has been raised up."

¹⁷For Herod was the one who had John arrested and bound him in prison on account of Herodias, the wife of his brother Philip, because he had married her. ¹⁸For John had said to Herod, "It is not lawful for you to have your brother's wife."

¹⁹Herodias had a grudge against him and wanted to kill him, but was not able to do so. ²⁰For Herod feared John, knowing him to be a just and holy man, and kept him safe. When he heard him, he was much perplexed, yet he used to enjoy hearing him.

²¹But an opportunity came when Herod on his birthday gave a banquet for his courtiers and officers and the leading men of Galilee. ²²When Herodias' own daughter came in and danced, she pleased Herod and his guests. The king said to the girl, "Ask me for whatever you wish, and I will give it to you." ²³And he made a strong oath to her, "Whatever you ask of me I will give you, even half of my kingdom." ²⁴She went out and said to her mother, "What shall I ask for?" She replied, "The head of John the Baptizer." ²⁵And going in immediately with haste to the king, she asked, saying, "I want you to give me at once on a platter the head of John the Baptist."

²⁶The king was deeply distressed, but because of the oath and his guests he did not wish to break his word to her. ²⁷So the king immediately sent an executioner with orders to bring his head. He went off and beheaded him in prison. ²⁸Then he brought his head on a platter and gave it to the girl, and the girl gave it to her mother.

²⁹When his disciples heard about it, they came and took his dead body and laid it in a tomb.

### 1. MEANING OF MARK 6:14–29

#### a. *6:14–16* King Herod thinks Jesus is John the Baptist raised from the dead.

Mark designates Herod Antipas, one of the sons of Herod the Great and the tetrarch of Galilee and Perea, as "king" Herod, who now hears about Jesus "for his name had become manifest" through the preaching and mighty deeds of healing and exorcism performed not only by Jesus himself but by his disciples (6:7–13). Jesus' "name" or identity, which he previously forbade expelled demons to make "manifest" (3:12) and which is included in that which was previously hidden and secret but will come to be "manifest" (4:22), is now made "manifest" through his divine and miraculous mighty deeds.

But although Jesus' "name had become manifest," there is ironically much confusion about his true identity. In contrast to the people of Jesus' home town, who spurned him as no more than a "carpenter" despite his "mighty deeds" (*dynameis*) (6:1–6), people are now identifying him as John the Baptizer raised from the dead because of the "mighty powers" (*dynameis*) at work in him. This identification of Jesus with John raised from the dead, which expresses something both true and false about the character of Jesus, functions as dramatic irony for the reader. While the people quite correctly place Jesus in close association with John, they do not realize what the reader knows, namely that Jesus is not John but that John himself pointed to Jesus as "the stronger one" who would come after him and baptize with the Holy Spirit (1:7–8) (6:14).

The irony continues as others identify Jesus as the wonder-working prophet Elijah, who was expected to reappear in the end time. But the reader knows that it is John himself who plays the role of Elijah as the messenger (1:2) and prophet (1:6) who prepares for the "way of the Lord" to be fulfilled by Jesus as "the stronger one" to come after John (1:7–8).[3] While this identification of Jesus with Elijah quite rightly places Jesus in close connection with the Elijah-like figure of John, the reader knows that Jesus, as "the stronger one" to come, is much more than Elijah. Similarly, the designation of Jesus as "a prophet like any of the prophets" ironically expresses something both true and false about Jesus. Although Jesus compared himself with a "prophet" dishonored by his own people (6:4), it is John who more aptly illustrates the classic role of a "prophet," as he wears the prophet's clothing (1:6), courageously preaches the word of God to "king" Herod and suffers the fate of a martyr's death like a prophet of old (2 Chr 36:15–16). While this designation of Jesus as a "prophet" quite appropriately associates Jesus closely with John and the fate of a prophet, the reader knows that Jesus is precisely not a "prophet" who is just like "any of the prophets" but, as the messianic "Son of God" (1:11; 3:12) and "Son of Man" (2:10, 28), is much more than a prophet (6:15).

As the "king" who put the "prophet" John to death by having him beheaded, Herod thinks, ironically for the reader, that he can confirm the opinion of those who identify the wonder-working Jesus as John raised from the dead and thus vindicated by God. Although the reader knows that Jesus is not the raised up John, Herod's identification of him as John ominously places Jesus in line to suffer the same fate as the prophet John and establishes Herod as another death-threatening enemy of Jesus (see

3:1–6; 8:15). But the reference to the divine vindication of John through his resuscitation from the dead subtly points to the eschatological resurrection of Jesus (6:16).

### b. *6:17–18* Herod had arrested John because of Herodias.

As a flashback in the narrative Mark now recounts the episode of John's death by Herod, thus explaining why Herod identifies Jesus as the raised up John. Herod had arrested John and bound him in prison (see 1:14) because he objected to Herod's adulterous and incestuous marriage to Herodias, the wife of Herod's brother Philip (6:17). "Like one of the prophets" (6:15) of old (Samuel, Elijah), John boldly and bravely stands up for the word of God against "king" Herod by pointing out that "it is not lawful," that is, it is against God's law and will (Exod 20:17; Lev 21:20), for Herod to marry his brother's wife, Herodias (6:18).

### c. *6:19–20* Herodias wanted to kill John.

Because John was a threat to her marriage, Herodias resented him and wanted to kill him. The fulfillment of her desire, however, was thwarted by the fact that Herod protected John from her murderous designs, since he feared John and knew that he was a just and holy man. Although John greatly perplexed Herod, he nevertheless enjoyed listening to him. Herodias could not tolerate the possibility that John might yet succeed in convincing Herod to repent of his sinful marriage to her.

### d. *6:21–25* After dancing for Herod, the daughter of Herodias requested the head of John.

Herodias' opportunity to kill John arose on the occasion of Herod's grand birthday banquet for his courtiers, military officers and the important men of Galilee (6:21). Herodias' own daughter, undoubtedly prompted by her mother, entered and danced in such a way as to please both Herod and his distinguished male guests. In a bragging display of royal grandiosity aimed at impressing and pleasing his eminent guests, Herod, now referred to exclusively and ironically as "king" (6:22, 25, 26, 27), thus emphasizing the contrast between the apparently strong and powerful male "king" and the apparently weak and lowly female "girl," promised to grant the "girl" whatever she wished (6:22). The "king" then pompously reinforced his promise by precariously placing himself under a strong oath to the "girl" with a boastful and rather rash and reckless offer of "even half of my kingdom" (see Esth 5:3, 6; 7:2) (6:23).

When the girl returned to her mother, seeking instructions on what to request, she received the sternly unhesitating and ghastly reply: "the head of John the Baptizer" (6:24). Promptly obeying her mother's directions and quickly seizing the opportunity, the girl returned "immediately with haste" and uttered a 'request' which sounds and ironically functions more like Herodias' 'command' to a "king" who has been pathetically manipulated by his own royal vanity and the feminine cunning of his own unlawful wife: "I want you to give me at once on a platter the head of John the Baptist." By morbidly requesting that the head of John be served "on a platter," the "girl" will transform the birthday banquet of the "king" into a macabre death feast for her mother (6:25).

### e. *6:26–28* Herod had John beheaded.

Knowing John to be a just and holy man whom he feared and did not want to kill (6:20), the "king" was "deeply distressed" by the request for John's head. But constrained by his foolish oath and trapped by his prideful concern to impress his guests, the "king" decided to honor his promise to Herodias' daughter (6:26). Rather than following his conscience and exercising his authority as "king" to save the "prophet" John from death, "king" Herod surrenders his royal power to the command of Herodias and her daughter as he orders an executioner to behead John in prison (6:27). Precisely fulfilling the command, even to the gory detail of bringing the head of John "on a platter," the executioner gave it to the "girl" and the "girl" gave it to her mother (6:28). Through their wicked and crafty conspiracy these females, Herodias and her daughter, have managed to emasculate the pretentious Herod by rendering his command and strength as "king" questionable. In ruthlessly accomplishing her deadly goal, the evil and unlawful wife, Herodias, has proven herself more powerful than "king" Herod, with the "prophet" John as the "just and holy" victim.

### f. *6:29* John's disciples buried his dead body.

With respectful reverence the disciples of John honor their master with a proper burial by laying his dead body in a tomb. This ominously prepares the reader to expect the disciples of Jesus to perform this same task for their master, who seems destined to fall as an innocent victim to a similar evil conspiracy (3:6) and to suffer the same fate of the "prophet" as John (6:14–16). John the Baptist has prepared "the way of the Lord" not only by preaching repentance and announcing the coming of "the stronger one" (1:2–8), but by preceding him in death.

### 2. MARK 6:14–29 AS MODEL FOR ACTION

Through the irony of identifying Jesus with John the Baptist raised from the dead and considering him to be a "prophet," we realize that it is precisely by suffering the fate of the innocent "prophet" and following John in death that Jesus will accomplish the "way of the Lord" and demonstrate his true identity as "the stronger one" who is the divinely authoritative Son of Man and messianic Son of God. Herod's assessment of Jesus as a resuscitated and thus vindicated John, prepares us for Jesus' divine vindication through his eschatological resurrection from the dead. We are thereby encouraged to persevere on the "way" of Jesus even though it will lead to his death (6:14–16).

As a courageous prophet who boldly preaches the word of God despite the risk of death, John the Baptist serves as a model for us who are called to be faithful Christian prophets and evangelists despite the hardships we will encounter. We are alerted to the possibility of being victimized, like John and Jesus, by the prideful, manipulative, deceitful and cunning ways of the powers of evil at work in those who oppose the word of God. But the disgusting weakness of the human and wicked "kingship" of Herod and Herodias induces us to accept and live under the "kingship" of God proclaimed and actualized by Jesus, "the stronger one" to come (6:17–28).

The disciples of John, who respectfully bury their master, portray ideal examples of the faithfulness we are called to imitate as Christian disciples who remain with their Lord even through and beyond his death (6:29).

## D. Mark 6:30–44: Jesus Miraculously Provides an Overabundant Meal for Five Thousand

[30]Then the apostles came together with Jesus and reported to him all that they had done and taught. [31]And he said to them, "Come away by yourselves to a deserted place and rest a while." For many people were coming and going, and they had no opportunity even to eat. [32]So they went away in the boat to a deserted place by themselves.

[33]But people saw them going and many came to know about it, and they hastened there on foot from all the towns and arrived before them. [34]As he went ashore, he saw a great crowd

and had compassion on them, for they were like sheep without a shepherd, and he began to teach them many things. [35]And when it had already become late, his disciples came to him and said, "The place is deserted and it is already late. [36]Dismiss them so that they can go to the surrounding farms and villages and buy themselves something to eat." [37]Replying he said to them, "You give them something to eat." But they said to him, "Are we to go and buy two hundred days' wages worth of bread and give it to them to eat?" [38]He asked them, "How many loaves do you have? Go and see." And when they had found out they said, "Five, and two fish." [39]Then he ordered them to make all recline in groups on the green grass. [40]So they sat down in rows by hundreds and by fifties. [41]And taking the five loaves and the two fish and looking up to heaven, he blessed and broke the loaves and gave them to his disciples to distribute to the people; and he divided the two fish among them all. [42]They all ate and were satisfied. [43]And they took up twelve baskets full of fragments and what was left of the fish. [44]Those who ate the loaves were five thousand men.

### 1. MEANING OF MARK 6:30–44

#### a. *6:30–32* Jesus invites his returning apostles to a deserted place to rest and eat.

The Twelve disciples whom Jesus had earlier sent out in pairs as "apostles" on a mission with his authority over unclean spirits (6:7) now reassemble around Jesus and report to their master the great success they have had in extending his ministry. They tell him "all that they had done and taught," namely, that they had preached the good news of the arrival of the kingdom of God calling for repentance and had expelled many demons and cured many who were sick (6:12–13) (6:30). In imitation of his own pattern of prayerful rest in a deserted place (1:35) and of attempts to withdraw from the constant thronging of the crowds (1:45; 3:9), Jesus invites his disciples to come away by themselves and join him in a "deserted place" so that they can "rest a while." For so many people were continually "coming and going" that they once again (3:20) had no leisure time even to eat a meal (6:31). And so, with the expectation of a private, restful meal with Jesus and with the possibility of a further private revelation of his more profound character (4:34–41) through their privilege of "being with him" (3:14), the Twelve went away with Jesus "in the boat to a deserted place by themselves" (6:32).

**b. *6:33-34* Jesus has compassion on the crowd who followed them.**

Continuing the theme of the constant attraction of huge crowds of people to be healed and taught by Jesus (1:32-34, 45; 3:7-12, 20; 4:1; 5:21), but apparently frustrating the plan for a private meal with his disciples, many people, learning of their departure, hurry on foot "from all the towns" and arrive at the deserted place ahead of Jesus and his disciples (6:33). As Jesus comes out of the boat, he sees a "great crowd" and despite his concern for a private meal with his disciples he is moved to have "compassion" upon them, "for they were like sheep without a shepherd."

In the biblical tradition for the people to be "like sheep without a shepherd" (Num 27:17; 1 Kgs 22:17) means that they have no leader or king who can mercifully restore and regather them, who have been "scattered" into disunity by exiles to various places (Deut 30:3; Tob 13:5), into a unified community of God's people, and who can truly rule and provide for them by healing and feeding them (Ezek 34:1-6). Since the past kings and leaders of Israel have failed to be such shepherds, God promises that he himself will function as the true shepherd-king of Israel by establishing and working through his own Davidic servant who will feed and be shepherd-king of his people (Ezek 34:7-24).

In contrast to the dubious "kingship" of Herod, selfishly concerned to shepherd and feed himself and the leaders rather than the people (6:17-29; Ezek 34:2-3, 8, 10), Jesus indicates that he will serve as God's promised shepherd-king (Ezek 34:23-24) with divine compassion for this shepherdless people. He demonstrates his compassionate leadership by beginning "to teach them many things" (6:34). Whereas the scribes, the Jewish religious leaders who, like Herod, have left the people shepherdless because they do not lead them on the way of God by teaching them with power or "authority" (1:22), Jesus acts as the true shepherd-king by attracting and teaching the people about the kingdom of God with a new and divine authority (1:14-15, 27; 4:1-2).

**c. *6:35-38* The disciples do not have enough food for the crowd.**

When it becomes late, the disciples present Jesus with two problems, each with a double meaning: By announcing that "the place is deserted" they not only alert Jesus to a potential danger for the people but remind him that this is to be the place of their private rest and meal with him (6:31-32). And by pointing out that "it is already late" they warn Jesus of a temporal restraint not only for the people but for their own restful meal with him (6:35). Their advice that Jesus should "dismiss" the people so that they have time to leave the deserted place and go to the surrounding farms and villages and buy food for themselves, and implicitly, so that the disciples themselves might eat with Jesus, introduces a dramatic tension as it precisely contradicts what Jesus should do as the compassionate shepherd-king of his people. For Jesus to dismiss and thus "scatter" the people without food would frustrate his role as God's true shepherd-king to restore and preserve the unity of his people and provide them with food (Ezek 34:1–24), as God through the leadership of Moses and Aaron fed the people of Israel in the wilderness during the Exodus event (Exod 16) (6:36).

Jesus rejects the disciples' suggestion to dismiss the crowd with the forceful command: "You give them something to eat." He thereby overrides their concern to feed themselves by giving them the responsibility to feed the people. But the disciples shrink from Jesus' command with a rhetorical question expressing their astonishment that Jesus would expect them to be able to provide food for such a large crowd: "Are we to go and buy two hundred days' wages of bread and give it to them to eat?" (6:37). Jesus then directs them to establish and witness for themselves exactly how much food is at hand. After they find out, they report that they have only five loaves of bread and only two fish, which clearly confirms their incapacity to feed the people and thus heightens the dramatic tension (6:38).

### d. *6:39–44* Jesus overabundantly feeds the crowd of five thousand.

Exercising his authoritative leadership as shepherd-king, and in contrast to the death-bringing "order" of "king" Herod (6:27), Jesus "ordered" the disciples to make all the people "recline in groups on the green grass." Although the disciples themselves cannot feed the people, they are to act as Jesus' intermediary servants for the meal to follow. In making the people "recline" or "sit down," the disciples are placing them in the normal posture for a meal or banquet, suggestive of the position people will assume in the eschatological banquet of the kingdom of God (Matt 8:11; Luke 12:37; 13:29). The image of the "green grass" not only adds a festive note to the banquet but contributes to the portrayal of Jesus as God's true shepherd-king by recalling the "good pasture" in which God as Shepherd abundantly feeds his people (Ps 23:2; Ezek 34:14; Isa 49:9).

That the people recline in "groups" and sit down in very orderly "rows by hundreds and by fifties" underlines the revelation of Jesus as the shepherd-king who rules over and reorders the scattered people, who have come from "all the towns" (6:33), for a unique anticipatory experience of God's eschatological feast. The motif of the people reclining in orderly groups of hundreds and fifties is reminiscent of the past salvific ordering of the people of Israel into similar numerical groups to be ruled and cared for by their leaders (Exod 18:21, 25). And the Qumran literature expresses the expectation for the restoration and regrouping of God's dispersed people in an eschatological banquet (6:39–40).[4]

Taking the very meager and insufficient "five loaves and the two fish," Jesus, in correspondence to the normal Jewish ritual for beginning a meal, "looks up to heaven" and "blesses" God as the source of the gift of food. Besides illustrating the meal aspect of the feeding, the motif of Jesus looking to heaven and blessing God for the food serves as the miracle-working gesture. It indicates that it is the life-giving and salvific power of God himself which will enable Jesus to feed the people. As the host of this unusual banquet Jesus "breaks the loaves" and gives them to his disciples as his assisting intermediaries to distribute to the people. He likewise had the meager "two fish" divided among "all" the people (6:41).

The dramatic tension of feeding such a large crowd with such insufficient means is miraculously resolved as "all ate and were satisfied." That "all" the people not only "ate" but were fully "satisfied" from only five loaves and two fish further indicates that Jesus has miraculously fed them through divine power, as it is God himself who so abundantly "feeds" and completely "satisfies" his people (Pss 132:15; 37:19; 78:29; 22:26; Joel 2:26) (6:42). Not only was there enough food to satisfy all of the people, but there was an overabundance, as "they took up twelve baskets full of fragments and what was left of the fish," which is much more than the paltry five loaves and two fish with which the meal began. This motif of overabundant food not only further illustrates the meal's character as an anticipation of God's eschatological feast (Isa 25:6; Jer 31:14; *2 Apoc. Bar.* 29:4–8), but enhances the divine power at work in Jesus as the shepherd-king who can overabundantly provide food for his people (6:43).[5] That those who ate of the loaves numbered "five thousand men" not only highlights the miraculous character of the meal by expressing the great number who were fed from so few loaves, but it also climaxes the theme of Jesus' reordering of the people into a unified whole, as the term "thousand" in the biblical tradition often refers to an organizational grouping within the people of Israel (6:44).[6]

By overabundantly feeding 5000 men with only 5 loaves and 2 fish through God's miraculous power, Jesus surpasses such wonder-working prophets of old as Elijah and Elisha. God worked through Elijah to miraculously increase the food of a widow and her son, who were about to die (1 Kgs 17:8–16). And Elisha through the powerful word of God commanded his skeptical servant to feed 100 men from only 20 loaves. Marvelously the men not only ate but had food left over (2 Kgs 4:42–44).

Although Jesus has revealed himself as God's special agent, his compassionate shepherd-king, who has the divine power to reorder and overabundantly feed his people as an anticipation of the great eschatological banquet of God's kingdom, when God's people will be definitively re-united and bountifully satisfied, amazingly neither the crowd nor the disciples respond to this unique revelation. Since the disciples are the ones who have witnessed the insufficient amount of food (6:37–38) and distrib-uted it, miraculously multiplied, to the people (6:41), their lack of re-sponse to this further demonstration of the profound character and iden-tity of Jesus arouses considerable suspense for the reader.[7]

## 2. MARK 6:30–44 AS MODEL FOR ACTION

Through this story we gain a further insight into and appreciation of the character of Jesus as God's compassionate shepherd-king equipped with the divine power to truly rule over, restore and generously nourish us as a community of God's people gathered around him as the focal point of our unity. We learn that Jesus possesses God's salvific power not only to heal and exorcise individuals but to overabundantly feed and fully satisfy our needs as a community. Rather than being "like sheep without a shep-herd," we have a true shepherd-king in Jesus who teaches us the ways of God's kingdom and can completely preserve, provide for and nourish us, so that we can follow the "way of the Lord" as a unified people with the hope of participating in the final, joyous and triumphant banquet of the kingdom of God.

As we identify with the disciples, we are reminded of our need for personal periods of rest and refreshment after ministering and helping others (6:30–32). But the concern for our own rest and personal needs cannot overrule our responsibility to provide for the urgent needs of others (6:35–38). Even when the need exceeds our human resources and abilities, with Jesus as our true shepherd-king we have available to us his divine power which can provide us with more than enough to meet the fundamental needs of others. Like the disciples we are empowered to act as Jesus' intermediaries, nourishing others for the "way of the Lord" (6:39–44).

## E. Mark 6:45–52: Jesus Rescues His Disciples by Miraculously Walking across the Stormy Sea

[45]Then immediately he forced his disciples to enter the boat and go ahead to the other side toward Bethsaida, while he dismissed the crowd. [46]And after he took leave of them, he went to the mountain to pray. [47]When evening came, the boat was in the

midst of the sea, but he was alone on the land. [48]And having seen them harassed in rowing, for the wind was against them, about the fourth watch of the night he came to them walking on the sea and he intended to pass by them. [49]But when they saw him on the sea walking, they thought that it was a ghost, and they cried out. [50]For all saw him and were frightened. And he immediately spoke with them, and he said to them, "Take courage, it is I; do not be afraid." [51]And he went up to them into the boat, and the wind ceased. But they were utterly astounded within themselves, [52]for they did not understand on the basis of the loaves, on the contrary, their hearts were hardened.

### 1. MEANING OF MARK 6:45–52

#### a. *6:45–46* After Jesus forces his disciples to cross the sea, he prays on the mountain.

Continuing the movement of his salvific "way" after overabundantly feeding the five thousand, Jesus "immediately" and mysteriously "forced" his disciples to reenter the boat they had taken to the deserted place (6:32) and to "go ahead" of him to the other side of the Sea of Galilee toward the village of Bethsaida. The expectation is that he will join the disciples after he has "dismissed the crowd" whom he has just miraculously fed (6:45). But rather than joining his disciples after he has taken leave of the crowd, Jesus unexpectedly "went to the mountain to pray." Since the last time Jesus prayed in solitude it resulted in the significant event of expanding his ministry to all of Galilee (1:35–39), his praying in solitude on the mountain alerts the reader to the possibility of a similar momentous happening. And so the mysteriously urgent "forcing" of the disciples to go ahead of him as well as the unexplained praying of Jesus on the mountain generate an aura of suspense (6:46).

#### b. *6:47–48* Jesus comes to the disciples by walking across the stormy sea.

The suspense increases with the notice that when it became evening, the boat of the disciples was already "in the midst of the sea" but Jesus was still "alone on the land." This presents further obstacles to the expectation of Jesus joining his disciples: It is becoming too late to travel and Jesus is separated from them by a distance of half of the sea and by their respective positions—Jesus is on the solid ground of the "land" whereas the disciples are in the midst of the often precarious "sea" (6:47).

The conflict is acutely heightened by the distress the disciples experience when a sea storm caused by a contrary wind makes it difficult for them to cross the sea. The disciples once again find themselves in a predicament of extreme trouble caused by the deadly danger of the stormy waters of a chaotic sea (4:35–41), except that now Jesus is not with them. Unable to help themselves they are once again in need of rescue which only the unique, creative and salvific power of God over the waters of chaos can provide. As Jesus earlier "saw" the great crowd who were in need as sheep without a shepherd and had compassion on them (6:34), so he now "sees" his disciples in distress as they are "harassed in rowing" without their "shepherd," thus arousing the expectation of his compassionate assistance.

After Jesus and the disciples have been separated most of the night, "about the fourth watch of the night," that is, the "morning watch" (3–6 a.m.), occurs the resolution of the dramatic conflict through the compassionate intervention of Jesus. As Israel of old was miraculously enabled to cross the sea through God's power over the waters and be rescued from the Egyptians in the "morning watch" of the Exodus event (Exod 14:24), so the disciples are miraculously rescued and enabled to cross the sea through Jesus' divine power over it in the "morning watch."

Beginning to fulfill the expectation that he would join his disciples, Jesus suddenly and unexpectedly "came to them walking on the sea." By "coming" to them he overcomes the obstacle of half of the sea separating him from his disciples, and by "walking on the sea" he overpowers the contrary wind as he triumphantly treads upon and tramples down the chaotic waves. By magnificently crossing the sea without a boat, Jesus indicates that the disciples in the boat can now cross the sea and thus be rescued from their distress. The motif of "walking on the sea" serves as the epiphanic action of this second Marcan sea-rescue epiphany and surpasses the earlier epiphanic action of Jesus rescuing his disciples by stilling the sea storm (4:35–41).

As he comes to them "walking on the sea," Jesus demonstrates to the disciples his possession of God's unique power over the waters of chaos. It was God as Creator who triumphantly "tread upon the high places of the sea," that is, "upon the back of the Sea-Monster" (Job 9:8), completely dominating the dark powers of chaos. In the Exodus tradition God saved the people of Israel by crossing the sea himself and leading his people across it through his unique power over water (Ps 77:20). Now equipped with this same uniquely divine power after praying to God (6:46), Jesus totally subdues the chaotic waters of the sea and rescues his disciples by leading them across it. By "walking on the sea" Jesus reinforces his previous self-revelation to his disciples as the one whom God has endowed with absolute power to save his people from any and every distress (4:39; Wis 14:1–4).[8]

That Jesus "intended to pass by them" means that he wanted to complete the epiphanic action by manifesting himself fully to his disciples. He wants to "pass by them" while walking on the sea so that they can see him performing this majestic divine action, which indicates their rescue. This accords with the Jewish tradition in which "passing by" functions as a technical term to express not the withdrawing away but the drawing near of a divine being in order to show himself before human eyes (Exod 33:18–34:6; 1 Kgs 19:11; Gen 32:31–32; LXX Dan 12:1).

**c. *6:49–50* Jesus identifies himself and comforts his frightened disciples.**

Jesus' desire to complete the epiphanic action by "passing" in front of the disciples is interrupted by their reaction of fright. As those privileged to witness the epiphany, the disciples "saw" Jesus "on the sea walking," but they "cried out" in fear, thinking they were seeing a ghost. Such reactions of fright are typical of the epiphany genre, highlighting the sudden unexpectedness as well as the mysterious, divine character of the epiphanic appearance (Luke 1:12, 29; 2:9; 24:5, 37; Matt 28:4; Mark 16:5). That the disciples think Jesus is a ghost is also a characteristic of the epiphany genre, in which there is often an element of ambiguity concerning the identity of the epiphanic being, which then allows the epiphanic being to properly identify himself (Luke 24:37; John 20:14–15) (6:49).

After Mark emphasizes the disciples' reception of the epiphany and their reaction of fear by explaining that "all" of the disciples actually "saw" him and were "frightened," Jesus immediately speaks with them and alleviates their fear by identifying himself with the words, "Take courage, it is I; do not be afraid." Such a comfort-bringing and self-identification formula is common in the epiphany genre.[9] Jesus calms the fear of his disciples and eliminates their confusion about his identity by assuring them that the one they see performing the uniquely divine action of walking on the sea is not a ghost but he himself (6:50).

**d. *6:51–52* Although rescued from the storm, the disciples do not understand the profound character of Jesus.**

Finally fulfilling the expectation that he would join his disciples in the boat, Jesus "went up to them into the boat," thus completing his marvelous epiphany before their eyes. As a result of his having overpowered the sea storm by trampling down the chaotic waves, the contrary "wind" which had caused the disciples' dangerous distress (6:48) "ceased," thus signalling their rescue as Jesus has made the sea once again crossable for them (4:39). As the response motif in the epiphany genre the disciples "were utterly astounded within themselves," thus indicating the extraordinary and overwhelming character of the epiphany.[10] Although Jesus' walking on the sea has dramatically heightened the previous epiphanic revelation of his more profound character by stilling the sea storm (4:35–41), so that the disciples should now presumably be able to answer their question about the deeper character of Jesus (4:41), they surprisingly regress by being completely overwhelmed and dumbfounded (6:51).

Mark then further explains the disciples' utter amazement. Although they have all actually seen Jesus' epiphanic action and experienced rescue because of it, they "did not understand" the true significance of Jesus as revealed by his walking on the sea, since they have not understood his significance "on the basis of the loaves," that is, as revealed in his multiplication of the loaves (6:30–44). Although the disciples, as "insiders" to whom the mystery of the kingdom of God has been given (4:10–11), experience this privileged revelation into the mystery of Jesus' person, they ironically respond as "outsiders" who "look and hear" but "do not see or understand" (4:12). Furthermore, the disciples were quite incapable at this point of understanding Jesus' profound character, since "on the contrary, their hearts were hardened" by God (divine passive). In the biblical tradition the "hardening of the heart" signifies a mysterious mixture of human resistance and incapacity with divine blinding, which prevents people from understanding and responding properly to the revelatory and salvific activity of God. Rather than thwarting God's overall plan of salvation, however, the "hardening of the heart" is part of it (see also 3:5) (6:52).

The disciples' response of utter astonishment, non-understanding and "hardening of the heart" to the splendid epiphany of Jesus walking on the sea represents the most dramatic expression thus far in the narrative of their inability to fully grasp Jesus' profound significance. And so the ongoing, bewildering suspense regarding the recognition and understanding of the true identity and profound character of Jesus by his disciples has greatly intensified.[11]

## 2. MARK 6:45–52 AS MODEL FOR ACTION

Through this second sea-rescue epiphany of Jesus we gain a deeper experience and appreciation of Jesus as the one God has endowed with an absolute power to save his people. We are reassured that Jesus possesses the uniquely divine power and compassion to protect and save us from any and every form of extreme danger and distress, as symbolized by the stormy waters of chaos, so that he can enable us "to cross the sea" and complete the salvific "way of the Lord" with him as our majestically powerful leader.

The disciples' utter amazement, lack of understanding and hardened hearts after witnessing Jesus walking on the sea caution us against a complacent presumption that we can ever fully grasp the inexhaustible greatness of Jesus' saving power and the depth of his person, which overwhelm our human understanding. We humbly realize that it is only through God's gracious assistance that our eyes, ears and hearts can be truly opened so that we can probe and grasp the mystery of the person and power of Jesus.

## F. Mark 6:53–56: At Gennesaret Jesus Is Recognized and the Sick Who Touch the Fringe of His Garment Are Healed

> [53]After crossing over, they came to land at Gennesaret and tied up there. [54]As they came out of the boat, people, immediately recognizing him, [55]ran about that whole district and began to bring the sick on pallets to wherever they heard he was. [56]And wherever he entered, in villages or towns or countryside, they laid the sick in the marketplaces and begged him that they might touch only the fringe of his garment; and as many as touched it were healed.

### 1. MEANING OF MARK 6:53–56

#### a. *6:53–55* At Gennesaret people bring their sick to Jesus.

Continuing the constant movement of his salvific "way," Jesus and his disciples, after "crossing over" the Sea of Galilee just made crossable by Jesus powerfully walking across it, "came" again to stable "land" after being on the unstable sea. That they come to land and tie up the boat at "Gennesaret" rather than "Bethsaida," where Jesus had earlier mysteriously "forced" them (6:45), arouses the tension of a yet to be fulfilled goal (see 8:22), symbolically characteristic of the disciples' yet to be fulfilled recognition of the true identity of Jesus (6:53).

As they "came out of the boat," the private domain of Jesus' special revelation to his disciples (6:32, 45–52; 4:35–41), and returned to the public domain, the people of the area "immediately recognized him." Through ironic contrast this "immediate recognition" adds to the tension created by the disciples' failure yet to recognize Jesus' more profound character (4:41; 6:52), the misunderstanding of his identity by Herod and others (6:14–16) and the rejection of him by his own town (6:1–6) (6:54).

Recognizing Jesus as a powerful healer, the people seize the opportunity as they scurry about "that whole district" and carry their sick on pallets to "wherever they heard he was." Jesus is continually on the move here, bringing his "way" of salvation throughout the whole district and in response the people are frantically striving to assist their sick in receiving the benefit of his marvelous healing power (6:55).

**b. *6:56* The sick who touch the fringe of his garment are healed.**

Wherever Jesus "entered" on his salvific "way," thoroughly traversing that whole district by going through "villages, towns and countryside," people, with obvious faith in his healing power, mercifully placed their sick compatriots in the public marketplaces, enabling them to encounter Jesus. That they humbly "begged" him that "they might touch only the fringe of his garment" climactically heightens their expression of faith in the greatness of Jesus' healing power: Whereas earlier, sick people pressed upon him to "touch him" (3:10), and the hemorrhaging woman with faith "touched his cloak" (5:27), now the sick need "touch only the fringe of his garment" to be healed, so great is the divine power at work in Jesus. In ironic contrast to the few sick people Jesus cured in his home town because of their lack of faith (6:5–6), now "as many as touched it were healed" (6:56).

This incident develops the theme of Jesus' ongoing mission throughout "all Galilee" (1:39), attracting huge crowds of people to be taught and healed. Whereas Jesus earlier healed all the sick from the whole town of Capernaum (1:32–34) and the many sick who came even from beyond Galilee in all directions (3:7–10), he now heals the sick people of the "whole district" around Gennesaret.

### 2. MARK 6:53–56 AS MODEL FOR ACTION

The people at Gennesaret serve as models of those who recognize the greatness of Jesus' healing power and who compassionately strive to bring their sick compatriots to Jesus for healing. Like them we are called to place our faith in the unlimited power of Jesus to heal our often fragmented, broken lives and restore us to wholeness, and to generously and charitably bring our fellow human beings into contact with the great and compassionate healing power of Jesus.

## G. Mark 7:1–13: Jesus Demonstrates That Pharisees and Scribes Annul God's Word with Their Human Traditions

¹Then the Pharisees and some of the scribes who had come from Jerusalem gathered around him. ²They had noticed that some of

his disciples ate their meals with unclean, that is, unwashed hands.

³(For the Pharisees and all the Jews do not eat without carefully washing their hands, observing the tradition of the elders.¹² ⁴And on their return from the marketplace they do not eat without purifying themselves. And there are many other things that they have traditionally observed, the purification of cups and jugs and kettles [and beds].)¹³

⁵So the Pharisees and the scribes questioned him, "Why do your disciples not live according to the tradition of the elders but eat a meal with unclean hands?" ⁶He said to them, "Well did Isaiah prophesy about you hypocrites, as it is written:

'This people honors me with their lips,
    but their heart is far away from me;
⁷In vain do they worship me,
    teaching as doctrines human precepts.' (LXX Isa 29:13)
⁸You neglect the commandment of God but observe human tradition."

⁹Then he said to them, "How well you have rejected the commandment of God in order to uphold your tradition! ¹⁰For Moses said, 'Honor your father and your mother' (Exod 20:12; Deut 5:16), and 'Whoever insults father or mother shall surely die' (Exod 21:17; Lev 20:9). ¹¹But you say, 'If a person says to father or mother, "Any support you might have had from me is *korban*," ' (that is, an offering), ¹²you allow him no longer to do anything for his father or mother. ¹³You nullify the word of God for your tradition that you have handed on. And you do many such things."

### 1. MEANING OF MARK 7:1-13

#### a. *7:1-2* Pharisees and scribes note that the disciples eat with unclean hands.

Without indication that Jesus has changed his location from the area around Gennesaret (6:53–56), "the Pharisees and some of the scribes who had come from Jerusalem gathered around him." Since the Pharisees had earlier opposed Jesus and were plotting to kill him (2:16–3:6), and Jerusalem scribes had previously accused Jesus of expelling demons by Beelzebul (3:20–30), the conjunction of this double group of enemies arouses ominous tension with the expectation of a serious controversial encounter between them and Jesus (7:1).

These menacing opponents of Jesus had observed some of his disciples eating their meals with "unclean," that is, "unwashed" hands. Their concern is not with the bodily hygiene of the disciples but with their apparent neglect to keep themselves ritually or cultically "cleansed" or "purified" of profane defilement in accord with the religious character of Jewish meals, which bonded the participants together in fellowship with God (see 2:15–17). This prepares the reader for the first element of the controversy story, the opponents' objection to the behavior of Jesus' followers as being contrary to what they consider to be the way (*halakah*) Jews are to live in accord with God's will or law (7:2).

### b. *7:3–4* All Jews keep the purification tradition of the elders.

In a parenthetical explanation of the opponents' concern with the disciples' "uncleanness" Mark not only informs his audience about the purification tradition of the Jewish elders, but through sarcastic rhetorical exaggeration persuades them to share his ridicule of it: Not only the Pharisees but an exaggerated "all" of the Jews observe their revered "tradition of the elders" by carefully washing their hands before eating (7:3). They even go so far as to wash themselves after returning with food from the public and ritually profane marketplace. Not only that, but they observe many other purification traditions, ridiculously purifying even the objects used for the meal—cups, jugs, kettles and even beds! (probably dining "couches," see 4:21) (7:4).

### c. *7:5–8* Jesus counters their objection with scripture.

Voicing their actual objection, the Pharisees and scribes question Jesus as to why his disciples, and by implication he himself as their master, apparently disregard the *halakah* contained in the revered "tradition of the elders" by eating with unclean hands. They imply that Jesus and his disciples do not live in accord with God's will or law as it is specified in the orally transmitted tradition of the ancient Jewish elders handed down from generation to generation (7:5).

Directly and aggressively meeting their accusation, Jesus initiates the counter-argumentation of the controversy with a charge of his own. He accuses the Pharisees and scribes of being "hypocrites" by fulfilling the prophesied word of God written in Isaiah (LXX 29:13): They are religious frauds because, while they pay lip service to God with their traditions designed to unite people closely to God, their own "heart," the true core of their inner being, ironically remains far distant from God (7:6). They worship God in vain, because they teach that their traditions are "doctrines" from God when in reality they are no more than mere "human precepts" (7:7). With sarcastic ridicule Jesus surprisingly turns the tables on his enemies as he accuses them of being the ones, rather than he or his disciples, who ironically "neglect" or "leave aside" the very "command-ment of God" while they "observe" or "cling" to the merely "human tradition" of the elders (7:8).

### d. *7:9–13* Jesus indicts them for annulling God's commandment.

Jesus then proceeds to the climactic "pronouncement" portion of the controversy. Not only do the Pharisees and scribes observe their merely human tradition instead of God's commandment but, as Jesus now dem-onstrates with biting sarcasm, they very cleverly reject God's own com-mandment in favor of "your," merely human and not God's, tradition. They ironically "uphold" their own human tradition about what God wants to the detriment of the very commandment of God! (7:9).

Further illustrating their hypocrisy, Jesus substantiates his charge with an appropriate example: He first recalls what Moses, the authentic mediator of God's commandments, stated as the fourth of the ancient and revered decalogue of commandments, namely, the positive directive to "honor your father and your mother" (Exod 20:12; Deut 5:16). In sup-port of this commandment he adds the extreme consequences of the fail-ure to observe it: "Whoever insults father or mother shall surely die" (Exod 21:17; Lev 20:9). This negative Mosaic injunction thus underlines the great seriousness of the positive commandment calling for honor and support of one's parents (7:10). To what "Moses said" as God's com-mandment Jesus contrasts what "you," the Pharisees and scribes, now "say," namely, that if a person declares that whatever material or finan-cial support he was obligated to give his parents is *korban,* that is, an "offering" dedicated to God (but not necessarily given to the temple, so that the person could still possess and use it himself), then that person is strictly bound by that declaration (7:11). By permitting a person to make such a *korban* declaration and forbidding the reversal of it, his opponents effectively prevent the person from doing anything to support his par-ents (7:12).

As Jesus has masterfully illustrated, rather than helping people to fulfill God's command for parental honor and support, "you" Pharisees and scribes actually "nullify" the very "word of God" for the sake of "your" merely human tradition which "you," not Moses, have handed on. Jesus concludes with a sharp intensification of his overpowering accu-sation: This has been only one example of the "many such things" that his enemies do. And so Jesus has impressively defeated his opponents' accu-sation with his own charge and superior argumentation, to which they can not respond. He has unmasked their hypocrisy and, as the climactic and triumphant pronouncement of the controversy, has reaffirmed the commandment of God over their merely human tradition (7:13).

### 2. MARK 7:1–13 AS MODEL FOR ACTION

In this controversy story the hypocritical Pharisees and scribes who oppose Jesus serve as negative models for what it means to follow the true way and will of God in order to live totally authentic human lives. Their hypocrisy warns us that our cherished religious traditions and customs, which are merely human precepts, can nullify the very word of God they are meant to supplement and support, if they serve our own selfish aims rather than God's plan. But by powerfully reaffirming God's word over human tradition, Jesus invites us to allow the original, genuine and clear word of God, such as the fundamentally humane commandment calling for parental respect and support, to purify the excesses that our various religious, social and cultural human traditions, customs and practices have introduced into our attempt to live authentic and fulfilled human lives by following the "way of the Lord."

## H.  Mark 7:14–23: To the Crowd and His Disciples Jesus Reveals a New Teaching about Interior Uncleanness

[14]Then summoning again the crowd, he said to them, "Hear me, all of you, and understand! [15]There is nothing entering a person from outside which can defile that person; but the things which come out of a person are what defile a person."[14]

[17]And when he had gone into the house away from the crowd, his disciples asked him about the parable. [18]He said to them, "Are even you likewise without understanding? Do you not realize that everything that goes into a person from outside cannot defile, [19]since it does not go into the heart but into the stomach and passes out into the latrine?" (Thus he declared all foods clean.)

[20]And he said, "But what comes out of a person, that is what defiles a person. [21]For from within, from the heart of people, come evil thoughts, sexual immoralities, thefts, murders, [22]acts of adultery, acts of greed, acts of malice, deceit, licentiousness, envy, blasphemy, arrogance, foolishness. [23]All these evils come from within and defile a person."

### 1. MEANING OF MARK 7:14–23

#### a. *7:14–15* Jesus reveals to the crowd what defiles a person.

Having muffled the opposing Pharisees and scribes to an ominous silence, Jesus "summons again the crowd," that is, the "crowd" whom he earlier "summoned" and publicly taught in parables (3:23, 20; 4:1–9, 26–34). Jesus exhorts them to "hear me, all of you, and understand!" The words "hear" and "understand" recall Jesus' earlier challenge to the crowd to really hear and understand the true significance of his parables, lest they again unfortunately fulfill the prophecy of Isaiah by "hearing" but "not understanding" (4:3, 9, 12). As it calls for an especially keen attentiveness, Jesus' urgent exhortation to "hear" and "understand" underlines the great importance and complexity of the new teaching to follow (7:14).

In reference to the objection that his disciples eat with "unclean" or "defiled" hands (7:5), Jesus pronounces a powerful antithetical aphorism —a brief, pointed saying which contains a sharp contrast: "There is nothing entering a person from outside which can defile that person; but the things which come out of a person are what defile a person."[15] With this concise and absolute aphorism Jesus forcefully challenges basic assumptions about "defilement" or ritual "uncleanness" and invites his audience to an entirely new understanding, vision and focus about what it is that really "defiles" a human being. But, like his opponents, the crowd remains silent, giving no indication that they have really "heard" and "understood" Jesus, thus adding to the dramatic suspense (7:15).

#### b. *7:17–19* Jesus explains to his disciples that food cannot defile.

When Jesus had entered the private domain of "the house" away from the public domain of the silent, non-understanding "crowd," his disciples asked him about "the parable," that is, the puzzling antithetical aphorism he has just uttered. This repeats the pattern which distinguishes between the crowd as "outsiders" who do not understand the parabolic teaching of Jesus and the disciples as "insiders" to whom, as those given the mystery of the kingdom of God, Jesus "explains everything" (4:10–12, 33–34) (7:17).

Jesus' poignant question, "Are even you likewise without understanding?," confirms that not only has the crowd not understood the aphorism but "even" his own disciples, despite their privileged reception of his special, private instruction (4:10–25, 33–34) and revelations (4:35–41; 6:30–52), are still "without understanding" of Jesus. As they "did not understand" about Jesus on the basis of the loaves but had "hardened hearts" after witnessing the revelation of his profound character on the stormy sea (6:52), so they are still "without understanding." With another forceful rhetorical question Jesus then explains the first half of his antithetical aphorism about defilement: Nothing which enters a person from outside can "defile," that is, prevent worship of and relationship with God, because it does not enter the "heart," the true inner core and interior, spiritual essence of a person, but merely enters the stomach and harmlessly passes out into the latrine. Mark then parenthetically clarifies and confirms the consequences for his readers, further persuading them away from the ludicrous Jewish preoccupation with the external "defilement" surrounding the eating of food (7:3–4): Jesus "thus declared all foods clean." And so the internal "heart" of a person rather than external food is to be the new focus for what really "defiles" and separates a person from God (7:18–19).

### c. *7:20–23* Jesus warns that defilement comes from within a person.

Explaining the second half of his parabolic aphorism, Jesus asserts that it is what "comes out" of the interior that really "defiles" and separates a person from God (7:20). For the staggering and overwhelming accumulation of the most evil thoughts and actions that plague human communal living and prevent true union and fellowship between people and God originate and come from "within," from the "heart," the interior core of human beings (7:21–22). As Jesus emphasizes, all such horrible and wicked immoral thoughts and deeds which seriously "defile" a person before God come from "within" (7:23).

In powerfully turning the focus of defilement away from mere external and peripheral concerns, Jesus has enabled his audience to see the true, interior locus of defilement by shocking them with a long list of the horrifying, repulsive and deplorable evil thoughts and deeds that can emerge from within, thus forcing them to take a long, sober and piercing look at the dark recesses of the human heart. Subtly and ironically removing the mask of his Jewish opponents' exaggerated and deceptive concern for external defilement, Jesus has warned his disciples (7:2–5) of their true, internal defilement of the "heart": They are the ones who "questioned" Jesus "in their hearts" (2:6–8), engaged in the "evil thoughts" (7:21) of "blasphemy" (7:22) against the Holy Spirit at work in Jesus (3:28–30), and demonstrated the "hardness of heart" which led to their plotting his "murder" (3:5–6; 7:21). In turning his disciples' attention to the importance of the human "heart" in relating to the ways of God (7:6, 19, 21), Jesus has advised them of the dangers of their own "hardened hearts" and invited them to avoid "defilement" by opening their "hearts" to "understand" his more profound character (6:52). But, like the opponents and the crowd, the disciples, despite this privileged and potent instruction by Jesus, remain speechless, thus intensifying the dramatic suspense of their non-understanding and "hardened hearts."

### 2. MARK 7:14–23 AS MODEL FOR ACTION

Through this new and authoritative teaching Jesus draws us away from a superfluous preoccupation with inessential external concerns in our relationship with God, and calls us rather to cultivate a clean and open "heart" within our inner selves in order to facilitate a proper and wholesome relationship not only with God but with our fellow human beings. Jesus alerts us to our need to contend with and overcome the horribly wicked and destructive "defilement" of thoughts and actions that can emerge from the human heart, not only of others but of ourselves, as we strive to follow the "way of the Lord." And the disciples' silent, non-understanding and stubborn "hardness of heart," despite their special instruction by Jesus, caution us against a complacent satisfaction with our own understanding of Jesus. They prompt us to look into our own hearts in order to remove any "defilement" that prevents us from remaining open to a new and deeper insight into the significance of Jesus and his powerful teaching, so that we can see how he enables a more authentically human and morally upright living in union with God.

## I. Mark 7:24–30: Jesus Exorcises the Daughter of a Greek Syrophoenician Woman with Cleverly Strong Faith

[24]From there he arose and went away to the region of Tyre. Then he entered a house and wanted no one to know it, but he could not escape notice. [25]So immediately a woman, whose little daughter had an unclean spirit, heard about him and came and fell down at his feet. [26]The woman was a Greek, a Syrophoenician by birth, and she begged him to drive the demon out of her daughter. [27]He said to her, "Let the children be satisfied first, for it is not right to take the children's bread and throw it to the little dogs." [28]But she answered and said to him, "Lord, even the little dogs under the table eat the little children's crumbs." [29]Then he said to her, "For saying this, you may go. The demon has gone out of your daughter." [30]When she went to her home, she found the little child lying in bed and the demon gone.

## 1. MEANING OF MARK 7:24-30

### a. *7:24-26* A Gentile woman begs Jesus to exorcise her daughter.

Jesus arose "from there," that is, from the house in which he had been privately instructing his disciples in the district of Gennesaret (7:17; 6:53). Not only continuing the movement of his salvific "way" but for the first time extending it beyond the area around the Sea of Galilee, Jesus "went away" to the Gentile "region of Tyre," the area around the prominent city of Tyre on the Phoenician coast to the northwest of Galilee. Whereas people from the area around Tyre and Sidon had earlier come to Jesus to be healed (3:8), he now goes to them. Some tension is present for the reader since Tyre (often coupled with Sidon to the north) traditionally represented a Gentile people who had achieved a proud power and superior wealth by harshly oppressing their Jewish neighbors (Isa 23; Joel 4:4-8; Zech 9:2-4).

Although Jesus went away to the Gentile region of Tyre, a further tension arises as he enters the private domain of a "house," not wishing to be recognized in public, and yet he was so well-known even in this region that "he could not escape notice." That Jesus could not remain in private generates a double tension: On the one hand, Jesus' desire to withdraw from the public domain because of the overwhelming demand upon his healing and teaching ministry is thwarted. This tension illustrates the greatness of his power and popularity as well as the large number of people he heals, since he is simply too powerful and well-known to remain hidden (1:35-39, 45; 2:1-2; 3:9-10, 20; 6:31-34). On the other hand, the need for Jesus to further instruct his non-understanding disciples in private has been interrupted (7:17-18; 6:52) (7:24).

As part of this dramatic tension a woman whose little daughter was possessed by an unclean spirit immediately comes and humbly does him homage by falling down at his feet (5:6, 22, 33). Demonstrating faith in the healing power of Jesus, she initiates the expected healing story with her urgent appeal for him to drive the demon out of her daughter. But the tension increases with the presence of a potential obstacle to the healing: The person requesting healing could be refused because of her sex, culture, religion, and ethnic origin—not only is she a socially subordinate woman but her religious and cultural status is "Greek" and her ethnic background is "Syrophoenician."[16] She thus cuts a sharp social contrast with Jesus, a Jewish male from Nazareth of Galilee. But her maternal concern for her daughter has brought about this unlikely and unusual encounter. And so the question is not whether Jesus *can* but whether he *wants* to heal this foreign woman's daughter (7:25–26).

### b. *7:27–28* She cleverly replies to Jesus' caustic reluctance.

In contrast to his quick and ready desire to act when Jairus, the Jewish male and socially prominent synagogue official, likewise "fell at his feet" and pleaded for a sick little daughter (5:22–24), Jesus rather gruffly rebuffs the woman's earnest request. With a symbolic, metaphorical expression Jesus heightens the suspense as he subordinates her personal plea to their religious and ethnic differences as Jew and Gentile. In reference to the priority God gave Jews for receiving his revelation and salvation, Jesus tells her to let the "children," that is, the Jewish people but most especially the disciples, be "satisfied first" with the revelatory and salvific benefits of God now available through Jesus. For, as Jesus continues, "it is not right," according to the Jewish priority in God's plan, to take the children's "bread," the revelatory and salvific benefits of Jesus, and throw it to the "little dogs," that is, house pets rather than dogs of the street or farm, but a somewhat derogatory designation for Gentiles.

That the "children" being "satisfied" by the "bread" of Jesus refers especially to his metaphorical "satisfying" of his disciples with the "bread" of his salvific self-revelation is indicated by the previous context: After Jesus invited them to come away with him to rest and "eat" (6:31), he literally "satisfied" with "bread" the large crowd that gathered as well as the disciples, as "all ate and were satisfied" (6:42). But after Jesus privately revealed to his disciples his absolute divine saving power by walking on the sea, they were utterly astounded for they had not understood what he had revealed about himself "on the basis of the loaves," that is, on the basis of his overabundant "satisfying" of the large crowd and themselves with a miraculous multiplication of "loaves" (literally "breads") (6:52). The private and profound revelation of Jesus that takes place in his literal overabundant feeding thus provides the basis for the reader to realize that the image of his "satisfying" the "children" with "bread" metaphorically characterizes the way that he "satisfies" his disciples with the "bread" of the special, private self-revelation and teaching reserved for them. And so Jesus is ordering the Syrophoenician woman not to interrupt him while he is trying to "satisfy" his still non-understanding disciples ("children") with the "bread" of his further instruction and self-revelation to them in the privacy of the house (7:17, 24) (7:27).

Undaunted by Jesus' brusque reluctance, the woman utters a clever, sparkling and charming reply illustrating the strength and insight of her faith. After acknowledging his superiority by humbly but urgently addressing him as "Lord," she astutely exploits the metaphorical image to her advantage by pointing out that even the "little dogs" (Gentiles) under the dining "table" in the household "eat" the "little children's" (Jews, especially disciples) "crumbs."[17] She thus delightfully demonstrates her insightful faith in the unlimited greatness and overabundance of Jesus' salvific power, which can provide more than enough "bread" (revelatory, salvific benefits) for the "little children" (Jews) so that even the "little dogs" (Gentiles, especially herself and her daughter), who are also part of the household, can receive the "crumbs" of the overabundance. Ironically, this is precisely the kind of insightful faith and "understanding" Jesus has been striving to bring his disciples ("little children") to have by "satisfying" them with the private revelations ("bread") of the unlimited greatness and overabundance of his saving power, especially in his overabundant feeding and powerful walking on the sea! (7:28).

### c. *7:29–30* Her charming reply wins the exorcism of her daughter.

Moved by the strength and insight of this Gentile woman's exemplary faith, Jesus grants her request "for saying this," that is, for boldly and brilliantly voicing her faith in the overwhelming greatness of Jesus' saving power in ironic contrast to the silence and non-understanding of the disciples (6:52; 7:18). He dismisses her with the powerful words of the healer, assuring this concerned mother that "the demon has gone out of your daughter" (7:29). The confirmation of the healing occurs when the woman returns to the communal setting of her "home" and finds her "little child" now lying in bed with the demon gone. A Gentile mother and child have both experienced the saving power of Jesus: The child has been mercifully exorcised and the mother has had the relationship with her daughter and thus the communal harmony of her "home" wonderfully restored. That Jesus has healed the child from afar further illustrates the overabundant magnitude of his salvific power (7:30).

### 2. MARK 7:24–30 AS MODEL FOR ACTION

The Greek Syrophoenician woman serves as a marvelous model of how a robust and perceptive faith in the overabundant saving power of Jesus can not only bring healing and peaceful harmony to ourselves and others, but can break down the racial, social, religious, cultural and sexual prejudices that separate the peoples of the world. This caring mother shocks, shames and charms us to imitate her bold and persistent faith in the unlimited greatness of Jesus' salvific power, so that we can likewise eliminate the social barriers and prejudices that plague not only our own lives but the lives of our fellow human beings. The sparkling faith and maternal care of this foreign woman enables us to realize and recognize that God's salvific activity is at work in all peoples and cultures of the world.

## J. Mark 7:31–37: Jesus' Healing of a Deaf and Mute Man Is Proclaimed Despite His Command for Silence

³¹Then again coming out of the region of Tyre, he went by way of Sidon to the Sea of Galilee, into the region of the Decapolis. ³²And people brought to him a deaf man who had a speech impediment and begged him to lay his hand on him. ³³So taking him away from the crowd privately, he put his fingers into his ears and, spitting, touched his tongue; ³⁴then looking up to heaven, he groaned and said to him, "*Ephphatha!*" (that is, "Be opened!"). ³⁵And immediately his ears were opened, his speech impediment was removed, and he spoke plainly. ³⁶He ordered them to tell no one; but the more he ordered them, all the more did they proclaim it. ³⁷And they were exceedingly astonished, saying, "He has done all things well; he even makes the deaf hear and the mute speak!"

### 1. MEANING OF MARK 7:31-37

#### a. *7:31-32* People beg Jesus to heal a deaf and mute man.

Continuing to extend the movement of the salvific "way of the Lord" (1:2–3), Jesus "came out" of the region of Tyre and "went" northward "by way of Sidon" (often coupled with Tyre as the principal twin cities of the region, 3:8) and then southward back "to the Sea of Galilee" and beyond it "into the region of the Decapolis." And so having journeyed beyond Galilee to the northwest, Jesus now travels beyond the focal point of the Sea of Galilee to the southeast, to the broad ten-city district of the Decapolis, the area throughout which the exorcised Gerasene demoniac had proclaimed how much Jesus had done for him, so that "all were amazed" (5:20) (7:31).

A healing story commences as people compassionately bring to Jesus a man with a double ailment: He is both "deaf" and has a "speech impediment," which means difficulty not only in receiving communication but in expressing it. He is thus hindered in the process not only of human social communication but also of hearing the word of God and properly responding to it. With hopeful faith in his healing power they "begged" Jesus to "lay" his powerful, healing "hand" (1:41; 5:23) on the man (7:32).

### b. *7:33–35* Jesus heals the man privately.

In initiating the healing gesture by taking the man "away from the crowd privately," Jesus relates him to the disciples whom he has likewise taken "away from the crowd" (7:17) and given revelations and explanations "privately" (6:31–32; 4:34). This man who is physically "deaf" and "mute" thus functions also as a symbolic representative of the disciples who are spiritually "deaf" and "mute" with their non-understanding and "hardened hearts" (7:18; 6:52), not having "ears to hear" (4:9, 12, 23), despite Jesus' special revelations and explanations of his more profound identity. In a gradual, painstaking and very graphic manner Jesus performs the powerful gesture and word of healing: He places his fingers directly into the man's deafened ears to unblock them, touches the man's bound tongue with the healing spittle of his own power to speak, "looks up to heaven" (6:41), the origin of divine healing power, painfully "groans" at the obstinate ailment, and in the native Semitic language pronounces the powerful word of healing, "*Ephphatha!*," which means, "Be opened!" Jesus thus commands the man to "be opened" to receive and give communication. This characterizes the gradual, painstaking and graphic manner in which Jesus has been revealing and explaining his profound identity, striving to "open" the ears and mouth of his "deaf" and silent disciples (7:33–34).

The confirmation of the healing occurs with the notice that suddenly and miraculously "his ears were opened, his speech impediment was removed, and he spoke plainly." Through the directly applied power of Jesus' dramatic actions and words the man's physical faculties of communication have been restored. What must Jesus do to likewise "heal" the spiritual faculties of his still "deaf" and "mute" disciples, so that they can hear, understand and "speak plainly" of his profound character? (7:35).

### c. *7:36–37* Despite Jesus' command of silence the astonished people proclaim him.

Once again expressing the mysterious desire that he not be made publicly known (1:24–25, 34, 44–45; 3:11–12; 5:43), which hints that his healing power does not totally capture his more profound identity and that there is more to be known about him, Jesus "ordered" the people not to tell anyone. His command for the people to be silent creates further tension for the reader as it stands in ironic contrast to his attempt to enable the disciples to hear, understand and acknowledge him, symbolized by his enabling the deaf and mute man to "speak plainly." But his healing power is simply too great and marvelous to remain hidden. The more Jesus ordered the people not to tell anyone, "all the more did they proclaim it" (7:36).

As a result, people are "exceedingly astonished" and acknowledge that "he has done all things well," thus relating the healing power of Jesus in recreating and restoring the faculties of the deaf and mute man to the original creative power of God who saw that "everything he made was very good" (Gen 1:31; Sir 39:16). Their excited exclamation that "he even makes the deaf hear and the mute speak!" indicates how Jesus is now fulfilling the prophetic promise of God that in the future "the ears of the deaf will be unstopped" and "the tongue of the mute sing for joy" (Isa 35:5–6). But this climactic admiration of the healing expresses a double irony for the reader: First, it functions as an ironic understatement, since the reader knows that Jesus has the power to do much more than this; indeed, he has an overabundant and absolute divine saving power (4:35–41; 6:30–52). Secondly, it functions also as an ironic overstatement, since the disciples are still "deaf" and "mute" to the revelations of his overabundant and absolute divine saving power (7:37).

### 2. MARK 7:31–37 AS MODEL FOR ACTION

The faith and exuberant exclamation of the people who compassionately bring the deaf and mute man to experience the healing power of Jesus, call us to likewise place our faith in the divine power and mercy of Jesus to unblock and restore the communicative faculties of ourselves and others, so that we can reach our full human potential by more properly and perfectly communicating not only with our fellow human beings but with our Creator.

Symbolic of the "deafness" and "muteness" of the disciples to the private revelations and explanations of Jesus' deeper character, this healing story makes us realize that Jesus has an overabundant and absolute divine saving power which exceeds even his wonderful power to heal physical ailments. But identifying with the deaf and mute man as an ironic symbol of the disciples, we are cautioned against an overconfident complacency that we can ever really hear and correctly speak about the true profundity of the person and power of Jesus without his continual "healing" and revelatory help. As we persist on the salvific "way of the

Lord," we are urged to allow our "ears" and "mouth" to "be opened" so that we can receive and give further communication about the true significance of Jesus.

## K. Mark 8:1–9: Jesus Miraculously Provides an Overabundant Meal for Four Thousand

> [1]In those days when there again was a great crowd who had nothing to eat, he summoned the disciples and said to them, [2]"I have compassion on the crowd, because they have been with me three days now and have nothing to eat. [3]If I send them away hungry to their homes, they will faint on the way, and some of them have come a great distance." [4]But his disciples answered him, "From where will anyone be able to satisfy them with bread here in this deserted place?" [5]Then he asked them, "How many loaves do you have?" And they said, "Seven." [6]He commanded the crowd to sit down on the ground. Then, taking the seven loaves he gave thanks, broke them, and gave them to his disciples to distribute, and they distributed them to the crowd. [7]They also had a few small fish. And blessing these he told them to distribute these also. [8]Then they ate and were satisfied. And they took up seven baskets of fragments left over. [9]There were about four thousand people, and he dismissed them.

### 1. MEANING OF MARK 8:1–9

#### a. *8:1–3* Jesus pities the crowd who have nothing to eat.

"In those days," when Jesus was in the region of the Decapolis (7:31), "there again was a great crowd who had nothing to eat," thus recalling for the reader Jesus' earlier miraculous and overabundant feeding of a "great crowd" (6:30–44). In contrast to the earlier feeding in which the disciples informed Jesus of the lack of food (6:35–36), Jesus now takes the initiative. He "summons" the disciples and informs them of his "compassion" on the crowd, reminiscent of his "compassion" on the earlier crowd, because "they were like sheep without a shepherd" (6:34). Here Jesus has "compassion" on the crowd because they have now been with him for a lengthy period of "three days" (see Exod 15:22), even longer than in the previous story (6:35), and hence "have nothing to eat" (8:1–2). Jesus does not wish to send the crowd away hungry to their homes, as the disciples suggested earlier (6:35), because they would collapse on the journey from lack of food, and the distance some of them have come is too great (8:3).

**b. *8:4–7* Jesus gives the food to his disciples to distribute.**

Surprisingly the disciples respond as if they had never witnessed or participated in Jesus' previous miraculous feeding! In expressing the human impossibility for "anyone" to feed the crowd, the very words of the disciples ironically indicate that they have learned and remembered nothing about Jesus from the previous situation: They ask "from where," not realizing that it was from God in heaven (6:41), "will anyone be able," not realizing that it was precisely Jesus as the "one" with divine power, "to satisfy them with bread here in this deserted place," not remembering that all were "satisfied" (6:42) with "bread" (6:38, 41) precisely in a "deserted place" (6:35) (8:4).

Exactly repeating his question from the previous story (6:38), Jesus asks them, "How many loaves do you have?" Their answer is "seven," which is even more than the "five" loaves of the previous story (6:38) (8:5). As in the earlier story (6:39–40), Jesus commands the crowd to "sit down" on the ground, thus preparing them for the unique banquet to follow. Again repeating what he had done before (6:41), Jesus takes the seven loaves and "gives thanks" to God as the giver of food and source of the miracle to follow, "breaks" the bread as the host of the meal, and again "gives" the loaves to his disciples to act as his intermediary servants in "distributing" the miraculously multiplied loaves. The disciples, once again not only witnessing but participating, "distributed them to the crowd" (8:6). As fish were part of the previous feast (6:38, 41), so also here Jesus calls down God's blessing upon a "few small fish" and the disciples likewise "distribute" them, now miraculously multiplied (8:7).

**c. *8:8–9* Jesus overabundantly feeds the crowd of four thousand.**

Precisely as in the previous wondrous feeding (6:42), the great crowd "ate and were satisfied," after Jesus multiplied the food through God's power. As there was an overabundance of leftovers earlier (6:43), so now they take up "seven baskets of fragments left over," much more than the seven loaves with which the banquet began (8:8). Whereas five thousand men were fed in the previous meal (6:44), now a similar but lesser large number of "about four thousand people" were miraculously fed by Jesus with only seven loaves and a few small fish. Having fulfilled his "compassion" (8:2) by once again fully "satisfying" the great crowd, Jesus "dismisses" them, amply nourished for their journey home (8:9).

Although they had witnessed and participated in Jesus' feeding of five thousand with only five loaves, the disciples not only fail to grasp that Jesus can therefore certainly feed four thousand with seven loaves (8:4), but they once again amazingly make no response whatsoever to this sec-

ond magnificent manifestation of Jesus' divine and compassionate power
to overabundantly feed and re-order his people in a unique anticipation of
the final age feast of God's kingdom. Jesus has not only marvelously
satisfied with bread a great crowd of four thousand, but he has also once
again "satisfied" the "children," his disciples, with the "bread" of his
special revelation of his more profound character (7:27). But despite this
additional revelation the disciples persist with their "non-understanding"
and "hardness of heart" (6:52; 7:18), still painfully "deaf" and "mute"
(7:31–37) to the true identity and character of Jesus (4:35–41; 6:30–52;
8:1–9). And so the acute and baffling suspense continues to build.

### 2. MARK 8:1–9 AS MODEL FOR ACTION

This second miraculous feeding story reinforces our faith in Jesus as
the one who, through God's splendid and unique power, can compassionately and bountifully nourish, sustain and unify us as a "great crowd" of
people who have "come a great distance" to follow the salvific "way of the
Lord." The disciples' continuing lack of response and understanding provides a model for our own human weaknesses and difficulties in fully
grasping the overabundant and unlimited greatness of the divine compassion and power of Jesus. We are urged to accept the continual guidance
Jesus himself provides, so that we can penetrate and appreciate the true
significance and deep mystery of his person.

## L.  Mark 8:10–12: Jesus Refuses the Pharisees' Request for a Sign

[10]Then immediately entering the boat with his disciples, he
came to the region of Dalmanutha. [11]The Pharisees came forward and began to argue with him, seeking from him a sign from
heaven to test him. [12]Sighing deeply in his spirit he said, "Why
does this generation seek a sign? Amen, I say to you, no sign will
ever be given to this generation!"

### 1. MEANING OF MARK 8:10–12

#### a.  *8:10–11* Pharisees test Jesus by requesting a sign from heaven.

After dismissing the crowd of four thousand, Jesus again enters the
boat expressly "with his disciples" who have not responded to his self-
revelation in the miraculous feeding and so remain non-understanding

and "hardened in heart" (6:52; 7:18). He continues the movement of his salvific "way" as he leaves the area of the Decapolis (7:31) and "comes" to the region of Dalmanutha (8:10).[18]

The Pharisees, the adversarial group whom Jesus previously silenced (along with scribes from Jerusalem) by demonstrating their hypocrisy (7:1–13) and who have been plotting his death (3:6), now come forward and begin to argue with him. They want Jesus to show them a "sign from heaven," that is, some kind of indication or extraordinary demonstration from God himself to legitimize and decisively confirm that Jesus operates through the power of God rather than Beelzebul (3:20–30). They do not innocently seek an indisputable basis to believe in Jesus; their deceptive and destructive aim is rather "to test him" (see 1:13) and ultimately discredit his claim for a faithful following. Their sinister request for a "sign from heaven" ironically underlines the disciples' failure to understand the profound identity of Jesus despite being given "the mystery of the kingdom of God" (4:11) and the special, private revelations which serve as "signs from heaven" of his overabundant and absolute divine power (4:35–41; 6:30–52; 8:1–9) (8:11).

### b. *8:12* Jesus refuses to give "this generation" a sign.

Extending his earlier emotional reaction of anger and deep grief at the Pharisees' "hardness of heart" (3:5), Jesus now expresses his exasperation at their continued perverseness by "sighing deeply in his spirit" and uttering the penetrating rhetorical question, "Why does this generation seek a sign?" By referring to the Pharisees as the derogatory "this generation," Jesus not only connects them with their faithless contemporaries (such as scribes and Herodians), but places them in the traditional biblical category of "this generation," that is, the past generation of faithless and perverse Israelites who continually tested and rebelled against God and his special agent, Moses, despite all of the saving wonders God had performed for them (Deut 32:5–20; Ps 95:8–11). Jesus' piercing question induces the reader not only to ponder the tragic mystery of human resistance to God but to realize that "this generation" seeks a sign, not in order to believe in, but to destroy Jesus.

With the serious and solemn introduction, "amen, I say to you," emphasizing the certainty and decisiveness of his words, Jesus definitively refuses their deceptive request and avoids their "test" as he warns that "no sign will ever be given to this generation!" Jesus' solemn warning functions as an appeal to believe in him based not on a "sign from heaven" but on the evidence or "sign" of God's power at work in him as already manifested in his miraculous healing and exorcistic ministry. It also further underlines the ironic non-understanding of the disciples despite being privileged with additional revelations or "signs" of the absolute divine power operative in Jesus (8:12).

### 2. MARK 8:10–12 AS MODEL FOR ACTION

Jesus' rejection of the Pharisees' insincere request for a "sign" to legitimize faith in him calls us to reexamine the basis for our decision to believe in Jesus. We reinforce and deepen our faith in him not by seeking and demanding, like the Pharisees, some clear, unambiguous and conclusive evidence or "sign" from God himself, but by properly interpreting the powerful healing and authoritative teaching of Jesus as evidence or "signs" of the arrival of God's kingdom, and by properly understanding, in contrast to the disciples, the revelation or "signs" of the unlimited greatness of the saving power of God at work in Jesus. The Pharisees' stubborn and perverse resistance to the power of God active in Jesus alerts us to ponder and reckon with the tragic mystery of the continued human opposition and defiance to the saving plan of God that we may encounter in ourselves and others as we follow "the way of the Lord."

## M. Mark 8:13–21: Jesus Interrogates His Disciples about the Overabundant Feedings

[13]Then leaving them and entering the boat again, he went away to the other shore. [14]They had forgotten to bring bread, and they had only one loaf with them in the boat. [15]He warned them, saying, "Watch out, beware of the leaven of the Pharisees and the leaven of Herod." [16]And they discussed among themselves that they did not have bread. [17]Realizing this he said to them, "Why do you discuss that you do not have bread? Do you not yet perceive or understand? Are your hearts hardened? [18]Having eyes do you not see, and having ears do you not hear? And do you not remember, [19]when I broke the five loaves for the five thousand, how many baskets full of fragments you took up?" They said to him, "Twelve." [20]"And the seven for the four thousand, how many baskets full of fragments did you take up?" And they said to him, "Seven." [21]Then he said to them, "Do you not yet understand?"

## 1. MEANING OF MARK 8:13-21

### a. *8:13-15* Jesus warns his disciples of the Pharisees and Herod.

After his stern refusal to give them a "sign" Jesus leaves the Pharisees behind. He enters the boat again, implicitly with his disciples (8:10), and continues the ongoing movement of his salvific "way" as he "went away" to the "other shore" of the Sea of Galilee. This motif of Jesus and his disciples crossing the sea in the private domain of the boat echoes the beginnings of the two previous sea-rescue epiphanies (4:35; 6:45), in which Jesus revealed himself as equipped with absolute divine saving power, and thus creates an expectation for a possible further revelation or explanation of Jesus to the disciples (8:13).

The suspense-arousing notice that the disciples "had forgotten to bring bread" but had "only one loaf" with them in the boat is reminiscent of the two previous miraculous feedings (6:30-44; 8:1-9), in which Jesus revealed himself with divine power to multiply small amounts of food into an overabundance. That the disciples have "only one loaf" with them in the boat should present no problem either for the obvious, literal level of meaning in which the "one loaf" signifies insufficient food which Jesus can miraculously multiply, nor for the more cryptic, metaphorical level of meaning in which the "one loaf" in the boat symbolizes Jesus himself who can reveal his profound character by "satisfying" his disciples with the "bread," the "one loaf" of his self-revelation (see 7:27). Although the disciples have "only one loaf" with them in the boat, the reader, through the previous overabundant feedings, knows that this "one loaf" is sufficient to satisfy them both physically with food and metaphorically with Jesus' self-revelation (8:14).

Continuing the "bread" metaphor, Jesus warns his disciples to beware of the "leaven" of the Pharisees and the "leaven" of Herod. In the biblical tradition "leaven," the yeast that so thoroughly and completely ferments a loaf of bread, is often used as a metaphor for the powerful and thorough influence of something mainly corruptive and destructive (Lev 2:11; 1 Cor 5:6-8; Gal 5:9). The "leaven" of the Pharisees and of Herod refers to their dangerous misunderstanding of the true identity of Jesus as a unique agent of God's saving power, which poses an ominous threat to the life of Jesus, the metaphorical "one loaf" (3:1-6; 6:14-29; 8:10-12). Jesus warns that this "leaven" of misunderstanding and hostility by the Pharisees and Herod can totally damage and corrupt the metaphorical "bread" of the self-revelation of his true character to his disciples (8:15).

### b. *8:16–19* Jesus reminds them of his overabundant feeding of five thousand.

In response to Jesus' warning about the danger of the metaphorical "leaven" of the Pharisees and of Herod, the disciples rather incongruously discuss among themselves that they do not have bread. This ironically conflicts with the fact that they actually do have "one loaf" with them in the boat (8:14), the literal "one loaf" of bread that metaphorically symbolizes Jesus' self-revelation. They overlook this "one loaf" endangered by the "leaven" of misunderstanding (8:16).

With his superior perception (see 2:8) Jesus realizes what his disciples are discussing and conducts a critical interrogation of their obvious failure to understand. That they are discussing their lack of bread despite having the "one loaf" leads Jesus to inquire whether they still do not "perceive" or "understand," and whether their "hearts" are still "hardened" (6:52) to what he has revealed about himself in his previous miraculous multiplications of insufficient bread (8:17). By questioning whether they have "eyes" but "do not see" and "ears" but "do not hear" (Jer 5:21; Ezek 12:2), Jesus likens his disciples, who have been given "the mystery of the kingdom of God" (4:11), to "those outside," who "see" and "hear" but tragically "do not understand" (4:12). He then forces them to "remember" and to explicitly recount the significance of his feeding of the five thousand. By asking them how many baskets full of leftover fragments they themselves, the witnessing participants, took up, Jesus leads them to the interpretive key of the miraculous feeding—its spectacular overabundance, indicative of Jesus' divine power to overabundantly feed his people. Their correct, concise and distinctly voiced answer of "twelve" demonstrates how Jesus is gradually unblocking their "ears" and removing their "speech impediment" so that they can "speak plainly" (7:31–37) and come to understand (8:18–19).

### c. *8:20–21* Jesus reminds them of his overabundant feeding of four thousand.

Continuing his painstaking, instructive interrogation of his disciples, Jesus forces them to recall and explicitly state how many baskets full of leftover fragments of bread they themselves took up after he miraculously satisfied the four thousand with only seven loaves. Again, they correctly and clearly voice the answer of "seven," pointing them to the significant overabundance of bread Jesus provided (8:20). Having opened their "eyes" and "ears" to "see" and "hear" that with their "one loaf" (8:14) they have both the literal and metaphorical "bread" revealing Jesus' divine power to overabundantly satisfy them, Jesus utters the climactic, suspenseful and critical question, "Do you not yet understand?" (8:21).

## 2. MARK 8:13–21 AS MODEL FOR ACTION

Jesus' warning about the "leaven" of misunderstanding and hostility as well as his meticulous instruction of his disciples about the overabundance of his miraculous "bread," guiding them to the critical question of their "understanding," invites us to penetrate and ponder the question of whether we ourselves, although we know the true identity of Jesus as God's chosen Son (1:11), really perceive and understand how great and how significant for human lives is the divine power at work in Jesus to overabundantly feed and satisfy us. Since only Jesus himself can open our eyes and ears to fully understand and appreciate the overabundant greatness of his person and power, we are urged to keep our eyes and ears fixed on him and his instructive guidance, so that we can truly "understand" as we follow his salvific "way." With Jesus as our "one loaf (bread)" we have the ability not only to "satisfy" ourselves and others who are "hungry" but to unite together in fellowship around Jesus the variously divided peoples and cultures of the world.

## N. Mark 8:22–26: At Bethsaida Jesus Gradually Heals a Blind Man

²²Then they came to Bethsaida. And people brought to him a blind man and begged him to touch him. ²³Taking the hand of the blind man, he led him outside of the village; and when he had spit on his eyes and laid his hands upon him, he asked him, "Do you see anything?" ²⁴And looking up he said, "I see people but they look like trees walking." ²⁵Then again he laid his hands upon his eyes, and he began to see clearly, and was restored and saw everything distinctly. ²⁶Then he sent him to his home, saying, "Do not even enter the village."

### 1. MEANING OF MARK 8:22–26

#### a. *8:22* At Bethsaida a blind man is brought to Jesus.

With his disciples, who still do not "see" and "understand," Jesus continues the movement of his salvific "way" as they "come" to "Bethsaida," a village on the northeastern shore of the Sea of Galilee. The

disciples have finally reached the goal toward which Jesus has been directing them since he "forced" them into the boat to go ahead of him "toward
Bethsaida" before he revealed to them his divine power to walk across the
sea (6:45; 8:13).

A healing story commences as people compassionately bring Jesus a
"blind man" and, with faith in his healing power, beg Jesus to touch him.
This recalls the very similar way that people brought a deaf and mute man
to Jesus and begged him to lay his hand on him (7:32). Just as the deaf and
mute man symbolically represented the disciples who are "deaf" and
"mute" to the revelations and explanations of Jesus' more profound identity, having "ears" but "not hearing" or understanding (8:18; 4:12), so this
blind man at Bethsaida likewise characterizes the disciples who are
"blind" to Jesus' true character, having "eyes" but "not seeing" and still
not understanding (8:18, 21; 4:12). In the biblical tradition blindness is
considered humanly incurable; God's healing of the blind and deaf is one
of the marvelous features of the future, definitive and final age of salvation (Ps 146:8; Isa 29:18; 35:5).

### b. *8:23–24* Jesus privately begins to bring the blind man to see.

Again echoing his healing of the deaf and mute man (7:33), Jesus
takes the blind man by the hand and leads him outside of the public
domain of the village for a private, personal encounter. After performing
the powerful healing gestures of spitting on his eyes and laying his hands
upon him, Jesus inquires, "Do you see anything?" This characterizes the
way that Jesus has been privately, personally and powerfully revealing
himself to his disciples, and recalls his critical question to them, "Do you
not yet understand?" (8:21), after he has painstakingly tried to open their
"eyes" to "see" (8:18) him and his true significance (8:23).

The blind man looks up and begins to see again. Although he can
now see people, he cannot yet see clearly enough, as "they look like trees
walking." This characterizes how the disciples, although they were able to
begin to "see" by correctly answering Jesus' questions about the overabundance of his miraculous feedings (8:19–20), still do not yet "see" or "understand" (8:21) clearly enough (8:24).

### c. *8:25–26* Jesus enables him to see clearly and sends him home.

After Jesus again lays his powerful healing hands upon the man's
partially seeing eyes, then the miraculous healing is confirmed as he begins to "see clearly," has his sight fully "restored," and "saw everything
distinctly." That Jesus has personally, privately and gradually enabled the
blind man to "see everything clearly" arouses the expectation that he will

likewise enable his disciples, whom he has just been personally, privately and gradually guiding and instructing (8:13–21), to "see everything clearly" by coming to understand Jesus' more profound character (8:25).

Jesus completes the man's personal experience of the salvation he brings as an indication of the arrival of God's kingdom by sending him to his home (see 5:19), thus restoring him as a fully healed human being to his family. That Jesus directs him not even to enter the public domain of the village continues the suspense of his previous, somewhat mysterious and usually unsuccessful, attempts to avoid public knowledge of his healing power (1:34, 44–45; 3:12; 5:43; 7:24, 36), as it seems to generate misunderstandings about his true identity and character (6:14–16; 8:10–12) (8:26).

### 2. MARK 8:22–26 AS MODEL FOR ACTION

Jesus' healing of the blind man at Bethsaida calls us to imitate the compassionate faith of those who brought the blind man to Jesus. We are urged to likewise bring not only others but ourselves to the divine healing, restorative and re-creating power available in Jesus with the faith that he can heal and strengthen the weaknesses and defects of our sight and insight, so that we can more properly and clearly "see" our fellow human beings and achieve our full potential within our respective human communities.

As we continue to follow Jesus on the salvific "way of the Lord," his personal, gradual and powerful healing of the blind man gives us the ardent hope and expectation that he has the power and compassionate desire to open our "eyes" to "see" and understand more and more clearly and completely the overabundant greatness of his divine saving power and the profound significance of his person for our lives and the lives of our fellow human beings.

## Notes

1. In recognizing the beginning of a new structural division at Mark 6:1 rather than at 6:6b and in keeping Mark 6:6b united with 6:6a as the conclusion of the pericope, we follow Manicardi, *Il cammino,* 29, 91.

2. This description of "irony" is indebted to the following: P. D. Duke, *Irony in the Fourth Gospel* (Atlanta: John Knox, 1985) 17; G. R. O'Day, "Narrative Mode and Theological Claim: A Study in the Fourth Gospel," *JBL* 105 (1986) 663; M. H. Abrams, *A Glossary of Literary Terms* (3d ed.; New York: Holt, Rinehart and Winston, 1971) 80. See also J. P. Heil,

"Reader-Response and the Irony of Jesus before the Sanhedrin in Luke 22:66–71," *CBQ* 51 (1989) 271–84.

3. See "Elijah" in Chapter I and the commentary on Mark 1:1–8 in Chapter II.

4. See 1 QSa 1:14f.; 1:27–2:1; 2:11–22; 1 QM 4:1–5; CD 13:1.

5. Priest, "Messianic Banquet," *IDBSup,* 591–92.

6. E. Lohse, *"chilias, chilioi," TDNT* 9.468.

7. See also J. P. Heil, "Interpreting the Miracles of Jesus," *McKendree Pastoral Review* 3 (1986) 36–41.

8. See also Hab 3:15; Isa 51:9–10; 43:16; and Heil, *Jesus Walking on the Sea,* 37–56.

9. Luke 1:13, 19, 30; 2:10; 24:39; Matt 28:5, 10; Mark 16:6; Acts 9:5; 22:8; 26:15.

10. For somewhat similar responses in other epiphanies, see Matt 28:8; Luke 24:41; Mark 16:8.

11. See also Heil, *Jesus Walking on the Sea,* 67–75, 118–44.

12. "Carefully" is an attempt to render the sense of the uncertain Greek word *pygmē,* which literally means "with the fist." Some have suggested that it means to wash with a "handful" of water, or with "cupped hand" or with "half-closed hand." See M. Hengel, "Mc 7,3 *pygmē:* Die Geschichte einer exegetischen Aporie und der Versuch ihrer Lösung," *ZNW* 60 (1969) 182–98; S. M. Reynolds, *"Pygmē* (Mark 7,3) as 'Cupped Hand'," *JBL* 85 (1966) 87–88; "A Note on Dr. Hengel's Interpretation of *pygmē* in Mark 7,3," *ZNW* 62 (1971) 295–96.

13. "And beds" is lacking in some manuscripts.

14. Verse 16, "If anyone has ears to hear, let him hear," is lacking in some of the best Greek manuscripts. It may have been transferred here by scribes from Mark 4:9, 23.

15. Tannehill, *Sword,* 88: "An aphorism is a short, pithy statement of a principle or precept, often containing something ingenious, striking, or witty. It expresses a truth of broad application and yet it frequently opposes truth as commonly seen."

16. W. L. Lane, *The Gospel According to Mark: The English Text with Introduction, Exposition and Notes* (NICNT; Grand Rapids: Eerdmans, 1974) 260: "She is designated a Syrophoenician because Phoenicia belonged administratively to the province of Syria and was distinguished from Libophoenicia with its center at Carthage in North Africa."

17. The "Greek" woman's brilliant cleverness extends to the fine points of the Greek language. After Jesus has somewhat unkindly referred to the Gentiles, and thus the woman, with the Greek diminutive "little dogs" (7:27), this distraught mother tenderly transforms his "children" (7:27), referring to Jews, to the diminutive "little children" (7:28), thus

associating them more closely with her sick "little daughter" (7:25). At the end of the story the narrator refers to her healed daughter as the "little child" (7:30), underlining this Gentile reception of a salvific benefit reserved "first" for the Jewish "little children."

18. Although notoriously difficult to identify and locate, Dalmanutha may well be identical to Magdala, an important city on the western shore of the Sea of Galilee. See Lane, *Mark,* 271 n. 6.

# VI

---

# Mark 8:27–10:52

## The Way of Jesus Leads to Suffering, Death and Resurrection.

### A. Mark 8:27–33: After Peter Confesses Jesus as the Christ, Jesus Teaches the Necessity That He Suffer, Die and Rise

[27]Then Jesus and his disciples went on to the villages of Caesarea Philippi. And on the way he asked his disciples, "Who do people say that I am?" [28]They said to him, "John the Baptist, others Elijah, still others one of the prophets." [29]Then he asked them, "But who do you say that I am?" Peter answered him, "You are the Christ!" [30]And he warned them to tell no one about him.

[31]Then he began to teach them that the Son of Man must suffer greatly and be rejected by the elders, the chief priests, and the scribes, and be killed, and after three days rise. [32]He spoke this word openly. Then Peter took him aside and began to rebuke him. [33]But he turned around and, looking at his disciples, rebuked Peter and said, "Get behind me, Satan! You are not thinking the things of God, but the things of human beings."

#### 1. MEANING OF MARK 8:27–33

##### a. *8:27–28* The disciples tell Jesus who people say he is.

With his disciples, who still "do not see" (8:18, 22–26) and still "do not understand" (8:21) his true identity, Jesus again expands the movement of his "way" beyond Galilee as he "went on" to the subordinate "villages" of the major city of Caesarea Philippi. Having journeyed to the areas of Tyre and Sidon in the northwest and the region of the Decapolis to the southeast (7:31), Jesus now takes his disciples to the far northeastern limits of the land.[1]

The explicit notice that Jesus was "on the way" recalls how the "way" of Jesus is to accomplish the salvific "way of the Lord" (1:2–3). While "on the way" immediately to the villages of Caesarea Philippi but ultimately to the accomplishment of God's "way" of salvation, Jesus continues his previous interrogation of his still non-understanding disciples (8:14–21) by presenting them with the question of his identity; "Who do people say that I am?" (8:27). Their answer of "John the Baptist," "Elijah," or "one of the prophets" echoes the ironic opinions expressed earlier by the people and Herod based on the manifestation of his "mighty powers" (6:14–16). While these complimentary opinions quite properly place Jesus in revered company, the reader knows that they are inadequate as designations of the profound identity of Jesus. They correspond to the indistinct and not yet complete "seeing" of the blind man at Bethsaida (8:24) (8:28).

### b. *8:29–30* Peter confesses Jesus to be the Christ.

After their recounting of the people's inadequate opinions Jesus places the question of his identity directly before his disciples: "But who do *you* say that I am?" In contrast to how the people identify him, Jesus asks who "you," the disciples who have received special, private self-revelations and explanations by Jesus, now "say that I am." Peter, the first to answer the call of discipleship (1:16) and the one whom Jesus renamed and placed at the head of the Twelve (3:16), functions as the spokesperson for the disciples as he identifies Jesus with the climactic confession, "You are the Christ!" This finally begins to resolve the previous, ongoing suspense regarding the disciples' stubborn lack of insight and understanding of the more profound character revealed by Jesus (4:41; 6:52; 8:21). In proclaiming Jesus to be "the Christ," that is, God's "anointed one" or expected "messiah" who would bring about the final, definitive age of God's salvation, Peter, as he confirms and reinforces the superscription of the narrative—"the beginning of the gospel of Jesus *Christ*," voices a much more adequate designation of Jesus which surpasses the opinions of the people.[2] Jesus has finally managed to bring his "deaf," "mute" (7:31–37) and "blind" (8:22–26) disciples to "see," "hear" and "speak" his true identity (8:29).

But as soon as his disciples recognize and acknowledge his true identity as "the Christ," Jesus immediately reintroduces the tension surrounding the significance of his person as "he warned them to tell no one about him." Jesus thus imposes upon his disciples the same mysterious and suspenseful silence that he has imposed upon the demons who know his true identity (1:24–25, 34; 3:11–12) (8:30).

### c. *8:31* Jesus teaches them that he must suffer, die and rise.

Why Jesus does not want his disciples to tell anyone about him becomes evident as he commences a new level of special revelations and explanations which further illustrate and specify his true identity. He "begins" anew to "teach" them about himself as the "Son of Man," that is, as the earthly embodiment of the heavenly, exalted messianic agent for the establishment of God's kingdom, who now exercises on earth the heavenly authority to forgive sins (2:10) and who is even now on earth the lord of the sabbath (2:28).[3] As the "Son of Man" Jesus "must" (*dei*), that is, in accord with the divine "necessity" of God's "way" or plan of salvation, "suffer greatly and be rejected by the elders, the chief priests, and the scribes," that is, by a comprehensive, threefold representation of authoritative Jewish leaders.[4] He must "be killed" and he must "after three days," that is, after the traditional, indefinite and short period of time when God intervenes on behalf of his own, "rise" from the realm of the dead.[5]

As the earthly embodiment of the heavenly, messianic "Son of Man" with divine authority (2:10, 28), who is also "the Christ" endowed with an overabundant and absolute divine saving power (6:30–52), Jesus now reveals that he "must" surprisingly and paradoxically suffer, die and rise. Jesus thus subsumes the ominous tension aroused by the sinister indications and attempts of his enemies to destroy him (2:20; 3:6, 22; 6:14–29; 8:11) into the "necessity" of God's "way" of salvation. He now adds to his accomplishing of the salvific "way of the Lord" by his "way" of teaching and healing the divine necessity of his suffering, dying and rising. As a new turning point in the plot of the narrative, Jesus now indicates to his disciples that he is not only "on the way" to the villages of Caesarea Philippi but "on the way" to his suffering, death and resurrection (8:31).

### d. *8:32–33* Jesus rebukes Peter for not thinking as God does.

Jesus spoke "this word" of new revelation about the necessity of his suffering, death and resurrection, which now becomes part of the "word" of the gospel of the arrival of God's kingdom (1:14–15, 45; 2:2; 4:14–20, 33), "openly" or "freely," that is, not in riddles or parables (4:33), not concealing anything, and with bold, confident acceptance of the content of what he is saying. Having just confessed Jesus to be the Christ in accord with the revelations of the greatness of his divine power, Peter "takes him aside" and begins to "rebuke" or "admonish" him, trying to deter him as the powerful Christ and divinely authoritative Son of Man from accepting the way of suffering, rejection and death (8:32).

But, as he is already "on the way" (8:27), Jesus "turns around," and looking directly at his disciples, "rebukes" Peter, their spokesperson and representative leader. Jesus orders him not to obstruct his "way" but instead to "get behind me," thus echoing his original command for Peter to become his disciple and follow him on his "way" by "coming after me" (1:17). By addressing him as "Satan," Jesus indicates that Peter's "rebuke" regarding the determination of Jesus to go the way of suffering, rejection and death amounts to a diabolical temptation from the very prince of demons, who diametrically opposes the ways of God (1:13; 4:15). As Peter is trying to prevent him from going on his "way," Jesus charges him with "not thinking the things of God, but the things of human beings." In other words, although it is contrary and paradoxical to normal human thinking for Jesus as the divinely powerful, authoritative Christ and Son of Man to accept the way of suffering, rejection, death and resurrection, it corresponds completely to God's plan of salvation and establishing his kingdom. Jesus is thus calling Peter and the rest of his disciples to abandon their past, human manner of thinking and to adopt a new, divine manner of thinking about God's way of salvation now revealed by Jesus (8:33).

### 2. MARK 8:27–33 AS MODEL FOR ACTION

That Jesus will not avoid the deadly opposition that has been mounting against him calls us, as we identify with Peter and the disciples, to accept along with him the necessity that he suffer, be rejected by the leaders of his own people, die and rise in accord with God's plan of salvation. We are prompted to ponder and probe the mysterious paradox of the divine necessity that Jesus, precisely as the Christ endowed with absolute divine saving power and as the Son of Man with heavenly authority on earth, "must" nevertheless suffer, die and rise. We are invited to persevere on the "way" of Jesus by allowing him to transform our ordinary, human manner of thinking into a new level of thinking in accord with the mysterious, salvific will of God.

## B. Mark 8:34–9:1: Jesus Calls the Crowd and His Disciples to Follow Him by Denying Self and Accepting the Cross

[34]Then summoning the crowd with his disciples, he said to them, "If anyone wishes to follow after me, let that person deny one-

self, take up one's cross and follow me. [35]For whoever wishes to save one's life will lose it, but whoever loses one's life for my sake and that of the gospel will save it. [36]What does it profit a person to gain the whole world and forfeit one's life? [37]What can a person give in exchange for one's life? [38]Whoever is ashamed of me and of my words in this faithless and sinful generation, the Son of Man will also be ashamed of that person, when he comes in his Father's glory with the holy angels." [1]And he said to them, "Amen, I say to you, there are some standing here who will not taste death until they see that the kingdom of God has come in power."

### 1. MEANING OF MARK 8:34–9:1

#### a. *8:34–38* Jesus calls the crowd and his disciples to follow him.

*8:34* Deny Self and Take Up One's Cross

That Jesus summons "the crowd" along with his disciples indicates that what he is about to say is not a private address directed only to his disciples but is open to the wider audience attracted to Jesus. Having announced his decision to go the way of suffering, rejection, death and resurrection (8:31), Jesus now issues new and challenging conditions for those individuals who want to continue on his "way" of salvation. With further elucidation of the "way" he has accepted for himself in accord with "the things of God" (8:33), Jesus urges others to imitate him. Anyone who wishes to continue as a follower of the "way" of Jesus must, first of all, "deny oneself," that is, act in a totally selfless manner without concern for personal advantage or convenience but open to "the things of God," as illustrated by Jesus, who "denies himself" in favor of the divine necessity of his suffering and death.

Furthermore, any follower of Jesus must "take up one's cross." For Jesus to take up his "cross" means that he willingly accepts upon his shoulders the crossbar used in the Roman execution of criminals by crucifixion, a common phenomenon in first-century Palestine.[6] Thus, for the follower of Jesus to "take up one's cross" means both to be willing to accept, like Jesus, the literal "cross" of a martyr's death by crucifixion and/or to accept the metaphorical "cross" of whatever opposition, rejection or suffering comes one's way in accord with God's will. The selfless attitude of "denying oneself" as well as the willingness to suffer adversity and death by "taking up one's cross" are the prerequisites Jesus challenges anyone to personally and individually choose for oneself in order to follow him on his "way" of accomplishing God's salvation.

*8:35* Lose One's Life To Save It

Jesus makes his demanding challenge of discipleship more attractive by uttering a concise, absolute antithetical aphorism expressing the outrageous but intriguing paradox that one now can actually gain life by losing it. This provocative saying compels its listeners to radically reexamine and ponder anew the common fears and concerns involved with "saving" and "losing" one's life.[7] Whoever wishes "to save one's life" by not denying oneself, taking up one's cross and following the "way" of Jesus will ironically experience the loss of the very life one has been striving to preserve. But whoever "loses one's life" by expending it for the sake of following Jesus and proclaiming the word of the gospel (1:1, 14–15), which now includes the divine necessity of his suffering, death and resurrection, will experience and discover the paradoxical wonder of saving or gaining one's life precisely by losing or expending it. With his intriguing offer of a radically new and revolutionary vision of the way one lives, Jesus is forcefully persuading his audience to choose to follow his "way" of accomplishing God's salvation.

*8:36–37* The Value of One's Life

With two thought-provoking rhetorical questions Jesus compels his listeners to realize and desire the supreme value of the life he promises. Developing the first half of the preceding paradoxical saying by extending the concept of "saving" into the commercial realm of financial and material "profit," "gain," "loss" and "payment," Jesus asks what "profit" a person who "gains" the whole world would acquire if that person were to "forfeit" one's life. The only answer is "nothing." Jesus is effectively prodding his audience away from a concern to preserve life by accumulating wealth and inducing them to choose the paradox of gaining the value of one's life by losing or spending it through following the "way" of Jesus (8:36). And this is reinforced by a second rhetorical question through which Jesus requires his listeners to appreciate that there is absolutely nothing that one can give as payment in "exchange" for the supreme value of one's very life (Ps 49:7–9) (8:37).

*8:38* The Triumph of the Son of Man

With a cogent warning that a decision not to follow him now would have unpleasant consequences in the future and final time of salvation, Jesus further persuades the crowd and his disciples to choose to follow his paradoxical "way" of accomplishing God's salvation by denying self, taking up the cross and losing life to gain it. Jesus advises against being "ashamed" of him for accepting the humiliating "way" of suffering, rejection and death, and of his "words," which call others to follow his "way" (8:34–37), in order to avoid being part of "this faithless and sinful generation" of people who oppose the "things of God" (8:33) revealed by Jesus (see 8:12). Whoever is "ashamed" of Jesus and his words by refusing to follow him now in this present time, Jesus will likewise "be ashamed of" when he, as the Son of Man, will not only suffer, die and rise (8:31) but "come" again triumphantly "with the holy angels" in the heavenly "glory" of God, his Father, to establish the kingdom of God at the end of time (Dan 7:13–14).[8] Jesus thus urges his listeners to choose to follow his paradoxical and humiliating "way" now, so that they can fully participate in the triumphant glory of the future and final age of God's salvation.

b. *9:1 Jesus assures that some will not die before seeing the kingdom of God in power.*

Solemnly underlining the importance and certainty of what he is about to say with the words, "amen, I say to you," Jesus pronounces a mysterious promise to the crowd and his disciples that some of them "will not taste death," and thus will not have to wait until the end of time (8:38), before "they see that the kingdom of God has come in power." Although Jesus, as the powerful Christ and authoritative Son of Man, has accepted the humiliating and shameful powerlessness of his suffering, rejection and death, the "power" with which the "kingdom of God" will "come" in and through the person and "way" of Jesus (1:14–15) will be visible to some before they die and before the end of time. With the assurance that some will see the power of God's kingdom yet in this age, Jesus further encourages his listeners to choose to follow his "way" of accomplishing God's salvation.

## 2. MARK 8:34–9:1 AS MODEL FOR ACTION

As we identify with the crowd and the disciples, Jesus invites us to continue to follow him on his "way" of suffering, rejection, death and resurrection by first of all ridding ourselves of a selfish preoccupation with our personal concerns and conveniences and adopting the selfless attitude of "denying ourselves." In addition, we must "take up our cross," that is, willingly accept in accord with God's will the "cross" of suffering, opposition, persecution, misunderstanding, misfortune and even death that we may encounter as Christians striving to follow the "way" of Jesus (8:34).

Provoking us to radically penetrate and probe anew our vision of what it means to "lose" and "save" our lives, Jesus offers us the intriguing opportunity to discover and experience the paradoxical wonder of real and authentic human living by "losing" or spending our lives for his sake and the sake of proclaiming his gospel, which likewise calls others to the mysterious paradox of "saving" our lives by "losing" them (8:35).

By cogently inducing us to realize that gaining our lives is worth infinitely more than any financial gain or accumulation of wealth, Jesus persuades us to avoid the ultimate futility of a life centered and "lost" on material success, but instead to desire and strive for the authentic life he offers us by following him on his paradoxical "way" of suffering, rejection, death and resurrection (8:36–37).

That Jesus' acceptance of the humiliation and powerlessness of suffering, rejection and death will lead not only to future resurrection but ultimately to the final, triumphant coming of the Son of Man in the heavenly glory of his Father (8:38), and that some people will witness the power of the coming kingdom of God even in this present age (9:1), encourages us to follow the paradoxical "way" of Jesus with the confident hope that we will surely see and participate in the triumphant glory and power of the future and final kingdom of God.

## C. Mark 9:2–8: After Jesus Is Transfigured before Three of His Disciples, God Enjoins Them To Listen to His Son

>²Then after six days Jesus took Peter, James and John and led them up a high mountain privately by themselves. And he was transfigured before them, ³and his clothes became dazzling, intensely white, such as no fuller on earth could bleach them. ⁴Then there appeared to them Elijah along with Moses, and they were talking with Jesus. ⁵Then Peter spoke and said to Jesus, "Rabbi, it is good that we are here! Let us make three tents, one for you, one for Moses and one for Elijah." ⁶For he did not know what to say, as they were terrified. ⁷Then a cloud came, casting a shadow over them, and a voice came from the cloud, "This is my beloved Son! Listen to him!" ⁸And suddenly, looking around, they no longer saw anyone but Jesus alone with them.

### 1. MEANING OF MARK 9:2–8

#### a. *9:2–3* Jesus is transformed into a heavenly figure before three disciples.

The unusual Marcan notice of a temporal interval, "after six days," between scenes alerts the reader to the unique and somewhat mysterious connection between what is about to take place on the "high mountain" and the previous scene of Jesus' calling the crowd and his disciples to follow him on his "way" of suffering, rejection, death and resurrection (8:27–9:1). In the biblical tradition it was "after six days" that God called to Moses out of the midst of the cloud for a special revelational encounter on a mountain (Exod 24:15–18).

That Jesus separates Peter, James and John, the special group of three within the Twelve (5:37; 3:16–17; 1:16–20), from the crowd and the rest of his disciples (8:34) and leads them up a "high mountain" prepares the reader for a unique, private revelation and/or explanation of Jesus to these chosen three disciples.[9] This is emphatically underlined by the fact that he takes them up the mountain "privately" (4:34; 6:31–32; 7:33) and "by themselves." Will these three disciples now prove to be part of the "some" Jesus solemnly promised would "not taste death until they see that the kingdom of God has come in power" (9:1)?

On a "high mountain," suggestive of closeness to the heavenly realm, Jesus is suddenly "transfigured," taking on the appearance of a heavenly being before these three specially chosen disciples (9:2). That Jesus has been transformed into a heavenly figure is dramatically confirmed as his clothes become "dazzling, intensely white" as no fuller (one who cleans woolen cloth) "*on earth*" could bleach them. Hence, Jesus' clothing has become "heavenly" clothing whiter than is possible "*on earth*" (see Dan 7:9; 12:3) (9:3).[10]

This sudden "transfiguration" or "transformation" of Jesus into a heavenly figure before three of his disciples signals the beginning of an "epiphany" genre. As a literary genre an epiphany portrays a sudden and unexpected manifestation of a divine or heavenly being before selected witnesses, which offers for their response a special insight or revelation into God's salvific ways.[11]

### b. *9:4* Elijah and Moses appear and talk with Jesus.

The epiphanic action continues as "Elijah along with Moses" also appear before the three disciples, and they are "talking with Jesus" in the heavenly realm. The epiphany thus portrays Jesus in close association with two revered prophetic figures of old who are now in heavenly glory. In the biblical tradition the prophet Elijah went up by a whirlwind into heaven without dying (2 Kgs 2:1–11); and because the place of Moses' burial was unknown (Deut 34:5–8), various Jewish traditions arose about his ascension into heaven possibly without dying.[12] Although the epiphany indicates that Jesus is destined to join Elijah and Moses in the glory of the heavenly realm, Jesus has already announced that, unlike Elijah and Moses who may have arrived at glory without dying, he will arrive at heavenly glory through the divine necessity of suffering, rejection and death (8:31, 38).

### c. *9:5–6* A terrified Peter wants to make a tent for each of them.

Peter, the leader and usual spokesman of the disciples, initiates a response to the epiphany on the part of the privileged witnesses. That he begins by addressing Jesus as "Rabbi" (teacher) already indicates the incongruity and inappropriateness of his response. The title of "Rabbi" for a heavenly figure whom Peter himself has confessed to be "the Christ" (8:29) seems to greatly undervalue the profound character of Jesus. Peter then exuberantly exclaims that "it is good that we are here!" And because of this fortunate presence of the three disciples Peter offers that they can build three "tents," one for each of these three heavenly figures. Peter is so fascinated by the heavenly glory that Jesus shares with Elijah and Moses that he wants to prolong this unique heavenly manifestation on earth by erecting three "tents" for them to dwell in (9:5).[13] The inappropriateness of this response is indicated by the parenthetical remark of the narrator that Peter really "did not know what to say." In fact, all three disciples "were terrified" and thus understandably overwhelmed by this mysterious epiphany of heavenly beings, a reaction of fear or awe common to the epiphany genre (9:6).

### d. *9:7–8* God's voice commands them to listen to his Son.

In reply to Peter's inadequate response (see 8:32) the epiphanic action resumes as a "cloud," symbolic of God's hidden presence (Exod 24:15–18; 40:34–35), comes and casts a shadow over the three heavenly figures.[14] Then the voice of God booms forth from the cloud: "This is my beloved Son! Listen to him!" These powerful words of God from the cloud echo his voice from heaven at the baptism of Jesus: "You are my beloved Son; with you I am well pleased!" (1:11). What the reader (1:1, 11) and demonic world (3:11; 5:7) have known throughout, namely, that Jesus is God's unique Son, God now finally reveals directly to the disciples. His voice from the cloud corrects Peter's misinterpretation of the epiphanic appearance of Jesus, which includes his desire to place Jesus on the same level as Moses and Elijah: "This" one, that is, Jesus rather than Elijah or Moses, is my unique "beloved Son," who will come in "his Father's glory" (8:38), and therefore is much more than a mere "Rabbi" (9:5) and greater even than the revered heavenly prophets, Elijah and Moses.

God's urgent command to "listen to him!" reinforces Jesus' own appeals to really "hear" and understand his teaching (4:3, 9, 23; 7:14), emphatically drawing special attention to his teaching that he must suffer, die and rise (8:31). It also alerts the disciples (and reader) to pay attention to what Jesus is yet to teach. Recalling the appeal to heed the words of the true prophet-like-Moses as the words of God himself (Deut 18:15, 18–19), God's command to "listen" to Jesus indicates his divine confirmation and approval of Jesus' teaching of the necessity of his suffering, death and resurrection as the very words of God. Because Jesus accepts this divine necessity, God fully approves him as his "beloved Son" (9:7).

The epiphanic action of Jesus' transfiguration into the heavenly realm with Elijah and Moses abruptly ends. As the disciples look around, "they no longer saw anyone but Jesus alone with them," thus underlining the fact that God's words apply uniquely to Jesus, who is now again "with them" on earth rather than with Elijah and Moses in heaven. The transformation of Jesus into the heavenly realm was thus a temporary, anticipatory glimpse of his future heavenly glory, not yet the permanent reality Peter prematurely attempted to make it (9:8).

This extraordinary epiphany dramatically reveals and reinforces that Jesus will surely "rise" from the dead and enter into the heavenly glory of his Father (8:38), but only by going the "way" of suffering, rejection and death. The final response to the epiphany remains in suspense: Will the disciples truly "listen" to the "beloved Son" and understand?

### 2. MARK 9:2–8 AS MODEL FOR ACTION

This stunning epiphany of Jesus' spectacular, anticipatory transfiguration into heavenly glory with Elijah and Moses emphatically assures us of his final triumph in and through his suffering, rejection and death. We are invited to participate in this future triumph and glory of God's unique "beloved Son" by intently "listening" to and thus obeying the paradoxical appeal to follow his "way" by denying ourselves, taking up our cross and losing our lives for his sake and the gospel's in order to gain them (8:34–35).

## D. Mark 9:9–13: Jesus Teaches His Disciples That Elijah Has Already Come

⁹And as they were coming down from the mountain, he ordered them to tell no one what they had seen, until the Son of Man had risen from the dead. ¹⁰So they kept the matter to themselves, questioning what rising from the dead meant. ¹¹Then they asked him, "Why do the scribes say that Elijah must come first?" ¹²He

told them, "Elijah will indeed come first and restore all things, yet how is it written of the Son of Man that he should suffer greatly and be treated with contempt? [13]But I tell you that already Elijah has come and they did to him whatever they pleased, as it is written of him."

### 1. MEANING OF MARK 9:9–13

#### a. *9:9–10* The disciples question what rising from the dead means.

Jesus and the select group of three disciples, Peter, James and John, come down "from the mountain," that is, from the place of the private revelation of the heavenly glory Jesus will share with Elijah and Moses, and return to the public domain. As he had earlier "warned them to tell no one about him" being the Christ (8:29–30), because his messiahship cannot be properly understood without the realization that as the "Son of Man" he must suffer, die and rise (8:31), so now Jesus orders them "to tell no one what they had seen" until he, as the Son of Man, has "risen from the dead." The implication is that a proper understanding of Jesus' transfiguration requires the realization that he, unlike Elijah and Moses, will enter into heavenly glory only after he has "risen *from the dead.*" And there is a further implication that once Jesus has "risen from the dead" his disciples are to openly and publicly proclaim, as part of the gospel, that Jesus is no longer in the realm of the dead but has triumphantly risen and entered into heavenly glory (9:9).

Unlike previous unsuccessful attempts by Jesus to restrict public knowledge of himself (1:44–45; 5:19–20; 7:24, 36), the disciples now obey his injunction to silence and "keep the matter to themselves." They keep the transfiguration of Jesus private, however, not because they understand the reason for Jesus' command for secrecy, but, on the contrary, they question "what rising from the dead meant" in the case of Jesus, whom they have just seen in heavenly glory. They obviously do not yet understand the divine necessity that as Son of Man Jesus must first "rise *from the dead*" before entering into heavenly glory (9:10).

#### b. *9:11–13* Jesus questions them about the suffering of Elijah and the Son of Man.

In line with their non-understanding and reluctance to accept the necessity of Jesus' suffering and death (8:32) the disciples question Jesus, pointing out the scribal teaching that Elijah, whom they have just seen in heavenly glory without having risen *from the dead,* "must" (*dei*), in accord with divine necessity, "come first." The disciples thus object to the necessity that Jesus suffer and die as Son of Man by appealing to the necessity that, according to common Jewish expectations (Mal 3:23), Elijah, who had ascended into heavenly glory without dying (2 Kgs 2:11), would return to earth as a prelude to the establishment of God's final, messianic age. The implication is that suffering and rising from the dead is not part of God's plan for final-age salvation and entrance into heavenly glory (9:11).

Jesus replies to his disciples' objection by affirming that "Elijah will indeed come first and restore all things" (see Sir 48:10) in preparation for the final age of God's salvation. But with a powerful, thought-provoking counter-question Jesus disallows any implication that Elijah's return conflicts with or excludes the divine necessity of God's recorded plan, as "written" in the Jewish scriptures, that the Son of Man "should suffer greatly and be treated with contempt" (Ps 22:7; Isa 53:3). Jesus thus indicates that as Son of Man he stands in the Jewish tradition of the "Suffering Servant" of Israel and/or "Suffering Just One" who suffers greatly and is treated with contempt in accord with God's plan of salvation (9:12).[15]

Continuing with a stunning, new revelation, Jesus shocks his disciples by announcing that not only has the expected return of the prophet Elijah already taken place with the coming of John the Baptist as the messenger-Elijah (1:4–8) but, moreover, he has already suffered a very humiliating death, when "they did to him whatever they pleased" (6:14–29), in accord with God's scriptural plan of salvation, "as it is written of him" (see 1 Kgs 19:2, 10, 14). The return of Elijah in the person of John the Baptist, who himself suffered and died in accord with God's plan, not only does not exclude the divine necessity that Jesus as Son of Man must suffer and "rise *from the dead*" before entering into heavenly glory, but prepares the "way" (1:2–3) for it and underlines its necessity in accord with God's "written" will. The tension, however, continues (8:32) as the disciples give no indication that they have obeyed the heavenly voice of God by "listening" to his "beloved Son" (9:7) in order to understand and accept the divine necessity that Jesus, as the Son of Man destined for heavenly exaltation, must suffer and "rise from the dead" (9:13).

## 2. MARK 9:9–13 AS MODEL FOR ACTION

The disciples' non-understanding and reluctance to accept the divine necessity that Jesus as the Son of Man destined for heavenly glory must suffer and rise from the dead invite us to ponder whether we ourselves really understand and truly accept the mysterious and paradoxical necessity that Jesus suffer and die on the "way" to his heavenly splendor. As we ourselves struggle to follow his "way" by denying ourselves, taking up our cross and losing our lives in order to gain them (8:34–35), we are reminded of our responsibility to publicly proclaim the gospel of the divine necessity of Jesus' suffering and death, now that he has already "risen from the dead" and achieved heavenly exaltation (9:9–10).

John the Baptist, as the returning Elijah who must "come first" to prepare the "way" for God's final age of salvation by himself suffering a humiliating death in accord with divine necessity, serves as a model who helps us to understand and accept the suffering and death of Jesus as a necessity within God's plan of salvation. John's own suffering and death, which precedes and prepares the salvific "way" of Jesus, acts as an ominous but encouraging and edifying example which can enable us to accept and follow our own way of suffering, rejection and eventual death in accord with God's will in order to share in the triumphant glory of Jesus (9:11–13).

### E. Mark 9:14–29: By Prayer Jesus Expels an Unclean Spirit from a Boy Whom the Disciples Could Not Cure

[14]Then coming to the disciples, they saw a great crowd around them and scribes arguing with them. [15]And immediately on seeing him, the whole crowd was greatly excited, and running up they greeted him. [16]He asked them, "What are you arguing about with them?" [17]Then someone from the crowd answered him, "Teacher, I have brought to you my son who has a mute spirit. [18]Wherever it seizes him, it throws him down; he foams at the mouth, grinds his teeth, and becomes rigid. I asked your disciples to expel it, but they were unable."

[19]Replying he said to them, "O faithless generation, how long am I to be with you? How long am I to bear with you? Bring him to me." [20]Then they brought the boy to him. And when he saw him, the spirit immediately threw the boy into convulsions, and falling to the ground, he rolled around, foaming at the mouth.

[21]Then he asked his father, "How long has this been happening to him?" He said, "Since childhood. [22]Many times it has thrown him both into fire and into water to kill him. But if you can do anything, have compassion on us and help us." [23]Jesus said to him, "If you can! All things are possible for one who believes!" [24]Immediately crying out, the father of the child said, "I do believe; help my unbelief!"

[25]Seeing that a crowd was quickly gathering, Jesus rebuked

the unclean spirit, saying to it, "Mute and deaf spirit, I command you, come out of him and never enter him again!" [26]Then crying out and violently throwing him into convulsions, it came out. Then he became like a corpse, which caused many to say, "He is dead!" [27]But taking him by the hand, Jesus raised him, and he stood up.

[28]When he entered the house, his disciples asked him privately, "Why could we not expel it?" [29]And he said to them, "This kind cannot come out by anything except prayer."

### 1. MEANING OF MARK 9:14–29

**a. *9:14–18* The disciples are unable to exorcise a boy with a mute spirit.**

When Jesus along with the three select disciples who have just witnessed his transfiguration on the mountain return to the rest of the disciples, a new tension emerges as they see a great crowd around these disciples and scribes, frequent opponents of Jesus (1:22; 2:6, 16; 3:22; 7:1; 8:31), arguing with them (9:14). As soon as all the crowd see Jesus, they are greatly excited, run up to him and greet him, obviously delighted to see him again after his absence from them during his transfiguration (9:15). After Jesus asks the scribes what they are arguing about with his disciples (9:16), "someone" from the crowd answers him and discloses the nature of the dispute. Respectfully addressing Jesus as "teacher," this "someone" reveals himself to be a distraught father who has brought to Jesus his son possessed by a "mute spirit." This initiates a healing story and the problem of a "mute spirit," after the disciples have remained "mute" and "deaf" with regard to hearing (see 9:7) and understanding the necessity of Jesus' suffering and death (8:31–9:13), alerts the reader to see this boy and his father as symbolic representatives of the disciples, just as the healing of the deaf and mute man (7:31–37) previously characterized the disciples' non-understanding of Jesus (8:17–18) (9:17).

The boy's father goes on to describe the dreadfully dehumanizing, epileptic symptoms of the demonic possession: Wherever the demon seizes the boy, "it throws him down; he foams at the mouth, grinds his teeth, and becomes rigid." This not only evokes a feeling of horror and sympathy, but indicates the great difficulty of this particular exorcism. This difficulty is further underlined as the man explains that he had asked the disciples, earlier given the authority to expel demons by Jesus (3:15; 6:7, 13), to exorcise it, "but they were unable." The disciples' inability to expel this demon, which apparently led to the argument with the scribes (9:14), the same group who earlier accused Jesus of exorcising by Beelzebul (3:22), calls into question the divine power and authority of Jesus himself. And so, a double suspense arises for the reader: Can Jesus, now that he has announced that he will go the powerless way of suffering and death (8:31), expel this particularly difficult demon? And why could the disciples not expel it while Jesus was absent? (9:18).

### b. *9:19-20* Jesus laments lack of faith.

Jesus addresses "them," that is, the father, the scribes and the crowd, as a "faithless generation," thus linking them not only with their faithless contemporaries who oppose Jesus (8:12, 38) but also with their faithless ancestors who continually rebelled against the ways of God (Deut 32:5, 20). He laments their lack of faith with rhetorical questions expressing his prolonged exasperation with them: "How long am I to be with you? How long am I to bear with you?" In view of Jesus' previous indications of his suffering and death (8:31–9:13) these rhetorical questions possess an ironic double meaning: On the one hand, they lamentfully express the long period of time Jesus has had to endure their lack of faith (see Num 14:27); but, on the other hand, they warn of the short period of time Jesus will still "be with them" before his approaching death, as foreshadowed by his absence from them during his transfiguration (9:19).

After Jesus asks for the possessed boy, they bring him. But as soon as the demon sees Jesus, it throws the boy into horrifying, epileptic convulsions so that he falls to the ground and rolls around, foaming at the mouth. This confirms the report of the father, reinforcing the dehumanizing effects of this terrible possession and further underlining the great difficulty of this particular exorcism (9:20).

### c. *9:21-24* The boy's father confesses his faith and begs Jesus to help.

Jesus asks the father how long his body has been plagued with this demonic possession. The father's reply, "since childhood," indicates the great length of the possession, further underscoring the difficulty of the exorcism (9:21). He then indicates the death-threatening seriousness of the ordeal: Many times the demon "has thrown him both into fire and into water to kill him." This dramatically intensifies the urgent need for the exorcism. Then in desperation the father utters his impassioned plea to Jesus on behalf of his son: "But if *you*," as opposed to the disciples who have failed, "can do anything, have compassion on us and help us." His desperate plea thus calls into question the healing power of Jesus, in light of his disciples' inability to expel the demon (9:22).

Repeating the father's words with surprise, "if you can!," Jesus chides his uncertain faith and proclaims that "all things are possible for one who believes!" This extremely potent pronouncement serves a fourfold function in the narrative: it calls for the father to acknowledge his faith in the divine healing power at work in Jesus; it indicates that Jesus will be able to expel the demon because of his own faith in God; it implies that the disciples failed to expel the demon because of their lack of faith; and, in the context of the announcement of the divine necessity that Jesus suffer, die and rise (8:31), it indicates that faith in God will enable both Jesus and his followers (8:34–35), symbolically represented by the father and son, to accomplish the difficult way of suffering, death and resurrection (9:23).

In response to Jesus' powerful pronouncement the father of the child immediately cries out his sincere confession of faith: "I do believe!" And he quickly adds a fervent, urgent prayer acknowledging his dependence upon God's power to further bolster his faith: "Help my unbelief!" The father thus proclaims his faith in the divine healing power at work in Jesus but earnestly pleads for Jesus to use this power to heal his son and thus further increase his faith lest he slip into "unbelief." With this brilliant demonstration of humble faith the father not only extricates himself from this "faithless generation" (9:19), but exemplifies the kind of faith the disciples need both to expel difficult demons and to follow Jesus' difficult way of suffering, death and resurrection (9:24).

### d. *9:25–27* Jesus expels the mute and deaf spirit.

The magnificent faith of the father wins healing "help" (9:22, 24) for himself and his child. In accord with his tendency to avoid public displays of his healing power (1:44–45; 3:9; 7:24, 36), as soon as Jesus sees that a crowd is rapidly gathering, he "rebukes" the unclean spirit with the powerful words of exorcism: "Mute and deaf spirit, I command you, come out of him and never enter him again!" Not only is the unclean spirit "mute" but also "deaf," intensifying the seriousness of the possession and extending the symbolic characterization of the disciples, who are both "mute" and "deaf" to the necessity of Jesus' suffering and death (8:31–9:13). Jesus effects a final and definitive cure of the boy, who has been afflicted "many times" (9:22) and "since childhood" (9:21), as he commands the demon not only to come out of him but to "never enter him again!" (9:25).

Overpowered by Jesus' command, the mute and deaf spirit "cries out" and after violently throwing the boy into convulsions one last time, finally "came out." As the boy "became like a corpse" many thought that he was actually "dead," with the demon (9:22) rather than Jesus thus prevailing (9:26). But Jesus, demonstrating the triumph of his divine healing and life-giving power over death-threatening demonic power, takes the boy by the hand, and "raised him, and he stood up." In "raising" the boy who appears to be dead so that "he stood up" or "arose" (see also 5:41–42; 1:31), Jesus symbolically alludes to his own death and resurrection (8:31; 9:9–10). Jesus' "raising" of the boy through his father's faith in the power of God through whom "everything is possible" (9:23) points to the faith by which not only Jesus himself but also his followers (8:34–38) can attain God's resurrection after suffering and death (9:27).

**e. *9:28–29* Jesus tells his disciples that only by prayer can they expel this kind of demon.**

As Jesus enters again into the private domain of "the house," his disciples ask him "privately" why they were not able to expel the demon. They thus initiate another special, private instruction (4:10–11, 34; 7:17–23; 8:14–21; 9:9–13) whereby Jesus reveals to them a deeper insight into himself and his "way" of actualizing the mystery of God's kingdom (9:28). Jesus explains that "this kind" of difficult, "mute" and "deaf" demon they cannot expel "by anything except prayer." The father has illustrated both the "prayer" and the "faith" needed to enable Jesus to expel the demon. He confessed his faith, "I do believe!" (9:24), in the God through whom "everything is possible for one who believes" (9:23), and uttered the ardent prayer, "help my unbelief!" (9:24), humbly acknowledging his dependence upon God's power to increase his faith and expel the demon. Only with such humble, faith-filled "prayer" for God's powerful help will the disciples be able, not only to expel "this kind" of "mute" and "deaf" demon from others, but also eliminate their own "muteness" and "deafness" to the necessity of following Jesus' "way" of suffering, death and resurrection (9:29).

### 2. MARK 9:14–29 AS MODEL FOR ACTION

The faith and prayer of the father serve as a model for the kind of confident yet humble prayer for faith in God's power that we need now that the earthly Jesus with his divine healing power is no longer with us. Jesus has prepared us for his absence by calling us, like the father and the disciples, to believe in and pray to the God through whom "all things are possible for one who believes" (9:23), so that God's saving power available through Jesus can operate in us to heal and restore the dehumanized lives of our fellow human beings who are overcome by the demonic power of evil. By imitating the sincere and humble prayer of the father, "I do believe; help my unbelief!" (9:24), we can eliminate our own stubborn "muteness" and "deafness" to Jesus' call that we follow him on the "way"

of suffering, rejection and death. The manner in which Jesus "raises" the
exorcised boy as if from "death" gives us the confident hope of likewise
being "raised" with Jesus after following him in suffering and death.

## F.  Mark 9:30–32: Jesus Teaches His Disciples the Necessity of His Death and Resurrection, but They Do Not Understand

> [30]Going on from there they passed through Galilee, but he did
> not want anyone to know it. [31]For he was teaching his disciples
> and telling them, "The Son of Man is to be delivered into the
> hands of people, and they will kill him, and three days after his
> death he will rise." [32]But they did not understand the saying, and
> they were afraid to question him.

### 1. MEANING OF MARK 9:30–32

#### a.  *9:30–31* To his disciples Jesus again announces his death and resurrection.

With his disciples Jesus continues the movement of his salvific
"way" as they "go on" from "there," the region around Caesarea Philippi
(8:27), and "pass through Galilee," now on the "way" to suffering, rejection, death and resurrection (8:31). That Jesus "did not want anyone to
know it" not only indicates his unwillingness to be deterred from his
"way," but also provides privacy for further instructing his disciples (9:30).

While on the "way" Jesus is teaching his disciples, repeating and thus
reinforcing his earlier announcement of the divine necessity of his suffering, death and resurrection (8:31). He tells them that as the heavenly,
messianic "Son of Man" now on earth he paradoxically "is to be delivered" by God (divine passive), in accord with the mysterious necessity of
God's plan, "into the hands of people," that is, into the power of those
people (Jewish leaders) who oppose him (see 2 Kgs 21:14; Ps 106:40–41).
These people will kill him, but after "three days," that is, after the indefinite, brief period of time when God intervenes on behalf of his own (see
8:31), he will rise from the dead (9:31).

#### b.  *9:32* The disciples do not understand and are afraid to question him.

As after Jesus' first announcement, when he rebuked Peter for thinking not "the things of God" but "the things of human beings" (8:32–33),

and when the three disciples questioned what "rising from the dead" meant (9:10–11), so now the disciples still "did not understand the saying." They have thus failed to heed God's voice at the transfiguration of Jesus: "This is my beloved Son! Listen to him!" (9:7). Not only do the disciples not understand but now they have regressed to silence, as "they were afraid to question him," thus making their understanding even more difficult. As they were unable to expel the "mute" and "deaf" spirit from the possessed boy because of their lack of prayer and faith (9:14–29), so now they are unable to eliminate their own "muteness" and "deafness" to the divine necessity of Jesus' death and resurrection. And so the tension of the disciples' non-understanding of Jesus continues to build.

### 2. MARK 9:30–32 AS MODEL FOR ACTION

The failure of the disciples to understand Jesus and their fear to even question him prompts us to ask ourselves whether we really understand and are willing to penetrate and probe what the mysterious and paradoxical necessity that Jesus suffer, die and rise means for the lives of ourselves and others as we strive to follow the "way" of Jesus.

## G. Mark 9:33–50: Jesus Teaches His Disciples about Service, Acceptance, and Respect for Others

[33]Then they came to Capernaum. And when he was in the house he questioned them, "What were you arguing about on the way?" [34]But they were silent; for on the way they had argued among themselves who was the greatest. [35]Then sitting down he called the Twelve and said to them, "If anyone wants to be first, let that person be last of all and servant of all." [36]And taking a child he placed it in their midst, and putting his arms around it he said to them, [37]"Whoever receives one such child in my name, receives me; and whoever receives me, receives not me but the one who sent me."

[38]John said to him, "Teacher, we saw someone expelling demons in your name, and we tried to prevent him because he does not follow us." [39]But Jesus said, "Do not prevent him. There is no one who will do a mighty deed in my name who will be able at the same time to speak ill of me. [40]For whoever is not against us is for us. [41]Anyone who gives you a cup of water to drink because you belong to Christ, amen I say to you, will surely not lose his reward."

[42]"Whoever causes one of these little ones who believe in me to sin, it would be better if that person had a great millstone put around his neck and were thrown into the sea. [43]If your hand causes you to sin, cut it off. It is better for you to enter into life maimed than with two hands to go into Gehenna, into the unquenchable fire.[16] [45]And if your foot causes you to sin, cut it off. It is better for you to enter into life lame than with two feet to be thrown into Gehenna. [47]And if your eye causes you to sin, pluck it out. It is better for you to enter into the kingdom of God with one eye than with two eyes to be thrown into Gehenna, [48]where 'their worm does not die, and the fire is not quenched' (Isa 66:24). [49]For everyone will be salted with fire."

[50]"Salt is good, but if salt becomes insipid, with what will you restore its savor? Have salt among yourselves and keep peace with each other."

### 1. MEANING OF MARK 9:33–50

#### a. *9:33–37* Jesus teaches his disciples to serve all others.

On his "way" through Galilee to suffering, death and resurrection (9:30–31) Jesus and his non-understanding disciples (9:32) "came" again to Capernaum (1:21; 2:1), the central city of Jesus' ministry around the Sea of Galilee. Jesus once again enters "the house," the private domain appropriate for a continuation of his special instruction to his disciples (7:17; 9:28, 30–31). Since the disciples are afraid to "question" Jesus and eliminate their non-understanding of his suffering, death and resurrection (9:32), Jesus "questions" them about what they were "arguing" about "on the way" (9:33). They once again fall silent because "on the way" they had been "arguing" among themselves about who was "the greatest." That they were "on the way" with Jesus to the lowliness and powerlessness of his suffering, rejection and death reinforces the inappropriateness of their "arguing" about who is "the greatest," which further underscores their lack of understanding (9:34).

Jesus then "sits down," the magisterial posture for authoritative teaching (see 4:1–2), and calls "the Twelve," those disciples specially selected from the others to be with Jesus and to be sent out with authority to preach and heal (3:13–19; 4:10; 6:7–13)—in other words, the leading disciples among whom would be those having the most claim of being "the greatest." That Jesus is in the magisterial "sitting" position and explicitly addressing "the Twelve" adds solemnity and importance to the teaching to follow. In direct response to the disciples' concern with great-

ness Jesus utters a shocking, paradoxical and powerful antithetical aphorism, calling for a complete reversal of thinking about what it means for
one to be great or prominent among others: "If anyone wants to be first,
let that person be last of all and servant of all." In a total upheaval of
normal considerations anyone who wants to be "great" or "first" must
become the absolutely "last" of all others and "servant," that is, one who
generously and hospitably meets personal needs and concerns, not only of
one's associates but of "all" others (9:35).

Concretely and dramatically demonstrating what it means to be "servant of all," Jesus "takes a child" and "places it in their midst," thus
turning their total attention to one who lacks the full rights and respect of
an adult person and has no status in society, the very epitome of lowliness
and insignificance, the exact opposite of one who is "great." He "puts his
arms around it," a gesture of hospitable welcome and personal acceptance
indicative of a complete care and concern for the individual (9:36). Inviting them to act similarly, Jesus proclaims that whoever "receives," that is,
hospitably welcomes as worthy of personal respect, one such insignificant
child "in my name," that is, for the sake of Jesus, acting as disciples in
accord with the attitude and command of the master, actually "receives"
Jesus himself. Furthermore, whoever "receives" Jesus by hospitably accepting one such child "receives" not only Jesus but "the one who sent
me," God the Father of Jesus, his beloved Son (1:11; 9:7). By serving and
accepting such lowly and insignificant human beings as children, the disciples will experience the true greatness that results from being a "servant of
all": Whoever receives and serves the least significant, a child, receives
and serves the most significant, God himself. And so Jesus is persuading
the Twelve to turn away from their concern for their own self-importance
and to accept the paradox of experiencing the greatness of receiving Jesus
and the God who sent him by serving all, even the most insignificant, in
order to better understand and accept the mysterious paradox that Jesus
suffer, die and rise in accord with the will of the God who sent him (9:37).

**b. *9:38–41* Jesus teaches his disciples to accept the service of others.**

John, brother of James and one of the select group of three within the
Twelve (1:19; 3:17; 5:37; 9:2), acts as spokesman for the Twelve and
informs Jesus that they had tried to prevent someone who was expelling
demons "in your name" because "he does not follow us." Although this
person was expelling demons in the "name" of Jesus and thus through the
same authority by which the Twelve themselves were able to exorcise
(3:14–15; 6:7–13), he does not belong to the special group comprised of
Jesus and the Twelve (9:38). Jesus, however, commands the Twelve not to

stop this strange exorcist. Since he is performing the mighty deed of expelling demons in the "name" of Jesus, that is, through his power and on his behalf, he surely will not harm Jesus. With these words Jesus not only calls the Twelve to expand their narrow-minded exclusivism into a broader-minded recognition and acceptance of one who acts in the "name" of and on behalf of Jesus, but also reminds them that they likewise are to operate not on behalf of themselves, preoccupied with their own self-importance and "greatness," but through and for the "name" of Jesus (9:39).

Proceeding to the general principle that "whoever is not against us is for us," Jesus leads the Twelve not only to realize that this strange exorcist acts on behalf of "us," both Jesus and the Twelve, but also to expand their horizon to welcome "whoever," that is, all those whose activities indicate that they are "not against us" but "for us" (9:40). Further illustrating how even strangers and outsiders can be "for us," Jesus solemnly assures ("amen I say to you") that "anyone" who graciously offers "you," the Twelve disciples, even "a cup of water to drink," a rather insignificant act of hospitality, recognizing that "you belong to Christ" (1:1; 8:29), will surely be rewarded by God in the final judgment. Jesus thus further broadens the mentality of the Twelve, called to be "servants of all," not only to welcome, acknowledge and value others, as God himself does, for even the most humble acts of hospitable service, but also to realize that the importance or "greatness" of being a disciple comes not from themselves but simply because they "belong to Christ" (9:41).

### c. *9:42–49* Jesus warns his disciples to eliminate causes of sin.

Jesus then warns the Twelve of the seriousness of their responsibility, as "servants of all," to provide a positive example to other believers. He advises each of the Twelve ("whoever") to avoid "causing to sin" or leading astray from their faith "one of these little ones who believe in me," that is, such persons as the strange exorcist (9:38–39) and those "little ones" who humbly offer a disciple even a cup of water to drink (9:41). The condemnation for a disciple who causes to sin or scandalizes such "little ones who believe" in Jesus will be so severe in the last judgment that it would be better for that disciple to suffer now the inescapable and harsh punishment of being thrown into the sea with a huge millstone around the neck. Jesus thus sternly advises the Twelve not to give scandal to or mislead the faith of others, especially by their inappropriate concern with their own rank and "greatness" (9:42).

With a rhetorically powerful and dramatically startling triple exhortation for the Twelve to decisively avoid whatever causes them to sin, Jesus emphatically underlines the extreme seriousness of their responsibility to be "servants of all" by not leading others to sin, especially by a preoccupation with their own self-importance. Each exhortation brutally shocks the listener with a command to forcefully remove ("cut off," "pluck out") an important part of one's person (hand, foot or eye) if it causes one to sin. Each leads the listener to realize and agree that it would certainly be preferable to enter into (eternal) life/the kingdom of God maimed, lame or half-blind than with body fully intact to suffer everlasting torment in Gehenna, the traditional place of eternal punishment of the wicked, with its "unquenchable fire" (9:43–47).[17] The horribly severe pain and permanence of this punishment is emphasized with an allusion to the final verse of Isaiah: Gehenna is the place where the "worm" which devours the rotting flesh of the dead people who have rebelled against God "does not die" and where the continual, stinging "fire" which intensely burns these wicked people "is not quenched" (Isa 66:24) (9:48). And that "everyone" in Gehenna will be "salted," that is, "seasoned" or "preserved," with the acutely penetrating flames of "fire" (rather than "salt," see Lev 2:13) further underlines the extreme anguish and finality of this everlasting punishment (9:49).

The intended effect of this rhetorically exaggerated and dramatically reinforced exhortation is not bodily mutilation but strict avoidance of all personal causes or temptations to sin. The Twelve are not to allow their personal faults, especially their concern for "greatness," to hinder themselves (9:43–49) or others (9:42) from attaining eternal life in God's kingdom.

### d. *9:50* Jesus urges his disciples to keep peace with one another.

Jesus then begins a final, summarizing exhortation with the announcement that "salt," the well-known seasoning and preservative of food, "is good." With a rhetorical question he forces the Twelve to realize the impossibility of their restoring the "savor," the quality of saltiness, the distinctive characteristic, of "salt" that has become "insipid." He thus urges them not to allow themselves to become insipid, but to "have salt" among themselves, that is, to maintain their distinctive role as the Twelve especially by being humble "servants of all" (9:35), and to thereby "keep peace with each other" by avoiding arguments over who of them is "the greatest" (9:33–34).[18]

### 2. MARK 9:33–50 AS MODEL FOR ACTION

As we identify with the Twelve disciples, Jesus teaches us to abandon any selfish concern for our own personal importance and greatness and discover the paradox of being "first" by becoming "last" and serving all, even the most insignificant of human beings, in order to receive, acknowledge and welcome, precisely in the people we serve, Jesus and the great God who sent him. Becoming hospitable, selfless servants of all people will enable us to better understand, accept and follow the paradoxical "way" of Jesus, who must suffer, die and rise in accord with the salvific plan of the God who sent him (9:33–37).

Jesus invites us to broaden our exclusivistic mentality by recognizing that others, even strangers and outsiders, can work for the cause of Jesus and ourselves: "Whoever is not against us is for us!" We are called not only to serve all others but to humbly accept even the most insignificant service from others, realizing that it is offered not because of our own importance but because we belong to Christ. We become important by serving others not for the sake of ourselves but for the sake of Jesus (9:38–41).

As disciples of Jesus we have a serious responsibility for acting as models of humble and selfless service for all those who believe in Jesus. We are to strictly avoid all temptations and causes of sin in our lives, so that we do not cause others to sin or stray from faith in Jesus, especially through a scandalous preoccupation with our own self-importance. We must eliminate the personal faults and failures that can prevent ourselves and others from achieving eternal life in the kingdom of God (9:42–49).

Jesus urges us to preserve our distinctive quality as disciples, especially by becoming humble servants of all people, rather than selfishly contend for rank and personal honor (9:50).

## H. Mark 10:1–12: Jesus Teaches the Crowds, Pharisees and Disciples about Divorce

[1]Then arising from there he went into the region of Judea and beyond the Jordan, and again crowds gathered to him and, as was his custom, he again taught them. [2]Then the Pharisees approached and asked him, "Is it lawful for a husband to divorce his wife?" They were testing him. [3]Replying he said to them, "What did Moses command you?" [4]They said, "Moses permitted him 'to write a bill of divorce and dismiss her' (Deut 24:1, 3). [5]But Jesus told them, "Because of your hardness of heart he wrote you this commandment. [6]But from the beginning of creation, 'male and female He made them' (Gen 1:27; 5:2). [7]'For this reason a man shall leave his father and mother and be joined

to his wife, [8]and the two shall become one flesh' (Gen 2:24). So they are no longer two but one flesh. [9]Therefore what God has joined together, no human being must separate!" [10]Then in the house the disciples again questioned him about this. [11]He said to them, "Whoever divorces his wife and marries another commits adultery against her; [12]and if she divorces her husband and marries another, she commits adultery."

### 1. MEANING OF MARK 10:1-12

#### a. *10:1-2* The Pharisees test Jesus on the lawfulness of divorce.

Jesus "arises" from his magisterial sitting position (9:35), thus concluding his special private instruction of the Twelve (9:33–50), and continues the movement of his "way" as he "went" into the region of Judea and beyond the Jordan river. Having announced his "way" of suffering, rejection, death and resurrection in the northern region around Caesarea Philippi (8:27–33) and having travelled "on the way" (8:27; 9:33–34) through Galilee (9:30) with a stop at Capernaum (9:33), Jesus now travels south to the regions of Judea and beyond (east of) the Jordan river, thus taking a decisive step on his "way" to suffering, death and resurrection. He now goes to regions from which great multitudes had earlier flocked to him (3:7–8). As previously throughout his ministry crowds continue to gather to him, and "as was his custom" he again teaches them (2:2, 13; 4:1–2; 6:34), thus initiating a scene of public teaching after the private teaching of the Twelve (10:1).

The Pharisees, one of the groups opposing Jesus and trying to destroy him (3:6), approach and ask Jesus whether it is "lawful," that is, in accord with God's will, for a husband to divorce his wife. The narrator adds that "they were testing him" (8:11; 7:1), thus indicating the deceptive intent of their question, meant to be a provocation to discredit Jesus before the crowds and establish grounds to accuse him (see 3:2). With their devious question of the lawfulness of divorce another controversy or pronouncement story has begun (10:2).

#### b. *10:3-4* They point out that Moses permitted divorce.

The counter-questioning of the controversy begins as Jesus asks the Pharisees what Moses had commanded them about divorce (10:3). With a reference to Jewish scripture (Deut 24:1–4) they reply that Moses permitted a husband to write a "bill of divorce," an official document freeing his wife for remarriage, and thus to "dismiss" his wife. And so the issue progresses to a question of the lawfulness of the actual practice of divorce as explicitly permitted by Moses (10:4).

## c. *10:5-9* Jesus proclaims that human beings must not separate what God has joined in marriage.

Continuing the counter-argumentation, Jesus acknowledges the "commandment" written by Moses but relativizes it with the proclamation that it was "because of your hardness of heart," that is, because of the obstinate refusal and rebellion against the salvific ways and will of God that was characteristic of the people of Israel and that the Pharisees continue to manifest in their opposition to Jesus (see 3:5), that Moses permitted divorce (10:5). With his own reference to scripture Jesus points to the original will of God, as indicated when he created human beings. From the very "beginning of creation," thus before the Mosaic permission because of hardness of heart, God fashioned human beings into two distinct sexes—"male and female He made them" (Gen 1:27; 5:2) (10:6). In accord with God's design for these two distinct but complementary sexes a man shall leave his parents and be joined to his wife in marriage, and "the two shall become one flesh" (Gen 2:24). And so in marriage a husband and wife, who were once "two" people of distinct and separate sexes, now become joined into "one flesh," that is, "one" composite human entity, "one" community of persons (10:7-8).

With a powerful, climactic pronouncement which concludes the argumentation, Jesus definitively answers the question of the "lawfulness" of divorce: "Therefore what God has joined together, no human being must separate!" Jesus thus reveals the divine institution and indissolubility of the marital union, which unites two people of distinct sexes into one complementary community of persons to achieve the Creator's design for human beings. No human being is allowed to separate the unity of persons that God himself has joined together in marriage (10:9).

## d. *10:10-12* Jesus teaches his disciples that divorce results in adultery.

The disciples, in the private domain of "the house," the place for their special instruction (7:17; 9:28, 33), continue to question Jesus about the issue of divorce (10:10). Jesus reinforces and sharpens his previous public teaching to the crowds and Pharisees by emphasizing to his disciples the fundamental equality and mutuality of the two persons united in marriage: Any husband who divorces his wife and marries another commits the serious sin of adultery, a direct violation of God's law (Exod 20:14; Deut 5:18), "against her"; and conversely, any wife who divorces her husband and marries another likewise commits the serious transgression of adultery. By proclaiming that a husband who divorces his wife and marries another commits adultery "against her," Jesus raises the status of the woman to one of equality to the man in marriage, since previously a man could not be accused of adultery.[19] Jesus thus insists upon the equal status and mutual responsibility of the two persons to uphold the one, indissoluble community they have formed in marriage (10:11–12).

### 2. MARK 10:1–12 AS MODEL FOR ACTION

Jesus' pronouncement of the divine indissolubility of the marriage union calls all husbands and wives to respect one another as equals with a serious mutual responsibility to preserve and promote the "one" community of persons they have become. As we strive to follow the difficult and paradoxical "way" of Jesus, we are urged not to "harden" but to open our hearts to Jesus' summons for a restoration of the Creator's plan for authentic human living. Rather than giving in to a permissive divorce mentality, we are obliged to advance and foster societal attitudes which value and uphold marriage as an indissoluble community of persons through which the distinct sexes complement one another and achieve their God-willed potential and fulfillment as human beings.

## I. Mark 10:13–16: Jesus Blesses Children and Teaches His Disciples To Be Childlike To Enter God's Kingdom

[13]And people were bringing children to him that he might touch them, but the disciples rebuked them. [14]When Jesus saw this he became indignant and said to them, "Let the children come to me, do not prevent them; for to such as these belongs the kingdom of God. [15]Amen I say to you, whoever does not receive the kingdom of God like a child will not enter it." [16]Then he put his arms around them and blessed them, placing his hands on them.

### 1. MEANING OF MARK 10:13–16

#### a. *10:13* The disciples rebuke those who bring children to Jesus.

As an appropriate consequence after the focus on marriage (10:1–12) children become the topic of Jesus' teaching. People were bringing children to Jesus so that he might "touch" them, that is, impart a blessing to them through his personal contact. That the disciples, however, "rebuke" those bringing the children indicates that they do not yet understand Jesus' teaching that they become servants of all by hospitably welcoming and respecting even children as the least significant members of society (9:35–37).

**b. *10:14–15* Jesus urges his disciples to be childlike to enter God's kingdom.**

When Jesus sees his disciples hindering the children, he becomes "indignant" and orders them to allow the children to come to him and not to "prevent" them. That the disciples are "preventing" the children further underlines their misunderstanding of Jesus and their own discipleship, since it recalls how they wrongly tried to "prevent" the strange exorcist because of their narrow-minded, exclusive mentality (9:38–39). But Jesus informs them that the "kingdom of God," which has now come near in the teaching and person of Jesus (1:14–15), belongs to such lowly, helpless, humble and dependent children (10:14).

Not only must the disciples permit the children to come to Jesus to receive the gift of God's kingdom, but Jesus urges that they themselves become like children in order to enter the kingdom of God. With a solemn introduction ("amen, I say to you") underscoring the truth and seriousness of his pronouncement, Jesus warns that whoever does not humbly "receive" the kingdom of God "like a child," that is, with the same humility, dependence and trust of a child, will not enter it. Jesus thus calls his disciples to realize that the kingdom of God now available through him is not to be acquired through human status or achievement but is to be gratefully "received" as a freely given gift. They will "receive" and experience God's kingly power only if they adopt the humble trust and dependent attitude of an unpretentious child (10:15).[20]

**c. *10:16* Jesus blesses the children.**

Demonstrating not only how the disciples should treat such lowly and insignificant persons such as children, but also how they themselves can receive the kingdom of God as a gift given to those who are childlike, Jesus hospitably welcomes the children by putting his arms around them in a gesture of loving acceptance and generously blessing them as he places his hands on them and thus extends to them his personal concern for their well-being.

### 2. MARK 10:13–16 AS MODEL FOR ACTION

Jesus serves as a model for how we are to extend loving care, personal concern and genuine respect to all children, who are often defenseless victims of abuse and mistreatment by adults. In order to discover and experience the freely given gift of God's kingship available to us as we strive to follow Jesus' "way" of suffering, death and resurrection, Jesus urges us to become as trusting, humble and dependent as children.

## J. Mark 10:17–31: On His Way Jesus Teaches His Disciples about the Difficulty of Leaving Riches for God's Kingdom

[17]As he was setting out on his way, a man ran up, knelt before him and asked him, "Good teacher, what must I do to inherit eternal life?" [18]Jesus said to him, "Why do you call me good? No one is good but God alone. [19]You know the commandments: 'Do not kill; do not commit adultery; do not steal; do not bear false witness; do not defraud; honor your father and your mother' (Exod 20:12–16; Deut 5:16–20)." [20]He said to him, "Teacher, all these I have observed from my youth." [21]Jesus, looking at him, loved him and said to him, "You lack one thing. Go, sell what you have and give to the poor, and you will have treasure in heaven; then come, follow me." [22]At that statement his face fell and he went away sad, for he had many possessions.

[23]Then Jesus looked around and said to his disciples, "How difficult it is for those who have wealth to enter the kingdom of God!" [24]The disciples were amazed at his words. So Jesus replying again said to them, "Children, how difficult it is to enter the kingdom of God! [25]It is easier for a camel to pass through the eye of a needle than for a rich person to enter the kingdom of God." [26]They were exceedingly astonished, saying to him, "Then who can be saved?" [27]Looking at them Jesus said, "For human beings it is impossible, but not for God. All things are possible for God!"

[28]Peter began to say to him, "Look!, we have left everything and followed you." [29]Jesus said, "Amen I say to you, there is no one who has left house or brothers or sisters or mother or father or children or lands for my sake and for the sake of the gospel, [30]who will not receive a hundred times more now in this present age, houses and brothers and sisters and mothers and children and lands—with persecutions—and eternal life in the age to come. [31]But many who are first will be last, and the last first!"

### 1. MEANING OF MARK 10:17–31

**a. *10:17–22* A rich man who seeks eternal life refuses to sell his possessions and follow Jesus.**

"Setting out on his way," Jesus continues the movement of his salvific "way" (8:27; 9:33–34) to suffering, death and resurrection (8:31; 9:31). While Jesus is on his "way," a man "runs up" to him, "kneels" in reverential homage before him, addresses him as "good teacher," and asks what he must do to "inherit eternal life," that is, what he must do in this life in order to secure and assure an eternal life in the age to come (10:17).

In surprisingly rejecting the man's seemingly harmless address of "good teacher" by pointing out that no one is "good" but God alone, Jesus indicates his own dependence upon God and places the man's request in the proper context of God's sovereignty. His request for eternal life can be answered ultimately only by the "good" God himself (10:18). Reminding the man of God's commandments, Jesus recites a list of well-known commandments from the Decalogue (Exod 20:12–16; Deut 5:16–20; with an additional "do not defraud," see Deut 24:14), those fundamental to authentic communal living (10:19). Addressing Jesus more properly only as "teacher," the man informs him that he has kept all of these commandments from his youth (10:20).

Jesus reacts favorably and shows his personal acceptance of the man by directly "looking at him" and expressing his "love" for him because he has kept the basic commandments of God. But Jesus informs the man that there is still one thing he lacks if he wishes to inherit eternal life from God. He commands him first to go and sell what he possesses and give the proceeds to the poor in order to have his "treasure in heaven" rather than on earth, and thus live in radical dependence upon God. And then, with the words, "come, follow me," Jesus invites the man to be a disciple (1:16–20; 2:14) and follow him on his "way" (10:17) to suffering, death and resurrection, that is, the paradoxical "way" of gaining one's life by losing it (8:34–37) (10:21). But unfortunately this demanding invitation of Jesus overwhelms the man as "his face fell and he went away sad." Although he seeks God's "eternal life" or "kingdom" (see 9:43–47), he is unable to sell what he has and live in trusting dependence on God like a child (10:15) by following the "way" of Jesus, "for he had many possessions" (see 4:18–19). And so the man tragically chooses his many possessions over God's eternal life (10:22).

### b. *10:23–27* Jesus teaches his disciples how hard it is for the rich to enter God's kingdom.

"Looking around" to gain his disciples' attention, Jesus lamentfully exclaims "how difficult" it is not only for this particular rich man who has refused to give up his possessions to follow Jesus but for all "those who have wealth to enter the kingdom of God!" (10:23). Since wealth was generally considered a blessing from God and more of a help than a hindrance in fulfilling God's commandments and other religious practices, Jesus' categorical statement about the rich "amazed" the disciples. Addressing them more directly and personally as "children," Jesus repeats and thus reinforces his shocking warning in a more absolute form: "How difficult it is to enter the kingdom of God!" (10:24).

Jesus then sharpens this "difficulty" to an obvious impossibility with the comically exaggerated statement that it is easier for a "camel," an extremely large animal, to pass through the "eye of a needle," an extremely small opening, than for "a rich person to enter the kingdom of God" (10:25). The disciples' "amazement" now progresses to an "exceeding astonishment" as they ask, "Then who can be saved?" In other words, if the rich whose possessions give them the means of keeping God's laws and helping others cannot be "saved" and enter the kingdom of God, then surely no one can be saved (10:26).

"Looking" directly at his despairing disciples, as he had "looked" at the rich man (10:21), Jesus utters a powerful, hope-bringing pronouncement: "For human beings it is impossible, but not for God. All things are possible for God!" (see Gen 18:14; Job 42:2). This recalls what Jesus had said to the father whose boy the disciples could not exorcise: "All things are possible for one who believes!" (9:23). Although it is impossible for human beings, especially the rich, to save themselves, Jesus assures that God has the power to bring people who believe in him to salvation. Jesus is thus calling his disciples to place their humble and trusting faith in the God through whom "all things are possible," so that he may enable them to follow Jesus on his "way" of suffering, death and resurrection and thus enter the kingdom of God (10:27).

### c. *10:28–31* Jesus assures his disciples of present rewards and eternal life.

Peter, the usual spokesman for the disciples (8:29, 33; 9:5), boldly reminds Jesus that in contrast to the reluctant rich man "we have left everything and followed you" (see 1:16–20), thus implicitly inquiring whether they will be appropriately rewarded (10:28). Underlining the certainty of his pronouncement with the solemn introduction, "amen, I say to you," Jesus assures his disciples that everyone who has left households, family relationships or possessions "for my sake and for the sake of the gospel" will be compensated. This recalls Jesus' earlier paradoxical promise about discipleship: "whoever loses one's life for my sake and that of the gospel will save it" (8:35). Jesus promises that those who follow him will "save" their lives and receive an extravagant "hundredfold" reward in this present age! They will receive a "hundred times more" households, family relationships and possessions, but also—and this is the surprising twist—"with persecutions."

Jesus has thus ridiculed his disciples' concern for additional earthly rewards by leading them to realize the rich reward they have already received by entering into the new household and family of Jesus' followers "who do the will of God" (3:31–35), and by reminding them of the sober reality that the present "reward" of a disciple includes the suffering of "persecutions." But nevertheless, Jesus assures his disciples that in the age to come they will receive the "eternal life" (10:17) that the rich man sadly refused in favor of his earthly possessions (10:29–30).[21]

With yet another paradoxical pronouncement Jesus recapitulates: "But many who are first will be last, and the last first!" This intriguing proclamation of the reversal of normal expectations serves both as a warning and an encouragement. It first of all warns that "many who are first" in earthly possessions or the wealth of this age, like the rich man (10:17–22), "will be last" in regard to eternal life in the age to come. But, recalling Jesus' earlier advice to the Twelve, "If anyone wants to be first, let that person be last of all and servant of all" (9:35), it promises that those who are "last" by leaving the wealth of this age to become followers of Jesus and servants of all will be "first" in the eternal life of the age to come (10:31).

## 2. MARK 10:17–31 AS MODEL FOR ACTION

The example of the rich man who refused to sell his possessions and follow Jesus prompts us to ask ourselves whether we are willing and able to live in radical and trusting dependence upon God in order to follow Jesus on his "way" of suffering, death and resurrection (10:17–22). But Jesus' shocking exclamations of how difficult it is to enter the kingdom of God call us to realize that as weak human beings it is impossible for us to follow Jesus without the help of God. Jesus thus encourages us to place our faith and hope in the God for whom "all things are possible!" (10:23–27).

The response of Jesus to Peter's concern for the rewards of discipleship reminds us not only to appreciate the familial dimension of discipleship—the many households and families of faith throughout the world that we are related to as members of the new household and family of Jesus, but also to prepare ourselves for the inevitable sufferings and persecutions of this age. We are assured, however, that we will attain eternal life in the age to come by becoming "last" and "servants of all" in this age in order to become "first" in the kingdom of God (10:28–31).

## K. Mark 10:32–34: On the Way to Jerusalem Jesus Tells the Twelve That He Will Suffer, Die and Rise

³²They were on the way, going up to Jerusalem, and Jesus was going before them. They were amazed, and those who followed were afraid. Taking the Twelve aside again, he began to tell them what was going to happen to him. ³³"Behold, we are going up to Jerusalem, and the Son of Man will be delivered to the chief priests and the scribes, and they will condemn him to death and deliver him to the Gentiles. ³⁴And they will mock him, spit upon him, scourge him, and kill him, but after three days he will rise."

### 1. MEANING OF MARK 10:32–34

#### a. *10:32* Those who follow Jesus to Jerusalem are amazed and afraid.

"They," that is, both Jesus and his disciples (10:28), continue "on the way" (8:27; 9:33–34; 10:17), Jesus' salvific "way" to suffering, death and resurrection (8:31; 9:31). Having travelled on this "way" to the villages of Caesarea Philippi (8:27), through Galilee (9:30), to Capernaum (9:33) and into the region of Judea and beyond the Jordan (10:1), Jesus and his disciples advance closer to the goal of his "way" as they now explicitly for the first time are "going up to Jerusalem," the Jewish religious and political center from which some of the scribes had earlier come to oppose Jesus (3:22; 7:1). Although the disciples are together with Jesus, he is clearly the one who is leading them on the "way" as he "was going before them."

With Jesus fearlessly and resolutely going ahead of them, the disciples follow him but are "amazed." As they were "amazed" by Jesus' shocking pronouncement about the danger of wealth (10:23–24), so now they are "amazed" at how boldly and bravely he is going ahead of them to the dangerous destiny that awaits in Jerusalem. Not only are the closest followers of Jesus, his disciples, amazed, but the wider group of "those who followed" are "afraid," that is, fearfully apprehensive of the impending threat that the "way" to Jerusalem poses. And so Jesus is leading the "way" followed by his amazed disciples and a further group of fearful followers.

Jesus then takes the Twelve, his special inner circle of disciples, aside again (9:35), thus separating them from the other followers as the ones to whom he will tell "what was going to happen to him." Jesus is fully aware of what will happen to him in accord with God's plan and will reveal this to the Twelve to prepare them for exactly what will happen to him as they follow him in light of the amazement and fear aroused by their going the "way" up to Jerusalem.

**b.** *10:33–34* **Jesus tells the Twelve that he will suffer, die and rise.**

With an introductory "behold" to draw the Twelve's attention to the great importance of his words, Jesus emphatically informs them that not only he himself but "we," Jesus and the Twelve, are now decisively and inevitably "going up to Jerusalem." And so the Twelve's special function of "being with" (3:14) Jesus now includes their "being with" him as he goes to the place of his suffering, death and triumph.

Uttering a third and much more detailed prediction of his suffering, death and resurrection, Jesus reinforces the first two predictions, further underscoring the inevitable certainty and necessity of his "way" as the fulfillment of God's "way" of salvation:

> *8:31*      . . . the Son of Man must suffer greatly and be rejected
> by the elders, the chief priests, and the scribes, and be
> killed, and after three days rise.
> *9:31*      . . . the Son of Man is to be delivered into the hands of
> people, and they will kill him, and three days after his
> death he will rise.
> *10:33–34* . . . the Son of Man will be delivered to the chief
> priests and the scribes, and they will condemn him to
> death and deliver him to the Gentiles. [34]And they will
> mock him, spit upon him, scourge him, and kill him,
> but after three days he will rise.

This third prediction reinforces that Jesus, as the divinely authoritative and messianic Son of Man, "will be delivered" in accord with the necessity of God's plan (divine passive) over to the Jewish leaders, "the chief priests and the scribes." But this third prediction adds that after the Jewish authorities condemn Jesus to death, they will further indicate their total rejection of him as the Jewish messiah by delivering him to the Gentiles (10:33). And the Gentiles will intensify his humiliation as "they will mock him" in derision, "spit upon him" in contempt, "scourge him" in punishment, and "kill him." But the ultimate outcome will be God's triumph over death, as after the brief period of "three days" Jesus "will rise" from the realm of the dead (10:34).

Although the first prediction evoked a rebellious rebuke of Jesus by Peter (8:32), and the second produced a fearful non-understanding of the disciples (9:32), this third and most dramatically precise prediction results in no immediate response by the Twelve, thus arousing suspense as to whether they understand, accept and are prepared to follow the "way" of Jesus.

### 2. MARK 10:32–34 AS MODEL OF ACTION

This third prediction of the divine necessity of Jesus' suffering, death and resurrection calls us to overcome initial shock and fearful apprehension by following the courageous leadership of Jesus, fully aware of the intense humiliation and suffering involved in the "way" of Jesus, yet confident of sharing in God's ultimate triumph over suffering and death.

## L. Mark 10:35–45: Jesus Teaches the Disciples the Need for Humble Service of Others in Imitation of Himself

35Then James and John, the sons of Zebedee, came to him and said to him, "Teacher, we want you to do for us whatever we ask of you." 36He said to them, "What do you want me to do for you?" 37And they said to him, "Grant that in your glory we may sit one at your right and the other at your left." 38But Jesus said to them, "You do not know what you are asking. Can you drink the cup that I drink or be baptized with the baptism with which I am baptized?" 39They said to him, "We can." Jesus said to them, "The cup that I drink, you will drink, and with the baptism with which I am baptized, you will be baptized; 40but to sit at my right or at my left is not mine to give but is for those for whom it has been prepared."

41When the ten heard this, they began to be indignant at James and John. 42Then summoning them Jesus said to them, "You know that those who are supposed to rule over the Gentiles lord it over them, and their great ones wield authority over them. 43But it shall not be so among you. Rather, whoever wants to be great among you will be your servant; 44and whoever wants to be first among you will be the slave of all. 45For the Son of Man did not come to be served but to serve and to give his life as a ransom for many."

### 1. MEANING OF MARK 10:35–45

#### a. *10:35–40* Jesus will not grant places of honor to James and John.

James and John, the pair of brothers who are the sons of Zebedee and whom Jesus named "Sons of Thunder" (3:17), were among the first disciples called by Jesus (1:16–20). Together with Peter, they form a special group of Three within the Twelve (3:16–17), privileged to witness Jesus' raising of Jairus' daughter (5:37) as well as Jesus' glorious transfiguration (9:2). They approach Jesus with a rather brazen request that he do for them "whatever" they ask of him, which rings particularly presumptuous and incongruous, since Jesus has just announced his impending suffering, death and resurrection in Jerusalem (10:33–34) (10:35).

After Jesus asks them what they want him to do for them (10:36), they disclose the selfishness of their request by asking that Jesus grant them to sit on his "right" and his "left," that is, to give them the special places of honor and power, when he enters his glory. Having witnessed Jesus' transfiguration, James and John are concerned about their own participation in the heavenly glory of Jesus, but without indication that they understand the necessity or significance of his suffering and death. Furthermore, their selfish request for the highest places in glory indicates that they are still concerned with personal greatness rather than with the humble service to which Jesus has called the Twelve (9:33–50) (10:37).

Jesus informs James and John that they "do not know" what is involved in the request they are making. Alluding to his impending suffering and violent death in Jerusalem by means of the double metaphor of "drinking the cup" and "being baptized with a baptism," Jesus asks them whether they are able to share his suffering and death by likewise "drinking the cup" which he drinks and "being baptized with the baptism" with which he is baptized. In the biblical tradition "to drink the cup" means to undergo the fate or destiny of painful suffering that God has allotted (Ps 75:8; Isa 51:17; Jer 49:12; Ezek 23:31–33). Similarly, "to be baptized" expresses the way one is totally overwhelmed and submerged by extremely violent suffering leading to death (Pss 42:7; 69:2, 15; Jonah 2:3–6) (10:38).

After James and John admit that "we can" drink the cup and be baptized, Jesus assures them that indeed they will "drink the cup" he drinks and "be baptized" with his "baptism" of violent suffering and death (10:39). But it is not Jesus' prerogative to grant places of honor, which have already been prepared for people by God. Jesus promises James and John not the places of honor they requested but only a share in his suffering and death in complete subordination to the will of God (10:40).

**b. *10:41–45* Jesus calls his disciples to selfless service of all.**

The arrogant request of James and John causes strife among the Twelve, as the other ten disciples become "indignant" when they hear it (10:41). In light of this dispute Jesus "summons" all of the Twelve together for another instruction on how they are to relate to one another. He reminds them how the high positions of authority and power are misused among the Gentiles. Although their leaders "supposedly" rule over them, they actually tyrannize their own by "lording it over them," and the "great ones" among the Gentiles ruthlessly and selfishly "wield authority" in dominance over them (10:42).

Jesus insists that such tactics are to be strictly avoided by the Twelve. With a rhetorically powerful double antithetical aphorism (see 8:35; 9:35) Jesus invites the Twelve to adopt an entirely new, radical and paradoxical vision of what it means to exercise authority and rule over others. In the first half of this double aphorism Jesus urges that whoever wants to be "great" among the disciples must become their "servant," that is, one who actively cares for the personal welfare of others (10:43). This is reinforced and carried forward by the second half of the aphorism, as "whoever wants to be *great*" is sharpened into "whoever wants to be *first*," the ultimate in greatness, and "will be your *servant*" is intensified into "will be the *slave of all*," that is, not just a voluntary servant but a completely subservient and humble "slave" not just of some but of "all." Jesus enjoins his disciples to experience a paradoxical "greatness" and prominence by becoming selfless servants and slaves of others, rather than competing for the highest places of honor and desiring to control and dominate others like the Gentiles. They are to become "servants" of others rather than "lording it over them"; they are to become "slaves of all" rather than "wielders of authority" over others (10:44).[22]

With a powerful, climactic pronouncement Jesus reveals why selfless service of all is so important and necessary for his disciples—it sums up the real significance of his own life and death. Although Jesus functions as the transcendent and divinely authoritative Son of Man, he does not use this position of high authority to dominate or to be passively "served" by others, but he "has come" as Son of Man to actively "serve" others, as has been illustrated by his teaching and healing ministry. And although he is on his "way" to Jerusalem to suffer and die (8:31; 9:31; 10:33–34), his life will not be passively taken away from him. Rather, he will actively and freely "give his life as a ransom for many," that is, he will offer his own life as the price to be paid in order to liberate "many," a common Semitic expression for "all" people.[23] The humble and selfless service exemplified by the life and death of Jesus thus represents the model the disciples are to imitate in becoming selfless servants and slaves of all (10:45).

### 2. MARK 10:35–45 AS MODEL FOR ACTION

Jesus' rejection of the request of James and John for places of honor and power by assuring them only of future suffering and death calls us to resist the desire for prestige and dominance of others, and instead to subordinate our lives to the salvific plan of God by accepting the suffering and death involved in following the "way" of Jesus. The example of totally selfless service that Jesus personally demonstrates to the point of offering his own life for the benefit of others provides a model for the generous and unlimited manner in which we are to become totally selfless servants and slaves with a personal concern for the welfare of all others.

## M. Mark 10:46–52: Leaving Jericho Jesus Heals the Blind Beggar Bartimaeus Who Then Follows Him on the Way

[46]Then they came to Jericho. And as he was leaving Jericho with his disciples and a considerable crowd, Bartimaeus, the son of Timaeus, a blind beggar, was sitting beside the way. [47]Hearing that it was Jesus of Nazareth, he began to cry out and say, "Jesus, Son of David, have mercy on me!" [48]And many were rebuking him, telling him to be silent. But he kept crying out all the more, "Son of David, have mercy on me!" [49]Jesus stopped and said, "Call him." So they called the blind man, saying to him, "Take courage; get up, he is calling you!" [50]Throwing aside his cloak and springing up, he came to Jesus. [51]And responding to him, Jesus said, "What do you want me to do for you?" The blind man said to him, "Master, I want to see." [52]Jesus said to him, "Go, your faith has saved you." And immediately he received his sight and followed him on the way.

### 1. MEANING OF MARK 10:46–52

#### a. *10:46–48* A blind beggar begs Jesus for mercy.

Jesus and his disciples advance the movement of his salvific "way" as they "came" to Jericho, the city in the Jordan valley from which pilgrims coming from Galilee began their direct ascent to Jerusalem. As Jesus "with his disciples and a considerable crowd" was leaving Jericho and coming ever closer to his destiny of suffering and death in Jerusalem (10:32–34), a blind beggar by the name of Bartimaeus, the son of Timaeus, was sitting beside the "way." The introduction of a "blind" man signals the beginning of a healing story and is reminiscent of the healing of the blind man at Bethsaida, who symbolically characterized the disciples' "blindness" and non-understanding of Jesus (8:22–26). And so the reader is alerted to compare blind Bartimaeus, the son of Timaeus, with the disciples, especially with James and John, the sons of Zebedee, who have just demonstrated a certain "blindness" to the necessity and significance of Jesus' suffering and death. That Bartimaeus is "sitting" beside the "way" not only places him in the position of begging from passers-by but also means that his blindness has immobilized him, preventing him from following the "way" of Jesus to Jerusalem (10:46).

As Bartimaeus hears that "Jesus of Nazareth," whose reputation as a healer has spread throughout the land (3:7–8), is passing by, he seizes the opportunity and utters a remarkable confession of faith which no one has yet dared to declare, namely that Jesus is the "Son of David," the one who fulfills the promises for a royal, messianic figure from the family of King David (2 Sam 7:12–16).[24] Bartimaeus thus cries out and begs Jesus whom he, though blind, recognizes as the Son of David to "have mercy" on him in his debilitating blindness (10:47). The great faith of Bartimaeus even overcomes the obstacle of those who are trying to silence him, as he cries out all the more, "Son of David, have mercy on me!" (10:48).

**b.  *10:49–50* Jesus calls and he comes.**

With his persistent and faith-filled begging, Bartimaeus succeeds in "stopping" Jesus as he makes his "way" to Jerusalem. Having "stopped," Jesus pronounces the authoritative command which enables blind Bartimaeus to come to him: "Call him." The people then "call" the "blind man," exhorting him to "take courage" and "get up" because Jesus is the one who is "calling" him (10:49). This is all the anxious Bartimaeus needs to hear. Fortified by the potent "call" of Jesus, he "throws aside" his beggar's "cloak," a symbol of his immobilization as a blind man, jumps up from his sitting position and "comes" to Jesus (10:50).

**c.  *10:51–52* Faith enables the blind man to see and follow Jesus on the way.**

Echoing his question to the sons of Zebedee (10:36), Jesus asks the son of Timaeus, "What do you want me to do for you?" Whereas James and John, "blind" to the true significance of Jesus' "way" of suffering and death as humble and selfless service of others, ask for places of honor in glory (10:37), the blind Bartimaeus, painfully aware of the debilitating "blindness" which prevents him from "seeing" and following the "way" of Jesus, asks that Jesus, the "master," enable him to see (10:51). Jesus then acknowledges the great faith of Bartimaeus and pronounces the powerful words of healing, "Go," that is, "be mobilized," for "your faith has saved you." The healing is confirmed as Bartimaeus "immediately" and miraculously receives his sight. Empowered by Jesus to "go" and to "see,"

Bartimaeus admirably uses his renewed sight and mobility to no longer "sit" beside the "way" but to follow Jesus on the "way" to his suffering, death and resurrection in Jerusalem (10:52).[25]

## 2. MARK 10:46–52 AS MODEL FOR ACTION

Bartimaeus provides us with a model for the kind of faith in Jesus we need in order to be able to follow Jesus on his "way" without being "blind" to the true significance of his suffering, death and resurrection as humble and selfless service of others. As we imitate the faith of Bartimaeus, we are prompted to prayerfully and persistently beg Jesus to assist us, assured that Jesus has the merciful will and power to "call" us to himself in order that he may enable us both to properly "see" and understand as well as faithfully follow his salvific "way" of selfless service of others through the humble acceptance of suffering and death.

## Notes

1. Caesarea Philippi was located on the southern slope of Mt. Hermon at one of the sources of the Jordan River. It was named after the Roman emperor, Caesar Augustus, who gave it to Herod the Great, and after Herod Philip, the son of Herod the Great and brother of Herod Antipas, who was tetrarch of the region.

2. On the "Christ" title, see Chapter I.

3. See "Son of Man" in Chapter I.

4. See "Scribes," "Elders," and "Priests/Chief Priests" in Chapter I.

5. For examples of God's special salvific intervention on behalf of his own "after three days," see Gen 22:4; 42:17; Exod 15:22; 2 Kgs 20:5; Jonah 2:1; Hos 6:2.

6. See J. M. Bassler, "Cross," *Harper's Bible Dictionary,* 194–95.

7. Tannehill, *Sword,* 99–100: "In the sharp antithesis, in which saving becomes losing and losing saving, we feel the grating vibration of two visions of life rubbing against each other. No effort is made to persuade us to accept the new perspective by reason or common sense. The speaker risks everything on the forcefulness of the words. . . . (The saying) must shake our deep assurance that we know what saving life and losing life mean. It attempts this by taking the meaning of our words away from us, turning them inside out, forcing us to face the possibility that we should fear what we have always wanted and should do what we have always feared. Such a shaking, if it begins in us, attacks our fear and concern themselves. Only this shaking of our deep, largely unconscious convic-

tions can do this. On the other hand, if the saying fit within our lives as something reasonable, the possibility of bringing about significant change would be lost. The saying would only be an additional item within the established vision of life, not a new beginning point. This the saying wishes to prevent, as its sharply paradoxical form makes clear."

For another example of an "antithetical aphorism," see Mark 7:15.

8. Note the implication that as the Son of Man Jesus is also the Son of God, his Father; see 1:1, 11; 3:11; 5:7.

9. Although the "high mountain" is not named or located, the very high Mt. Hermon was near the villages of Caesarea Philippi (8:27).

10. W. Michaelis, *"leukos,"* *TDNT* 4.246–50.

11. For previous examples of the epiphany genre in Mark, see 4:35–41; 6:45–52. For the differences between the literary genres of "theophany," "epiphany" and "vision," see Lentzen-Deis, *Taufe,* 100–107.

12. J. Jeremias, *"Mōusēs,"* *TDNT* 4.853–55.

13. On the problem of the background of the "tents," see W. Michaelis, *"skēnē,"* *TDNT* 7.379–80.

14. A. Oepke, *"nephelē,"* *TDNT* 4.905, 908.

15. See "Suffering Servant and Suffering Just One" in Chapter I.

16. Verses 44 and 46 are omitted in important early manuscripts. They appear to be later scribal additions that simply repeat verse 48.

17. "Gehenna" refers to the "valley of Hinnom" southwest of Jerusalem, where children were once sacrificed by fire to foreign gods (Jer 7:31; 32:35). Jeremiah pronounced its imminent judgment and destruction (Jer 7:32; 19:4–6) and King Josiah destroyed and desecrated its places of sacrifice (2 Kgs 23:10). In Jewish apocalyptic literature and the NT "Gehenna" became a symbol for the place or state of the eternal punishment of the wicked. See W. E. Lemke, "Gehenna," *Harper's Bible Dictionary,* 335.

18. On Mark 9:33–50, see Stock, *Boten,* 112–30; H. Fleddermann, "The Discipleship Discourse (Mark 9:33–50)," *CBQ* 43 (1981) 57–75; U. C. von Wahlde, "Mark 9:33–50: Discipleship: The Authority That Serves," *BZ* 29 (1985) 49–67.

19. J. M. Efrid, "Adultery," *Harper's Bible Dictionary,* 13–14.

20. J. Marcus ("Entering into the Kingly Power of God," *JBL* 107 [1988] 673) offers the following paraphrase of Mark 10:15: "Unless you receive God's kingly power with an acknowledgment of total dependence, in the manner that a little child receives everything from its parent's hand, you will never have a share in it."

21. On 10:29–30, see Tannehill, *Sword,* 147–52.

22. Tannehill, *Sword,* 105: "Thus vss. 43b–44 are full of paradoxical tension, for greatness and being a slave do not go together. To be sure,

something happens to the ideas of being "great" and "first" when they enter into this paradox. What happens is not that we are given a new goal for which to strive, a clear and reasonable ideal of greatness, but that greatness is taken out of our hands, for it is promised to the one who has decided in his life to make no claims to greatness. For such a one greatness can only come as a strange and wonderful gift and be based on something quite different from his achievements for himself in the world."

23. J. Jeremias, "*polloi,*" *TDNT* 6.536–45.

24. See "Son of David" in Chapter I.

25. Explicit references to the "way" of Jesus not only characterize this section (8:27–10:52) of the Marcan narrative (8:27; 9:33, 34; 10:17, 32, 46, 52) but form a literary inclusion introducing (8:27) and concluding it (10:52).

# VII

---

# Mark 11:1–13:37

*On His Way Jesus Brings Forth New Teachings in and about the Temple of Jerusalem.*

## A. Mark 11:1–11: Jesus Triumphantly Enters Jerusalem and Returns to Bethany with the Twelve

¹When they drew near to Jerusalem, to Bethphage and Bethany at the Mount of Olives, he sent two of his disciples ²and said to them, "Go into the village opposite you, and immediately as you enter it you will find a colt tied on which no one has ever sat. Untie it and bring it here. ³If anyone says to you, 'Why are you doing this?' say, 'The Master has need of it and will send it back here immediately.' " ⁴So they went off and found a colt tied at a gate outside on the street, and they untied it. ⁵Some of the by-standers there said to them, "What are you doing, untying the colt?" ⁶They answered them just as Jesus had told them, and they permitted them to do it. ⁷Then they brought the colt to Jesus and put their cloaks over it. And he sat on it. ⁸And many spread their cloaks on the way, and others spread leafy branches that they had cut from the fields. ⁹Those preceding him as well as those following kept crying out: "Hosanna! Blessed is he who comes in the name of the Lord! (Ps 118:26). ¹⁰Blessed is the coming kingdom of our father David! Hosanna in the highest!" ¹¹Then he entered Jerusalem and went into the temple. Looking around at everything, since it was already late, he went out to Bethany with the Twelve.

### 1. MEANING OF MARK 11:1-11

#### a. *11:1-3* Jesus sends two disciples for a colt that no one has sat upon.

Continuing on the salvific "way" of the Lord after leaving Jericho, Jesus with his entourage of disciples, the crowd (10:46) and Bartimaeus (10:52) "drew near" to Jerusalem, the capital Jewish city but ominous place where Jesus is destined to suffer, die and rise (10:32–34). Suspense is generated as they "draw near" but do not yet enter Jerusalem, stopping at the villages of Bethphage and Bethany located on the Mount of Olives, the mount directly opposite the eastern side of the temple mount of Jerusalem across the Kidron valley.

Poised for their entrance into Jerusalem, Jesus takes majestic control of the preparations as he commissions two disciples to go into the "village opposite" them. Illustrating his prophetic foreknowledge, Jesus predicts that as they enter the village they "will find a colt tied on which no one has ever sat." They are to "untie" it and "bring" it to Jesus. That "no one has ever sat" on this colt indicates its appropriateness for the sacred and unique role it will play in God's plan (see Num 19:2; Deut 21:3; 1 Sam 6:7) to be carried out by Jesus. This special "colt" alludes to the "colt of an ass" (Zech 9:9; see also Gen 49:10–11) upon which the humble, messianic "king" of Jerusalem would triumphally ride into his city (11:1–2).

Jesus further instructs the two disciples that if anyone questions why they are doing this, they are to inform them that the "master" or "lord" has need of this colt but will return it immediately. Jesus thus reveals himself as the "master" or "lord" (see 2:28; 5:19) for whom this special animal will play a unique but temporary role in the majestic entrance of Jesus as "lord" into Jerusalem (11:3).

#### b. *11:4-6* The disciples procure the colt.

In obedience to the instructions of Jesus the two disciples go into the village and find there the destined colt tied at a gate in the street. As they untied it, some of the bystanders question what they are doing in untying the colt (11:4–5). But when the disciples answered "just as Jesus had told them," they were permitted to take the colt (11:6). That everything happens precisely as Jesus has predicted not only underlines his superior knowledge and majestic control of the entry into Jerusalem in accord with God's plan, but further assures the reader that the previous predictions of Jesus about the divine necessity of his suffering, death and resurrection (8:31; 9:31; 10:33–34) will likewise take place precisely as Jesus has predicted.

**c. *11:7–10* Jesus rides the colt in triumphal procession into Jerusalem.**

The disciples then bring the colt to Jesus and put their cloaks over it in preparation for Jesus to ride it. In the manner of a royal enthronement (see 1 Kgs 1:38–40; 2 Kgs 9:13) Jesus, "the lord," majestically "sat" on this unique colt "on which no one has ever sat" (11:2, 7). In homage to the "lord" Jesus many spread their cloaks "on the way," that is, on the salvific "way" (10:32, 52) of the lord Jesus into Jerusalem to execute the "way of the Lord" God (1:3). Others spread leafy branches they had cut from the fields, adding to the festive and triumphal character of the entrance (11:8).

The excited procession of those preceding and following Jesus as he rides the colt into Jerusalem keep crying out exuberantly. Beginning with a traditional liturgical acclamation of praise to God, "Hosanna!" (literally, "save us"), the crowd joyfully applies to Jesus a direct citation from one of the psalms of ascent to Jerusalem (Ps 118:26): "Blessed is he who comes in the name of the Lord!" They thus acknowledge Jesus as a unique messianic agent, *the* "one who comes" to accomplish the salvific will of the "Lord" God (11:9). Further elaborating, they enthusiastically exclaim, "Blessed is the coming kingdom of our father David!" They thus express their hope that with the "coming" into Jerusalem of Jesus, whom Bartimaeus had recognized as "Son of David" (10:47–48), the long-awaited, messianic "kingdom of our father David" (see 2 Sam 7:12–16) is now "coming." They conclude their processional chant with an intensifying "Hosanna in the highest!" (11:10).

For the reader, who knows that Jesus is coming as "the lord" into Jerusalem to inaugurate not merely the kingdom of David but the kingdom of God (1:15; 9:1), the exuberant exclamation of the triumphal procession functions as ironic understatement. The question for the reader is whether the disciples and crowd, who were earlier amazed and fearful while following Jesus up to Jerusalem (10:32), now understand that Jesus is triumphantly entering Jerusalem to suffer, die and rise (10:33–34) or, like James and John (10:35–45), are focused only on the coming "glory" of Jesus.

**d. *11:11* After viewing everything in the temple, Jesus went to Bethany with the Twelve.**

The triumphal procession reaches its goal as Jesus, the "lord" (11:3) and the "one who comes" with the authority of God (11:9), enters the sacred temple of Jerusalem, the central Jewish religious institution and dwelling place of God.[1] After intently, authoritatively but mysteriously "looking around at everything" in the temple precincts, he leaves "since it was already late." He curiously returns for the night to the village of Bethany on the Mount of Olives "with the Twelve," those specially commissioned "to be with him" (3:14) and those who have not yet indicated that they understand that Jesus must suffer, die and rise in Jerusalem (10:32–45). And so suspense has arisen as to how Jesus, who has triumphantly entered the temple of Jerusalem under the authority of God, will exercise this authority after he has observed everything in the temple but left it until the next day.

### 2. MARK 11:1-11 AS MODEL FOR ACTION

The majestic decisiveness and foreknowledge with which Jesus prepares to enter Jerusalem assures us that he is the messianic "lord" endowed with the authority to bring God's plan of salvation to a triumphant fulfillment. As we follow the joyful and spirited procession of Jesus into the temple of Jerusalem, we are invited to acclaim and acknowledge that Jesus is *the* "one who comes" with the divine authority of the Lord God to bring about not a Davidic kingdom of earthly and political glory but the magnificent kingdom of God, not in a powerful, military manner but by humbly suffering, dying and rising in accord with the salvific will of God.

## B. Mark 11:12–14: Coming from Bethany with His Disciples Jesus Curses a Fig Tree for Not Bearing Fruit

¹²The next day as they were leaving Bethany he was hungry. ¹³And seeing from a distance a fig tree in leaf, he went to see if he might find anything on it. When he came to it he found nothing but leaves; for it was not the season for figs. ¹⁴And responding he said to it, "May no one ever eat fruit from you again!" And his disciples heard it.

### 1. MEANING OF MARK 11:12-14

#### a. *11:12-13* Leaving Bethany Jesus looks for fruit on a fig tree.

On the next day as Jesus and the Twelve are leaving Bethany on the Mount of Olives, where they had spent the night after the triumphal entry into the temple of Jerusalem (11:11), Jesus is hungry. Presumably Jesus and his disciples are returning to the temple where Jesus had authoritatively entered as "the one who comes in the name of the Lord" but, after enigmatically "looking around at everything," had abruptly departed (11:12).

As the hungry Jesus sees from a distance a fig tree in leaf, he comes closer to see if perhaps he might find some fruit on it, even though it was not yet the season for figs. Although his coming to see "if he might find anything" on it when it is not yet the time for fully ripened figs expresses the tentativeness and uncertainty of Jesus' expectation of fruit, that the fig tree is already "in leaf" means that it should have at least some immature but edible fruit, since the fig tree produces its fruit even before its leaves.[2] But when Jesus comes he finds "nothing but leaves" and therefore no fruit to satisfy his hunger. The leaves prove to be a false indication of the fruit the fig tree should have produced (11:13).

**b.  *11:14* The disciples hear Jesus curse the fruitless fig tree.**

Since the fig tree in leaf has not fulfilled its purpose by producing the fruit Jesus expected, he pronounces a severe condemnation of it: "May no one ever eat fruit from you again!" Jesus will not allow the fig tree to ever again deceive anyone as it deceived Jesus by producing leaves but no fruit to satisfy his hunger. This harsh and stinging indictment reverberates in the ears of the disciples who "heard it."

In the biblical tradition the image of seeking but not finding the fruit that should be produced symbolizes the failure of human beings to achieve their God-given purpose by producing the "fruit" God expects (Mic 7:1–2; Jer 8:13). Such failure to bear expected "fruit" can be threatened with destruction (Matt 3:8–10; Luke 3:8–9). Jesus' sharply ominous condemnation of the fruitless fig tree thus serves as a symbolic warning not only for the listening disciples but also for the Jerusalem temple, which Jesus has thoroughly examined (11:11) before examining the fig tree, to fulfill their God-given purpose as Jesus expects.

### 2. MARK 11:12–14 AS MODEL FOR ACTION

Jesus' stern condemnation of the fruitless fig tree warns us of our need to "produce fruit" by fulfilling our expected purpose as disciples called to hear and understand the mystery of the person of Jesus as we follow him on the "way" to suffering, death and resurrection.

## C. Mark 11:15–19: After Jesus Teaches That the Temple Is for All Peoples, the Jewish Leaders Seek To Destroy Him

> [15]Then they came to Jerusalem, and on entering the temple he began to drive out those selling and buying in the temple, and he

overturned the tables of the money changers and the seats of those who were selling doves. [16]He would not allow anyone to carry anything through the temple. [17]He was teaching and he said to them, "Is it not written:

'My house shall be called a house of prayer for all peoples' (Isa 56:7)?

But you have made it a den of robbers" (Jer 7:11).

[18]The chief priests and the scribes heard it and were seeking how to destroy him, for they feared him because the whole crowd was astounded at his teaching. [19]And when evening came, they went out of the city.

### 1. MEANING OF MARK 11:15–19

**a. *11:15–16* Jesus forcefully disrupts the temple cult.**

Continuing the movement of his salvific "way," Jesus and his disciples "came" again to Jerusalem, returning as expected after spending the night in Bethany (11:11). When Jesus again enters the temple, which he had thoroughly examined the day before (11:11), he begins to forcefully disrupt the temple cult as he "drives out" the people "selling" as well as those "buying" the items used to perform sacrificial worship in the temple. He continues this disturbance by dramatically "overturning" the tables of the "money changers," those who exchanged the secular Roman coins for the Jewish coins appropriate to pay the temple tax and to buy the things needed for cultic sacrifice within the sacred temple precincts. He also overturns the seats of those who were selling the "doves" needed for various purification sacrifices (Lev 12:6; 14:22; 15:14, 29; Luke 2:22–24) (11:15). Finally, Jesus brings to a complete halt the business of temple worship as he forbids "anyone" at all to carry anything through the temple (11:16).

Jesus' symbolic gesture of cursing the fruitless fig tree on the way from Bethany to the Jerusalem temple (11:12–14) has prepared the reader to interpret the forceful action of Jesus in the temple as a powerful and authoritative prophetic gesture condemning the temple and warning of its destruction. Just as the fig tree, although it has leaves, has failed to produce fruit and thus fulfill its expected, God-given purpose, so the temple, although it conducts the business in preparation for sacrificial worship, evidently has not fulfilled its expected, God-given purpose. Jesus' condemnatory disruption of the temple cult, climaxed by his forbidding anyone to carry anything through the temple area echoes his strong condemnation of the fruitless fig tree, which he forbids to ever produce fruit for anyone again:

> *11:14* "May no one ever eat fruit from you again!"
> *11:16* He would not allow anyone to carry anything through the temple.

### b. *11:17* Jesus indicts those in the temple.

Having brought a halt to temple worship, Jesus introduces his own authoritative "teaching" in the temple. In the course of this teaching he explains and reinforces his powerful prophetic gesture of condemnation of the temple with his authoritative words, by which he pointedly and provocatively contrasts God's stated purpose for the temple with its failure to "produce fruit" like the doomed fig tree and achieve its true purpose.

With a potent rhetorical question referring to the will of God as "written" in the authoritative scriptures, Jesus first reminds his listeners of the expected, God-willed purpose for the temple. As God's messianic agent, "the one who comes" to the temple "in the name of the Lord" (11:9), Jesus speaks with the authority of God himself as he proclaims anew God's intention and promise for his temple: "My house shall be called a house of prayer for all peoples" (Isa 56:7). Jesus thus indicates that it is God's will that the temple preserve the sovereignty of God by truly being the house of God ("*my* house"), that it be truly a house of authentic prayer to God, and that it be a house of prayer not limited to an exclusive and privileged group of Jewish people but universally open "for all peoples" of the world. With its future formulation ("shall be called") Jesus' proclamation can be heard by the reader not only as an expression of God's intention of what the temple should be but also as a future promise for a "temple" that can truly be a place of genuine prayer to God for all human beings. The triumphal and masterful manner in which Jesus has entered and condemned the Jerusalem temple arouses the expectation of whether and how he himself might fulfill this promise.

Jesus then directly accuses those engaged in the business of the temple cult (11:15–16) of long having made and of continuing to make (perfect tense of the Greek verb "to make") the temple a "den of robbers" (Jer 7:11). Instead of making the temple the true "house" and dwelling place of the sovereign God, they have transformed it into their own "den" and hiding place for themselves as "robbers." In sharp contrast to God's purpose that the temple be a "house," a communal household, where all human beings can truly pray to God, they have turned it into a "den" of those who, as "robbers," ravage others rather than enable them to truly pray to God. Like the prophet Jeremiah before him (Jer 7:11–14) Jesus sternly indicts the people for making the temple a "den of robbers" destined for destruction.

### c. *11:18–19* The chief priests and scribes seek to destroy Jesus.

The "chief priests" and the "scribes," those Jewish religious leaders already predicted by Jesus as the ones who will reject him (8:31) and to whom he will be delivered to be condemned to death (10:33), "heard" of Jesus' forceful gesture and authoritative teaching condemning the temple. The disruptive actions of Jesus undermine the authority the chief priests exercise over the temple and the powerful words of Jesus threaten the teaching authority of the scribes. In response to the threat Jesus poses to them, the chief priests and scribes continue to fulfill their role in accord with Jesus' predictions as they "were seeking how to destroy him" (see 3:6). They seek to kill Jesus because "they feared him," that is, they feared him as a threat to their own leadership and authority over the temple and "the whole crowd" of the Jewish people who are "astounded at his teaching" with a divine authority surpassing that of the scribes (1:22). The whole crowd is "astounded" at the teaching of Jesus which effectively indicts their leaders, especially the chief priests and scribes, as inadequate for making the temple a "den of robbers" rather than enabling it to achieve its true purpose as God's house of prayer for all human beings. The people's attraction to the impressive and superior teaching of Jesus with its promise of enabling all peoples to authentically pray to God thus frightens the chief priests and scribes into trying to eliminate Jesus as a threat to their own inferior authority and leadership (11:18).

Having completed this second day in the temple of Jerusalem, which included Jesus' powerful cursing of a fruitless fig tree as a symbolic foreshadowing of his authoritative condemnation of the temple for failing to achieve its true purpose (11:12–17), "when evening came" Jesus and his disciples "went out of the city" of Jerusalem presumably to again spend the night in Bethany (11:11). Suspense has been aroused regarding the Jewish leaders' attempt to destroy Jesus, which stands in tension with the whole crowd's astonishment over his powerful and provocative teaching in the Jerusalem temple (11:19).

### 2. MARK 11:15–19 AS MODEL FOR ACTION

Jesus' forceful disruption of the temple's inadequate worship and his imposing teaching warning of the temple's destruction serve as a model for us to examine our worship of God for unauthentic elements which can render our worship useless. Jesus teaches us to keep our worship authentic by acknowledging and respecting the sovereignty of God and by forming a communal household of genuine prayer to God, a prayer characterized by a global and universal attitude of openness to all other peoples of the world. We are persuaded to focus upon the person and divine authority of Jesus as the one who can empower us to become God's communal household of authentic prayer open to all human beings.

## D. Mark 11:20–25: Passing by the Withered Fig Tree, Jesus Teaches His Disciples about Faith, Prayer and Forgiveness

> [20]As they passed by in the morning, they saw the fig tree withered to its roots. [21]Peter remembered and said to him, "Rabbi, look! The fig tree that you cursed has withered!" [22]Responding Jesus said to them, "Have faith in God! [23]Amen, I say to you, whoever says to this mountain, 'Be lifted up and thrown into the sea,' and does not doubt in his heart but believes that what he says happens, it shall be done for him. [24]Therefore I tell you, all that you ask for in prayer, believe that you have received it, and it shall be done for you. [25]And whenever you stand praying, forgive, if you have anything against anyone, so that your Father who is in heaven may also forgive you your transgressions."[3]

### 1. MEANING OF MARK 11:20–25

#### a. *11:20–21* Peter points out that the fig tree Jesus cursed has withered.

On the next day as Jesus and his disciples "pass by" on their return from Bethany to Jerusalem, they see that the fig tree which Jesus condemned on the preceding day for its failure to produce fruit (11:12–14) is now "withered to its roots" and thus totally destroyed. This dramatic illustration of the effectiveness of Jesus' powerful words of condemnation reinforces his strong condemnation of the temple (11:15–19), assuring the reader that the temple, like the fruitless fig tree, is doomed to destruction (11:20).

Peter, spokesman for the disciples who "heard" Jesus condemn the fruitless fig tree (11:14), "remembers" and, addressing Jesus as "rabbi" or "master" of the disciples, expresses his utter surprise and bewilderment by exclaiming: "Look! The fig tree that you cursed has withered!" The implication is that Peter and the disciples do not understand and so need Jesus to explain what consequences the withered fig tree has as a warning not only of the destruction of the temple but of the necessity for the disciples themselves to "produce fruit" and fulfill their God-willed purpose (11:21).

**b. *11:22–25* Jesus bids his disciples to pray with faith in God and with forgiveness toward others.**

Responding to the bafflement of his disciples, Jesus first of all exhorts them to "have faith in God!," that is, to have a complete confidence and trust in God (11:22). With the solemn introduction, "amen, I say to you," underlining the importance and certainty of what he will say, Jesus teaches how faith in God empowers prayer. Employing the rhetorical exaggeration of lifting up and throwing a mountain into the sea to symbolically express what is humanly impossible, Jesus proclaims the unlimited power available to anyone who prays with complete faith in God. Jesus insists that whoever "does not doubt" in his "heart," his inner being, but confidently "believes" that what he says actually happens, even something as impossible and miraculous as moving a mountain, God will do it for that person (11:23). Having already taught his disciples that what is impossible for human beings is possible for God (10:27) so that "all things are possible for one who believes" (9:23) in God, Jesus assures that "all" that "you," the disciples as a community, "ask for in prayer" with such a great and confident faith that you believe that you have already received it, God with his unlimited power will bring it about. In order for the community of disciples to offer effective prayer, they must have a total and absolute faith in the boundless power of God (11:24).

Having appealed for his disciples to have faith in God as a first condition for effective prayer, Jesus adds a second: forgiveness. He exhorts the disciples that whenever they stand praying as a community they are to "forgive" whatever they have against "anyone." Such a forgiveness of "anyone" will constitute the disciples as an inclusive community open to reconciliation and peaceful, harmonious relations with all other human beings. It is necessary for the disciples to forgive all others in order that God, "your Father who is in heaven," may in turn forgive them their transgressions against God (Sir 28:2). Only when their sins have been forgiven by God can the disciples offer effective prayer with the confident faith of receiving all that they request through the unlimited power of God. Faith in God and forgiveness, the divine forgiveness of the community who forgives their fellow human beings, are the prerequisites for authentic and effective prayer (11:25).

Jesus has indicated what the disciples must do to "produce fruit" and fulfill their God-willed purpose: They are to offer authentic and effective prayer by being a community of disciples who pray with total faith in the unlimited power of God to answer their needs and who have their sins forgiven by God after they have forgiven the offenses of their fellow human beings. At the same time that they fulfill their own purpose as a community which offers authentic and effective prayer with an inclusive and universal attitude of forgiveness toward all other human beings, the disciples fulfill the purpose that the condemned and doomed Jerusalem temple has failed to achieve. They become the communal household of the sovereign God, "a house of prayer for all peoples" (11:17).

### 2. MARK 11:20–25 AS MODEL FOR ACTION

As we identify with the disciples, Jesus exhorts and empowers us to pray authentically and effectively by placing our complete and confident faith in the unlimited power of God to grant whatever we request and by forgiving anyone who has anything against us so that we may receive the forgiveness of our own sins from God. Through our total faith and God's forgiveness we are assured of the efficacy of our prayer. By forgiving others we become an inclusive community with a global and universal attitude of openness to all of our fellow human beings and fulfill our purpose as followers of Jesus by becoming the true communal household of the sovereign God, a community of effective prayer open to all peoples and cultures of the world.

## E. Mark 11:27–33: The Authority of Jesus in the Temple Is Questioned by the Chief Priests, Scribes and Elders

[27]Then they came again to Jerusalem. And as he was walking in the temple, the chief priests and the scribes and the elders came to him [28]and said to him, "By what authority are you doing these things? Or who gave you this authority to do them?" [29]Jesus said to them, "I will ask you one question. Answer me, and I will tell you by what authority I do these things. [30]Was the baptism of John of heavenly or of human origin? Answer me." [31]Then they discussed it among themselves and said, "If we say, 'Of heavenly origin,' he will say, 'Then why did you not believe him?' [32]But shall we say, 'Of human origin'?"—they feared the crowd, for all

held that John really was a prophet. [33]So answering Jesus they said, "We do not know." Then Jesus said to them, "Neither will I tell you by what authority I do these things."

<h3 style="text-align:center">1. MEANING OF MARK 11:27–33</h3>

**a. *11:27–28* The Jewish leaders question the authority of Jesus.**

After having entered and examined the Jerusalem temple on the first day (11:11) and after having disrupted and condemned the temple worship on the second day (11:15–17), Jesus and his disciples come again to Jerusalem on this third day. Jesus "was walking in the temple" and thus continuing to demonstrate his authority over it. Three groups of Jewish leaders, the chief priests, the scribes and the elders, approach Jesus as he is walking in the temple. The chief priests and the scribes represent those who are seeking "how to destroy him" after hearing of his condemnation of the temple (11:18). That they are now joined by "the elders" recalls Jesus' first prediction of his passion, according to which it is precisely these three groups of Jewish leaders who will reject Jesus and have him put to death (8:31). This means that their coming to Jesus now is to be viewed as part of their malicious plot to eliminate him as a threat to their own authority (11:27).

With hostile intent the Jewish leaders demand that Jesus tell them the quality ("by what authority") and origin ("who gave you") of his "authority" to do "these things," the things Jesus has done (11:1–11, 15–17) and is still doing (11:27) in the temple, indicative of his claim to authority over it. This double demand of the Jewish leaders, with its implication that Jesus is without authority because they know he has not been authorized by them, represents their attempt to exercise and demonstrate their superior authority. The reader, of course, knows the divine quality and origin of Jesus' authority (1:22, 27; 2:10) as the "one who comes in the name of the Lord" (11:9). The question is how Jesus will now demonstrate this to the opposing Jewish leaders (11:28).

**b. *11:29–30* Jesus asks them about the origin of John's baptism.**

Already beginning to illustrate his superiority, Jesus reverses the situation and asserts himself as the questioner rather than the questioned. He informs his opponents that he will ask them "one question." Framed by his own double demand to them, "answer me" (11:29, 30), indicating that he is the one in authority, Jesus says that he will tell them "by what authority" he does "these things" regarding the temple, if they tell him whether the baptism of John was of divine or human origin. In demanding that the Jewish leaders take a position on the authority of John's baptism, Jesus is indirectly enabling them to realize the correct answer to their own questions about the origin of Jesus' authority, since, as the reader knows, John's baptism of repentance was authorized by God as a preparation for the "way" of Jesus, the "stronger one" to come after John with the divine authority to "baptize with the Holy Spirit" as God's beloved Son (1:2–11). If the Jewish leaders will correctly answer the question of the divine origin of John's authority, they will be forced to confess the divine authority of Jesus.

### c. *11:31–33* They plead ignorance and Jesus refuses an answer.

As the Jewish leaders discuss Jesus' powerful question among themselves, they realize that Jesus has placed them in a dilemma. They perceive that if they say that John's baptism was of heavenly origin, they indict themselves for not believing him (11:31). Their fear of being discredited by the crowd who considered John to be truly a "prophet" and hence one sent by God's authority prevents them from saying that John's baptism was of human origin (11:32). Unwilling to either deny or affirm the divine origin of John's baptism, the Jewish leaders insincerely admit "we do not know." In allowing them to admit their inability to distinguish between divine and human authority, Jesus has cleverly disclosed their inadequacy to question his authority, so that he need not tell them "by what authority" he does "these things" in the temple. Jesus has thus masterfully exercised and demonstrated his own superior, divine authority over the Jewish leaders who stubbornly refuse to acknowledge and believe in the divine origin of John's baptism and hence of Jesus' authority (11:33).

### 2. MARK 11:27-33 AS MODEL FOR ACTION

Jesus' demonstration of his superior, divine authority over the Jewish leaders responsible for the inadequate worship of the Jerusalem temple calls us to place our faith in the divine authority of Jesus to enable us to offer authentic worship by becoming the communal household of God which prays effectively with a complete confidence in God's power to answer our prayers and with forgiveness toward all others (11:20–25). In fulfilling our purpose of being a community of authentic worship, we are to follow the example of Jesus by relying upon the authoritative power God will grant us through prayer to withstand opposition. The stubborn refusal of the Jewish leaders to acknowledge the divine authority of John and Jesus advises us to examine our willingness to recognize and submit to God's sovereign authority over our lives by undergoing the personal conversion John the Baptist urges so that we may faithfully follow Jesus on his "way" to suffering, death and resurrection.

## F. Mark 12:1–12: Jesus' Parable about Wicked Tenants Causes the Jewish Leaders Trying To Arrest Him To Leave

[1]Then he began to speak to them in parables. "A man planted a vineyard, put a hedge around it, dug a wine press and built a tower. Then he leased it to tenant farmers and went on a journey. [2]At the proper time he sent a servant to the tenants to acquire from them some of the fruit of the vineyard. [3]But seizing him they beat him and sent him away empty-handed. [4]Again he sent them another servant, and that one they beat over the head and treated shamefully. [5]He sent yet another, and that one they killed; and many others, some they beat, others they killed. [6]He had still one other, a beloved son. He sent him to them last of all, saying, 'They will respect my son.' [7]But those tenants said to one another, 'This is the heir. Come, let us kill him, and the inheritance will be ours.' [8]So they seized him and killed him, and threw him out of the vineyard. [9]What then will the owner of the vineyard do? He will come, put the tenants to death, and give the vineyard to others. [10]Have you not read this scripture passage:
    'The stone which the builders rejected
      has become the cornerstone;
    [11]by the Lord has this been done
      and it is wonderful in our eyes' (Ps 118:22–23)?"
[12]Then they were seeking to arrest him, but they feared the crowd, for they realized that he had addressed the parable to them. So they left him and went away.

### 1. MEANING OF MARK 12:1–12

#### a. *12:1–5* A man leased his vineyard to tenant farmers who beat and killed the servants he sent them.

Continuing his hostile encounter with the chief priests, scribes and elders in the temple, Jesus begins to speak to them "in parables," that is, in a more indirect and cryptic fashion, after he has refused an explicit answer to their questions about the quality and origin of his authority over the temple because of their unwillingness to acknowledge the heavenly origin of John's baptism and hence of Jesus' authority (11:27–33). In light of the purpose of speaking "to those outside in parables" (4:11), that Jesus now speaks to the Jewish leaders "in parables" means that he will only intensify and make even more evident their stubborn "blindness," "deafness," non-understanding and unwillingness to repent and believe (4:12).

Jesus then narrates a parable about a "man" who planted a "vineyard" and provided it with the care, protection and components it needs to successfully produce as he "put a hedge around it, dug a wine press and built a tower." The owner of the vineyard then leased it to "tenant farmers" and left on a journey. The expectation is that these "tenants" will pay their rent to the owner with the produce of the vineyard. The obvious allusion to the "Song of the Vineyard" in Isaiah 5:1–7 indicates that the "man" who planted the vineyard represents God and that the "vineyard" represents the "house of Israel" (Isa 5:7; Ps 80:9–10, 15–16; Jer 2:21; Hos 10:1). The "tenant farmers" would then represent the Jewish leaders responsible for guiding and enabling the chosen people of Israel to fulfill their purpose by "producing the fruit" God expects (12:1).

As expected, "at the proper time," the owner sent a "servant" to the tenants to collect from them some of the fruit of the vineyard (12:2). But instead of giving produce from the vineyard, they seized the servant, beat him and sent him away with nothing (12:3). This begins to characterize how in the biblical tradition the past leaders of Israel continually rejected, abused and killed God's prophets (1 Kgs 18:13; 2 Chr 36:15–16; Neh 9:26), who were often referred to as "servants" sent by God (Jer 7:25–26; 26:4–6; Amos 3:7; Zech 1:6). The owner (God) sent another servant (prophet) whom the tenants (Jewish leaders) simply "beat over the head and treated shamefully" (12:4). In his persistent solicitude and forbearance the owner (God) continued to send "yet another" servant (prophet) whom they killed and "many others," but the wicked tenants (Jewish leaders) continued to beat and kill them (12:5).

### b. *12:6–9* Since they killed his beloved son, the owner will destroy the tenants and give the vineyard to others.

The owner (God) had "still one other" to send, a "beloved son," representing Jesus himself whom God's heavenly voice has twice declared to be my "beloved Son" (1:11; 9:7). The owner sent his own son to the tenants "last of all," that is, as the climax to the entire line of servants (prophets), but, as God's own beloved Son, worthy of more respect than the prophets, so that the owner expects that surely "they will respect my son" (12:6). Rather than showing respect, however, the tenants were even more strongly motivated to kill and dishonor the owner's beloved son than the servants (prophets). Apparently thinking that the owner has died and that his son has come as the heir to take over the vineyard, the tenants decided among themselves to kill the beloved son so that they may have his inheritance for themselves (12:7). So the tenants seized the owner's beloved son, killed him and shamefully compounded this dishonor and total rejection by throwing him out of the vineyard, not even allowing him a proper burial within his own vineyard. This characterizes what the Jewish leaders as the "tenants" are seeking to do to Jesus as God's beloved Son (12:8).

Jesus then dramatically heightens the suspense by directly asking his listeners, the chief priests, scribes and elders, what the owner of the vineyard, who has now lost not only many servants but his beloved son, will do. Having subtly and cleverly disclosed to his opponents his knowledge of their plan to kill him, Jesus is in effect asking the Jewish leaders, the wicked "tenants," what God, the "owner" of the vineyard, will do to them after they kill Jesus, God's beloved Son. Answering his own question, Jesus sternly warns that the owner (God) himself will come, put the tenants to death, and give the "vineyard," the community of God's people whom the tenants (Jewish leaders) have misguided by killing not only God's prophets but his beloved Son, to others (12:9).

### c. *12:10–11* God made the stone the builders rejected into the cornerstone.

Continuing his reproachful warning by asking the Jewish leaders, who are certainly very familiar with their scriptures, "Have you not read this scripture passage?," Jesus boldly interprets their rejection and killing of him as part of the triumphant fulfillment of God's plan of salvation as explicitly recorded in scripture. He cites the scripture passage (Ps 118:22–23) that tells of how the people see the paradoxical and triumphant marvel the Lord God has performed by transforming a "stone" which the "builders" of a structure have "rejected" as unfit and useless for the building into the "cornerstone," the most essential and architecturally crucial component upon which the entire edifice stands. The "stone" alludes to Jesus as God's beloved Son whom the "builders," the chief priests, scribes and elders entrusted by God with the responsibility of "building" the temple into the true communal household of God, a "house of prayer for all peoples" (11:17), will "reject" (see 8:31) by killing and "throwing out of the vineyard" (12:8).[4] But by raising Jesus from the dead and exalting him to glory (8:31, 38; 9:2–4, 31; 10:34, 37) God will marvelously and triumphantly establish the "rejected stone," his beloved Son, as the crucial "cornerstone" of a new edifice or "house," the community of disciples who pray effectively with a confident trust in God and forgiveness of others (11:20–25), the new "house of prayer for all peoples." Jesus thus proclaims God's ultimate triumph over his rejection by the Jewish leaders.

### d, *12:12* The Jewish leaders seek to arrest Jesus, but fear the crowd and go away.

Although Jesus' parable has warned the Jewish leaders of their disastrous destiny if they reject and kill him, it does not, as expected (4:11–12), bring them to repentance. On the contrary, they continue their pernicious plot against him as they are "seeking to arrest him." The Jewish leaders fear, however, the crowd, who has been attracted to his teaching in the temple (11:18), because they have perceived that Jesus has directed the parable, which discloses their inadequacy to truly lead God's people to God and thus threatens their authority over the crowd, against them. Temporarily frustrated, the Jewish leaders "left him and went away."

### 2. MARK 12:1–12 AS MODEL FOR ACTION

The stubborn refusal of the Jewish leaders to repent and accept Jesus as God's beloved Son warns us of our need for continual conversion to faith in Jesus as the one authorized by God to enable us, the "others" entrusted with the "vineyard" of God's people (12:9), to fulfill our responsibility of leading and forming people into a community which "produces fruit" by achieving the purpose God expects. We are invited to marvel and rejoice in God's triumphant establishment of Jesus, the "rejected stone/son," into the crucial "cornerstone," the essential, undergirding foundation and support, for God's "house," his communal household of authentic and effective prayer embracing all peoples and cultures of the world (11:17). With Jesus as our supportive "cornerstone" we are called and empowered, by the same divine power that raised the "rejected stone" and beloved Son of God from death, to build and guide ourselves and others into the universal household of God's people by praying effectively with a total trust in the unlimited power of God and with forgiveness of others so that God may forgive us (11:20–25).

## G. Mark 12:13–17: Jesus Amazes the Pharisees and Herodians Sent To Trap Him with the Issue of Paying Taxes to Caesar

[13]Then they sent to him some Pharisees and Herodians to trap him in his speech. [14]They came and said to him, "Teacher, we know that you are sincere and do not concern yourself with anyone's opinion; for you do not regard a person's status but sincerely teach the way of God. Is it lawful to pay the census tax to Caesar or not? Should we pay or should we not pay?" [15]But knowing their hypocrisy he said to them, "Why are you testing me? Bring me a denarius to look at." [16]They brought one and he said to them, "Whose image and inscription is this?" They said to him, "Caesar's." [17]So Jesus said to them, "Repay to Caesar what belongs to Caesar and to God what belongs to God!" And they were utterly amazed at him.

### 1. MEANING OF MARK 12:13–17

#### a. *12:13–14* Pharisees and Herodians ask Jesus if it is lawful to pay taxes to Caesar.

Thwarted in their attempt to arrest Jesus by the precarious position his parable (12:1–11) has placed them in regard to the crowd (12:12), the chief priests, scribes and elders (11:27) send to Jesus "some Pharisees and Herodians," those who are likewise seeking to destroy him, "to trap him in his speech." This brings together in a united front against Jesus the various groups of Jewish authorities seeking his death (3:6; 11:18). That the Pharisees are a primarily religious group and the Herodians political suggests that the verbal "trap" may have religious and political ramifications (12:13).[5]

The Pharisees and Herodians address Jesus with what appears to be an elaborate compliment but which, because of their deceitful intentions, must be taken as a sarcastically exaggerated attempt to set up the "trap." The careful chiastic arrangement of their address, in which references to the sincerity of Jesus' teaching frame and contrast references to his refusal to be influenced by human opinion or status, intimates that their "trap" will involve a conflict between his lack of concern for human opinion or status and his sincere teaching of the "way of God":

> *a* Teacher, we know that you are sincere
> *b* and do not concern yourself with anyone's opinion;
> *b* for you do not regard a person's status

*a* but sincerely teach the way of God.

Their statement that Jesus sincerely teaches the "way of God" expresses an ironic understatement for the reader, who knows that indeed Jesus not only truly "teaches" the "way of God" in direct contrast and opposition to the Jewish leaders (1:22, 27; 11:17–18; 11:27–12:12) but also through his teaching, healing miracles and suffering, death and resurrection accomplishes the salvific "way of the Lord" God (1:2–3).

Presenting Jesus with an embarrassing and treacherous dilemma, similar to the one with which he previously denigrated the authority of the chief priests, scribes and elders (11:27–33), the Pharisees and Herodians spring their trap by asking whether "it is lawful," that is, God's will or the "way of God," to pay the "census tax," the Roman tax assessed on the basis of the census of people and property and especially hated by the Jews, to "Caesar," the Roman emperor, or not. That this is a question of what is the law or will of God in the matter of paying the Roman tax signals the beginning of a controversy or pronouncement story. Their reinforcing question, "should we pay or should we not pay?," indicates that this is no mere theoretical inquiry but a pressing practical issue. The suspense of the dilemma is whether Jesus will teach payment of the tax and thus open himself to a charge by his fellow Jews of respecting the human status of the Roman emperor over the "way of God" or whether he will teach non-payment of the tax, upholding God's authority but risking the dangerous consequences of refusing to respect the political authority of the Roman emperor and government (12:14).

**b. *12:15–16* Jesus asks them whose image is on a denarius.**

With his superior power of perception Jesus knows the "hypocrisy" of their insincere inquiry. He unmasks their devious and diabolical intentions as he begins his counter-questioning and argumentation by asking, "Why are you testing me?" (see 1:13; 8:11; 10:2). Then asserting his own authoritative control over his opponents, Jesus commands them to bring him a "denarius," the Roman coin used in paying the tax, to look at (12:15).[6] After they bring forth a denarius, Jesus acts as the masterful teacher they have complimented as he forces them to state whose image and inscription is on the Roman coin. Their correct and obvious answer, "Caesar's," increases the suspense as the reader now wonders what is the point of this dramatic demonstration with the coin (12:16).

**c. *12:17* Jesus commands them to give to God what belongs to God.**

Jesus then boldly utters the powerful aphoristic pronouncement which not only extricates him from the perilous trap of his opponents but continues to illustrate his new and authoritative teaching in the temple (11:17–18):

> "Repay to Caesar what belongs to Caesar
> and to God what belongs to God!"

The aphoristic form and parallel construction of this forceful pronouncement, which concisely contrasts "what belongs to Caesar" with "what belongs to God," directs the audience to consider the danger and difficulty of relating life to both Caesar and God. The saying prevents thinking of either separately. Political life cannot be separated from the claims of God and the religious dimension of life cannot ignore the political dimension and problems of society. The powerful pronouncement thus reminds its listeners of the possible conflict between the claims of political government and of God.[7]

But with its final and climactic emphasis upon "God" and "what belongs to God" the pronouncement clearly asserts that the claims of God embrace, overshadow and relativize the claims of the state. Answering his opponents' question about the dilemma of paying the tax, Jesus cleverly commands them "to repay to Caesar what belongs to Caesar," that is, to give back to Caesar the coins which bear his "image" and "inscription." With this witty reply involving who actually owns the coins Jesus rather flippantly minimizes the concern for paying the tax. They are simply to give to Caesar the coins that belong to him in the first place. Thus devaluing the concern to pay the tax, Jesus, with an acute and astute variation on the same words, issues the overriding command to repay "to God what belongs to God," that is, to give to God what in accord with the biblical tradition bears his "image" and "likeness," namely, the totality of the human person (Gen 1:26–27). Whereas Caesar's claims are limited to the coins that belong to him, the claims of God are not so limited. Every human being created by God belongs to God and so Jesus' powerful pronouncement appeals for his listeners and all human beings to give to God their complete allegiance.

With his sharp and brilliant pronouncement Jesus has masterfully extricated himself from the dilemma with which his opponents have tried to trap him. By teaching the payment of the tax Jesus cannot be delivered to the Roman authorities as a political rebel. But neither can he thereby be accused by his fellow Jews of respecting human and political status over the religious authority of God, for he indeed truly teaches the "way of God" by urging his audience to submit the totality of their persons to the absolute claim of the sovereign God, which embraces and surpasses the claim of political government.

Overpowered by the superior intelligence and authority of Jesus' teaching and defeated in their attempt to trap him in his speech, the Pharisees and Herodians "were utterly amazed at him." But the threatening tension of their opposition lingers as their amazement does not lead them to repent and submit to the "way of God" Jesus truly teaches.[8]

### 2. MARK 12:13–17 AS MODEL FOR ACTION

Jesus' brilliant teaching of the "way of God" in the temple, according to which God's absolute claim on human lives and the world surpasses the limited claim of political government, provides us with a model to follow and promote as we become God's true communal household of prayer for all peoples (11:17). With its power to utterly amaze us Jesus' compelling command to repay "to God what belongs to God" exhorts us to submit ourselves totally and unreservedly to the sovereign dominion of God, an absolute dominion which embraces and exceeds all other claims for our allegiance, even those of ruling political authorities. By teaching complete dedication to the sovereign claim of God over us and the world as the true "way of God," Jesus reveals his own attitude of total submission to the will of God. It is his attitude of complete trust in God that enables him to accomplish the salvific "way of the Lord" (1:2–3) by undergoing suffering, death and resurrection, and that serves as an example to empower us to follow this "way" of Jesus by likewise submitting ourselves completely to the will of God.

## H. Mark 12:18–27: Jesus Teaches the Sadducees That God Will Raise the Dead to Life

[18]Then Sadducees, who say there is no resurrection, came to him and put a question to him, saying, [19]"Teacher, Moses wrote for us, 'If someone's brother dies, and leaves behind a wife but does not leave a child, his brother must take the wife and raise up descendants for his brother' (Deut 25:5). [20]Now there were seven brothers. The first took a wife but died and left no descendants. [21]So the second took her and died, leaving no descendants, and the third likewise. [22]And the seven left no descendants. Last of all the woman also died. [23]At the resurrection when they arise whose wife will she be? For the seven had her as wife." [24]Jesus said to them "Are you not mistaken for this reason, that you know neither the scriptures nor the power of God? [25]For when they rise from the dead, they neither marry nor are given in

marriage, but are like angels in heaven. [26]As for the dead being raised, have you not read in the Book of Moses, in the passage about the bush, how God spoke to him, saying, 'I am the God of Abraham, the God of Isaac, and the God of Jacob' (Exod 3:6)? [27]He is not the God of the dead but of the living! You are greatly mistaken."

### 1. MEANING OF MARK 12:18–27

**a.  *12:18–23* Sadducees ridicule resurrection with an example of seven dead brothers who had married the same woman.**

Another group of Jewish religious leaders, the priestly and aristocratic "Sadducees," whom Mark characterizes simply as those "who say there is no resurrection," approach Jesus while he is teaching in the temple and question him.[9] That they come to Jesus after the previous antagonistic groups of Jewish authorities, the chief priests, scribes and elders (11:27) as well as the Pharisees and Herodians (12:13), suggests that they have come to likewise challenge his authoritative teaching. And their denial of the resurrection from the dead indicates the issue of their controversy, which implicitly conflicts with the salvific "way" of Jesus, according to which he must suffer, die and *"after three days rise"* (8:31; 9:31; 10:34; see also 9:9–10) (12:18).

The Sadducees address Jesus as "teacher," echoing the address of the deceitful Pharisees and Herodians (12:14) and further indicating that they are challenging the "teaching" of Jesus. They begin the controversy story with a reference to the practice of levirate marriage which "Moses wrote for us" in scripture. It stipulates that if someone's brother dies childless, he must take the widow as wife and raise up descendants for his dead brother in order to continue his name (Deut 25:5–6; Gen 38:8) (12:19). Having established a scriptural basis explaining how one wife could be legitimately married to more than one husband, the Sadducees proceed to mock the very idea of resurrection from the dead with a ludicrous example designed to illustrate its utter absurdity. According to their example, after the first of seven brothers died childless, each of the rest in turn took the wife to raise up descendants for the dead brother but died childless himself. Finally the woman herself died (12:20–22). Confident that such a ridiculous example has exposed the idea of resurrection as utter folly, the Sadducees sarcastically ask Jesus whose wife the woman will be "at the resurrection when they arise," since all seven brothers had her as wife (12:23). And so, with this provocative mockery of resurrection the Sadducees have intrigued the reader by apparently presenting a formidable challenge to Jesus' teaching authority and ability.

**b. *12:24–27* Jesus exposes their error with his pronouncement that God is not the God of the dead but of the living.**

Jesus responds to the Sadducees' ridicule of resurrection with his own counter-question, by which he accuses them of being "mistaken" because they "know neither the scriptures," although they have quoted them to begin their mockery, "nor the power of God," to which they have neglected to make any mention (12:24). Jesus then subverts their ridicule of resurrection by asserting that when people rise from the dead, there is no question of them being married. In the resurrection men "neither marry" nor are women "given in marriage." Rather they will be transformed from earthly beings into heavenly beings and become "like angels in heaven."[10] In other words, it is not the idea of resurrection that is absurd, but the Sadducees' conception of it. They wrongly think that resurrection from the dead includes such limited and earthly categories as marriage, and fail to realize that resurrection is a divine phenomenon transcending our human understanding (12:25).

Having diverted the ridicule of the Sadducees' question about marriage for the resurrected back upon them, Jesus then demonstrates how they do not know the scriptures which point to the dead being raised. Countering their mischievous quotation of what "Moses wrote for us" (12:18), Jesus reminds them of the dramatic scriptural passage about the burning bush in the "Book of Moses" where God revealed his identity to Moses by proclaiming that he is the God of the promises to the patriarchs: "I am the God of Abraham, the God of Isaac, and the God of Jacob" (Exod 3:6) (12:26). Since Abraham, Isaac and Jacob were already dead when God uttered this to Moses, it indicates "the power of God" (12:24) to raise them from the dead, because, as Jesus authoritatively pronounces, God "is not the God of the dead but of the living!" In other words, since God in his covenantal fidelity does not promise to be the saving God and deliverer of those who are "dead" but of those who are "living," Abraham, Isaac and Jacob cannot remain dead but will live through the power of God, so that there is a resurrection of the dead! Reinforcing and intensifying the charge with which he began his response to the Sadducees (12:24), Jesus concludes by advising them: "You are greatly mistaken" (12:27).

Jesus' powerful proclamation that God "is not the God of the dead but of the living!" serves as the climactic and emphatic pronouncement of the controversy story, which illustrates the superiority of Jesus' teaching of the resurrection over the Sadducees' mocking challenge to reduce it to absurdity. Jesus has called the Sadducees to correct their false and ridiculous way of thinking about the resurrection in their inadequate, earthly terms and to open themselves to the transcendent, life-giving power of God. That God "is not the God of the dead but of the living!" cuts with a double edge: It summons the Sadducees away from a morbid concern with what happens to those who have died and urges them to place their hopeful faith in the God of the "living"—those presently living and who will still live in the future—assured that God has the power to raise those who have died to a new and glorious life.

### 2. MARK 12:18–27 AS MODEL FOR ACTION

Through his authoritative teaching of the Sadducees Jesus invites us to an authentic and wholesome way of thinking about resurrection of the dead by abandoning the often silly and morbid concerns, curiosities and conjectures of our narrow human categories and realizing that resurrection is a divine phenomenon exceeding our capacity to fully understand it. Jesus teaches that the authoritative scriptures and the life-giving power of God assures us that God will raise the dead to new life. Jesus' vigorous pronouncement that God "is not the God of the dead but of the living!" encourages us to continue to follow the "way" of Jesus with confidence in God's marvelous power to raise him from the dead. As we form God's communal household of effective prayer embracing all peoples (11:17) and submit ourselves to God's sovereignty (12:17), we are urged to live our lives with faith and hope in the "God of the living," the God who has the mighty power not only to sustain us while we are living but to raise us to new life after we have died.

## I. Mark 12:28–34: After Jesus Answers a Scribe's Question about the Greatest Commandment, No One Dares to Question Him

> [28]Then one of the scribes came up and heard them disputing, and seeing that he answered them well, asked him, "Which commandment is the first of all?" [29]Jesus answered, "The first is this: 'Hear, O Israel! The Lord our God, the Lord is One! [30]And you shall love the Lord your God with all your heart, and with all your soul, and with all your mind, and with all your strength'

(Deut 6:4–5). [31]The second is this: 'You shall love your neighbor as yourself' (Lev 19:18). There is no other commandment greater than these." [32]Then the scribe said to him, "Well said, teacher! You are right in saying, 'He is One and there is no other than he' (Deut 6:4; 4:35). [33]And 'to love him with all your heart, and with all your understanding, and with all your strength' (Deut 6:5), and 'to love your neighbor as yourself' (Lev 19:18) is worth more than all whole burnt offerings and sacrifices." [34]And when Jesus saw that he answered with understanding, he said to him, "You are not far from the kingdom of God." And no one dared to ask him any more questions.

### 1. MEANING OF MARK 12:28–34

#### a. *12:28* A scribe asks Jesus which is the greatest commandment.

An individual scribe comes up and hears Jesus disputing with the Sadducees in the temple. Although belonging to the group of scribes, who are opposing Jesus' teaching authority (11:27–28) and seeking to destroy him (11:18), that this scribe is impressed with how "well" Jesus has answered the challenge of the Sadducees indicates that his approach is friendly and that he is favorably disposed toward the teaching authority of Jesus. His question to Jesus about which of all of the many Jewish commandments of the Torah, God's law, is the "first" or greatest of all, then, is intended not as a hostile trap (12:13) or a mockery of Jesus' teaching (12:18–23), but as a sincere inquiry. The scribe, himself a professional scholar of the Torah, genuinely wants Jesus, whom he recognizes as an authoritative and competent teacher, to tell him which of all the commandments sums up the essence and spirit of God's will and is therefore the most important to perform.

#### b. *12:29–31* Jesus states that the two greatest commandments are to love God totally and one's neighbor as oneself.

Jesus informs the scribe that the "first" or greatest commandment is contained in the familiar *Shema* ("hear") (Deut 6:4–5), which Jews recited regularly in their daily worship. It begins with the rousing command, "Hear, O Israel!," calling for the people of Israel to pay particular and wholehearted attention to the words that follow. Exclaiming that "the Lord our God, the Lord is One!," it proclaims the utter uniqueness and absolute sovereignty of the God of Israel as the "One" and only "Lord" worthy of undivided devotion (12:29). Because of the uniqueness and sovereignty of the One Lord God each person is commanded to "love" him with the totality of one's being in a complete and unreserved fashion. That this devoted love for the One Lord God must be total and complete is rhetorically reinforced through a quadruple repetition in which the word "all" is accentuated and followed by a fourfold description of one's total personal capacities (heart-soul-mind-strength) (12:30):

> And you shall love the Lord your God
> with all your heart,
> and with all your soul,
> and with all your mind,
> and with all your strength.

Jesus then goes beyond the scribe's request by adding a "second" commandment, namely, that "you shall love your neighbor as yourself" (Lev 19:18). In correspondence to the first commandment, the words "as yourself" express the total and complete manner with which one is to extend loving care and concern to one's fellow human being. Jesus explains that there is no other commandment "greater" or more important than these two, which assert the fundamental attitude of love toward God and neighbor necessary to do all that God commands. Jesus' bringing together of these two otherwise separate commandments of "love" and designating them both together as the greatest commandments signifies that true love and authentic worship of God are not complete without love of neighbor and that genuine love of neighbor must include love and worship of the unique and sovereign Lord God (12:31).

### c. *12:32-33* The scribe agrees and adds that love of God and neighbor is worth more than all temple sacrifices.

As he had been impressed with how "well" Jesus had answered the Sadducees (12:28), so now the scribe is impressed with how "well" Jesus, the "teacher," has answered his question. He approves what Jesus has taught and demonstrates his understanding of it by repeating and elaborating upon it. Agreeing with Jesus that God is the unique and sovereign Lord, the scribe admits that God "is One" (Deut 6:4) and further proclaims his uniqueness: "there is no other than he" (Deut 4:35) (12:32). He reinforces Jesus' repeated emphasis upon a completely committed love of God with the totality of one's person by his own triple repetition in which an accentuated "all" is followed by a threefold description of one's total personal capacities (heart-understanding-strength):

to love him
with all your heart,
and with all your understanding,
and with all your strength.

But after approvingly repeating Jesus' second commandment, "to love your neighbor as yourself" (Lev 19:18), the scribe pronounces that Jesus' double commandment of total love of God and neighbor is more valuable than "all" of the "whole burnt offerings" and other "sacrifices" performed in the temple cult (see 1 Sam 15:22; Hos 6:6). By subordinating the entire sacrificial cult of the temple, described with a generalizing "all" of its various offerings and sacrifices, to Jesus' double commandment of love of God and neighbor, the scribe has in effect called into question the worth and adequacy of worship in the Jerusalem temple. His implicit denigration of temple worship, made more poignant by the fact that he is listening to Jesus' teaching while in the temple (11:27), coincides with and further develops Jesus' earlier condemnation of the temple for failing to achieve its purpose of becoming God's "house of prayer for all peoples" (11:17). A completely committed and total love of God and neighbor rather than temple sacrifice makes possible authentic and effective worship of the One Lord God (12:33).

**d. *12:34* Jesus tells the scribe that he is not far from the kingdom of God.**

Seeing that the scribe has responded "with understanding" to his teaching in the temple, Jesus authoritatively pronounces that he is "not far from the kingdom of God." In other words, the scribe is close to experiencing and living under the final, decisive and definitive "kingdom of God," whose inauguration and establishment is the whole point of Jesus' teaching, healing, suffering, death and resurrection (1:15; 4:11, 26, 30; 9:1, 47; 10:14–15, 23–25). But Jesus' approving compliment of the scribe raises the question of what the scribe still needs to understand in order not just to come close but to enter fully into God's kingdom.

That "no one dared to ask him any more questions" serves a double narrative function: It indicates the brilliantly superior authority and power of Jesus' teaching in the temple, which has brought to a closing silence all of the previous inquiries of his teaching in and authority over the Jerusalem temple by various groups of Jewish leaders (11:27–12:34). And it sets the stage for Jesus himself now to take the initiative and answer the engaging question he has implicitly raised as to what teaching is still needed for the scribe (and reader) to fully understand and enter into the kingdom of God.

### 2. MARK 12:28–34 AS MODEL FOR ACTION

This vivacious exchange between Jesus and an intelligent scribe summons us to combine a wholehearted and completely committed love of the sovereign Lord God with a sincere and genuine love for our fellow human beings. By submitting ourselves to God as that which belongs to him (12:17), by realizing that God is a God of the living with power to raise the dead to life (12:24–27), and by loving God and our neighbor with the totality of our beings (12:29–31), we can achieve our purpose of becoming God's community of authentic worship and effective prayer inclusive of all peoples (11:17), which surpasses the inadequacy of temple sacrifices (12:33). For our worship to be authentic and our prayer effective, we must combine our faith in the unlimited power of God to answer our prayers (11:22–24) with a totally devoted, undivided and unreserved love for our sovereign Lord God. And for us to become God's true household of prayer embracing all peoples and cultures of the world, we must combine our forgiveness of others (11:25) with a comprehensive care and concern for all our neighbors.

## J. Mark 12:35–37: The Great Crowd Gladly Hears Jesus Question the Scribes' Assertion That the Christ Is the Son of David

[35]Then responding Jesus said, while teaching in the temple, "How can the scribes say that the Christ is the Son of David?
[36]David himself, inspired by the Holy Spirit, said:

'The Lord said to my Lord,

"Sit at my right hand,

until I place your enemies under your feet" ' (Ps 110:1).
[37]David himself calls him 'Lord'; so how is he his son?" And the great crowd heard him gladly.

### 1. MEANING OF MARK 12:35–37

#### a. *12:35* Jesus asks how the scribes can say that the Christ is the Son of David.

Jesus responds to the previous silence he has created and will presumably indicate what is still lacking for the sincere scribe to enter fully into the kingdom of God (12:34). Since no specific group or individual is named as Jesus' audience, he is apparently addressing the people or crowd in general "while teaching in the temple." The explicit notice that Jesus is still teaching in the temple reminds the reader of his authority and "lordship" over the Jerusalem temple, which he triumphally entered as the "lord" who comes in the name of the Lord God (11:1–11) and which his "teaching" condemned as a place of inadequate worship (11:15–19). He is thus still demonstrating the content of his authoritative teaching as superior to that of the Jewish leadership (11:27–12:34).

After having been variously questioned by others, Jesus takes the initiative and presents his own question. He asks how "the scribes" can say that "the Christ" is the "Son of David." By questioning a doctrine of "the scribes" (see 9:11–12), Jesus is not only continuing to demonstrate the superiority of his teaching to that of his scribal opponents (1:22; 2:6, 16; 3:22; 7:1, 5; 8:31; 9:11, 14; 10:33; 11:18, 27), but is indirectly indicating what the sincere "scribe" still needs to understand in order to enter the kingdom of God (12:34). Although on the surface Jesus is questioning whether the theoretical "Christ" or messiah is the "Son of David," the reader knows that this is more than a theoretical question and that he is actually asking whether he himself, already affirmed as "the Christ" (1:1; 8:29; 9:41), is the "Son of David."[11] Jesus is thus calling into question the correctness of Bartimaeus' acclamation of him as "Son of David" (10:47–48) and of the crowd's expectation that he will establish "the kingdom of our father David" (11:9–10).

### b. *12:36–37* David himself calls him "Lord."

Continuing his provocative inquiry, Jesus explains that David himself, the traditional author of the Psalms, spoke under the inspiration of the Holy Spirit and therefore with divine authority when he said that "the Lord," that is, God himself, commanded "my Lord," that is, the Christ or messiah, that he should sit enthroned at the powerful and authoritative "right hand" of God, while God himself gives him a triumphant victory over his "enemies" by placing them in submission "under your feet" (Ps 110:1). Jesus thus not only subtly implies that as the Christ he is the one David calls "Lord," but also indirectly proclaims his future enthronement at God's right hand in heavenly triumph over his enemies (see 12: 10–11) (12:36).

Jesus then brings his penetrating query to a pointed climax by asking that if David himself calls the Christ "Lord," then "how" or in what sense is the Christ David's Son? Jesus' question projects a double meaning for the reader: How can one whom David calls "Lord" be David's *son?;* and how can one whom David calls "Lord" be *David's* son? This double-edged question thus invites the reader to reflect on both the lordship and the sonship of Jesus. It leads the reader not only to conclude that "the Christ," and therefore Jesus himself, is more appropriately understood as the "Lord" rather than the "Son" of David ("how is he his *son?*"), but also to realize whose "Son" Jesus as "Lord" really is, if not David's ("how is he *his* son?"), namely the beloved "Son of God" (1:1, 11; 3:11; 5:7; 9:7; 12:6). In other words, Jesus' intriguing question causes his listeners to realize that as the Christ he is more appropriately understood as the "Lord" rather than the "Son" of David, and as the messianic Lord who is the Son of "God" rather than the Son of "David."

And so Jesus has indirectly indicated what the sincere scribe still needs to understand and acknowledge in order to enter the kingdom of God, namely, that Jesus is the messianic "Lord" and "Son of God" who thus greatly surpasses the expectations of a messianic "Son of David." But rather than contradicting the absolute sovereignty of God as the "One" and only "Lord" worthy of total love and allegiance, as both Jesus and the scribe have asserted (12:28–34), the messianic lordship of Jesus coincides with the sovereign lordship of God. Jesus' probing question prods his audience to understand that as the "Lord" he is also the beloved "Son of God" who accomplishes the salvific "way" of the "Lord" God (1:2–3) and whom the "Lord" God will enthrone as messianic "Lord" and Son at his right hand in triumph over his enemies.

Although not necessarily indicative that they understand, that "the great crowd heard him gladly" underlines their favorable disposition to the teaching of Jesus in the temple as a new and authoritative teaching more attractive than that of the scribes (see 1:22, 27). But the great crowd's approving attraction to Jesus continues to express the tension that Jesus' teaching has aroused between the amiable crowd and their hostile leaders, who are seeking to kill him (11:18, 32; 12:12) (12:37).

## 2. MARK 12:35-37 AS MODEL FOR ACTION

Jesus' provocative question directing us to his lordship and divine sonship as the Christ invites us to enter into and experience the kingdom of God (12:34) in our lives, a kingdom whose divine power far surpasses our human hopes, by submitting ourselves to the messianic lordship of Jesus as part of our total devotion to the One Lord God (12:17, 26, 28–34). As we follow the "way" of Jesus through suffering and death, we may look forward to participating in the glorious triumph and heavenly exaltation over all opposition and enemies that our sovereign Lord God has granted Jesus as our messianic "Lord" and God's beloved "Son" enthroned at God's right hand with divine power and authority.

## K. Mark 12:38–40: Jesus Warns against and Denounces the Hypocrisy of the Scribes

³⁸And in his teaching he said, "Beware of the scribes, who like to go around in long robes and accept greetings in the market-places, ³⁹the best seats in synagogues, and places of honor at banquets. ⁴⁰They devour the houses of widows and as a pretense pray at length. They will receive a most severe condemnation."

### 1. MEANING OF MARK 12:38–40

**a. *12:38–39* Jesus warns against the self-serving behavior of the scribes.**

Jesus is still publicly teaching in the temple the great crowd which is gladly listening to him after he has demonstrated the deficiency of scribal teaching about the messiah (12:37). In the course of his authoritative "teaching" Jesus warns the people not to imitate the self-serving behavior of the scribes. After having indicated the need to realize that as the Christ he is the messianic "Lord" and "Son of God," Jesus indirectly indicates what kind of behavior the sincere scribe and others need to avoid in order to fully enter into the kingdom of God (12:34).

The scribes' self-serving desire for societal distinction, honor, respect and privilege over their fellow Jews is illustrated by their fondness for parading around in "long robes" of distinction which call attention to themselves as scribes, for greetings of respect in the public marketplaces, and for privileged places of honor in synagogues and at social banquets. This proud and self-centered attitude stands in stark contrast to the humble and selfless attitude Jesus himself exemplifies and calls his disciples to imitate. Jesus earlier stated that as the Son of Man he "did not come to be served but to serve and to give his life as a ransom for many" (10:45). He urged his disciples, concerned with their own greatness and privileged status (9:33–37; 10:35–45), to imitate his selfless service by becoming the "last" (9:35) and the "servant" (9:35; 10:43) and the "slave" (10:44) of all. He directed them to follow him in embracing the lowliness and humility of a "child" (9:36–37; 10:13–16) as the attitude of those to whom the kingdom of God belongs (10:14): "Amen I say to you, whoever does not receive the kingdom of God like a child will not enter it" (10:15). Child-like humility and selfless service of others rather than the scribal desire for self-serving honor and privilege is the kind of behavior necessary for the sincere scribe (and reader) who is "not far from the kingdom of God" (12:34) to enter into it.

### b. *12:40* Jesus denounces the selfish conduct and phony worship of the scribes.

The scribes also take for themselves and rapaciously "devour" the "houses" or property of "widows," those who, together with orphans and foreigners, represent in the biblical tradition the lowliest and most needy members of society, worthy of special care and protection.[12] But abusing their privileged position, the scribes selfishly rob widows rather than assist them. To their failure to provide for needy widows the scribes add their unauthentic worship. They "pray at length" not with a sincere devotion to God but merely "as a pretense" demonstrating their false piety. The scribes' combination of ruthlessly robbing widows with phony worship of God sharply contradicts Jesus' double commandment of love, which calls for a combination of a completely committed love and devotion to God with a total love and care for others (12:28–34). As the sincere scribe recognized, implementing the double commandment of love of God and neighbor enables a true worship which surpasses the temple's sacrificial cult (12:33). That the scribes devour the houses of widows and pray insincerely thus further illustrates their failure to bring about authentic worship in the temple by making it God's "house of prayer for all peoples" rather than a "den of robbers" (11:17). Their false praying contrasts the effective praying and true worship Jesus enjoins his disciples to exhibit by having faith in the unlimited power of God and forgiveness for others (11:22–25).

Reinforcing his stern warning for the people to strictly avoid the selfish conduct and fake worship of the scribes, Jesus authoritatively advises that "they will receive a most severe condemnation" from God in the last judgment.[13]

### 2. MARK 12:38–40 AS MODEL FOR ACTION

Jesus' reproachful warning against the conduct of the Jewish scribes serves as a negative example calling us to avoid such self-serving behavior toward others, and insincere worship of God. In order to fully experience the kingdom of God in our lives we are urged to shun the desire for social honors and privileges and to adopt the humility typical of a child (10:13–

16) and the selfless service of others manifested by Jesus (10:45). And to become God's community of effective prayer inclusive of all peoples (11:17) we are summoned to practice the double commandment of love by combining a wholehearted and sincere devotion to God with a committed care and concern for others (12:28–34), especially the most needy (such as widows) among us.

## L. Mark 12:41–44: To His Disciples Jesus Praises a Poor Widow's Donation to the Temple Treasury

> [41]Then he sat down opposite the treasury and observed how the crowd put money into the treasury. Many rich people put in large sums. [42]A poor widow also came and put in two small coins worth a few cents. [43]Summoning his disciples, he said to them, "Amen I say to you, this poor widow put in more than all those contributing to the treasury! [44]For they have all contributed from their surplus, but she, from her poverty, has contributed all she had, her whole living."

### 1. MEANING OF MARK 12:41–44

#### a. *12:41–42* Jesus observes a poor widow giving a few cents to the temple treasury in contrast to the large sums of the rich.

Still in the temple Jesus sits down opposite the temple "treasury," the place which contained the receptacles for collecting the contributions used to operate the temple cult, and watches how the crowd are placing their monetary contributions into the treasury. These contributions, since they supported the temple worship, were themselves acts of devotion to God. In contrast to the "many rich people" who were contributing, a "poor widow" comes and, in contrast to the "large sums" of the rich, puts in the treasury only "two small coins, worth a few cents."[14] That the "poor widow," one of the group whose property the scribes "devour" (12:40), puts in both of her "two" small coins without holding one back for herself underlines the totality of her offering.[15]

#### b. *12:43–44* The poor widow gives more than everyone—her whole living.

Jesus then calls to himself his disciples, who have accompanied him throughout his teaching in the temple, and draws their attention to the contribution of this poor widow. Beginning with the solemn words, "Amen I say to you," which underline the importance and truth of what he will say, Jesus pronounces the shocking paradox that this poor widow has put in "more" than "all" those contributing to the temple treasury! (12:43). Explaining this paradoxical reversal of values, Jesus asserts that while all the others have contributed out of their "surplus" wealth, this poor widow, out of her "poverty," has made a total contribution by giving "all" she had, that is, her "whole" living. With his divine authority Jesus thus teaches his disciples that the worth of the poor widow's contribution, although of extremely small monetary value, astoundingly surpasses, as an act of devotion to God, the greater monetary value of "all" the others who contributed, because her contribution is a *total* offering to God whereas those of all the others are only partial (12:44).

The poor widow's total offering to God serves as an outstanding example which Jesus has pointed out not only for his disciples but for the sincere scribe, who is "not far from the kingdom of God" (12:34), to imitate. In ironical contrast to the arrogant, selfish and greedy scribes who "devour the houses of *widows*" (12:38–40), the humble poverty of this poor *widow* indicates another quality which facilitates entrance into the kingdom of God. The sharp contrast between her "poverty" and the "surplus" wealth of the rich recalls how difficult it is for the rich to make the total commitment necessary to enter God's kingdom (10:17–31). Earlier Jesus had amazed his disciples with his warning of "how difficult it is for those who have wealth to enter the kingdom of God!" Indeed, he asserted, "it is easier for a camel to pass through the eye of a needle than for a rich person to enter the kingdom of God" (10:23–25). The partial contributions to God by the rich in the temple treasury confirm these words of Jesus. The poverty of the widow reminds the disciples and the sincere scribe of their need for detachment from material possessions in order to make the total commitment to God necessary to enter his kingdom.

The *totality* of the poor widow's offering serves as a concrete example illustrating the total and complete commitment to God demanded by the double commandment of love that Jesus stated and the sincere scribe reinforced (12:28–34). That the poor widow contributed "all" she had, her "whole" living, echoes the sevenfold repetition of the total manner by which one is to love God with "all" one's being:

> *12:30* And you shall love the Lord your God
>      with *all* your heart,
>    and with *all* your soul,
>    and with *all* your mind,
>    and with *all* your strength.
> *12:33*    with *all* your heart,
>    and with *all* your understanding,
>    and with *all* your strength.

*12:44* she has contributed (to God)
     *all* she had,
     her *whole* living.

The sincere scribe correctly affirmed the requirement of total love and dedication to God and thus "is not far from the kingdom of God" (12:34). To fully enter the kingdom of God he must now actually practice what he has proclaimed by imitating the poor widow's wholehearted commitment to God.

As addressed to the disciples, the total contribution of the poor widow illustrates the radically trusting faith in God's power that Jesus has earlier urged his disciples to have (11:22–24). Just as the poor widow's radical faith enables her to offer an act of total devotion to God which is more valuable than "all those contributing to the treasury" in the temple (12:43), so the radical faith of the disciples will enable them to pray effectively (11:24) as God's true household of prayer inclusive of all peoples (11:17) and to commit themselves totally to God as an act of authentic worship which "is worth more than all whole burnt offerings and sacrifices" in the temple (12:33).[16]

### 2. MARK 12:41–44 AS MODEL FOR ACTION

The poor widow's admirable donation to God of "*all* she had, her *whole* living," presents us with a triple model to imitate: First, the humble *poverty* of the poor widow persuades us to detach ourselves from material wealth in order to dedicate ourselves unreservedly to God and thus experience his kingship in our lives. Secondly, the astounding and absolute *totality* of the poor widow's offering challenges us not just to recognize the commandment for a totally committed love and devotion of God but to take the risk of actually putting it into practice. Thirdly, the radical *faith* of the poor widow urges us to place our trust and faith in God in a complete and wholehearted manner, so that we may offer authentic worship by praying with effectiveness as God's community of prayer open to all peoples of the world.

## M. Mark 13:1–2: Leaving the Temple Jesus Foretells Its Destruction to One of His Disciples

[1]As he was coming out of the temple one of his disciples said to him, "Look, teacher, what stones and what buildings!" [2]But

Jesus said to him, "Do you see these great buildings? There will not be left here a stone upon a stone that will not be thrown down."

### 1. MEANING OF MARK 13:1-2

#### a. *13:1* A disciple points out the beauty of the temple to Jesus.

After having triumphantly entered Jerusalem and observed everything in the temple, Jesus left it on the first day (11:1–11). And after having dramatically condemned the temple for failing to achieve its God-willed purpose, he likewise left it on the second day (11:15–19). Now, after having authoritatively taught in the temple the authentic way of relating to God, but with continued opposition from the Jewish leaders (11:27–12:44), Jesus continues the movement of his salvific "way" as he "comes out" of the temple and leaves it for the third and climactic time.

As Jesus is leaving the temple precincts, "one of his disciples," impressed with the magnificence of the temple's external and physical beauty, exclaims to Jesus, "Look, teacher, what stones and what buildings!" Such fascination with the striking exterior splendor of the temple stands in ironic contrast to what Jesus has just taught within it. Not only has Jesus condemned the temple for being a "den of robbers" rather than God's "house of prayer for all peoples" (11:17), but "one of the scribes," in ironic contrast to "one of his disciples," has proclaimed that the double commandment of total love of God and neighbor surpasses the entire sacrificial cult of the temple (12:28–34). And, moreover, Jesus has just pointed out to the disciples that the poor widow's radical faith in donating her whole meager living to God is worth more than all other monetary contributions to the temple's treasury which maintains its great buildings (12:41–44). Jesus' sharp denigration of the temple's worship clashes with the terribly incongruous exclamation of its external beauty by this disciple, who obviously has not understood the significance and implications of Jesus' teaching in the temple.

#### b. *13:2* Jesus predicts the total destruction of the temple.

Acknowledging the naive disciple's awe over the external grandeur of the temple's buildings, "Do you see these great buildings?," Jesus makes explicit the implications of his previous condemnation and denigration of the temple by powerfully and prophetically predicting with his divine authority its complete and utter destruction: "There will not be left here a stone upon a stone that will not be thrown down." The emphatic repetition of the negatives, "*will not be* left/*will not be* thrown down," rhetorically reinforces the certainty, decisiveness and totality of the temple's devastation. The magnificent "stones" and great "buildings" which have impressed the disciple will be completely dismantled without "a stone upon a stone."[17]

Jesus thus warns this overawed disciple away from attachment to the physical beauty of the Jerusalem temple, which will ultimately be annihilated. More important than the external splendor of the temple is the teaching of Jesus in the temple, according to which the interior disposition of total faith in and love for God, as declared by the sincere scribe (12:33) and admirably exemplified by the poor widow (12:43), far exceeds the worship of the temple. The temple will be destroyed because it is not constructed by God upon the foundation "stone" of the person and teaching of Jesus. Not one "stone" will be left upon another "stone" among the great "buildings" of the temple complex because the "builders," the Jewish leaders, have rejected the "stone," Jesus as God's beloved Son, which God has destined as the "cornerstone" for his own true and authentic "building" (12:1–12) or "household" (11:17), the community of those who pray effectively with a comprehensive faith, forgiveness (11:22–25) and love (12:28–34, 41–44).

### 2. MARK 13:1–2 AS MODEL FOR ACTION

Jesus' powerful prediction of the utter destruction of the magnificent temple of Jerusalem calls us away from an excessive preoccupation with the externals of worship and toward a sincere concentration upon the interior essence of relating to and worshipping God. The temple's destruction makes it even more urgent and necessary for us to allow God to empower us to form his communal household based upon the person and authoritative teaching of Jesus, the "cornerstone" (12:10–11). Jesus teaches us how to become the new and authentic community of God's people, the community of true worship inclusive of all peoples of the world, by praying effectively from a sincere interior disposition of radical faith in God's power, mutual forgiveness, and totally unreserved love for God and others.

## N. Mark 13:3–8: To Four Disciples on the Mount of Olives Jesus Foretells Events Commencing the End of the Age

³Then as he was sitting on the Mount of Olives opposite the temple, Peter, James, John and Andrew asked him privately, ⁴"Tell us, when will these things happen, and what will be the

sign when all these things will be accomplished?" [5]Jesus began to say to them, "Watch out that no one deceives you. [6]Many will come in my name saying, 'I am he,' and they will deceive many. [7]When you hear of wars and reports of wars do not be alarmed; such things must happen, but it is not yet the end. [8]For nation will rise against nation and kingdom against kingdom. There will be earthquakes in various places, there will be famines. These are only the beginning of the birth pangs."

### 1. MEANING OF MARK 13:3–8

**a. *13:3–4* Four disciples ask Jesus about the time and sign of the end of the world.**

After having left behind the temple, inadequate to be God's "house of prayer for all peoples" (11:17) and destined for utter destruction (13:2), Jesus "sits" down on the Mount of Olives opposite the temple. That Jesus is "sitting on the Mount of Olives," from which he had triumphantly begun his activity in the Jerusalem temple (11:1–11) and which is separated from the temple mount by the Kidron valley, underscores that he has ended his temple activity by definitively abandoning and distancing himself and his disciples from the doomed temple. But that he is sitting "opposite the temple," as he had "sat down opposite the treasury" in the temple to observe the contributors (12:41), indicates that the temple is still in view and still the focus of attention. What does its future demise mean?

After Jesus has deflated the individual, unnamed disciple's fascination for the temple's beautiful stones and buildings with his powerful pronouncement of its utter destruction (13:1–2), a special group of four named disciples, "Peter, James, John and Andrew," question him privately. As the first four disciples to be called by Jesus when he began his ministry in Galilee (1:16–20), they appropriately question him now that his ministry is nearing its conclusion in Jerusalem (see 10:33). That they question Jesus "privately" (see 4:10, 34; 6:31–32; 7:17; 9:2, 28) prepares the reader for another special, private revelation or teaching of Jesus to his disciples (13:3).

Although prompted by Jesus' prediction of the destruction of the temple, the disciples' double question goes beyond this and refers to the end of the world. In asking "when will *these things* happen" and "what will be the sign when *all these things* will be accomplished," the four disciples, in accord with their apocalyptic-eschatological milieu, are asking not just about the destruction of the temple but about all of the cataclysmic events which will bring history and the world to an end so that

God can establish his final and definitive salvation. That the questions about the time and the sign "when all these things will be accomplished" concern the "end" is confirmed by their allusion to the apocalyptic book of Daniel. When Daniel asks, "How long shall it be till the end of these wonders?" (Dan 12:6), he is referring to the "time of the end" (Dan 12:4, 9, 13), when "all these things would be accomplished" (Dan 12:7) (13:4).[18]

**b.  *13:5–6* Jesus warns them not to be misled by impostors.**

From his magisterial position of "sitting" indicative that an extended teaching will follow (see 4:1–34; 9:35–50), Jesus begins his response. Rather than answering immediately and directly the disciples' question of the time and sign of the end, Jesus responds indirectly by advising them not to let anyone "deceive" them with regard to the end (13:5). Jesus then prepares his disciples for what to expect in the future time between his resurrection from the dead (8:31; 9:9, 31; 10:33–34) and his final, triumphant coming as the messianic Son of Man in the glory of his Father (8:38) by warning them that many will come "in my name," that is, claiming the power and authority of the Christ, and declare, "I am he," that is, claiming the dignity and identity of the Christ. But these are merely false messiahs who will "deceive" or lead astray many. The disciples, however, should not be deceived because the coming of these impostors is *not* the time or sign of the end (13:6).

**c.  *13:7–8* Wars, earthquakes and famines are only the beginning of the end.**

Continuing to prepare his disciples for the future time before the end, Jesus cautions them "not to be alarmed" when they hear of wars and reports of wars throughout the world. Such calamities are subsumed within the plan of God and "must" (*dei*) (see 8:31; 9:11; Dan 2:28) happen before the end. But when they happen it is *not* yet the time or sign of the end (13:7). For, as Jesus explains, in accord with God's plan recorded in scripture it can be expected that "nation will rise against nation" (2 Chr 15:6) and "kingdom against kingdom" (Isa 19:2). The natural catastrophe of "earthquakes" throughout the world as well as disastrous "famines" will continue to take place. But these terrible events are *not* the time or sign of the end; on the contrary, they are only the beginning of the "birth pangs," that is, the period of intense suffering, comparable to a woman's labor pains in giving birth, before the "birth" of the end-time or messianic age. That these horrible misfortunes are "only the beginning" of birth pains before the time of the end implies the possibility of even more intense suffering. Jesus thus prepares his disciples not only to expect such future distress but also to be ready for even more severe travails.

## 2. MARK 13:3-8 AS MODEL FOR ACTION

In preparing his disciples for the time between his resurrection and final coming in glory Jesus is likewise preparing us to deal with present and future events before the end of the world. We are advised not to allow anyone to divert us away from our faith in the true authority and identity of Jesus as the Christ. We are not to be unduly alarmed by the various wars, natural catastrophes and disasters that are sure to occur throughout the world, but to be ready to withstand these and even greater sufferings before the end of time when Christ will come again in glory to establish God's definitive salvation.

## O. Mark 13:9-13: Jesus Warns about Future Persecution and the Need for the Gospel To Be Preached to All

⁹"Watch out for yourselves. They will deliver you to the courts and you will be beaten in synagogues. And you will stand before governors and kings for my sake to testify to them. ¹⁰Indeed the gospel must first be preached to all peoples. ¹¹When they lead you away and deliver you up, do not worry beforehand about what you are to say. But say whatever will be given you at that hour, for it will not be you who are speaking but the Holy Spirit. ¹²Brother will deliver brother to death, and the father his child, and children will rise up against parents and have them put to death. ¹³You will be hated by all because of my name. But the one who perseveres to the end will be saved."

### 1. MEANING OF MARK 13:9-13

### a. *13:9-11* The Holy Spirit will assist the disciples to testify to their faith and preach the gospel to all peoples.

With a general introductory warning focusing upon the disciples themselves, "watch out for yourselves," Jesus continues to prepare his disciples and all other future followers of him for the time after his death and the end of the world. He forewarns that not only will they be "delivered" over to the Jewish courts by an indefinite "they" and be beaten in Jewish synagogues, but that they will also be forced to stand before Gentile governors and kings "for my sake to testify to them." Jesus thus advises his followers that they can expect a fate of persecution similar to his own. As he has predicted, he too will be "delivered" to both Jewish and Gentile authorities to be condemned to death (10:33-34; 9:31). The disciples will stand before foreign governors and kings "for my sake," that is, because of their adherence to and faith in Jesus and the gospel. And they will be forced "to testify to them," that is, to publicly give witness to their faith and the gospel, so that these Gentile rulers can either repent and believe in the gospel (see 1:14-15) or reject it and be left to the judgment of God (see 6:11). "To testify to them," then, is a form of preaching the gospel to them (13:9).[19]

Proceeding from the idea that testifying to Gentile rulers presents an opportunity for preaching the gospel to other peoples, Jesus states that indeed the gospel "must," in accord with divine necessity, "first," that is, before the end of the world (13:7), be preached to all peoples. This both comforts and exhorts the disciples. It comforts them by assuring them that the persecutions they will experience are not yet the intense sufferings that will accompany the end of the world because it is God's plan that there be time for the gospel "first" to be preached to all peoples throughout the world. But it also exhorts the disciples to fulfill their responsibility of offering the gospel to all peoples, whether by testifying in persecution or by missionary preaching (3:14-15; 6:7-13), in order to bring about the end-time of God's salvation. And that disciples are called to extend the gospel to "all peoples" corresponds to their task of forming God's new communal household of prayer inclusive of "all peoples" of the world (11:17) (13:10).

Jesus then encourages his disciples to withstand their future persecutions with his authoritative promise of divine assistance. He reassures them that when they are led away and delivered up, they need not worry beforehand about what they will say in testimony to their persecutors. They may say whatever "will be given" them by God (divine passive) at that critical hour, because God's own "Holy Spirit" will be speaking through them, thus assisting them to testify and preach the gospel. The authority and assurance of Jesus' promise of the Holy Spirit's help is reinforced by the fact that he himself has been endowed with God's Spirit (1:10) and John the Baptist has proclaimed him as the "stronger one" to come who "will baptize you in the Holy Spirit" (1:8) (13:11).

### b. *13:12-13* The one who perseveres through persecution will be saved.

Disciples can be expected to be persecuted and put to death even by members of their own families, as a brother "will deliver" a believing brother to death, and a father his believing child, and children will rise up against their believing parents and have them put to death (Mic 7:6). This corresponds to the pattern of Jesus himself, who experienced resistance from his own family (3:21) and was betrayed or "delivered" to death by Judas Iscariot, one of the Twelve (3:19) and a member of Jesus' new "family" of disciples (3:31–35) (13:12). Disciples, then, will be hated by "all," even closest associates, "because of my name," that is, because of their faith in the person of Jesus as the Christ (1:1; 8:29). But Jesus exhorts and encourages his disciples with the hopeful promise that whoever "perseveres" in testifying and preaching the gospel (13:9–11) "to the end," that is, until death or until the end of the world (13:7), "will be saved" by God (divine passive). And this assured hope of God's future salvation for followers who persevere on the "way" of Jesus is reinforced by the pattern of Jesus' own suffering and death, which is followed by resurrection (8:31; 9:31; 10:33–34). With this hope of God's future salvation Jesus empowers his disciples to endure extreme persecution, even to death (9:13).

### 2. MARK 13:9-13 AS MODEL FOR ACTION

Jesus inspires and exhorts us to persevere through future suffering and persecution with his divinely authoritative promise of the assistance of God's Holy Spirit and the assurance of God's ultimate salvation. We are encouraged that God, who gives us the time, the opportunity and the responsibility to proclaim the gospel to all peoples of the world, will give us the help of his Holy Spirit to publicly testify to our faith and thus preach the gospel even to those who persecute us. The assured hope of God's final salvation enables us to endure the most severe persecutions for the sake of our faith in Jesus and of our preaching the gospel, even those from closest associates and even those that result in death.

## P. Mark 13:14–23: Jesus Prepares His Disciples for the Great Tribulations Prior to the End of the Age

> [14]"When you see the desolating abomination standing where he should not (let the reader understand), then let those in Judea flee to the mountains, [15]and let a person on a housetop not go down or enter to take anything from his house, [16]and let a person in a field not turn back to take his cloak. [17]Woe to pregnant women and nursing mothers in those days. [18]Pray that this not happen in winter. [19]For those days will be tribulation such as has not been from the beginning of God's creation until now, nor

ever will be. [20]If the Lord had not shortened those days, no one would be saved; but for the sake of the elect whom he chose, he shortened the days. [21]If anyone says to you then, 'Look, here is the Christ! Look, there he is!' do not believe it. [22]For false Christs and false prophets will arise and will give signs and wonders in order to mislead, if possible, the elect. [23]But be watchful! I have told you everything beforehand."

### 1. MEANING OF MARK 13.14–23

**a. *13:14–19* The desolating abomination is the sign for the intense tribulation of the last days.**

After having prepared his disciples for the future crises, distresses and persecutions which they will encounter but which are not yet the last days signalling the end of the world (13:5–13), Jesus finally begins to answer his disciples' questions of the "time" and the "sign" of the destruction of the temple and hence of the end of the world (13:2–4). They will know that the last days have arrived and the end is near "when" they "see" the sign of "the desolating abomination standing where he should not." The "abomination" or "sacrilege" that makes "desolate" originally referred to the altar to the foreign god Zeus which was erected in the Jerusalem temple (ca. 167 B.C.) under the Syrian ruler Antiochus IV (Dan 9:27; 11:31; 12:11; 1 Macc 1:54; 6:7).[20] It desecrated the temple with idolatrous worship and rendered it "desolate" by forcing the Jews to abandon it. Later the term "desolating abomination" became a symbol for the mysterious thing or person who would desecrate the temple in the future as a sign of its coming destruction and the beginning of the last days prior to the end of the world.

That this "desolating abomination" will stand "where he should not" means that he will stand where he "must" (*dei*) (see 13:7, 10) not according to the divine necessity of God's plan, namely, inside the Jerusalem temple. The sinister "desolating abomination" will thus effect a profanation of the sacred temple contrary to the plan of God. The disciples are to see in this "desolating abomination" a prophetic sign which points them away from the temple and toward the end-time, final salvation of God.

The parenthetical remark, "let the reader understand," makes an appeal to the audience as the "reader," the one who "reads" and studies the OT scriptures, to realize that the mysterious "desolating abomination" refers to the desecration of the temple mentioned by the scriptures in the prophetic book of Daniel (Dan 9:27; 11:31; 12:11) and that it is a sign indicative of the last days and the end of the world.[21]

When the disciples see the sign of the "desolating abomination" standing in the temple, "then" is the time for those in Judea, the region surrounding Jerusalem, to "flee" not to the temple but "to the mountains" for refuge from the intense distress of the last days (13:14). So quick will this end-time distress come and so urgent will be the need for flight that the person on his housetop will not have time to go back into his house and take anything with him for the trip (13:15), and likewise the person working in a field will not even have time to retrieve his cloak for the journey (13:16). The anguish of "those days" will be particularly acute for pregnant women and nursing mothers because of the difficulty for them to flee quickly (13:17). The disciples should "pray" to God that this distress not occur during the winter season when travel is more arduous (13:18). Jesus then announces that the "tribulation" of "those days" will be the most horrible, severe and intense since God created the world and that there will never be such distress again (Dan 12:1). In other words, this will be the time of the excruciating afflictions preliminary to the end of the world and God's final salvation (13:19).

### b. *13:20–22* The Lord shortened those days for the elect, who should beware of deceptive impostors.

So intense and terrible will "those days" of tribulation be that if the Lord God had not shortened the period of those days, not a single human being would be able to persevere and "be saved" (see 13:13). But for the sake of the "elect," those people whom God has specially "chosen," he did in fact shorten those days of fierce afflictions. With this authoritative revelation into the salvific plan of God, Jesus consoles his listeners, who are to consider themselves to be among God's "elect," by assuring them that for the sake of their salvation God has mercifully reduced the most severe period of suffering the world has ever experienced (13:20).

Jesus further prepares his disciples by warning that if "then," at that time of the most acute tribulation, anyone tries to divert their attention to the end-time arrival of the messiah with excited exclamations that he is "here" or "there," they are not to believe it (13:21). Those days of intense distress will not yet be the time for the triumphant final coming of the Christ. But even God's "elect" must vigilantly persevere through this terrible time. Even they will not be immune from the "false Christs" and "false prophets" who will arise and attempt, "if possible," to mislead them with their impressive "signs and wonders" (Deut 13:1–3) into thinking that the end has come and the Christ has arrived (13:22).

**c. *13:23* Jesus has told his disciples everything beforehand.**

With his rousing command to "be watchful!" Jesus brings to a climax his urgent warnings and appeals that his disciples be vigilant (13:5, 9) in the future time between his death and final coming. He sums up his discourse to this point by powerfully pronouncing, "I have told you everything beforehand." In contrast to the "false prophets" who will arise to deceive the disciples, Jesus acts as God's authoritative and true prophet who, in answer to the disciples' request to know when "all" these things will be accomplished (13:4), has predicted "everything" they will encounter before it has happened, which includes future deceptions, disasters (13:5–8), persecutions (13:9–13) and extreme tribulations (13:14–22). With the words of this authoritative and powerful prophecy Jesus has equipped his disciples to endure whatever may befall them before his triumphant coming to establish God's definitive salvation at the end of time.

### 2. MARK 13:14–23 AS MODEL FOR ACTION

Jesus' prophetic predictions assure us that all possible future afflictions we may suffer are embraced by God's plan of salvation. Equipped with the encouraging words of Jesus' powerful prophecy, we will be able to persevere through even the most excruciating tribulations prior to the end of the world because, as Jesus' followers, we are among God's mercifully protected "elect." But even as among God's elect we are advised to be on guard against deceptions that distract us from an authentically confident and hopeful expectation of Jesus' future glorious return as the Christ to bring about God's final salvation.

## Q. Mark 13:24–27: Jesus Describes the End and the Coming of the Son of Man To Gather His Elect

> <sup>24</sup>"But in those days after that tribulation
> the sun will be darkened,
>    and the moon will not give its light,
> <sup>25</sup>and the stars will be falling from the sky,
>    and the powers in the heavens will be shaken.
> <sup>26</sup>And then they will see 'the Son of Man coming in the clouds'
> with great power and glory (Dan 7:13–14). <sup>27</sup>And then he will

send out the angels and gather his elect from the four winds, from the end of earth to the end of heaven."

**1. MEANING OF MARK 13:24–27**

**a. *13:24–25* After the tribulation of the last days the cosmic cataclysm will occur.**

Having prepared his disciples to endure future sufferings before the end of the world (13:5–23), Jesus now declares that only "after" the intense "tribulation" of "those days" preliminary to the end (13:19) will the disintegration of the cosmos finally take place. With allusions to the Jewish scriptures (Isa 13:10; 34:4; Ezek 32:7–8; Joel 2:10, 31; 4:15) and in accord with apocalyptic-eschatological expectations Jesus poetically describes the end of the world in the terrifying terms of the failure and fall of celestial bodies: The sun and the moon will fail to give light (13:24); the stars will fall from their places in the sky; and thus the "powers in the heavens" which establish and govern the order of God's creation (Gen 1:1–19) "will be shaken." In other words, the structural foundation and framework of the cosmos will collapse, indicative that the universe is coming to an end (13:25).

**b. *13:26–27* Then the Son of Man will appear in glory to gather his elect.**

But this shaking of cosmic powers will not be the last event in God's plan, for "then" people will "see" the messianic "Son of Man," that is, Jesus himself after he has suffered, died and risen (8:31; 9:31; 10:33–34), "coming in the clouds" from God's heavenly domain, endowed with the "great power and glory" of God (Dan 7:13–14). This glorious appearance of Jesus as the Son of Man will thus stand in sharp contrast not only to the appearance of false Christs and false prophets with their misleading "signs and wonders" (13:21–22, 6) but also to the unholy appearance of the "desolating abomination" which will desecrate the temple and initiate the terrible tribulations of the last days (13:14–19). When he comes again in glory as the transcendent Son of Man, the messianic agent of God, Jesus will be equipped with the divine power and authority to establish the final and definitive kingdom of God (13:26).

As the divinely powerful Son of Man Jesus will "then" constitute the ultimate community of God's kingdom by sending out "the angels," God's heavenly messengers (see 8:38), to "gather" together into one, final community "his elect," the divinely chosen followers and believers of Jesus (13:20, 22), "from the four winds, from the end of earth to the end of heaven" (Deut 30:4; LXX Zech 2:6, 10; Isa 43:5–6). No matter where the "elect" may be forced to flee and be scattered abroad by future afflictions, Jesus, when he returns in glory as Son of Man, will have the power to "gather" those who have persevered to the end (13:13) and draw them all together into the ultimate community of universal scope within the kingdom of God (13:27).

### 2. MARK 13:24–27 AS MODEL FOR ACTION

With this powerful prophetic prediction of his triumphant final coming as the heavenly Son of Man, Jesus has given his disciples, and hence all of us who believe in him and follow his "way," the consoling and confident hope of ultimately participating in the worldwide community of God's kingdom as his "elect" after we have patiently endured the disasters, persecutions and extreme tribulations we will encounter before the end. We need not be distraught, despondent or discouraged by the future crises and problems we will meet; on the contrary, Jesus has empowered us to persevere through and to ultimately triumph over all future distress with the assured hope and confident expectation of our participation in the final, universal community of God's salvation.

## R. Mark 13:28–31: Jesus Teaches about the Nearness of These Events and the Enduring Value of His Words

²⁸"Learn a lesson from the fig tree. As soon as its branch becomes tender and sprouts leaves, you know that summer is near. ²⁹So also, when you see these things happening, know that he is near, at the gates. ³⁰Amen I say to you, this generation will not pass away until all these things have taken place. ³¹Heaven and earth will pass away, but my words will not pass away."

### 1. MEANING OF MARK 13:28–31

#### a. *13:28–29* When the events Jesus foretold happen the Son of Man will be near.

Having assured his disciples of his glorious return as the Son of Man to effect God's final salvation after the end of the world (13:24–27), Jesus directs them to learn a "lesson" (literally, "parable," "comparison") from the natural phenomenon of the growth of a fig tree. Once the branch of the fig tree becomes tender with the rising of its sap in the spring and begins to sprout leaves, it is common knowledge that summer is near. In other words, summer follows inevitably and soon after the budding fig tree sprouts its leaves (13:28). Similarly, when the disciples see "these things happening," namely, the appearance of the "desolating abomination" with ensuing end-time tribulations followed by the disintegration of the cosmos (13:14–25), they may know and be assured that the Son of Man, the returning Jesus himself, is so "near" that he is "at the gates" ready to enter the world "in the clouds with great power and glory" (13:26) to gather his elect into God's kingdom (13:27). Just as the sprouting fig tree signals the inevitable and imminent arrival of summer so the occurrence of the end-time events predicted by Jesus means his inevitable and imminent arrival as the transcendent and triumphant Son of Man (13:29).

**b. *13:30–31* The enduring words of Jesus ensure his predictions.**

With the words, "amen I say to you," underlining the truth and certainty of the assertion to follow, Jesus proclaims that "this generation," that is, this "present age" of faithless and sinful people opposed to God's ways (see 8:12, 38; 9:19), "will not pass away" and thus come to an end "until *all* these things" predicted by Jesus, namely, future distress and persecutions (13:5–13) as well as end-time tribulations (13:14–25) followed by the triumphant arrival of the Son of Man (13:26–27), take place.[22] In other words, all of the things predicted by Jesus are sure to occur before this present age comes to an end. By underscoring the certainty of his powerful prophetic prediction that he will surely return as the heavenly Son of Man after future sufferings, Jesus bolsters the consolation and hope of his disciples (13:30). Whereas "heaven and earth (the universe) will pass away" and thus come to an end as Jesus has already indicated (13:24–25), "my words," especially the divinely authoritative and powerful words of this prophetic discourse (13:5–37), "will not pass away" but have an enduring value surpassing that of the created universe. The enduring value of the words of Jesus further assures his disciples of the certainty of his final coming in triumph to establish God's kingdom after future afflictions (13:31).

### 2. MARK 13:28–31 AS MODEL FOR ACTION

With the unsurpassably enduring value of the divinely authoritative words of Jesus in this prophetic discourse (13:5–37) we are equipped to endure the most extreme troubles and sufferings of the future with the assured hope of the inevitable and certain coming of Jesus as the triumphant and glorious Son of Man to gather us into God's kingdom after the world has ended.

## S. Mark 13:32–37: Since They Do Not Know the Time of the Son of Man's Coming Jesus Exhorts All To Be Watchful

[32]"But of that day or hour no one knows, not even the angels in heaven, nor the Son, but only the Father. [33]Be watchful! Be alert! For you do not know when the time will come. [34]It is like a man away on a journey, who has left his house and given his servants the authority, each with his work, and ordered the gatekeeper to be on the watch. [35]Watch, therefore; for you do not know when the lord of the house will come, whether in the evening, or at midnight, or at cockcrow, or in the morning, [36]lest he come suddenly and find you sleeping. [37]What I say to you, I say to all: 'Watch!' "

### 1. MEANING OF MARK 13:32-37

**a. *13:32–33* The disciples must be watchful since only the Father knows exactly when the Son of Man will come.**

Although the triumphant coming of Jesus as the Son of Man with power and glory to finally establish God's kingdom is inevitable and certain (13:28–31), no one knows the exact "day" or "hour" of his coming, not even the angels in heaven who will accompany him (8:38; 13:27), nor the Son of Man himself, but only God the Father with his absolute sovereignty (13:32). Since the disciples and future followers of Jesus will not know the exact time when the Son of Man will come, Jesus urges them to be constantly "watchful" (13:5, 9, 23) and "alert" for it (13:33).

**b. *13:34–36* The disciples must be alert servants diligently awaiting the return of the lord of the house.**

With an allegorical comparison Jesus instructs his disciples how they are to consider their situation and conduct their lives after he has died and before his final coming in glory as Son of Man. The situation will be like that of a "man away on a journey," representative of Jesus after he has died. This "man" (Jesus) has left his "house" or "household," that is, the new familial community of followers of Jesus (see 3:31–35; 10:28–31) who comprise God's new "house" or communal household of prayer for all peoples (11:17). But he has given his "servants" (literally "slaves"), that is, the disciples whom Jesus has called to be "servants" (9:35) and "slaves" (10:44) of all in imitation of himself who came as Son of Man not to be served but to serve (10:45), "authority" over his "house" or communal household. The "servants" (disciples) may exercise the "man's"

(Jesus') "authority" or power over the "house" or community especially by healing and preaching the gospel (see 3:14–15; 6:7–13; 13:10). That the "man" (Jesus) has left "each with his work" means that each individual disciple has a task and responsibility toward the "house" or community. And that he has ordered the "gatekeeper" to be on watch means that he is to watch the "gates" (13:29) for the future coming of the Son of Man (13:34).

Jesus then exhorts his disciples as the "servants" of his community ("house") to be ever vigilant and "watch" for they do not know when the "lord" (Jesus, see 11:3) of the "house" (community) will come as Son of Man in power and glory. He could come at any time of the "day" (or period of history), evening, midnight, dawn or morning (13:35). The disciples are to "watch" by diligently performing their "work" and fulfilling their responsibility toward the community lest the Son of Man come suddenly and find them "sleeping" rather than diligent and vigilant, and thus unprepared to participate in the final salvation and kingdom of God that the Son of Man will bring about (13:36).

### c. *13:37* All followers of Jesus must be vigilant.

In his closing and summary exhortation Jesus makes explicit the implicit application of his entire discourse (13:3–37) to all disciples. What Jesus authoritatively ("I") says to "you," Peter, James, John and Andrew (13:3), he authoritatively ("I") says to "all," that is, to all the other disciples and future followers of the "way" of Jesus. His closing exhortation is the single, keynote command: "Watch!" This sums up the attentive attitude all future followers of Jesus must have as they diligently perform their work for the "lord of the house" while looking forward to the future glorious coming of the Son of Man.

### 2. MARK 13:32–37 AS MODEL FOR ACTION

As we await with confident hope his inevitable and certain coming as the triumphant Son of Man to finally establish the kingdom of God, Jesus urges us to be ever watchful and alert, since only God knows the exact time when the Son of Man will come. While we are attentively waiting, we are to consider ourselves as servants in the new community of Jesus' "house" with Jesus' authority and power to heal others and preach the gospel. Each of us has been given a work to perform and a responsibility to fulfill toward the Christian community, the "household" of the Lord. We are urged to diligently and vigilantly perform our work and fulfill our responsibility so that we may be alert and ready to fully participate in the final and definitive salvation, the kingdom of God that Jesus as Son of Man will come to establish in triumphant power and glory.

## Notes

1. See "Temple" in Chapter I.
2. W. J. Cotter, " 'For It Was Not the Season for Figs,' " *CBQ* 48 (1986) 62–66.
3. Mark 11:26, "But if you do not forgive, neither will your Father in heaven forgive your transgressions," probably inserted by copyists in imitation of Matt 6:15, is omitted in the best manuscripts.
4. The close connection between the "stone" of the Psalm verse and the beloved "son" of the parable is enhanced by a wordplay between the Hebrew words for "stone" (*eben*) and "son" (*ben*). See K. Snodgrass, *The Parable of the Wicked Tenants: An Inquiry into Parable Interpretation* (WUNT 27; Tübingen: Mohr-Siebeck, 1983) 113–18.
5. See "Pharisees" and "Herodians" in Chapter I.
6. A denarius was a Roman silver coin with the monetary value of a day's wage for a laborer; see also 6:37.
7. Tannehill, *Sword,* 174.
8. For a fuller discussion of the rhetorical power of Mark 12:13–17, see Tannehill, *Sword,* 171–77. His closing comments are noteworthy: "To be sure, this text has frequently been used to protect the Christian citizen from the claims of God by defining "the things of God" in a narrow sense and isolating them from concerns of the state. As we have seen, this is wrong for a number of reasons. It falsely assumes that vs. 17 is meant to be a clear rule of behavior which must refer to clearly separable realms. It neglects the fact that the final reference to God is formally the climactic element in the story and that, in contrast to the case with the "things of Caesar," the story suggests no limit to the "things of God." It fails to see that the inquirers' concern with the tax is wittily minimized so that God's claims may be the dominant concern even in relation to the state. These conclusions agree with the dominant view of the Bible as a whole, which makes clear that the God of whom it speaks is not one who limits himself to private religion and personal morality."
9. See "Sadducees" in Chapter I.
10. According to Jewish apocalyptic literature angels do not marry (*1 Enoch* 15:7). That the resurrected will be like angels in the future world corresponds to apocalyptic thought: The resurrected will "dwell in the heights of that world and be like the angels and like the stars" (*2 Apoc. Bar.* 51:10).

11. For the biblical background on the expectation of a Davidic messiah, see "Son of David" in Chapter I.

12. See, for example, Exod 22:21–23; Deut 10:18; 24:17; Isa 1:17, 23; 10:2; Ezek 22:7; Pss 94:6; 146:9; Job 22:9; 24:3.

13. On Mark 12:38–40 see H. Fleddermann, "A Warning about the Scribes (Mark 12:37b–40)," *CBQ* 44 (1982) 52–67; Biguzzi, *Io distruggerò*, 79–83.

14. Literally, "two *lepta*," two of the smallest coins in the Jewish monetary system, "worth a *quadrans*," the smallest coin in the Roman monetary system. Mark thus expresses the extremely small amount of the widow's contribution in terms that can be understood throughout the Roman Empire.

15. Intensifying the low sociological status of the poor widow is the fact that she is a woman; see "Women and Children" in Chapter I.

16. On Mark 12:41–44, see Biguzzi, *Io distruggerò*, 83–85.

17. Lane, *Mark*, 451–52: "The most striking feature of this prophecy is its emphatic definiteness. The double negatives (*ou me*), which occur twice in verse 2, already suggest the total nature of the devastation, while the description "stone upon stone" removes all possible misconception about the extent of the destruction envisaged."

18. For an extensive illustration of the rich OT background, especially from Daniel, for the discourse of Mark 13, see L. Hartman, *Prophecy Interpreted: The Formation of Some Jewish Apocalyptic Texts and of the Eschatological Discourse Mark 13 Par.* (ConBNT 1; Lund: Gleerup, 1966) 145–77.

19. Note that the two previous occurrences of "for my sake" are followed by "and for the sake of the gospel" (8:35; 10:29). This close connection between being a disciple "for the sake" of "Jesus" and "for the sake of" preaching the "gospel" indicates that "to testify to them," following "for my sake" in Mark 13:9, is oriented to the preaching of the gospel.

20. R. H. Hiers, "Abomination that makes desolate," *Harper's Bible Dictionary*, 6.

21. Each of the three previous occurrences of the word "read" in the narrative (2:25; 12:10, 26) refers to the "reading" of the OT scriptures.

22. "This generation" is a comprehensive term not limited to the contemporaries of Jesus but embracing the entire "present age" as opposed to the "age-to-come" in accord with apocalyptic-eschatological thought. The "kingdom of God" is the Marcan term for the expected "age-to-come" of God's eschatological salvation.

# VIII

---

# Mark 14:1–15:47

*Jesus Accomplishes the Way of Suffering and Death.*

## A. Mark 14:1–2: Two Days before Passover the Chief Priests and Scribes Seek To Kill Jesus without a Tumult

¹It was two days before the feast of Passover and Unleavened Bread. And the chief priests and scribes were seeking how to arrest him by deceit and put him to death. ²For they said, "Not during the feast, lest there be a tumult of the people."

### 1. MEANING OF MARK 14:1–2

#### a. *14:1* The chief priests and scribes are seeking to arrest and kill Jesus.

The temporal notice that it was two days before the annual springtime feast of Passover and Unleavened Bread places the events to follow within the context of this most important Jewish festival. Many Jewish pilgrims came to Jerusalem to celebrate the week-long familial feast of Passover and Unleavened Bread, during which they commemorated their participation in the past saving deeds of God on behalf of the people of Israel, especially the exodus from slavery in Egypt (Exod 12), and looked forward with hope to participating in God's future and final salvation.[1] That it was only "two days" before this great and solemn feast means that Jerusalem is filling with pilgrims and that all attention is focused upon preparing for the imminent celebration.

The "chief priests and scribes," representing the persistent enemies of Jesus throughout the narrative both in Galilee and now in Jerusalem, are still seeking to arrest Jesus and have him put to death. After Jesus

273

condemned the temple and thus the Jewish leaders responsible for it (11:15–17), they "were seeking how to destroy him" (11:18). And after Jesus told the parable of the wicked tenants against them (12:1–11), they "were seeking to arrest him" (12:12). The one significant development is that now they are seeking to arrest and kill him "by deceit":

> *11:18*  The chief priests and the scribes heard it and were seeking how to destroy him.
>
> *12:12*  Then they (the chief priests, scribes and elders, see 11:27) were seeking to arrest him.
>
> *14:1*  The chief priests and scribes were seeking how to arrest him *by deceit* and put him to death.

Having unsuccessfully challenged the authority of Jesus in the temple (11:27–33) and having failed to "trap him in his speech" (12:13) and thus to discredit his teaching before the people, the chief priests and scribes must now resort to "deceit" or "treachery." That they seek to arrest and kill Jesus "by deceit" not only underlines their wickedness and opposition to God, but indicates the innocence of Jesus whose divinely authoritative teaching in the temple could not be legitimately discredited or undermined by the Jewish leaders.[2]

From Jesus' previous passion predictions (8:31; 9:31; 10:33–34) the reader knows that the chief priests and scribes will ultimately succeed in arresting Jesus and having him put to death, but suspense is now aroused with regard to exactly how this will happen, how it is related to the Passover feast, and what is involved in their "deceit."

### b. *14:2* They wish to avoid a riot of the people during the feast.

The chief priests and scribes explicitly express their desire not to arrest and kill Jesus during the Passover feast "lest there be a tumult of the people." Since the Passover feast is only two days away, they will have to quickly dispose of Jesus before the feast or wait until the week-long celebration has ended. Their cautious desire introduces a double tension for the reader. First, will they be able to avoid arresting and killing Jesus during the Passover feast and thus prevent his death from appropriately taking place while the Jewish people are celebrating the past saving deeds of God and looking forward to his final deliverance and salvation?

And second, will they be able to avoid relating the Jewish people to the death of Jesus? The desire of the chief priests and scribes to prevent a "tumult of the people" continues the previous tension involving the favorable attraction of the "crowd" to Jesus. After Jesus condemned the temple cult (11:15–17), the chief priests and scribes were seeking how to destroy him, "for they feared him because the whole *crowd* was astounded at his teaching" (11:18). And after the chief priests, scribes and elders realized that Jesus had directed the parable of the wicked tenants against themselves, they were seeking to arrest him, "but they feared the *crowd*" (12:12; 11:32). Now, these Jewish leaders are concerned not just with the "crowd" attracted to Jesus in the temple but with causing a "tumult," a riot or commotion (see 5:38), among the "people," that is, the "people" composed of Jerusalem residents and pilgrims who have come to celebrate the Passover, and who thus represent the "people" (*laos*) of Israel as God's specially chosen "people" (see 7:6).[3] That the Jewish leaders fear a tumult of the "people" thus indicates that the death of Jesus has a significance for the entire chosen "people" of Israel as they celebrate the feast of Passover and commemorate God's salvific activity.

### 2. MARK 14:1–2 AS MODEL FOR ACTION

That the Jewish leaders seek to arrest and kill Jesus "by deceit" makes us realize the innocence and superior authority of the teaching of Jesus, who will die in accord with God's plan, not because of any wrongdoing on his part but because of the wickedness of the leaders of his own people. We are invited to emulate the innocence and fidelity of Jesus to God by accepting and promoting his divinely authoritative teaching as we follow his "way," even in the face of deceit from those who oppose us.

The concern of the enemies of Jesus to prevent his death from causing a tumult during the feast of Passover among the "people" attracted to him induces us to deepen our understanding of the salvific significance of the death of Jesus by realizing that it has a profound meaning for the entire people of God as *the* salvific event which climaxes the past saving and liberating deeds of God commemorated in the great Passover feast.

## B. Mark 14:3–9: At Bethany a Woman Anoints Jesus for Burial

[3]While he was in Bethany reclining at table in the house of Simon the leper, a woman came with an alabaster flask of perfumed ointment, costly genuine spikenard. She broke the alabaster flask and poured it on his head. [4]There were some who were indignant among themselves, "Why has there been this waste of perfumed ointment? [5]For this perfumed ointment could have been sold for more than three hundred days' wages and given to the poor." And they were infuriated with her. [6]Jesus

said, "Let her alone. Why do you make trouble for her? She has done a good work for me. [7]For you always have the poor with you, and whenever you wish you can do good to them, but you will not always have me. [8]She has done what she could. She has anticipated anointing my body for burial. [9]Amen I say to you, wherever the gospel is proclaimed in the whole world, what she has done will be told in memory of her."

### 1. MEANING OF MARK 14:3-9

#### a. *14:3* At Bethany a woman anoints Jesus with expensive ointment.

While the chief priests and scribes are plotting how to arrest and kill him by deceit (14:1-2), Jesus is "in Bethany reclining at table in the house of Simon the leper." That Jesus is in Bethany continues to express his radical separation from the condemned and doomed Jerusalem temple and the Jewish leaders responsible for it (11:15-19; 13:2). Rather than stay in Jerusalem during his controversial teaching in the temple Jesus spent his nights with his own community of followers in Bethany (11:1, 11, 19). His opposition to the chief priests and scribes is further underlined as he "is reclining at table," participating in table fellowship with his own followers "in the house of Simon the leper." In Galilee the Jewish leaders objected to Jesus' eating and thus establishing a communal bond with such social outcasts as public sinners and toll collectors (2:15-17). That Jesus is now in the house of one "Simon the leper" means he is again associating, in opposition to the chief priests and scribes, with social outcasts and those who "need a physician" (see 2:17), since the Jewish leadership banned anyone with the disease of leprosy from worship in the temple and full participation in the community of Israel (1:40-44). In stark contrast to the Jewish leaders seeking to deceitfully arrest and kill Jesus, his own followers, who include social and religious outcasts, are enjoying table fellowship with him in the communal setting of the "house" of an outcast, Simon the leper.

During the meal an unnamed "woman" comes "with an alabaster flask of perfumed ointment" whose great value and extreme expensiveness is emphasized by the further specification that this perfumed ointment was "costly genuine spikenard."[4] The woman then breaks open the alabaster flask and, as a gesture of hospitality often offered in the context of a meal or banquet (Pss 23:5; 133:2; 141:5; Luke 7:46), anoints Jesus by pouring the precious and fragrant ointment over his head.

**b. *14:4–5* Some object to the waste with concern for the poor.**

A conflict arises and tension mounts as some of those participating in the table fellowship angrily object to the woman's kind and hospitable gesture. Interpreting her action as a "waste" of expensive ointment, they question what she has done (14:4) and point out that the valuable ointment could have been sold for a very handsome sum, "more than three hundred days' wages," and the proceeds given as alms to support the poor.[5] They are expressly "infuriated" with the woman and thus implicitly upset also with Jesus who has allowed such "waste." They value giving alms to the poor as more important than the hospitable anointing of Jesus. The tension calls for resolution and proper interpretation by Jesus (14:5).

**c. *14:6–9* Jesus accepts her anointing as the anticipation of his burial.**

Jesus firmly counters their furious indignation and comes to the defense of the woman with the words "let her alone" and "why do you make trouble for her?" He then gives the proper interpretation of the woman's hospitable anointing with costly ointment. Rather than an extravagant "waste" of money and a missed opportunity for exercising almsgiving as an important duty demanded by Jewish piety, the woman's gesture was a "good work," that is, an act of charitable love also demanded by Jewish piety, which she performed not "for the poor" but "for me," Jesus himself. Her "good work" toward Jesus thus stands in pointed contrast to the Jewish leaders' deceitful death plot against him. As a practice of Jewish piety the value of this "good work" or "act of love" surpasses that of almsgiving in three ways: It is performed for a specific person (Jesus) rather than a general group (the poor); it requires and demonstrates a personal commitment of love rather than just an impersonal giving; and it is occasioned by a particular situation and time of urgent need rather than by the general and continual condition of the poor.[6] And so Jesus indicates that the woman's costly anointing of him at this time is to be valued as a superior act of love toward him surpassing that of giving alms to the poor (14:6).

Further explaining the woman's generous gesture toward him, Jesus emphasizes the uniqueness of his situation of need by pointing to his future absence, thus indicating his majestic awareness of the deceitful death plot against him (14:1–2). He reminds his followers that since they will always have the general group of the poor with them (see Deut 15:11), they may and should fulfill their obligation of almsgiving and do good to the poor whenever they wish. But the important point for them to realize is that they will not always have Jesus with them (see 2:18–20). That is what makes this occasion of communal table fellowship uniquely urgent and the woman's act of loving devotion by hospitably anointing Jesus so extremely valuable (14:7).

Jesus continues by pointing out that the woman "has done what she could," literally, "she used what she had." In other words, she did what she could by using the cherished perfumed ointment she had in her possession to demonstrate her loving devotion toward Jesus as he is nearing his death. She recognizes and honors the approaching death of Jesus as an event worthy of her most expensive and precious possession. Jesus proclaims her lavishly hospitable anointing as a prophetic gesture anticipating his upcoming burial. Because she acknowledges and esteems the death of Jesus, this unnamed woman serves as a refreshingly unexpected model of discipleship. She stands in sharp contrast to the male disciples unable to understand and accept the necessity of Jesus' death. That Jesus acclaims her for doing all she could and using what she had as an act of total and personally committed love of him on his way to death is reminiscent of his praise for a similar unnamed and exemplary woman, the poor widow, who "contributed all she had, her whole living" (12:44) to the temple treasury as an act of completely committed and wholehearted love and devotion to God (14:8).[7]

With the solemn introductory words, "amen I say to you," underlining the truth and certainty of what he is saying, Jesus further extols the woman's loving acknowledgment of his approaching death by announcing that in the future, worldwide proclamation of the gospel, her generous act of love in anointing him before his burial will be told as part of the gospel message in memory of her. Because the death of Jesus is such an essential part of the gospel message, her hospitable gesture in recognition of the precious value of Jesus' death will be forever memorialized in the global proclamation of the gospel. Occurring within the context of the Passover feast (14:1–2), which commemorates the saving event of the Exodus as well as all of God's other saving deeds, past, present and future, the precious value of the death of Jesus will be commemorated forever and everywhere that the gospel is proclaimed throughout the world as the definitive saving deed of God because of the great reverence of this anonymous woman. This indicates that the followers of Jesus have the duty not only to preach the gospel "to all peoples" before the end of the world (13:10) but to include in their global evangelization the memory of this extraordinary woman's loving acknowledgment of the precious death of Jesus as a crucial part of the gospel message (14:9).

## 2. MARK 14:3–9 AS MODEL FOR ACTION

The nameless woman's hospitable anointing of Jesus as an act of loving devotion in recognition of the precious value of his death serves as a model moving us to likewise accept the necessity of the death of Jesus as we follow his "way" and to devote ourselves with a full personal commitment to the extraordinary value of his death as the definitive act of God's salvation, to be commemorated forever and everywhere in the gospel. As we promote the "way" of Jesus by preaching the gospel throughout the world, we must recall for all other peoples and cultures this woman's magnificent act of love so that they can likewise accept the necessity of and appreciate the eminent value of the death of Jesus as *the* saving event for the people of God. The woman's example of generous giving of all she could to Jesus at his critical moment of need on the way to his death inspires us to abundantly give of ourselves to those in need, especially the poor who will always be among us.

## C. Mark 14:10–11: Judas Iscariot, One of the Twelve, Seeks To Betray Jesus to the Chief Priests

> [10]Then Judas Iscariot, one of the Twelve, went to the chief priests in order to betray him to them. [11]When they heard him they were pleased and promised to give him money. So he was seeking how to opportunely betray him.

### 1. MEANING OF MARK 14:10–11

#### a. *14:10* The disciple Judas offers to betray Jesus to the chief priests.

In keen, ironic contrast to the nameless and socially insignificant woman who has just compassionately anointed Jesus for burial (14:3–9), a named, male disciple, Judas Iscariot, who has the status of being one of Jesus' specially chosen "Twelve" disciples with the privilege of "being with him" (3:14), now leaves the communal gathering of table fellowship with Jesus at Bethany (see 11:11) with the intention of betraying him. Judas, unlike the hospitable woman who anticipates and lovingly accepts Jesus' death, thus refuses to remain in fellowship with Jesus on his way to imminent death. Whereas Judas, along with the other disciples called to form the Twelve, had earlier answered Jesus' summons by "coming to him" (3:13) in order "to be with him" (3:14) in a close communal bond, he now breaks that bond with Jesus as "he went to the chief priests," the enemies seeking how to deceitfully arrest and kill Jesus (14:1), with the purpose of betraying him to them:

> *3:13* They (the Twelve) came to (*apēlthon pros*) him (Jesus).
> *14:10* He (Judas) went to (*apēlthen pros*) the chief priests.

From the time that Jesus chose the Twelve the reader has known that Judas would be the one "who betrayed him" (3:19). That Judas is now offering to "betray" him to the "chief priests" means that the necessity that Jesus be "delivered" or "betrayed" in accord with God's salvific plan, as repeatedly predicted by Jesus (8:31; 9:31; 10:33–34), is now being fulfilled:

> *9:31* The Son of Man is to be delivered/betrayed (*paradidotai*) into the hands of people . . .
> *10:33* The Son of Man will be delivered/betrayed (*para-dothēsetai*) to the chief priests . . .
> *14:10* Judas . . . went to the chief priests in order to betray/deliver (*paradoi*) him to them.

Although a tragic betrayal of one of the trusted Twelve, Judas' wicked intentions against Jesus are embraced within God's plan of salvation. Ironically and paradoxically, Judas, who refuses to remain in communal fellowship with Jesus as he approaches his death, will play a prominent role in bringing about that death by betraying Jesus in accord with God's plan.

### b. *14:11* The chief priests promise Judas money to betray Jesus.

When the chief priests, who, together with the scribes, are "seeking how to arrest him by deceit and put him to death" (14:1), hear Judas' offer to betray Jesus, they are "pleased" because they have now presumably found a way to arrest and kill Jesus "by deceit" so as not to cause a disturbance of the people during the Passover feast (14:2). The "deceit" or "treachery" will take the form of secret betrayal by Judas, "one of the Twelve," a member of the group of followers closest to Jesus.

That the chief priests promise to give Judas money for his betrayal of Jesus underlines how both the chief priests and Judas stand in ironic contrast to the nameless woman who generously anointed Jesus for burial (14:3–9). Whereas the woman expended her precious ointment worth more than three hundred days' wages to demonstrate her devotion and appreciation of the death of Jesus, the chief priests will spend their money not for devotion to the dying Jesus but for deceitful betrayal leading to his death. And whereas the woman generously donated all that she could as an act of love toward the dying Jesus, Judas, a trusted disciple, will take money in return for a treacherous and tragic act of betraying Jesus to death.

Judas now establishes a bond with the Jewish leaders and becomes the bribed agent in their plot to arrest Jesus and have him put to death. As the chief priests and scribes were "seeking how" to arrest and kill Jesus "by deceit," so now Judas enters into their treacherous plot and is "seeking how" to opportunely "betray" him:

> *14:1*  The chief priests and scribes were seeking (*ezētoun*) how (*pōs*) to arrest him by deceit and put him to death.
>
> *14:11*  He (Judas) was seeking (*ezētei*) how (*pōs*) to opportunely betray him.

The suspense regarding whether Jesus will be arrested and put to death during the feast of Passover and whether it will cause a tumult or riot among the people (14:2) now focuses upon Judas' deceitful plan to betray Jesus to the chief priests.

### 2. MARK 14:10–11 AS MODEL FOR ACTION

The horror of Judas, one of the Twelve disciples closest to Jesus, breaking his bond of fellowship with Jesus and offering to betray him to death serves as a warning advising us to remain in close communal fellowship with Jesus as we follow his "way" so that we, like the admirable woman who anointed Jesus for burial (14:3–9), may accept the necessity for and appreciate the great value of the death of Jesus as *the* saving event within God's plan of salvation for his people. The chief priests' promise to give Judas money for deceitfully betraying Jesus to death alerts us to imitate the generous giving of the anointing woman by rejecting a self-serving use of ourselves and what we own in favor of a selfless giving of ourselves in devoted service to others and Jesus, who came not "to be served but to serve and to give his life as a ransom for many" (10:45).

## D. Mark 14:12–16: The Disciples Prepare for Jesus To Eat the Passover Meal with Them

¹²On the first day of the feast of Unleavened Bread, when they sacrificed the Passover lamb, his disciples said to him, "Where

do you want us to go and prepare in order for you to eat the Passover?" [13]Then he sent two of his disciples and said to them, "Go into the city and a man will meet you, carrying a jar of water. Follow him [14]and wherever he enters, say to the master of the house, 'The Teacher says, "Where is my guest room where I may eat the Passover with my disciples?" ' [15]Then he will show you a large upper room furnished and ready. Prepare for us there." [16]The disciples then went off, entered the city, and found it just as he had told them; and they prepared the Passover.

### 1. MEANING OF MARK 14:12–16

**a. *14:12* The disciples ask where Jesus wants to eat the Passover.**

That it is already "the first day of the feast of Unleavened Bread," when "they," the priests in the temple, sacrificed the Passover lambs used in the various local celebrations of the Passover meal in Jerusalem means that the chief priests and scribes did not succeed in arresting Jesus and having him put to death before the Passover feast has begun.[8] And so the suspense as to whether or not the Jewish leaders can avoid killing Jesus during the week-long Passover feast so as to prevent a tumult of the people continues (14:1–2).

In contrast to Judas, the disciple who left table fellowship with Jesus (14:3–9) and "went away" to the chief priests for the purpose of betraying him to them, the disciples who remain in table fellowship with Jesus ask him where he wants them to "go away" and prepare for the purpose of his eating the Passover meal:

> *14:10* Judas Iscariot, one of the Twelve, went (*apēlthen*) to the chief priests in order (*hina*) to betray him to them.
>
> *14:12* His disciples said to him, "Where do you want us to go (*apelthontes*) and prepare in order (*hina*) for you to eat the Passover?"

Whereas Judas has broken his communal bond with Jesus, there are still disciples with him who are concerned with continuing their communal bond of table fellowship by preparing for Jesus to eat the solemn Passover meal with them. That Jesus has already been anointed for his burial (14:8) lends added significance to this particular Passover meal as it places the impending death of Jesus in the context of the Passover feast, which celebrates the past, present and future saving deeds of God on behalf of his people.

**b.** *14:13–15* **Jesus directs the disciples to the room ready for the Passover meal.**

That Jesus then sends two disciples into Jerusalem to prepare the Passover meal with authoritative instructions demonstrating his superior prophetic knowledge of the future recalls his similar instructions to the two disciples sent to procure the colt for his triumphal entrance into Jerusalem and the temple:

> *11:1–2* He sent two of his disciples and said to them, "Go into the village opposite you . . .
>
> *14:13* He sent two of his disciples and said to them, "Go into the city . . .

Whereas Jesus earlier authorized his disciples to prepare for his triumphal entrance into the Jerusalem temple as "lord" or "master" (11:3) through his masterful command and prophetic foreknowledge, he now authorizes his disciples to prepare for the final Passover meal which he, "*the* Teacher," will eat with "his disciples" in Jerusalem. This indicates Jesus' strong desire and intention to eat the Passover with his disciples in view of his impending death, despite the concern of the Jewish leaders to prevent that death from taking place during the Passover (14:2). Jesus has a masterful control and prophetic foreknowledge of God's plan for his death superior to the enemies plotting it.

Jesus predicts that a "man carrying a jar of water" will meet the disciples. This nameless "man" with his "jar of water" complements the nameless "woman" with her "alabaster flask of perfumed ointment" from the previous scene of table fellowship (14:3–9). As the "woman" with her flask of precious ointment performs a prophetic gesture anticipating the burial of Jesus, so the "man" with his jar of ordinary water will serve as a distinctive sign leading the disciples to the room where Jesus will eat the Passover meal in view of his approaching death.[9]

After Jesus instructs the disciples to follow the man with the jar of water into whatever household he enters, he empowers them to use his eminent authority as "*the* Teacher." They are to tell the master of that household: "The Teacher says, 'Where is my guest room where I may eat the Passover with my disciples?' " Whereas many have addressed Jesus as "teacher" throughout the narrative,[10] this is the first time Jesus refers to himself as "teacher," that is, as "*the* Teacher," the one who "teaches" a "new teaching" with divine "authority" and "not as the scribes" (see 1:21–28). By identifying himself for the first time as "*the* Teacher," Jesus not only brings to a climax the previous references to him as "teacher" but recalls and confirms the powerful divine authority of all of his previous "teachings" throughout the narrative.[11] Not only is this the first and climactic time that Jesus refers to himself as "*the* Teacher," but it is the first and only time that he refers to his disciples as "*my* disciples." This underlines the close teacher/disciple bond uniting Jesus with his followers, a bond Jesus strongly desires to reinforce and deepen with "*my* disciples" through the table fellowship of this extraordinary Passover meal, which will anticipate his death (14:13–14).

Once the disciples have utilized the commanding authority Jesus has given them as disciples of "*the* Teacher" by authoritatively addressing the master of the household they have entered, he will then show them "a large upper room furnished and ready." There they may "prepare" the Passover meal to be shared by "us," Jesus and his disciples (14:15).

### c. *14:16* The disciples follow Jesus' instructions and prepare the Passover meal.

In obedience to the authoritative directives of Jesus the disciples go off and enter the city of Jerusalem and find that everything happens precisely as Jesus had foretold. Through the powerful prophetic predictions of Jesus and his divine authority as "*the* Teacher" the disciples are now able to "prepare" for this special Passover meal before the imminent death of Jesus, already anointed for burial (14:8). That everything happens exactly as Jesus has foretold underlines his superior prophetic knowledge of the future events of God's plan and further assures the reader of the truth and certainty of all that Jesus, "*the* Teacher," has taught and predicted, especially the predictions he taught about his passion, death and resurrection (8:31; 9:31; 10:33–34) as well as his teaching (13:1) about the future events before his final coming in glory (13:5–37).

### 2. MARK 14:12–16 AS MODEL FOR ACTION

The scene of the disciples' "preparation" for their final Passover meal with Jesus "prepares" us to join ourselves in a close bond of fellowship to Jesus as we follow his "way" of suffering and death. The divinely authoritative teaching of Jesus, *the* Teacher, empowers us, his disciples, to prepare ourselves to be united to Jesus as he approaches his death so that we can appreciate and celebrate the profound significance of that death for us as *the* salvific event which climaxes the past saving and liberating deeds of God memorialized in the Passover meal. Jesus' demonstration of his prophetic knowledge of the future enables us to prepare ourselves for the necessity and certainty that he will not only suffer, die and rise in accord with God's plan but also return in glory to finally establish the kingdom of God.

## E. Mark 14:17–21: While Eating with the Twelve, Jesus Foretells His Betrayal by One of Them

<sup>17</sup>When it was evening he came with the Twelve. <sup>18</sup>And as they reclined and were eating, Jesus said, "Amen I say to you, one of you will betray me, one who is eating with me." <sup>19</sup>They began to be distressed and to say to him, one by one, "Surely it is not I?" <sup>20</sup>He said to them, "One of the Twelve, the one who dips with me into the dish. <sup>21</sup>For the Son of Man indeed goes as it is written of him, but woe to that man by whom the Son of Man is betrayed. It would be better for that man if he had never been born."

### 1. MEANING OF MARK 14:17–21

#### a. *14:17–18* Jesus predicts that one of the Twelve will betray him.

"When it was evening," and thus time for the Passover meal, Jesus came to Jerusalem "with the Twelve," the twelve disciples specially chosen "to be with him" (3:14), so that he can fulfill his strong desire to share the intimate table fellowship of his final Passover meal with them (14:14) as he approaches his death (14:8). The close communal bond established by the table fellowship of the Passover meal enables the Twelve's privilege of "being with him" to be fully and climactically actualized, as it joins the Twelve intimately with Jesus on his way "to give his life as a ransom for many" (10:45) within the context of the most solemn commemoration of God's salvific activity for his people (14:17).

After the Passover meal has begun and they have "reclined" and "were eating," Jesus introduces another authoritative prophetic prediction with the solemn words, "Amen I say to you," underscoring the importance, truth and certainty of what he will say. Indicating his awareness of Judas' deceitful plot against him (14:10–11), Jesus announces that "one of you," that is, one of the Twelve now in table fellowship with him, "will betray me." He then reinforces the incongruity of this serious offense with the intimacy of table fellowship as he adds, "one who is eating with me." With their allusion to Psalm 41:9: "Even my bosom friend in whom I trusted, who ate of my bread, has lifted his heel against me" (see also Ps 55:12–14), these words place Jesus in the biblical tradition of the "suffering just one," the person who humbly remains loyal to God despite opposition and persecution, even from closest friends and companions, with the high hope that God will vindicate his faithfulness in ultimate triumph (see Ps 41:10–12).[12] That one who is "eating" the Passover meal "with Jesus" will betray him represents a most grievous violation not only of the close bond of the table fellowship within the sacred Passover meal but of the special privilege of the Twelve "to be with" Jesus (14:18).

**b.** *14:19–21* **Jesus assures his disciples that although his betrayal is part of God's plan, his betrayer is culpable.**

Shocked by Jesus' startling pronouncement, the Twelve react by becoming "distressed" or "saddened." As they had been personally and individually called and named by Jesus to be members of the Twelve (3:13–19), so now personally and individually, "one by one," they anxiously and apprehensively ask, "surely it is not I?," each one unsure of his own commitment, nervously hoping that Jesus will exempt him. As previously they were selfishly concerned with their own greatness and status (9:33–34; 10:35–37), so now they seem more concerned with their individual innocence than with the tragic betrayal of Jesus by one of his and their close associates (14:19).

Rather than reassuring the non-betrayers, Jesus insistently repeats and reinforces his alarming pronouncement. He further specifies and emphasizes that the betrayer is "one of you" with the scandalous statement that he is "one of the Twelve." And he accentuates his betrayer's grave violation, as one who is "eating *with me,*" of the intimacy of table fellowship and of the privilege of being one of the Twelve "*with him*" (3:14) by adding that he is "the one who dips *with me* into the dish":

> *3:14* He appointed twelve that they might *be with him . . .*
> *14:18* One of you will betray me, one who is eating *with me*
> *14:20* One of the Twelve, the one who dips *with me* into the dish.

The betrayer is so closely associated *with Jesus* that he even "dips" bread *with him* "into the dish" of the meal. This further indicates how Jesus is the "suffering just one" betrayed by a close companion but to be ultimately vindicated by God because of his humble fidelity (Ps 41:9–12) (14:20).

With complete foreknowledge and determined acceptance of his role in God's future plan of salvation, Jesus proclaims that as the Son of Man he indeed "goes," that is, he will "go" his "way" by being delivered/

betrayed to suffer, die and rise, "as it is written of him" in accord with God's plan recorded in the sacred Jewish scriptures. Although Jesus' betrayal by one of the Twelve is embraced by God's salvific will, the betrayer, held fully and personally responsible, is to be sadly pitied for abandoning the Twelve's intimate communal bond with Jesus and betraying him: "but woe to that man by whom the Son of Man is betrayed":

9:12 How *is it written* of the Son of Man that he should suffer greatly and be treated with contempt?

9:31 The Son of Man is to be *delivered/betrayed* into the hands of people, and they will kill him, and three days after his death he will rise.

10:33 The Son of Man will be *delivered/betrayed* to the chief priests and the scribes, and they will condemn him to death and deliver him to the Gentiles . . .

14:10 Judas . . . went to the chief priests in order to *betray/deliver* him to them.

14:21 For the Son of Man indeed goes as *it is written* of him, but woe to that man by whom the Son of Man is *betrayed/delivered.*

So unfortunate and accursed is the fate of the betrayer that it sadly would have been better if he had never even been born (see Job 3:3; Sir 23:14). And so the negative example of the one member of the Twelve who should never have been born for betraying Jesus to death stands in stark contrast to the positive model of the woman who will be forever and everywhere memorialized in the proclamation of the gospel for anointing the body of Jesus for death:

14:9 Wherever the gospel is proclaimed in the whole world, what she has done will be told in memory of her.

14:21 But woe to that man by whom the Son of Man is betrayed. It would be better for that man if he had never been born.

## 2. MARK 14:17–21 AS MODEL FOR ACTION

The anxiously uncertain and fearful question that each member of the Twelve, shocked by the prediction of the betrayal of Jesus, "one by one" asks, "surely it is not I?," provokes each of us to question our own personal and communal commitment to Jesus on his "way" to death. Warned that any of us could "betray" Jesus by abandoning his "way," we are advised to examine whether we truly understand, accept and appreciate the crucial need for us to remain closely united to Jesus and to one another in communal fellowship if we are to follow the "way" of Jesus to final glory through the necessity of his suffering and death. The example of Jesus as the "suffering just one" encourages us to likewise humbly accept and endure the suffering, persecution and opposition that we will encounter, even from close associates, as we follow the "way" of Jesus with the confident conviction that God will ultimately lead us to glorious triumph.

## F. Mark 14:22–25: Jesus Interprets the Meal as Symbolic of His Death for All and as an Anticipation of God's Kingdom

> [22]While they were eating, he took bread, said the blessing, broke it, and gave it to them, and said, "Take it; this is my body." [23]Then he took a cup, gave thanks, and gave it to them, and they all drank from it. [24]He said to them, "This is my blood of the covenant, which will be poured out for many. [25]Amen I say to you, I shall never again drink of the fruit of the vine until that day when I drink it new in the kingdom of God."

### 1. MEANING OF MARK 14:22–25

**a. *14:22* Jesus designates the bread of the meal as his body.**

While the disciples and Jesus are "eating" the special Passover meal the disciples have prepared through the authoritative command of Jesus, the Teacher (14:12–16), he performs the role of host or head of the meal by taking "bread," "blessing" or thanking God for it, "breaking" it for distribution and "giving" it to his disciples. In the ritual of the Passover meal the father or head of the household pronounced the traditional symbolic interpretations upon the various elements of the meal, so that the participants could not only commemorate but actually share in and sacramentally relive the salvific experience of the original Passover meal when God liberated his people from slavery in the Exodus from Egypt and gave them the hope and expectation of God's future and final salvation. In his last Passover meal with his disciples, Jesus, as their Teacher and host, transforms the meaning of this meal for them as he places a new symbolic interpretation upon the bread and wine.

After directing them to "take" the bread which he has blessed and broken for them, Jesus designates it as the symbolic and sacramental equivalent of his "body," that is, his very person: "this *is* my body." The "bread" thus becomes the very "body" or person of Jesus (*to sōma mou,* 14:22), which "body" (*to sōma mou,* 14:8) has already been anointed for death and burial. By giving them the Passover "bread," which is his "body" destined for death, to eat, Jesus enables his disciples to sacramentally share in his death as *the* salvific event that climaxes all the past saving deeds of God for his people commemorated and experienced in the Passover meal which arouses hope for God's future and definitive salvation. The Twelve's special privilege "to be with" Jesus (3:14) thus reaches its high point in this unique Passover meal as they eat the bread/body of Jesus, which unites them in table fellowship "with him" on his way to death.

This final, climactic Passover meal of Jesus recalls for the reader the meal fellowship he has shared with his disciples and others throughout the narrative (1:31; 2:15–28; 3:20; 6:30–44; 8:1–9; 14:3–9), especially that of the miraculously overabundant feedings. That Jesus identifies his own person destined for death with the bread of the Passover meal coincides with yet develops the earlier metaphorical meaning of the "one loaf (bread)" (8:14) which the disciples had with them in the boat after Jesus had twice miraculously multiplied small amounts of bread and fish for large numbers of people (6:30–44; 8:1–9). This "one loaf (bread)" symbolized the person of Jesus, who had revealed his profound character as the one with divine power to overabundantly satisfy and unify in communal meal fellowship with him his disciples and the large crowds (8:13–21). The "one loaf (bread)" symbolic of Jesus with his power to satisfy and unify now becomes the Passover "bread" identical to the very person of Jesus anointed for death, the bread/body with which he feeds and closely unites his disciples with him and his saving death.

The ritual gestures of "taking-blessing-breaking-giving" that Jesus performs in offering the "bread" which is his "body" to his disciples recalls the corresponding gestures he used in both of the previous miraculous meals with the crowds:

> *6:41* And *taking* the five *loaves* and the two fish and looking up to heaven, he *blessed* and *broke* the loaves and *gave* them to his disciples to distribute to the people.
>
> *8:6* *Taking* the seven *loaves* he *gave thanks, broke* them, and *gave* them to his disciples to distribute, and they distributed them to the crowd.
>
> *14:22* He *took bread,* said the *blessing, broke* it, and *gave* it to them, and said, "*Take* it; this is my body."

In the miraculous meals the pattern Jesus established by his gestures of taking-blessing-breaking-giving the bread concluded with his disciples distributing the bread to the crowds, thus making them intermediary distributors to the people of the bread they received from Jesus. This pattern within the miraculous meals implies that when the disciples "take" the Passover bread/body which Jesus "gives" them, they are not only to feed themselves but to once again distribute it to the people in future celebrations of this new Passover meal. The very nature of the Passover meal as a repeatedly celebrated commemorative feast indicates that the disciples are to repeatedly celebrate this new Passover meal of Jesus in the future. In giving them the Passover bread which is his very person destined for death, Jesus has not only left his disciples a new way "to be with him" (3:14) after he has died, but he has enabled them to feed, satisfy and unify other people "with him" and his saving death.

**b. *14:23-25* Jesus designates the wine as his blood.**

Still within the Passover meal, Jesus "takes" a "cup" of wine, "gives thanks" to God for it, and "gives" it to his disciples, who in turn "all drank from it." Within the interlocking relationship formed between the earlier miraculous meals and this climactic Passover meal, that "all" the disciples "drank" from the cup Jesus gave them complements the notice that "all" the disciples and people "ate" and "were satisfied" when Jesus gave them the loaves and fish:

> *6:42*   They all (*pantes*) ate and were satisfied.
> *14:23*  They all (*pantes*) drank from it (the cup).

Whereas the bread and fish Jesus gave in the miraculous meal (6:30–44) satisfied and united in meal fellowship with him "all" the disciples and people who "ate" it, the cup of wine Jesus now gives in the Passover meal unites with him on his way to death "all" the disciples who "drank" it.

That "all drank from the cup" Jesus gave them fulfills for all of the disciples on the literal level the previous promise Jesus made to James and John that they would "drink the cup" that he "drinks," as a metaphor for sharing in his suffering and death before they enter into "glory" with him (10:35–40). The literal "drinking" from "the cup" that Jesus gives all the disciples, then, indicates their sacramental participation in the suffering and death of Jesus through this new Passover meal and thus prepares them for their own future sufferings and deaths (13:9–13) (14:23).

As he had reinterpreted the Passover "bread" as his own "body" destined for death, so now Jesus reinterprets the cup of wine that all the disciples have drunk within the Passover meal as the symbolic and sacramental equivalent of his own "blood" about to be shed in his death: "This *is* my blood of the covenant, which will be poured out for many." By designating the cup of wine as "my blood of the covenant," Jesus relates the blood to be shed by his death to the sacrificial "blood of the covenant" which Moses threw against the altar, representative of God, and upon the people (Exod 24:3–8) with the words: "Behold the blood of the covenant which the Lord has made with you in accordance with all these words" (Exod 24:8). The ceremony establishing the "covenant" concluded with a meal which united the people of Israel in the covenantal relationship with God (Exod 24:9–11).

In the biblical tradition "covenant" referred to the fundamental relationship uniting God to Israel as his specially chosen people, the pledge of mutual fidelity and loyalty according to which God would be their saving God and they would be his people.[13] But the people of Israel repeatedly failed to uphold their role in God's covenant with them. Consequently, God, through prophecies such as that pronounced by Jeremiah, promised to establish a new, permanent and definitive "covenant" with his people. This new "covenant" would be profoundly internal to the people, "written upon their hearts," and characterized by a universal knowledge of God and the forgiveness of sins (Jer 31:31–34; 32:37–41). By referring to his blood as "my blood of the covenant," Jesus indicates that the blood of his death will effect the fulfillment of *the* "covenant," the new and definitive "covenant" according to which God unites himself permanently and profoundly with his people in a salvific and liberating relationship.[14] Jesus thus further transforms the Passover meal into a covenant meal, whereby those who drink the wine designated as his blood of *the* covenant are sacramentally and profoundly united into this new and final covenantal relationship God establishes with his people through the salvific death of Jesus.

That Jesus' blood, which effects *the* covenant with God, "will be poured out for many" emphasizes the nature of Jesus' death as a covenantal sacrifice for the atonement of sins. As the blood of sacrificed animals was "poured out" by priests on the altar as a sin offering to atone for the sins of the people (Lev 4:7, 18, 25, 30, 34), so the blood which will be "shed" or "poured out" by the death of Jesus represents a sacrifice for the atonement of sins "for," that is, "on behalf of" (*hyper*) "many" people. The forgiveness of sins (see 2:1–12, 15–17; 3:28; 11:25) brought about by the sacrificial death of Jesus is part of the new and definitive "covenant" God establishes with his people (Jer 31:34). That the atoning blood of Jesus will be poured out on behalf of "many," a common Semitic expression for "all" people,[15] indicates the universal nature of *the* covenant which brings forgiveness and salvation to "all." This corresponds to and develops Jesus' previous pronouncement that the selfless offering of his life will effect a salvific liberation for "many" = "all" people:

> *10:45* For the Son of Man did not come to be served but to serve
> and to give his life as a ransom for *many* (all).
>
> *14:24* This is my blood of the covenant, which will be poured
> out for *many* (all).

Thus, *the* covenant established through the sacrificially atoning blood of Jesus is intended to include "all" people (14:24).

With the solemn introductory words, "Amen I say to you," reinforcing the authority and certainty of what he will say, Jesus announces that this is his last meal: "I shall never again drink of the fruit of the vine." That Jesus will no longer drink wine, the festive drink produced from the "fruit (grapes) of the vine" means not only that his death is very imminent but that it will prevent him from partaking of the joyous and convivial meal fellowship he has continually shared with his followers. But the death of Jesus will not bring a definitive conclusion to the joy and festivity of his table fellowship. On the contrary, "on that day" of God's end-time fulfillment of his salvific activity (see 13:24–27, 32), after Jesus' glorious triumph over death through his resurrection, he will drink "new" festive wine and thus again be united in joyous meal fellowship with his followers in the fully and finally established "kingdom of God."

The celebration of this transformed Passover meal of Jesus, then, enables its participants to sacramentally anticipate and share in not only the saving death of Jesus, which effects *the* new covenant for all people, but also the triumph of Jesus over death through his resurrection. In their celebration of the new Passover meal of Jesus, his followers look forward with joyful hope to their future participation in the ultimate banquet of the kingdom of God when they will share in Jesus' final triumph over death (see Isa 25:6–8). This powerful prediction of the joyous and festive table fellowship celebrating Jesus' conclusive triumph over death in God's kingdom thus stands in sharp contrast to his previous prediction of his sad and woeful betrayal to death by one of the Twelve eating with him (14:18–21) (14:25).

## 2. MARK 14:22–25 AS MODEL FOR ACTION

The scene of Jesus' last Passover meal with his Twelve disciples serves as a model for our celebration of the table fellowship that unites us with Jesus and one another in the eucharist, the new Christian Passover and sacrificial covenant meal which anticipates the final triumphant meal of God's kingdom. In the eucharist Jesus commands us to "take" the bread which is his body destined for death so that with the salvific effects of his death we can spiritually nourish and unite not only ourselves but others with him, in order that we may complete his "way" of suffering and death. The eucharistic wine which is the blood of Jesus' death invites us to realize and experience the new and profound "covenant" whereby God joins all of us into his covenant people whom he will loyally and faithfully bring to final and definitive salvation through the sacrificial death of Jesus which effects the forgiveness of sins. Through our sacramental participation in the saving death and resurrection of Jesus in the eucharist we joyfully anticipate and look forward with confident hope to our future triumph over suffering and death in the festive meal fellowship we will all share with Jesus in the final banquet of God's kingdom.

## G. Mark 14:26–31: Jesus Predicts Abandonment by His Disciples and Peter's Denial of Him

[26]After singing a hymn, they went out to the Mount of Olives. [27]Then Jesus said to them, "All of you will fall away, for it is written:
   'I will strike the shepherd,
     and the sheep will be scattered' (Zech 13:7).
[28]But after I have been raised up, I will go before you to Galilee." [29]Peter said to him, "Even if all fall away, I will not." [30]Then Jesus said to him, "Amen I say to you, this very night before the cock crows twice you will deny me three times." [31]But he vehemently insisted, "Even if I must die with you, I will not deny you." And they all spoke similarly.

### 1. MEANING OF MARK 14:26–31

**a. *14:26–28* Jesus predicts that all will abandon him, but that he will precede them to Galilee after his resurrection.**

The "singing of a hymn" by Jesus and his disciples marks the jubilant conclusion of the unique Passover meal,[16] which has united the disciples in a close bond of fellowship with Jesus by enabling them to sacramentally anticipate both his death and his future triumph. With their "singing a hymn" the intimate relationship of the disciples' "being with" (3:14) Jesus is at a high point as they conclude the meal. Jesus and his disciples continue the movement of his "way" as they once again "went out" of

Jerusalem (see 11:11, 19; 13:1) and returned not to the communal setting of Bethany (11:1, 11; 14:3–9) but to the Mount of Olives, the place where Jesus had prepared his disciples for their separation from him after his death and resurrection and before his coming in glory at the end of time (13:3–37) (14:26).

In stunning contradiction to their sharing of communal meal fellowship with him, Jesus tells his disciples that "all of you will fall away." "All" of the disciples who have just been closely united to Jesus on his way to death as they "all" drank from the Passover cup of wine designated as the very blood of Jesus will "fall away" and thus be separated from Jesus:

> *14:23* They all (*pantes*) drank from it (the cup).
> *14:27* All (*pantes*) of you will fall away.

Jesus' prediction of desertion by "all" of the disciples complements his earlier prediction of betrayal by "one" of the Twelve. Not only will "one" of the Twelve eating the Passover meal with Jesus violate his close bond with Jesus by betraying him to death (14:18–20), but "all" of the disciples who have just participated in that meal fellowship will also impede their intimate union with Jesus by "falling away" from him.

That all the disciples will "fall away" from Jesus, or literally "be scandalized" by him, means that they will be like those in Jesus' parable who initially hear the word with joy, but, having "no root" in themselves, "when tribulation or persecution because of the word arises, they immediately *fall away*" (4:17). The disciples' "falling away" or "being scandalized" thus indicates the shallowness of their faith, which prevents them from following and remaining with Jesus on his "way" to suffering and death.[17]

But like Judas' betrayal (14:21), the disciples' desertion accords with what "is written" explicitly in the scriptural plan of God: "I will strike the shepherd, and the sheep will be scattered." In his adaptation of this quotation from Zechariah 13:7, Mark accentuates how the suffering and death of Jesus are the doing of God himself. "I," that is, God himself, "will strike" with suffering and death "the shepherd," that is, Jesus, and consequently "the sheep," that is, the disciples, "will be scattered." The image of Jesus as "shepherd" recalls the introduction to his first miraculously overabundant meal, when "he saw a great crowd and had compassion on them, for they were like sheep without a shepherd" (6:34). Jesus then demonstrated how he is "shepherd" by uniting in meal fellowship his disciples and the crowd as the shepherdless "sheep" (6:35–44). Now, the close union that Jesus as "shepherd" has just established in his last Passover meal with his disciples will be broken as they "will be scattered" like "sheep" who disperse when their "shepherd" is killed (14:27).

But this "scattering" of the disciples will only be temporary. After Jesus, the "shepherd," has been raised from the dead, he will "go before" his disciples, the "sheep," and return "to Galilee." As Jesus had earlier "gone ahead" of his followers, leading them on the "way" to Jerusalem where he will suffer and die, so he will "go before" his disciples to Galilee with the implication that they are to follow him:

> *10:32* They were on the *way,* going up to Jerusalem, and Jesus was *going ahead* of them. They were amazed, and those who *followed* were afraid . . .
>
> *14:28* But after I have been raised up, I will *go before* you to Galilee.

Jesus' suffering and death and the disciples' desertion in Jerusalem will not be the end of the "way" of Jesus. His salvific "way" will continue anew after his resurrection in Galilee where it began. "Galilee" thus represents the place of both the beginning and the renewed continuation of the dynamic "way" of Jesus. In Galilee the close bond broken by the deserting disciples will be reestablished with the risen Jesus. Unlike the betraying Judas whose fate is so woeful that it would be better if he had never been born (14:21), the temporarily deserting disciples will be reunited with the risen Jesus in Galilee to follow anew his "way" of salvation (14:28).

### b. *14:29–31* Jesus predicts that Peter will deny him three times.

Peter, the leader (3:16) and usual spokesman of the disciples (8:29, 32; 9:5; 10:28; 11:21), directly contradicts the authoritative prediction of Jesus: "Even if all fall away, I will not." With his customary impetuosity Peter now speaks only for himself. Whereas the disciples had earlier reacted with timid sadness to Jesus' prediction that "one" of them would betray him (14:18–19), Peter, with brash overconfidence, protests the prediction that "all" of the disciples will desert him. He insists that he will prove the exception (14:29).

Reinforcing and developing his shocking prediction of desertion by all his disciples, Jesus counters Peter's impulsive protest with a further, more intense and individualized prediction directed at Peter. With the solemn introductory formula, "amen I say to you," emphasizing the certainty of what he will say, Jesus predicts that Peter, the first-called and leader of the disciples, will shamefully "deny" him. Jesus underlines how quickly and repeatedly Peter will "deny" him by stating that "this very night" before the cock has the chance to crow "twice" as a signal of dawn, Peter will "three times," that is, definitively, deny him. Unable to fulfill Jesus' demand that a disciple must "deny" oneself, "take up one's cross" and follow Jesus on the "way" to suffering and death (8:34), Peter will fail miserably as a disciple by "denying" Jesus rather than himself. Not only will Peter not prove to be an exception to the desertion by all the disciples, but he will sharpen his separation from Jesus by blatantly denying him (14:30).

Continuing to resist the authoritative, prophetic foreknowledge of Jesus, Peter vehemently objects: "Even if I must die with you, I will not deny you." His bold and brazen statement functions as dramatic irony for the reader. Peter still does not seem to realize what the reader knows, namely that a disciple "must" indeed "die with" Jesus. Not only has Jesus demanded that a disciple must lose his life for Jesus' sake (8:35), but he has indicated that his disciples will participate in his suffering and death (13:9–13), which they have already anticipated by "drinking the cup" of his blood in the Passover meal (10:38–39; 14:22–24). Nor does Peter understand what has been consistently demonstrated for the reader, namely that what Jesus, *the* Teacher, foretells happens with exact certainty (14:12–16), so that Peter cannot possibly avoid denying Jesus. Ironically, it is precisely because Peter has not grasped the necessity of suffering and "dying with" Jesus (8:32–33; 9:5–8; 10:28–31) that he will "deny" him. For the reader the irony expresses the mysterious paradox that the necessity for a disciple to die with Jesus does not preclude denial of him— both dying with Jesus and denying him are embraced by God's plan as predicted by Jesus.

Although Peter insistently and presumptuously maintains that he will be the one exception to desertion of Jesus by all the disciples, "they all spoke similarly," likewise protesting their abandonment of Jesus. And so "all" of the disciples, despite having anticipated the suffering and death of Jesus by drinking his cup of wine/blood (14:23), fail to understand that they cannot avoid abandoning Jesus because "all" of them "will be scattered" in accord with the "written" plan of God (14:27). But the hope is sure that after Jesus' resurrection they will be reunited with him (14:28) (14:31).

## 2. MARK 14:26–31 AS MODEL FOR ACTION

Jesus' authoritative prediction of all of his disciples' desertion and Peter's denial of him warns us against a presumptuous overconfidence in our ability to remain faithfully united with Jesus as we follow his "way" of suffering and death. Can we be sure that we will not abandon and deny

Jesus rather than ourselves, especially when we encounter opposition, persecution, suffering and death for the sake of Jesus and his gospel (8:34–35; 13:9–13)? But despite our failures to remain united with Jesus in suffering and death, the promise of his resurrection empowers us to be reunited with him in order to follow anew and complete his "way" to God's salvation by suffering and dying in close union with him.

## H. Mark 14:32–42: Through Prayer at Gethsemane Jesus Accepts His Death While the Disciples Are Overcome with Sleep

³²Then they came to a place named Gethsemane, and he said to his disciples, "Sit here while I pray." ³³He took with him Peter, James, and John, and began to be greatly troubled and distressed. ³⁴Then he said to them, "I am very sorrowful, even to death. Remain here and watch."

³⁵And going forward a little, he fell to the ground and prayed that if it were possible the hour might pass by him. ³⁶He said, "*Abba,* Father, all things are possible for you! Take this cup away from me, but not what I will but what you will!"

³⁷He returned and found them sleeping. He said to Peter, "Simon, are you asleep? Could you not watch for one hour? ³⁸Watch and pray, so that you may not undergo the test. The spirit is willing but the flesh is weak."

³⁹Withdrawing again, he prayed, saying the same thing. ⁴⁰Then returning again, he found them sleeping, for their eyes were heavy; and they did not know what to answer him.

⁴¹He returned the third time and said to them, "Are you still sleeping and taking your rest? It is enough. The hour has come. Behold, the Son of Man is betrayed into the hands of sinners. ⁴²Get up, let us go! Behold, my betrayer is at hand!"

### 1. MEANING OF MARK 14:32–42

**a. *14:32–34* While Jesus prays at Gethsemane, he exhorts his disciples to keep watch.**

Jesus and his disciples advance the movement of his salvific "way" as they "came" to a specific "place" on the Mount of Olives (14:26) known as "Gethsemane." Although still with his disciples, Jesus begins to separate himself from them for the purpose of praying alone. He directs them to "sit here while I pray." Jesus had prayed alone at a critical turning point of his salvific "way" when, through prayer, he came to the decision to extend his salvific ministry beyond Capernaum to all of Galilee (1:35–39). And it was from a position of private prayer signalling his close communion with God that Jesus revealed to his disciples his divine power to walk on the sea and save them from the sea storm (6:45–52). Jesus' desire to again pray alone thus leads the reader to expect another critical or momentous event on the "way" of Jesus (14:32).

Withdrawing from the larger group of disciples, Jesus once again takes with him the special smaller group composed of Peter, James and John. Only these three disciples were chosen to accompany Jesus to witness the revelation of his power to raise the daughter of Jairus from the dead (5:37–43). Jesus took only these three with him to witness the revelation of his heavenly glory in the scene of his transfiguration (9:2–8). And it was to these three along with Andrew that Jesus revealed the events to take place after his resurrection and before his final coming at the end of the world (13:3–37). That Peter, James and John again accompany Jesus as he goes to pray prepares the reader for another significant revelation by Jesus.

The expected critical event commences with a notable change in the emotional state of Jesus as he "began to be greatly troubled and distressed." With allusions to the biblical psalms of lament and in accord with his portrayal as the "suffering just one" (Pss 40:12–13; 42:9–11; 55:5–6; 116:3–4; Sir 51:6–12), Jesus announces the great seriousness of the situation to Peter, James and John: "I am very sorrowful, even to death" (see Pss 42:5, 11; 43:5). Here Jesus reveals that the quite human fear of his approaching death (14:8, 22–25) is now overwhelming him with a deep distress and sorrow commensurate with that death. Jesus then directs the three to "remain here and watch," further separating himself from his disciples as he goes to pray alone:

> *14:32* Sit here while I pray.
> *14:34* Remain here and watch.

Thus, Peter, James and John are to remain behind and "watch" while Jesus goes forward to "pray."

Jesus' command for these three disciples to "watch" recalls his earlier command for the disciples and for "all" others to "watch" in the period after his resurrection and before his final coming in glory (13:32–37). To "watch" means to be awake and alert, ready and prepared for the critical time or "hour" leading to God's final and definitive salvation. That the disciples are to "watch" while Jesus "prays" thus places them in a position that serves as a paradigm for the time of "watching" for the final and triumphant coming of Jesus after his death and resurrection (14:33–34).

### b. *14:35–36* Through his prayer Jesus accepts God's will.

Jesus then separates himself from Peter, James and John a short distance as he "goes forward a little." Although Jesus goes forward to pray alone, his praying has significance for the disciples, who, though separated, are still in close vicinity to Jesus. Indeed, the praying of Jesus has been consistently defined in reference to the disciples. They are explicitly told to "sit here" (14:32) and "remain here and watch" (14:34) while Jesus goes forward to pray.

That Jesus then "falls to the ground" corresponds to and accentuates the overburdening effect of his great distress and anxiety in view of his imminent death. On the ground from the depths of his anguish he prays that "if it were possible the hour might pass by him." Jesus thus prays that "if it were possible" in accord with God's will, he would prefer not to undergo "the hour," the critical and upcoming time of his suffering and death (14:35).

In his prayer Jesus addresses God as "*Abba*, Father." "*Abba*" is the Aramaic word for "father," connoting intimacy, affection and reverence.[18] Throughout the narrative Jesus has been identified as the special "Son of God" (1:1, 11; 3:11; 5:7; 9:7). Now, Jesus, especially in correspondence to the heavenly proclamations of God himself, "You are my beloved Son; with you I am well pleased!" (1:11) and "This is my beloved Son!" (9:7), endorses and exploits his unique sonship as he affectionately but reverentially begs God as his intimate and loving Father for deliverance from his imminent death.

Acknowledging the absolute and ultimate power of God, Jesus proclaims that "all things are possible for you!" He thus demonstrates and actualizes his faith in the unlimited power of God to save, a faith that he earlier exhorted others to exhibit. With the words, "all things are possible for one who believes!" (9:23), Jesus called the father of the boy with the mute spirit which the disciples could not expel to acknowledge his faith in the power of God at work in Jesus to cure his son (9:14–29). With the words, "all things are possible for God!" (10:27), Jesus invited his disciples to place their faith in the supreme power of God to bring people, even the rich, to salvation (10:17–31):

*9:23* All things are possible for one who believes!
*10:27* All things are possible for God!
*14:36* All things are possible for you!

In addition, Jesus urged his disciples to "have faith in God!" (11:22), assuring them that "all that you ask for in prayer, believe that you have received it, and it shall be done for you" (11:24). And so, when Jesus proclaims in prayer that "all things are possible for you!," he expresses his knowledge and firm belief that God's deliverance of him from death is a distinct and real possibility.[19]

With his faith in the limitless power of God Jesus entreats his Father to "take this cup away from me." "This cup," like "the hour," refers to the suffering and death that Jesus must "drink." His plea for God to take away this "cup" stands in shocking contradiction not only to his earlier assurance that James and John would "drink the cup" that Jesus "drinks" and thus share in his suffering and death (10:38–39), but also to the giving of the Passover "cup" of his wine/blood which all the disciples drank as a sacramental participation in his suffering and death (14:23–24). In accord with his prayer of lament, that Jesus wants God to remove "this cup" brings to a climax the expression of his deep dread and sorrowful distress at the prospect of approaching death.

The dramatic tension of the contradiction between the divine necessity that Jesus suffer and die and his quite human trepidation to undergo that suffering and death is resolved through the very praying of Jesus as he utters the words, "but not what I will but what you will!" In thus submitting his own will to the sovereign will of God, Jesus exemplifies the hallmark that is to characterize his new "family" of followers: "whoever does the will of God is my brother and sister and mother!" (3:35). For those he calls to follow him on his "way" to suffering and death, Jesus now demonstrates what it means to "think the things of God" rather than the "things of human beings" (8:33) and to "deny oneself" (8:34) in order to take up one's cross and follow him, namely, to deny one's own will in favor of God's will.

Jesus' acceptance of God's will over his own will in prayer, even though he knows and believes that God has the power to take away his "cup" of suffering and death, develops his earlier teaching about prayer. Although disciples are to pray with faith in God's absolute power to grant their request (11:22–24), they must realize that God, though he possesses unlimited power, does not always choose to exercise that power to remove suffering and death. The will of God remains sovereign. But the Gethsemane prayer of Jesus illustrates how one can voice one's deepest fears and concerns with firm faith that God can alleviate them, and yet ultimately submit one's own will to God's will precisely in and through such prayer. Jesus thus demonstrates the power of prayer to enable one to "deny oneself" and conform his own will to the sovereign will of God (14:36).

### c. *14:37–38* Jesus exhorts the sleeping disciples to watch and pray.

Returning to the three disciples after his prayer, Jesus "found them sleeping" rather than awake and "watching" as he had commanded (14:34). That he "finds them sleeping" is precisely what he warned them against in his discourse preparing them for the time before his final coming: "Watch, therefore; for you do not know when the lord of the house will come, whether in the evening, or at midnight, or at cockcrow, or in the morning, lest he come suddenly and *find you sleeping.* What I say to you, I say to all: 'Watch!' " (13:35–37). The disciples' "sleeping," then, not only indicates their inability to stay awake and "watch" during this critical time while Jesus prays before his suffering and death, but also points to their potential failure to be prepared for Jesus' final coming by "sleeping" rather than "watching."

Jesus' two reproachful questions to Peter, "Simon, are you asleep?" and "Could you not watch for one hour?," stand in ironical contrast to Peter's previous protest that he would be the exception to the disciples' desertion of Jesus (14:29). That he cannot watch for even "one hour" while Jesus prays for deliverance from death sharply contradicts his boast that even if he must die with Jesus, he will not deny him (14:31). Not even Peter, spokesman and leader of the disciples, can avoid "sleeping" and the failure to "watch" while Jesus prays (14:37).

Developing his previous commands, Jesus now commands the disciples to "watch and pray."[20] His addition of the command to "pray" indicates the significance and power of his own prayer. Now that he has prayed, he commands and empowers his disciples to likewise "pray":

*14:32* Sit here while I *pray.*
*14:34* Remain here and *watch.*
*14:35* ... he fell to the ground and *prayed* ...
*14:38* *Watch* and *pray* ...

That Jesus "prays" precisely while the disciples sleep and are unable to "watch" indicates that the prayer of Jesus is not only the model for the disciples to emulate in their prayer but the basis or empowerment for their own praying. The sleeping disciples can now "watch and pray" only because Jesus watched and prayed.

Jesus enjoins his disciples to watch and pray in order that they not "undergo the test." The "test," "trial" or "temptation" refers to God's final struggle with and conquering of the powers of evil, which is now reaching a crescendo with the suffering and death of Jesus. The dreaded "test" embraces not only this critical "hour" of Jesus' suffering and death, but the future time of the disciples' own persecution, sufferings and deaths (13:9–13). Although the praying of the disciples will not guarantee the elimination of their sufferings and distress, the powerful prayer of Jesus has demonstrated how they, in and through his praying, can deny themselves and conform their wills to the sovereign will of God through their praying, and thus withstand the terrible "test."

The disciples need to watch and pray because of the fundamental and constant tension that "the spirit is willing but the flesh is weak." In other words, although the "spirit," that part of the human person attuned to God and the spiritual, transcendent realm, is "willing" or "eager" to obey God's will, the "flesh," that part of the human person attuned to oneself and the earthly, limited and mortal realm, is "weak" and thus disinclined to obey the will of God. This basic tension has been demonstrated by Peter and the disciples, whose "spirit" is willing to die with Jesus (14:31) but whose "flesh" prevents them from staying alert and watching. Jesus illustrates how to overcome this tension between "spirit" and "flesh" in and through prayer. In his prayer of lament Jesus, distressed and sorrowful over his imminent death, fully voiced his own concerns of the "flesh" as he begged God to take away his "cup" of suffering and death. But in and through his prayer he allowed his "willing spirit" to predominate over the "weak flesh" as he submitted his own will to that of God (14:38).

### d. *14:39–40* After praying again Jesus finds the disciples still sleeping.

Jesus withdraws from his disciples again and repeats his prayer (14:39). But when he returns he finds them still sleeping, "for their eyes were heavy; and they did not know what to answer him." That "their eyes were heavy" further illustrates the weakness of their "flesh," unable to watch and pray. And that "they did not know what to answer him" indicates their complete and utter bewilderment, as it echoes Peter's perplexed incomprehension at the transfiguration of Jesus (9:5–6). This continued inability of the disciples to stay awake and understand the significance of this critical time underlines and intensifies their stark contrast to the ardent and profound praying of Jesus. That they fail to watch and pray while Jesus continues to pray enhances the importance of the power of Jesus' prayer for them (14:40).

### e. *14:41–42* After praying a third time and finding his disciples asleep, Jesus announces the arrival of his betrayer.

After he has prayed a decisive and definitive "third time," Jesus returns to find his disciples still unable to stay awake, watch and pray: "Are you still sleeping and taking your rest?" With his terse pronouncement, "it is enough," Jesus marks the conclusion of the disciples' pathetic and shameful sleeping as well as his own impassioned praying. His announcement that "the hour has come" begins to illustrate the powerful transforming effect his prayer has had for him. Whereas he had begun praying that if it were possible "the hour" of his suffering and death might pass by him (14:35), now that he has subordinated his own will to the sovereign will of God through prayer (14:36), he is able to proclaim with resolute acceptance that "the hour has come." Continuing to demonstrate how his prayer has enabled him to overcome his fearful distress and deep sorrow over his approaching death, Jesus announces: "Behold, the Son of Man is betrayed into the hands of sinners." He thereby not only indicates his resolved recognition of the divine necessity of his suffering and death, but authoritatively and climactically proclaims that his previous predictions are presently being fulfilled:

> *9:31* The Son of Man *is to be* delivered/betrayed into the hands of people, and they will kill him, and three days after his death he will rise.
> *10:33* The Son of Man *will be* delivered/betrayed to the chief priests and the scribes, and they will condemn him to death and deliver him to the Gentiles . . .
> *14:41* Behold, the Son of Man *is* betrayed/delivered into the hands of sinners.

Now that he has completed his prayer, Jesus' announcement of his betrayal sets in motion the events leading to his suffering and death (14:41).

Jesus' exhortation to the disciples, "get up, let us go!," indicates the powerful effect Jesus' prayer has for them. Before he withdrew to pray, Jesus commanded his disciples to "sit here" and "remain here" while he prayed:

> *14:32 Sit here* while I pray.
> *14:34 Remain here* and watch.
> *14:35* . . . he fell to the ground and *prayed* . . .
> *14:42 Get up,* let us go!

But after he has prayed, Jesus empowers his disciples to "get up" from their inert, sleeping position and enables them to "go" with him—"let *us* go!" Now that Jesus has been strengthened through his prayer, he and his disciples can "go" together to play their respective roles in God's plan— the bewildered disciples to be "scattered" (14:27) and Jesus to be betrayed.

With the climactic exclamation, "behold, my betrayer is at hand!," Jesus not only reinforces the announcement of his imminent betrayal but illustrates his determined readiness, now that he has submitted to God's will through prayer, to face his betrayer (14:42).

## 2. MARK 14:32–42 AS MODEL FOR ACTION

The Gethsemane prayer of Jesus serves as a sterling model and effective empowerment for our own praying. We can pray authentically only because Jesus, at the most serious and intensely critical time before his suffering and death, with deep dread and fearful sorrow over that death, resolved the tension between "willing spirit" and "weak flesh" by humbly submitting his own will that he be rescued from death to the sovereign will of God that he undergo suffering and death. In and through this profound prayer of Jesus we are enabled to likewise "deny ourselves" and follow Jesus' "way" of suffering and death by subordinating our own weak and egoistical wills to the supreme and salvific will of God.

Jesus' prayer exemplifies how we can give full and honest expression in our prayers to our deepest human fears and desires to be spared from our difficulties, sufferings and death, and yet still accept the sovereign will of God. We must realize that although we are called to pray with firm faith in the absolute and unlimited power of God to save and rescue us (11:22–24), God will not always choose to eliminate the pain and problems of our lives. Nevertheless, it is precisely in and through such sincere and humble praying that we are enabled to conform our own limited and weak, selfish wills to the omniscient and ultimate, salvific will of God.

The pathetic failure of the disciples to "watch and pray" illustrates how difficult it is for us to fulfill Jesus' command to be alert and ready for his final coming (13:32–37) and to pray on our own. Based upon our own resources, we tend to be lulled to "sleep," overburdened and bewildered with our own selfish concerns, rather than to remain awake and vigilant for God's salvific activity. But if we rely upon Jesus' magnificent prayer of total and humble submission to the sovereign will of God, we are empowered to watch and pray, strengthened to face whatever crisis we may encounter in playing our part to accomplish the salvific "way" of God, and alert and prepared for the final, triumphant coming of Jesus in glory.

## I. Mark 14:43–52: After Judas Betrays Him, Jesus Is Arrested and Abandoned by His Disciples

⁴³Then immediately, while he was still speaking, Judas, one of the Twelve, arrived, and with him a crowd with swords and clubs, from the chief priests, the scribes, and the elders. ⁴⁴His betrayer had arranged a signal with them, saying, "The man I shall kiss is the one; arrest him and lead him away securely." ⁴⁵When he came, he immediately went over to him and said, "Rabbi." And he affectionately kissed him. ⁴⁶Then they laid hands on him and arrested him. ⁴⁷One of the bystanders drew his sword, struck the high priest's servant, and cut off his ear.

⁴⁸Replying, Jesus said to them, "Have you come out as against a robber, with swords and clubs to capture me? ⁴⁹Day after day I was with you in the temple teaching, yet you did not arrest me. But let the scriptures be fulfilled!"

⁵⁰Then leaving him, they ran away, all of them. ⁵¹And a young man was following with him wearing nothing but a linen cloth about his body, and they arrested him. ⁵²But leaving behind the linen cloth, he ran away naked.

### 1. MEANING OF MARK 14:43–52

#### a. *14:43–47* Jesus is betrayed by Judas and violently arrested.

While Jesus "was still speaking," that is, precisely as he was announcing the arrival of his betrayer (14:42), Judas, again designated as "one of the Twelve," reinforcing the tragic horror that it was one of Jesus' closest followers who betrayed him (14:10, 17–20), "arrived" in suspenseful fulfillment of the authoritative pronouncement of Jesus:

> *14:42* Behold, my betrayer is at hand!
> *14:43* Judas, one of the Twelve, arrived . . .

That Judas arrives immediately in accord with Jesus' announcement accentuates Jesus' control and command, in conjunction with God's plan, over the evil and deceitful machinations of his enemies.

Having tragically separated himself from the close bond of following Jesus by "being with him" as befits "one of the Twelve" (3:14), Judas is no longer a follower with Jesus but a leader of those against Jesus, who now has "with him" a crowd with swords and clubs. That Judas brings with him a "crowd" armed "with swords and clubs" adds to the suspense by creating an expectation of a violent betrayal and possible resistance by Jesus and/or his disciples. The armed crowd accompanying Judas is from "the chief priests, the scribes, and the elders," that is, the full range of Jewish leaders plotting the death of Jesus (8:31; 10:33; 11:18, 27). Not only are the chief priests and scribes, through Judas and the crowd, fulfilling their wicked scheme "to arrest him by deceit and put him to death" (14:1), but in so doing they are, ironically, fulfilling God's plan as predicted by Jesus (8:31; 9:12, 31; 10:33; 14:21) (14:43).

Judas is then designated as "his betrayer," further confirming Jesus' announcement and underlining the tragedy that one of the trusted Twelve is the betrayer:

> *14:42* Behold, *my betrayer* is at hand!
> *14:43* Judas, *one of the Twelve,* arrived . . .
> *14:44* *His betrayer* had arranged a signal . . .

That Judas had previously arranged a signal with the armed crowd, whereby he would "kiss" Jesus as the one they should seize, intensifies the treachery and further underscores the tragedy of his betrayal. He will deceitfully betray Jesus with a false demonstration of affection, sadly abusing the close bond he enjoyed with Jesus as "one of the Twelve." This betrayal by a close friend advances the portrayal of Jesus as the "suffering just one" (14:17–21; Pss 41:9; 55:12–14). Judas' command to "arrest" the one he kisses shows how his betrayal enables the Jewish leaders to fulfill their desire to "arrest" Jesus by deceit (14:1). His additional caution to "lead him away securely" contributes to the tone of violence with the expectation of possible resistance to the arrest (14:44).

Judas immediately comes up to Jesus and addresses him as "Rabbi," deceitfully betraying him with a title of respect and honor (9:5; 10:51; 11:21). He then gives the signal for the arrest as he not only "kissed" him but "kissed him with affection," intensifying his tragic treachery (see 2 Sam 20:8–10; Prov 27:6) (14:45).[21]

The armed crowd then violently "laid hands" on him, thus illustrating that they are the "sinners" into whose "hands" the Son of Man is betrayed in accord with Jesus' pronouncement (14:41). That the crowd "arrested" Jesus finally accomplishes the "arrest" the chief priests and scribes have been intently plotting as part of their plan to destroy him:

> *11:18* The chief priests and the scribes heard it and were seeking how to destroy him.

*12:12* They were seeking to *arrest* him.

*14:1* The chief priests and scribes were seeking how to *arrest* him by deceit and put him to death.

*14:46* Then they laid hands on him and *arrested* him.

The expected resistance comes not from Jesus but from "one of the bystanders," who, in reaction to the violent arrest of Jesus by the crowd wielding "swords and clubs," draws his own "sword" and cuts off the ear of the servant of the high priest. This anonymous bystander retaliates against the forceful arrest of Jesus by violently striking an important member of the arresting crowd, the very "servant of the high priest," and cutting off his ear, inflicting him with a painfully humiliating and disgraceful wound. But such violent retaliation exhibits a complete misunderstanding of Jesus' arrest. That the bystander "strikes" the servant of the high priest with his "sword" indicates his unwitting and futile resistance to the scriptural will of God (Zech 13:7), according to which Jesus (not the high priest's servant) is the "shepherd" whom God (not a bystander) will "strike" with suffering and death (14:27).[22] The bystander's violent retaliation thus demonstrates his confused and inappropriate response to the arrest of Jesus (14:47).

**b. *14:48–49* Jesus announces the fulfillment of the scriptures.**

Making his own response to the inappropriate violence surrounding his arrest, Jesus indignantly and sarcastically asks the crowd whether they mistake him for a "robber," since they have come out to capture him with "swords and clubs." The ironic implication is that the crowd rather than Jesus represent the real "robbers" who employ "swords and clubs" as weapons of unwarranted and unjust violence, an irony enhanced by Jesus' earlier denunciation of the Jewish leaders as the "robbers" who have degraded the Jerusalem temple into a "den of robbers" (11:17). The confused and misdirected crowd has been sent by real "robbers" to violently capture one who is no "robber" (14:48).

The reproachful irony continues as Jesus proclaims that "day after day," that is, continually and in broad daylight, "I was with you," in other words, there was no need to "come out" to capture him, as he was in the temple publically and authoritatively "teaching" the people the genuine ways of God, not behaving like a "robber." Although they had an obvious opportunity to arrest him while he was openly teaching in the temple, they did not do so. Jesus' ironic rebuke recalls how the Jewish leaders, although they wanted to arrest and destroy Jesus, could not do so because of the people's favorable reception of Jesus' divinely authoritative teaching (11:18; 12:12, 37). Since they could not legitimately arrest Jesus while he was teaching in public (14:2), they must resort to treachery and violence in the secluded darkness of Gethsemane. Jesus thus sarcastically unmasks their ruthless deceit while exonerating himself as innocent and no "robber."

Jesus' exclamation, "but let the scriptures be fulfilled!," explains why the armed crowd sent by the Jewish leaders can only now arrest him. It is not that they have triumphed over Jesus, nor that he is a "robber," but that they are playing their role in fulfilling God's scriptural plan (9:12; 14:21). His vigorous exclamation echoes and reinforces his previous powerful prayer:

> *14:36* but not what I will but what you will.
> *14:49* but let the scriptures be fulfilled!

That Jesus has allowed himself to be arrested without violent resistance on his part further illustrates how his prayer has enabled him to submit himself to the will of God as recorded in the scriptures. And his mighty exclamation serves as the signal for the disciples to now fulfill their role in God's scriptural plan (14:49).

### c. *14:50-52* All of Jesus' followers abandon him.

As soon as Jesus calls for the scriptures to be fulfilled, the disciples answer by all running away and abandoning him, thus fulfilling Jesus' previous prediction that they would all fall away from him in accord with the scriptural quote, "I will strike the shepherd, and the sheep will be scattered" (Zech 13:7) (14:27). That the disciples all "leave" Jesus signals a reversal and renunciation of their discipleship. When the first disciples were called by Jesus, they "left" behind their occupations, families and everything to follow him. Now they sadly and shamefully "leave" behind Jesus and run away:

> *1:18* Immediately leaving (*aphentes*) their nets, they followed him.
> *1:20* Immediately he called them, and leaving (*aphentes*) their father Zebedee . . . they went after him.
> *10:28* Peter began to say to him, "Look!, we have left (*aphēkamen*) everything and followed you."
> *14:50* Then leaving (*aphentes*) him, they ran away, all of them.

The emphasis that "all" fled further underlines the fulfillment of

Jesus' previous prediction that they would "all" fall away from him (14:27) despite the objections and protests of "all" (14:31). And that they "all" ran away stands in paradoxical contrast to the fact that "all" of them drank from the Passover cup of Jesus' wine/blood, sharing the close bond of fellowship with Jesus on his way to suffering and death:

> *14:23* They all (*pantes*) drank from it (the cup).
> *14:27* All (*pantes*) of you will fall away.
> *14:50* They ran away, all (*pantes*) of them.

Although all the disciples had deserted Jesus, an anonymous "young man" was still "following with" Jesus and he was "wearing nothing but a linen cloth about his body," meaning that he is not armed with weapons to violently resist the arrest of Jesus and thus stands in sharp contrast to the anonymous and confused bystander armed with a sword (14:47). The armed crowd "arrested" the young man just as they had "arrested" Jesus (14:46). This young man, then, stands for the reader as a possible candidate to fulfill the role of an ideal disciple. All others have fled, but he is still "following with" (*synēkolouthei*) Jesus, indicating his chance not only to be a disciple and close follower of Jesus, but also, because he is unarmed and has been "arrested" with Jesus, to fulfill Peter's and "all" the disciples' forsaken promise to "die with" (*synapothanein*) Jesus (14:31) (14:51).

But alas, even this would-be follower of Jesus fails to be the ideal disciple who follows Jesus on his way to suffering and death (8:34). Panic-stricken, he leaves behind his only piece of clothing, escaping his arrest with Jesus, sadly and shamefully running away naked. This young man's abandonment of Jesus intensively reinforces that of all the disciples and definitively illustrates the radical failure and impossibility for anyone at all to "follow with" Jesus at this most critical time on his way to suffering and death. In accord with the mysterious paradox of God's scriptural will, it is necessary that all the friends and companions of Jesus desert him as the "suffering just one" who dies alone. But that all abandon Jesus in fulfillment of his prediction (14:27) reinforces the certainty of his promise to go before his disciples to Galilee and reestablish communion with them after his resurrection (14:28).

### 2. MARK 14:43–52 AS MODEL FOR ACTION

Jesus' nonviolent submission to his forceful and unjust arrest, even though he has faithfully and innocently taught and demonstrated the true ways of God, encourages and strengthens us to likewise avoid violent retaliation to unjust aggression and submit ourselves with total faith and reliance upon the salvific will of God to ultimately rescue and save us. Jesus' example enables us to endure senseless suffering, persecution, and even betrayal by trusted friends as we persevere on the salvific "way" of the Lord.

Judas' deceitful betrayal, the bystander's violent resistance, and the fearful desertion of all the disciples and the young man serve as negative models warning us to examine the sincerity, fortitude and tenacity of our commitment to follow Jesus on his "way" to suffering and death. The betrayal of Judas alerts us to our potential to sadly betray and renounce our discipleship despite our close communion with Jesus. The violent and confused bystander advises us that the "way" of Jesus involves submission to suffering and opposition without violent resistance. And the cowardly abandonment of all the disciples as well as the young man cautions us on how radically difficult and ultimately impossible it is for us, despite our best intentions, to fully follow Jesus' "way" of suffering and death. Jesus must accomplish his "way" alone, but through his resurrection he empowers us to overcome our human failures to follow him.

## J. Mark 14:53–65: After Jesus Admits His True Identity, He Is Condemned to Death

[53]Then they led Jesus away to the high priest, and all the chief priests and the elders and the scribes came together. [54]Peter followed him at a distance right into the high priest's courtyard and was sitting with the guards, and warming himself at the fire. [55]The chief priests and the whole Sanhedrin kept seeking testimony against Jesus to put him to death, but they found none. [56]For many gave false witness against him, but their testimonies did not agree. [57]Some stood up and gave false witness against him, saying, [58]"We heard him say, 'I will destroy this sanctuary made with hands and within three days I will build another not made with hands.' " [59]Yet not even so did their testimony agree. [60]The high priest stood up before the assembly and questioned Jesus, saying, "Have you no answer? What are these men testifying against you?" [61]But he was silent and answered nothing. Again the high priest asked him and said to him, "Are you the

Christ, the Son of the Blessed One?" [62]Then Jesus said, "I am;
and

> 'you will see the Son of Man
> seated at the right hand of the Power (Ps 110:1)
> and coming with the clouds of heaven' " (Dan 7:13).

[63]The high priest tore his garments and said, "What further need
have we of witnesses? [64]You have heard the blasphemy. What do
you think?" They all condemned him as deserving to die. [65]Then
some began to spit on him, and to cover his face, and to strike
him, saying to him, "Prophesy!" And the guards greeted him
with blows.

## 1. MEANING OF MARK 14:53–65

### a. *14:53–54* While Jesus is led to the high priest, Peter sits in the courtyard.

In response to Judas' command that after they arrest Jesus they "lead
him away" securely (14:44), the crowd now "leads Jesus away" to the
"high priest," the highest ranking Jew and head of the Sanhedrin, whose
servant's ear was severed in the violence accompanying Jesus' arrest
(14:47).[23] An assembly of the Sanhedrin, the highest Jewish council and
court, takes place as "all" the chief priests and the elders and the scribes
came together, the full range of Jewish leaders who had commissioned the
crowd to arrest Jesus (14:43). Now that the Jewish leaders have finally
succeeded in arresting Jesus, the expectation is that they will accomplish
their plot to destroy him by condemning him to death (11:18; 12:12;
14:1). But in so doing they will be fulfilling God's plan as previously
predicted by Jesus (8:31; 9:12, 31; 10:33–34) (14:53).

Although all followers have deserted Jesus (14:50–52), Peter is still
following him "at a distance." With its allusion to Psalm 38:12, "My
friends and companions stand aloof from my plague, and my kinsmen
stand afar off," Peter's following from afar contributes to the portrait of
Jesus as the "suffering just one." Peter's separation from Jesus in reference to the high priest indicates the disintegration of his discipleship and
the beginning of his denial of Jesus. Although Peter follows Jesus even
into the courtyard of the high priest, he is no longer "with (*meta*) Jesus" as
befits one of the Twelve (3:14), but is sitting "with (*meta*) the guards" of
the high priest, warming himself "at" or "before" (*pros*) the fire rather
than standing ready to die with (14:31) Jesus "before" (*pros*) the high

priest (14:53). That Peter is "warming himself at the fire" means that it is night time, thus preparing for the fulfillment of Jesus' prediction of his denial of him "this very night" (14:30) (14:54).

### b. *14:55–59* False witnesses accuse Jesus of intending to destroy and rebuild the sanctuary of the temple.

As expected, the chief priests and the entire Sanhedrin, which has now assembled, are seeking testimony to put Jesus to death. That "they found none" underlines the innocence of Jesus as the "suffering just one" (14:55). Even though many give false witness against Jesus, their testimonies do not agree with one another. The Sanhedrin is thus further frustrated in its attempt to condemn Jesus to death, since there must be agreement by two or more witnesses for the death sentence (Num 35:30; Deut 17:6; 19:15). That false witnesses have arisen against Jesus adds to his portrayal as the innocently "suffering just one," who, though unjustly and falsely attacked by fellow human beings (Pss 27:12; 35:11–12), is to be vindicated by God (Wis 2:12–20; 5:1–5) (14:56).

As an example of the false witness against Jesus, some stood up in the assembly of the Sanhedrin (14:57) and claimed to have heard him say, "I will destroy this sanctuary made with hands and within three days I will build another not made with hands." This statement functions as a profoundly dramatic irony for the reader. Although the false witnesses intend to falsely attribute to Jesus a serious threat of destroying the temple sanctuary and a ridiculous boast of rebuilding it in three days, they are unwittingly and ironically proclaiming on a deeper level a true prophecy about Jesus for the reader.

While Jesus never claimed that he would be the one to destroy the "sanctuary" (*naos*), the building which contained the Holy of Holies as the place of God's unique presence and of the most important and sacred acts of authentic worship, the very epitome of the special sacredness of the entire temple (*hieron*) complex, he did predict the utter destruction of all the impressive buildings of the temple (13:1–2).[24] In so doing, Jesus had hinted at the inadequacy of the many magnificently beautiful buildings of the temple with its central sanctuary "made by hands" to be a permanent dwelling of God and locus of genuine worship. And Jesus was the one who had condemned the temple as being worthy of destruction for failing to achieve its purpose to be God's "house of prayer for all peoples" (11:12–17, 20–21). When these false witnesses transform Jesus' prediction of the entire temple's ultimate demise into an intensely serious yet knowingly false accusation that *he himself* would destroy the sacred "*sanctuary*" of the temple as inadequate because only "*made with hands*," they are ironically developing Jesus' prediction into a true and more profound prophecy allowing the reader to realize that indeed Jesus himself will effect the destruction of the "sanctuary," the heart and epitome of the entire temple complex, revealing it as an inferior structure made with merely human hands.

The false witnesses compound their false accusation by attributing to Jesus what they intend to be understood as a ridiculous boast of power, namely, that within a short period, "three days," he would "build" another, new and different "sanctuary," one "not made by hands." For the reader this falsely intended boast of power ironically proves to be a true revelation and profound prophecy of the power Jesus will exercise through his death and resurrection. The "three days," the ridiculously short period of time to rebuild the sanctuary according to the false accusation, recalls the "three days" after which Jesus would rise from the dead in accord with his previous predictions (8:31; 9:31; 10:34). It is through his death and resurrection, then, that Jesus will "build" an entirely new and superior "sanctuary," one constructed not by human hands but by the divine power manifested in Jesus' resurrection. This new "sanctuary," however, will not be another material, humanly made building, as supposed by the false witnesses, but a spiritual, God-made structure, the community founded upon Jesus, whom God will make the "cornerstone" of his new communal edifice by raising him from the dead. This has been indicated by Jesus' parable about the wicked tenants in which he revealed that by his death as God's Son he would become the "stone" rejected by the "builders," the Jewish leaders in charge of the sanctuary "made by hands," whom God, by raising him from the dead, would make the "cornerstone" of a new edifice "not made by hands," the community of Jesus' followers (12:1–12).

As a new "sanctuary" this community will perform the authentic worship the old sanctuary failed to achieve. It will be a community characterized as God's familial household of prayer for all peoples (11:17), a community that prays with faith in God's limitless power and with forgiveness for one another (11:22–25), a community that practices total love of God and fellow human beings, the kind of love that surpasses and renders inferior "all whole burnt offerings and sacrifices" (12:33) performed in the sanctuary "made by hands." Through the dramatic irony of this "false" witness which is a "true" prophecy, the reader experiences the profound paradox that it is precisely through the death of Jesus, the aim of this "false" accusation, that he will exercise the divine power of his resurrection to establish a new, superior "sanctuary," one "not made by hands," the community that performs authentic worship as God's "house of prayer for all peoples" (11:17) (14:58).

That not even this testimony of the false witnesses agrees reinforces the innocence of Jesus as the "suffering just one" and the frustration of the Jewish leaders to find sufficient testimony to sentence Jesus to death. The "false" testimony which is a "true" prophecy is not enough to condemn Jesus. Suspense is sustained as something more is needed (14:59).

**c. *14:60–62* To the high priest Jesus affirms his true messianic identity.**

As some false witnesses had "stood up" to testify against Jesus but without producing enough testimony to condemn him to death, so the high priest himself "stood up" before the assembly and asks Jesus whether he has an answer for what these false witnesses are testifying against him (14:60). That Jesus "was silent and answered nothing" further illustrates how he is the "suffering servant" of God (Isa 53:7) and "suffering just one" (Pss 38:12–14; 39:9), who, though totally innocent, silently endures the false testimony of his accusers, willing to undergo the unjust death which is their aim, so that he can enable their false accusation (14:57–58) to be revealed as a true prophecy by the vindication of his death through his resurrection by God. Drawing out the implication of the false testimony that only the messiah and Son of God has the divine power to build the sanctuary "not made by hands," the high priest again interrogates Jesus, seeking testimony to put him to death (14:55) by asking him the climactic question which echoes the superscription of the entire narrative (1:1), "Are you the Christ, the Son of the Blessed One?" The high priest thus invites Jesus to confirm, at the risk of being condemned to death, the earlier climactic confession by Peter that he is the Christ (8:29) and the previous proclamations by God and the demons that he is the Son of God (1:11; 3:11; 5:7; 9:7) (14:61).

By directly responding to the high priest's question with the words, "I am," Jesus not only boldly affirms his true and profound messianic identity but courageously accepts the death to which his confession leads. He then valiantly proclaims his ultimate vindication and triumph to the assembly (and readers) by promising that "you will see the Son of Man seated at the right hand of the Power (Ps 110:1) and coming with the clouds of heaven (Dan 7:13)." It is as the transcendent messianic figure of the "Son of Man" that Jesus must suffer, die and rise in accord with God's scriptural will (8:31; 9:9, 12, 31; 10:33, 45; 14:21, 41). And it is as the Son of Man that Jesus, through his death and resurrection, will be exalted and vindicated in ultimate triumph with power over his enemies, with power to build the "sanctuary not made with hands," and with power to come again in glory to effect the final salvation of the kingdom of God.

In conjunction with his previous revelation (12:35–37) that he is the messianic "lord" and Son of God to whom the Lord God says, "Sit at my right hand, until I place your enemies under your feet (Ps 110:1)" (12:36), Jesus' promise that he will be "seated at the right hand of the Power" indicates his future vindication and triumph over the enemies who are now condemning him to death. That Jesus will be enthroned at the right hand of God, designated as "the Power," reinforces that he will indeed have the divine power needed to build the "sanctuary not made by hands" and thus to demonstrate as a true prophecy what the false witnesses voiced as a ridiculously impossible boast of power (14:57–58). And, recalling his previous prediction that at the end of time "they will see 'the Son of Man coming in the clouds' with great power and glory (Dan 7:13–14)" (13:26), Jesus assures his listeners that after his death and resurrection he will be enabled to "come with the clouds of heaven" equipped with the divine power and glory to establish the kingdom of God's final and definitive salvation for his elect (13:27).

Jesus' fearless confession and bold proclamation to the high priest serve not only as a provocative instigation for his opponents to put him to death in accord with God's plan, but also as a comforting and consoling hope for the followers of his "way." Jesus' brave answer to the high priest further illustrates the strength he gained for himself and his disciples through his Gethsemane prayer to accept his death as the will of God (14:32–42). His courageous response models what he had advised his disciples regarding their future persecution: "When they lead you away and deliver you up, do not worry beforehand about what you are to say. But say whatever will be given you at that hour, for it will not be you who are speaking but the Holy Spirit" (13:11). Jesus' authoritative prediction to the high priest thus encourages his followers by assuring them of the assistance of God's power, through his death and resurrection, to lead them to ultimate vindication and triumph with him (14:62).

### d. *14:63–65* Jesus is condemned to death and abused.

The high priest responds by dramatically "tearing his garments" (2 Kgs 18:37–19:4; Jdt 14:19), underlining the extreme offensiveness of Jesus' statements. His question, "what further need have we of witnesses?," implies that the testimony of Jesus himself "agrees" with the "false" testimony ("true" prophecy) of the false witnesses, so that the Sanhedrin now has enough agreement of witnesses to condemn Jesus to death (14:55–59). For the reader the high priest's confidence of not needing any more witnesses ironically points to the need for Jesus' followers to confirm his testimony by giving witness to their faith in Jesus and his gospel (13:9) (14:63).

With his assertion that "you have heard the blasphemy," the high priest not only labels Jesus' bold confession and proclamation with the serious charge of "blasphemy," that is, a grasping infringement upon and blatant dishonoring of the sovereign power and authority of God (see 2:7; 3:28–29), but also further links Jesus' testimony to the "blasphemy" of the ironically true prophecy attributed to him by the false witnesses:

> *14:58* We *heard* him say, "I will destroy this sanctuary . . .
> *14:64* You have *heard* the blasphemy.

In response to the high priest's question, "what do you think?," the Sanhedrin finally pronounces their desired death sentence, as they all "condemned" him as "deserving to die." That they unjustly judge Jesus, whom the reader realizes is totally innocent because of the truth of his powerful proclamations, as "deserving" or "guilty" (see 3:29) of a crime punishable by death ironically underscores how he is the innocently "suffering just one." And that they "condemned" Jesus to death expresses the irony of the Jewish leaders failing to realize what the reader already knows, that their "condemnation" to death is actually fulfilling God's plan precisely as predicted by Jesus:

> *10:33* the Son of Man will be delivered to the chief priests and
>         the scribes, and they will *condemn* him to death . . .
> *14:64* They all *condemned* him as deserving to die.

It is precisely by condemning Jesus to death in order to destroy him and render him powerless that his opponents will ironically enable him to exercise the divine power of his resurrection over death, triumphantly vindicating his unjust death (14:62) and empowering him to build, within the "three days" of his resurrection from death, the new "sanctuary not made by hands" (14:58) (14:64).

Some of the members of the Sanhedrin then begin to contemptuously "spit" on him, to cruelly cover his face and strike him, mocking him to "prophesy!" By spitting upon, abusing and mocking him, they are adding to the picture of Jesus as the "suffering servant" and "just one" to be vindicated by God (Isa 50:6).

Their taunt for Jesus to "prophesy!" brings to a climax the dramatic irony that pervades this scene. They mock as ridiculous Jesus' "prophecy" of his power to build the "sanctuary not made by hands" (14:58), his "prophecy" of his ultimate vindication and triumph as the exalted Son of Man (14:62), and thus his prophetic claim to be the Christ and Son of God (14:61). But they who have covered Jesus' face are the ones who are tragically "blinded." They do not "see" that precisely by spitting upon him, abusing him and mocking his power to prophesy, they are ironically fulfilling God's plan as prophetically predicted by Jesus: "And they will mock him, spit upon him, scourge him, and kill him, but after three days he will rise" (10:34). Furthermore, Jesus' previous prophecy of Peter's denial (14:30) is in the process of being fulfilled, since Peter has associated himself with the "guards" (14:54), who are now adding to the cruel suffering of Jesus by "greeting him with blows." The irony that Jesus' past prophecies are being fulfilled precisely through the derisive mockery of his power to prophesy assures the reader of the future fulfillment of his prophecies to rise from the dead with power to form a new community of authentic worship and to come again as the messianic Son of God and Son of Man with divine power to establish the final salvation of God's kingdom (14:65).

## 2. MARK 14:53–65 AS MODEL FOR ACTION

The courageous confession of Jesus before the high priest serves as a model empowering us to emulate him by fearlessly testifying to our faith in Jesus as Christ and Son of God even in the face of persecution. Jesus' bold strength and ability to defiantly stand up to opponents and proclaim his true messianic identity and future triumph encourages us to likewise rely upon the power of God to strengthen us to encounter suffering and opposition as we follow the "way" of Jesus (13:9–13). The portrayal of Jesus as the "suffering servant" and innocently "suffering just one" who will be vindicated because of his fidelity to God invites us to likewise place our faith in God to bring us to ultimate vindication and triumph over suffering and death.

The ironic fulfillment of the prophecies of Jesus assures us that by his submission to the powerlessness of death he has gained divine power to form us into the new communal "sanctuary not made by hands," so that we can perform authentic worship of God as a community of prayer open to all peoples and cultures of the world (11:17), characterized by faith in the boundless power of God, forgiveness of one another (11:22–25), a totally committed love for God and fellow human beings (12:28–34), and motivated with a vibrant and assured hope of the future coming of Jesus as the messianic Son of God and Son of Man with the divine power to bring about the ultimate and definitive salvation of the world.

## K. Mark 14:66–72: After Peter Denies Jesus Three Times, He Remembers Jesus' Prediction and Weeps

⁶⁶While Peter was below in the courtyard, one of the high priest's maids came. ⁶⁷Seeing Peter warming himself, she looked intently at him and said, "You too were with the Nazarene, Jesus." ⁶⁸But he denied it saying, "I neither know nor understand what you are saying." Then he went out into the outer court. (And the cock crowed.)²⁵ ⁶⁹The maid saw him and began again to say to the bystanders, "This man is one of them." ⁷⁰But again he denied it. And after a little while again the bystanders said to Peter, "Surely you are one of them; for you too are a Galilean." ⁷¹But he began to curse and to swear, "I do not know this man of whom you speak." ⁷²And immediately the cock crowed a second time. Then Peter remembered the word that Jesus had said to him, "Before the cock crows twice you will deny me three times." He broke down and wept.

### 1. MEANING OF MARK 14:66–72

#### a. *14:66–68* To the high priest's maid Peter denies being with Jesus.

That "Peter was below in the courtyard" of the high priest, as "one of the high priest's maids came" prepares for a dramatic contrast with the previous scene (14:53–65) of Jesus courageously confessing his true messianic identity before the high priest (14:66). The maid "sees Peter warming himself," thus reminding the reader that Peter is still separated from Jesus (14:54), not in a position to "die with him" as he had promised (14:31). Looking intently at Peter, the maid identifies him as having formerly been in the company of Jesus, "You too were with the Nazarene, Jesus." Whereas the high priest, the highest ranking Jewish male, confronted Jesus with the extremely serious question of his identity as "the Christ, the Son of the Blessed One" (14:61), the maid of the high priest, a female of considerably less authority, confronts Peter with the less serious question of his association with Jesus identified only as "the Nazarene." Encountering Peter as having been "with" (*meta*) Jesus, the maid underlines for the reader Peter's abandonment of his special privilege as one of the Twelve to be "with" (*meta*) Jesus (3:14) (14:67).

Whereas Jesus had fearlessly and insistently affirmed his true messianic identity to the high priest (14:62), to the maid of the high priest Peter cowardly and emphatically denies his special association "with" Jesus, "I neither know nor understand what you are saying." Peter's double denial of neither "knowing" nor "understanding" rings as an ironic understatement in the ears of the reader. Although Peter was the one who had confessed Jesus to be the Christ (8:29), he truly does not understand what is involved in the privilege of "being with" Jesus as one of the Twelve disciples, namely, to "deny oneself" and follow with Jesus on his "way" to suffering and death (8:31–38). Despite his protest to "die with" Jesus (14:31), Peter tragically neither knows nor understands his discipleship. As he goes out into the outer court, Peter further distances himself from Jesus (see 14:54), timidly shrinking from affirming his association with him. If the words, "and the cock crowed," are original, they remind the reader how Peter's denial is fulfilling Jesus' prediction (14:30) (14:68).

**b. *14:69–71* Peter denies being a disciple and knowing Jesus.**

The drama of Peter's denial intensifies as the maid sees him withdrawing and now charges him before a group of people, "the bystanders," with being a disciple of Jesus, "this man is one of them." Her accusation functions as another ironic understatement, since Peter is not merely "one" of the disciples, he is the first-called (1:16–18), preeminent leader (3:16) and spokesman of the disciples (1:36; 8:29, 32; 9:5; 10:28; 11:21), the one who vehemently protested that he would be the exception to all others by dying with Jesus rather than denying him (14:27–31) (14:69).

Peter then denies his discipleship a second time. After a little while the drama continues to intensify as no longer merely the maid but the whole group of "bystanders" now confronts Peter with his discipleship, "Surely you are one of them; for you too are a Galilean." This additional evidence that he is a "Galilean" brings to a climax the ironic understatements of the accusations made against Peter. For the reader, that Peter is truly a "Galilean" means not merely that he is from the same geographical region as Jesus, but that it was as a "Galilean" that Peter was first called to be a disciple (1:16) to follow Jesus on his ministry of teaching and healing throughout all of Galilee (1:14–15, 28, 35–39). And that Peter is indeed a "Galilean" means that he is one of the disciples Jesus has promised to be reunited with in Galilee after his resurrection (14:28) (14:70).

Confronted with such incriminating evidence by the entire assembly of bystanders, Peter panics in cowardice as he begins "to curse and to swear," decisively and definitively denying his discipleship for the third time, "I do not know this man of whom you speak." His cursing and swearing stands in tragic contrast to his earlier earnest protest that he would die with Jesus rather than deny him (14:31). Peter's admission that he "does not know this man" to whom his accusers are referring reinforces the ironic understatement of his first denial. Although he confessed

Jesus to be the Christ (8:29), Peter really does not know Jesus. He does not understand what "this man" has just confessed to the high priest and the Sanhedrin, namely, that he is the Christ and Son of God precisely because he suffers and dies, but who will come again as exalted Son of Man in final triumph (14:62) (14:71).

### c. *14:72* Peter remembers Jesus' prediction and weeps.

As the cock crows a second time, Peter remembers Jesus' previous prediction that "before the cock crows twice you will deny me three times" (14:30). Despite his protest Peter has sadly and disloyally denied Jesus, exactly as Jesus had predicted. Because he was unable to stay awake, watch and pray with Jesus (14:37), Peter does not have the strength to follow and die with Jesus (14:31). But his response of "weeping" is an expression of deep remorse indicative of his repentance. Although he has failed miserably as leader of the disciples, there is the strong hope that he will be reconciled with Jesus after his resurrection in Galilee (14:28).

#### 2. MARK 14:66–72 AS MODEL FOR ACTION

Peter's tragic triple denial of Jesus and his discipleship provokes us to examine our understanding of and commitment to Jesus. Do we really know who Jesus is and what is involved in following him as a disciple? Do we understand that confessing our faith in Jesus as the Christ and Son of God includes the call to deny ourselves, take up our crosses and follow him on his "way" to suffering and death? Although our faith may falter, we have the opportunity to repent, like Peter, and recommit ourselves as disciples of Jesus. The cowardly denial of Jesus by Peter, the leader of the Twelve, illustrates how difficult it is for us, because of our human weaknesses, to follow Jesus in the face of suffering, persecution and death. But the courageous confession of Jesus empowers us to overcome our human inabilities so that we can follow his "way" with the hope of final triumph (14:62).

## L. Mark 15:1–5: The Jewish Leaders Deliver Jesus to Pilate Who Asks about His Kingship and Wonders at His Silence

[1]As soon as it was morning the chief priests with the elders and scribes, that is, the whole Sanhedrin, held a council. They bound Jesus, led him away, and delivered him to Pilate. [2]Pilate ques-

tioned him, "Are you the king of the Jews?" Replying he said to him, "You say so." [3]And the chief priests accused him of many things. [4]Pilate again questioned him, saying, "Have you no answer? See how many accusations they bring against you!" [5]But Jesus made no further answer, so that Pilate wondered.

### 1. MEANING OF MARK 15:1–5

a. *15:1–2* **The Sanhedrin hands Jesus over to Pilate who asks if he is the king of the Jews.**

When it was "morning" after the "night" of Peter's denial (14:30, 66–72) and of Jesus' trial before the Sanhedrin (14:53–65), the chief priests, who have emerged as the leading instigators in the Sanhedrin's earnest attempt to put Jesus to death (14:55), "held a council" with the elders and scribes, the rest of the entire Sanhedrin. Now that they have "all condemned him as deserving to die" (14:64), the implication is that this "council" is for the purpose of arranging Jesus' execution (see 3:6). They then bind the condemned Jesus, lead him away and deliver him to Pilate, the Roman governor of Judea, so that he can sanction their death sentence and carry out Jesus' execution. That they "delivered him to Pilate" continues to illustrate how the Jewish leaders are ironically achieving God's plan precisely as predicted by Jesus, whom they derisively taunted to prophesy (14:65):

> *10:33* The Son of Man will be delivered to the chief priests and the scribes, and they will condemn him to death and *deliver him to the Gentiles.*
>
> *15:1* They bound Jesus, led him away, and *delivered him to Pilate.*

Pilate's question to Jesus of whether he is the "king of the Jews" parallels that of the high priest about Jesus' messianic identity:

> *14:61* Are you the Christ, the Son of the Blessed One?
>
> *15:1* Are you the king of the Jews?

In view of Jewish traditions about a Davidic, kingly messiah, the two questions are nearly equivalent.[26] Pilate's question, however, carries more political connotations of sedition to the Roman government. Since Jesus has been bound as a prisoner, forcefully led away and delivered by the leaders of the Jewish people to the Roman governor, treatment hardly appropriate for a "king of the Jews," Pilate's question is to be understood as a ridiculing mockery.

Jesus' curt and ambiguous reply to Pilate, "you say so," stands in sharp contrast to his bold and unequivocal affirmation to the high priest, "I am" (14:62). Neither clearly affirming nor denying his kingship, Jesus' answer to Pilate's ridicule, "*you* say so" or "it is *you* who say so," throws the burden of his designation as king back on his questioner. Jesus does not claim the title of "king of the Jews" for himself, but neither does he reject it. Whether, and in what sense he is, the "king of the Jews" is to be determined by Pilate, the one who "says" Jesus is a king. The reader, who knows that Jesus is indeed "the king of the Jews" in the sense that he is the messianic Son of God through suffering, dying and rising as the Son of Man (14:61–62), experiences the irony that Pilate is unwittingly playing his role in establishing and demonstrating how Jesus is truly "the king of the Jews" precisely by mocking and ridiculing his kingship. Pilate's derisive questioning of Jesus as "the king of the Jews" paradoxically illustrates how and in what sense the reader can declare Jesus to be the true "king of the Jews" (15:2).

**b. *15:3–5* Jesus does not answer the charges of the chief priests, so that Pilate wonders.**

After the chief priests accused Jesus of "many things" (15:3), Pilate again questions Jesus, asking him if he wishes to reply to the many charges the chief priests have hurled against him. Pilate's question to Jesus again echoes that of the high priest during Jesus' trial before the Sanhedrin:

> *14:60* The high priest stood up before the assembly and questioned Jesus, saying, "*Have you no answer?* What are these men testifying *against you?*"
>
> *15:4* Pilate again questioned him, saying, "*Have you no answer?* See how many accusations they bring *against you!*"

Since the high priest was referring to the uneven testimony of the many false witnesses that arose against Jesus (14:56–57), the implication is that the accusations of the chief priests against Jesus are likewise false (15:4).

That Jesus "made no further answer" to Pilate, declining to defend himself against the false charges of the chief priests, likewise echoes his silence to the high priest regarding the unjust testimony of the false witnesses:

> *14:61* But he was silent and answered nothing.
> *15:5* But Jesus made no further answer.

Jesus' reticence continues to contribute to his portrayal as the innocent "suffering servant" and "suffering just one" (Isa 53:7), who, though abandoned by friends and surrounded by false accusers, silently endures and perseveres through persecution, faithfully relying upon God for his vindication. Pilate "wonders" or "marvels" in amazement that one whom he questioned as "the king of the Jews" can remain defenselessly silent before his accusers. But for the reader the silence of Jesus further illustrates his ironic kingship. He is "the king of the Jews" precisely and paradoxically as the silently "suffering servant" and "just one" of God (15:5).

Jesus' powerful response to the Roman governor and his silent endurance of persecution further models and reinforces what he promised would be the lot of his followers: "They will deliver you to the courts and you will be beaten in synagogues. And you will stand before governors and kings for my sake to testify to them. Indeed the gospel must first be preached to all peoples. When they lead you away and deliver you up, do not worry beforehand about what you are to say. But say whatever will be given you at that hour, for it will not be you who are speaking but the Holy Spirit" (13:9–11).

### 2. MARK 15:1–5 AS MODEL FOR ACTION

Jesus' silent suffering of the false and unjust charges of his opponents calls us to realize that the paradoxical power of his kingship lies in his willingness and ability to endure the powerlessness of persecution for the sake of God's ultimate triumph. The amazing example of Jesus' masterful response to Pilate's mocking question of his kingship and of his silent endurance of persecution empowers us to likewise withstand whatever sufferings, unjust accusations or false charges we may encounter as we live, preach and bear witness to the gospel of Jesus' kingship and God's kingdom.

## M. Mark 15:6–15: Pilate Releases Barabbas Instead of Jesus Whom He Scourges and Delivers To Be Crucified

[6]Now on the occasion of the feast he used to release to them one prisoner whom they requested. [7]There was a man called Barabbas in prison with the rebels who had committed murder in the rebellion. [8]The crowd came up and began to ask him to do for them as he was accustomed. [9]Pilate answered them, saying, "Do you want me to release to you the king of the Jews?" [10]For he knew that it was out of envy that the chief priests had delivered

him up. [11]But the chief priests stirred up the crowd to have him release Barabbas for them instead. [12]Answering again Pilate said to them, "What then do you want me to do with the one you call the king of the Jews?" [13]They cried out again, "Crucify him!" [14]Pilate said to them, "Why, what evil has he done?" But all the more they cried out, "Crucify him!" [15]So Pilate, wishing to satisfy the crowd, released to them Barabbas, and after he had Jesus scourged, delivered him to be crucified.

### 1. MEANING OF MARK 15:6-15

#### a. *15:6-10* Pilate offers to release Jesus as the king of the Jews.

That it was "the occasion of the feast (*heortēn*)" when the Jewish leaders arrested Jesus and brought him to Pilate renews the suspense aroused by their desire not to arrest Jesus and put him to death during the Passover feast (14:1) in order to avoid a commotion or riot of the people: "Not during the feast (*heortē*), lest there be a tumult of the people" (14:2). If the chief priests have not been able to avoid arresting Jesus during the feast, will they be able to prevent a tumult of the people caused by his death during the feast?

That it was customary for Pilate to release a prisoner whom the Jews requested during the feast generates suspense as it creates the possibility for the release of the prisoner Jesus (15:6). The mention of another prisoner, however, one called Barabbas, compounds the suspense by introducing another candidate for release. As a rebellious criminal arrested along with other rebels guilty of murder, Barabbas stands in sharp contrast to Jesus, an innocent prisoner arrested as if he were a violent "robber" (14:48) and unjustly condemned to death (15:7).

As "the crowd" comes up and begins to ask Pilate to grant them a prisoner in accord with his custom for the feast (15:8), Pilate offers them the opportunity to acknowledge and accept Jesus as their "king" by requesting his release: "Do you want me to release to you the king of the Jews?" (15:9). Pilate's offer is motivated by his knowledge that Jesus is innocent, having been delivered to him by the chief priests because of their "envy" of him. Pilate's knowledge accords with that of the reader who knows of the Jewish leaders' fearful jealousy of the favorable reception of Jesus' authoritative teaching by the crowds to the detriment of their own authority and leadership over the people (1:22; 11:18; 12:12, 37). The insinuation that Jesus is the true "king" and hence authoritative leader of the Jews underlines the tense conflict between Jesus and the Jewish leaders regarding their authority and leadership over the people.

The suspense heightens with the possibility that the crowd, previously impressed by Jesus, might accept Pilate's offer to release Jesus and thus thwart the plot of the chief priests to have the Roman governor put Jesus to death (15:10).

### b. *15:11–14* The chief priests incite the crowd to ask Pilate to release Barabbas but to crucify Jesus.

The chief priests continue to illustrate how they are the wicked "robbers" who mislead the Jewish people (11:17) as they "stir up" the crowd to have Pilate release Barabbas, the rebellious and murderous criminal, instead of Jesus, their innocent and true king. Their preference for one guilty of murder in a rebellion underscores how they are rebelling against their true king and murdering him. By "stirring up" the crowd, the chief priests are ironically causing the riotous and rebellious "tumult" of the people which they had hoped to prevent (14:1–2). But they cannot avoid involving the people in their plot of rejecting and killing their true king (15:11).

Pilate then allows the crowd to decide the fate of the one who is truly their king: "What then do you want me to do with the one you call the king of the Jews?" (15:12). But the crowd, persuaded and misdirected by their chief priests, totally reject their true king as they vehemently and tragically continue to cry out, "Crucify him!"[27] They want the Roman governor to execute as a seditious criminal the one whom they sadly fail to accept as their true and innocent king (15:13). Pilate's protesting question, "Why, what evil has he done?," emphasizes the complete innocence of Jesus as the "suffering just one" of God. The crowd, although unable to charge Jesus with anything "evil," nevertheless overwhelms and drowns out Pilate's protest with their insistent demand, "Crucify him!" By calling for the death of Jesus as the innocent "suffering just one," however, the crowd contributes to the profoundly paradoxical and ironical kingship of Jesus. They cannot prevent the one whom they reject and want to kill from becoming their king. Precisely by demanding the crucifixion of the innocent "suffering just one," they are ironically and paradoxically accomplishing God's plan by establishing Jesus as their true king (15:14).

### c. *15:15* Pilate releases Barabbas and delivers Jesus to be crucified.

Although Pilate knows that Jesus is innocent, he "wishes to satisfy the crowd" incited by the chief priests, allowing them to be responsible for the rebellious murder of their true king. In accord with their wish he released to them Barabbas, a rebellious murderer like themselves, and had the innocent Jesus "scourged." He then "delivered" Jesus to be crucified.

That Pilate had Jesus "scourged" and "delivered" him to death illustrates how he is ironically playing his role in accomplishing God's plan as predicted by Jesus:

> *10:33–34* The Son of Man *will be delivered* to the chief priests and the scribes, and they will condemn him to death and *deliver* him to the Gentiles. And they will mock him, spit upon him, *scourge* him, and kill him, but after three days he will rise.
>
> *15:1* They bound Jesus, led him away, and *delivered* him to Pilate.
>
> *15:15* After he had Jesus *scourged,* (Pilate) *delivered* him to be crucified.

The chief priests, the crowd and Pilate all play their roles in demonstrating and establishing the ironical kingship of Jesus. They determine the fate of Jesus to be their true king precisely by perpetrating his death as the innocently "suffering just one" to be vindicated by God.

That Jesus silently endures his being hated and handed over to death by the crowd of his own people, who had earlier been favorably attracted to his authoritative teaching, demonstrates and reinforces his earlier promise to the disciples on the Mount of Olives: "Brother will deliver brother to death, and the father his child, and children will rise up against parents and have them put to death. You will be hated by all because of my name. But the one who perseveres to the end will be saved" (13:12–13). By patiently persevering through rejection and death, Jesus becomes the true "king of the Jews" and shows the way for his followers to be likewise saved by God.

## 2. MARK 15:6–15 AS MODEL FOR ACTION

The paradoxical kingship of Jesus over the very people who rejected him and perpetrated his death strengthens his power to lead and save us as our true king. Even if we rebel against and reject him and his powerless "way" of suffering and death, he becomes and remains our powerful king precisely as God's innocently "suffering just one." Jesus' silent and patient perseverance through the jealous hatred and murderous rebellion of his own people encourages us with the assurance of sharing in his ultimate triumph as our king after we endure the jealousy, hatred, rejection and persecution that we will encounter as we follow on the "way" that Jesus, our true king, leads us.

## N. Mark 15:16–20: After Mocking Jesus as King of the Jews, the Soldiers Lead Him Out To Crucify Him

<sup>16</sup>The soldiers led him away inside the palace, that is, the praetorium, and called together the whole cohort. <sup>17</sup>Then they clothed him in purple and, weaving a crown of thorns, placed it on him. <sup>18</sup>And they began to salute him, "Hail, King of the Jews!" <sup>19</sup>And they kept striking his head with a reed and spitting upon him, and they knelt before him in homage. <sup>20</sup>And when they had mocked him, they stripped him of the purple cloak, dressed him in his own clothes, and led him out to crucify him.

### 1. MEANING OF MARK 15:16–20

#### a. *15:16–18* A whole cohort of soldiers dresses and salutes Jesus as king of the Jews.

Just as those who arrested Jesus had "led him away" to the residence of the high priest for his trial before the "whole" Sanhedrin (14:53–55; 15:1), so now the Roman soldiers "led him away" to the "palace" or "praetorium," the official residence of the Roman ruler, and assembled the "whole" cohort or battalion of soldiers. This gathering of the "whole" cohort of Gentile soldiers around Jesus thus parallels that of the "whole" Jewish Sanhedrin (15:16).

Whereas the "whole" Sanhedrin condemned Jesus to death (14:64), rejecting him as their messianic king (15:1–15), the "whole" cohort of soldiers performs a cruel parody of an official royal investiture of Jesus, further illustrating for the reader his ironical kingship. They dress him in "purple," honorable clothing appropriate for a king or ruler, but add an incongruous "crown of thorns" to ridicule the honor of the purple robe.[28] This "crown" woven from "thorns" serves not only as a mockery of a royal coronation but as a device for painful abuse (15:17).

Mimicking the regal acclamation accorded a Roman emperor or king, the soldiers salute Jesus with a ridiculing, "Hail, King of the Jews!" The irony for the reader is that these Gentile soldiers, precisely by mocking Jesus as the "king" rejected by his own Jewish people, are unwittingly clothing, crowning and hailing him as the true "king of the Jews" (15:18).

### b. *15:19-20* After abusing and mocking him, they lead him out to crucify him.

Continuing the mockery of Jesus' kingship, the soldiers "kept striking his head with a reed." That they strike his "head" increases the pain inflicted by the crown of thorns. And that they strike him with a "reed," a parody of the ruler's staff or scepter, underlines the powerlessness of this "king" who helplessly suffers brutal abuse from the very "reed" or scepter with which he should be powerfully ruling. Their "spitting upon him" not only serves as a shameless gesture of deep contempt (Num 12:14; Deut 25:9) highly inappropriate for an authoritative ruler, but recalls how these Gentile soldiers are fulfilling God's plan as predicted by Jesus, namely, that the Jewish leaders would deliver him to the Gentiles, who would "mock" him and "spit" upon him and "scourge" him (10:33–34). Their ridicule of the reverence due him as king by "kneeling before him in homage" ironically foreshadows and exemplifies the genuine reverence to be accorded Jesus as the paradoxical "king," enduring abuse as the "suffering just one" of God rather than displaying royal power and authority (15:19).

After they had "mocked" (10:34) him as king, the Gentile soldiers "stripped" him of the "purple cloak" symbolic of royal status and honor and dressed him again in his own ordinary clothing. They thus continue to ironically reveal the radically new and profoundly paradoxical character of Jesus' kingship. The purple robe of royalty is quite inappropriate for Jesus who shows himself to be a "king" unlike the Gentile rulers and "great ones" who "lord" and "wield authority" over their subjects (10:42). That Jesus wears his own clothes rather than regal purple accords with the "greatness" he demonstrates as the "servant" king (10:43) and "slave of all" (10:44), who came as the Son of Man not "to be served but to serve and to give his life as a ransom for many" (10:45). As they then "led him out to crucify him," the Gentile soldiers play their ironic role, in accord with the wish of the Jewish people that he be "crucified" (15:13–14), to establish Jesus as the true "king of the Jews" precisely and paradoxically in and through his rejection, ridicule, suffering and death (15:20).

### 2. MARK 15:16–20 AS MODEL FOR ACTION

The mockery and ridiculing reverence by which the Gentile soldiers ironically established Jesus as the true "king of the Jews" calls us to pay him homage and honor as our "king" who demonstrates his greatness and power to save us not by ruling in royal splendor but by silently and patiently enduring brutal abuse as the "suffering just one" of God. Jesus' model of humble perseverance through persecution for the sake of our salvation empowers us to likewise humbly endure suffering, ridicule and abuse as we follow the "way" of Jesus, our king.

## O. Mark 15:21–32: Jesus Is Crucified and Mocked by Passers-By, Chief Priests, Scribes and Those Crucified with Him

[21]They compelled a passer-by, Simon of Cyrene, who was coming in from the country, the father of Alexander and Rufus, to carry his cross.
[22]And they brought him to the place of Golgotha (which is translated Place of the Skull). [23]They gave him wine drugged with myrrh, but he did not take it. [24]Then they crucified him and divided his clothes, casting lots for them to see what each should take.
[25]It was the third hour when they crucified him. [26]The inscription of the charge against him read, "The King of the Jews." [27]And with him they crucified two robbers, one on his right and one on his left.[29]
[29]Those passing by reviled him, shaking their heads and saying, "Aha! You who would destroy the sanctuary and rebuild it in three days, [30]save yourself by coming down from the cross!"
[31]Likewise the chief priests, with the scribes, mocking him among themselves, said, "He saved others; he cannot save himself! [32]Let the Christ, the King of Israel, come down now from the cross that we may see and believe!" Those who were crucified with him were also taunting him.

### 1. MEANING OF MARK 15:21–32

#### a. *15:21* They force Simon of Cyrene to carry Jesus' cross.

That the soldiers executing Jesus "compelled" a certain passer-by named Simon of Cyrene, a diaspora Jew from the city of Cyrene on the Mediterranean Sea in northern Africa, "to carry his cross" makes this Simon, in the absence of the disciples, a substitute model of discipleship. Although forced, this Simon literally illustrates what Jesus demands of a disciple: "If anyone wishes to follow after me, let that person deny oneself, take up one's cross and follow me" (8:34). That they must "compel" a passer-by to carry the cross underscores the disciples' total abandonment of Jesus. "Simon" of *Cyrene* is forced to carry the cross in the absence of "Simon" called and named Peter by Jesus in *Galilee* (3:16; 14:70), the leader of the disciples who vowed to die with Jesus (14:31). In contrast to all the disciples who left Jesus and ran away (14:50), Simon of Cyrene "comes" into the city "from the country" and becomes a substitute disciple. The "father" of the brothers Alexander and Rufus, in the absence of the "sons" of Zebedee, James and John, who left their father to follow Jesus (1:19–20; 3:17; 10:35), must now replace the disciples and carry the cross. Whereas Simon of Cyrene was "compelled" to carry the cross, the reader has been summoned to freely follow Jesus on his "way" of suffering and death by denying self and willingly taking up the cross.

**b. *15:22–24* After Jesus refuses drugged wine at Golgotha, they crucify him and divide his garments.**

The soldiers then "brought" Jesus outside the city to the place of crucifixion called "Golgotha," whose translation as "Place of the Skull" projects the ghastly aura of death (15:22). As a humane gesture to lessen his pain, they give him "wine drugged with myrrh,"[30] which furthers the portrayal of Jesus as the "suffering just one," who, in the midst of shame and insults inflicted by foes, is given vinegar or strong wine to drink (Ps 69:20–22). That Jesus refuses to take the drugged wine accords with his promise to "never again drink of the fruit of the vine until that day when I drink it new in the kingdom of God" (14:25). Jesus thus declines the drugged wine in order to fully experience the "cup" of suffering and death willed for him by God (14:36) as the "way" to the establishment of the final and triumphant banquet of God's kingdom (15:23). When the soldiers crucify Jesus, they contribute to his portrait as the "suffering just one" by "dividing his clothes and casting lots for them" (Ps 22:19) to determine what each should take. Crucified as the "suffering just one" of God, Jesus dies utterly alone and forsaken, not only abandoned by his closest followers but bereft of even his own clothing (15:24).

**c. *15:25–27* Jesus is crucified as king of the Jews with two robbers.**

It was the "third hour" (9 a.m.), that is, soon after the early morning meeting of the whole Sanhedrin seeking his death (15:1), that the soldiers crucified Jesus (15:25). That the inscription of the "charge" against Jesus reads "The King of the Jews" continues the theme of the ironical and paradoxical kingship of Jesus. In crucifying him as guilty of the "charge" of falsely claiming to be "the King of the Jews," they are ironically installing him as their innocent and true King (15:26).

The innocent Jesus, who was unjustly arrested as if a "robber" (14:48), while the guilty revolutionary and murderer Barabbas was released (15:6–15), is now incongruously crucified in a mock royal enthronement as king between two "robbers." These two robbers, presented as the royal attendants of the enthroned Jesus, "one on his right and one on his left," serve as substitute disciples for James and John who had requested to "sit one at your right and the other at your left" (10:37) in the glory of Jesus after promising to "drink the cup" of and to be "baptized" with the suffering and death of Jesus (10:38–39), but who are now sadly absent. Disciples rather than "robbers" should be dying with Jesus (14:31) in order to participate in his "glory." By crucifying Jesus as a mock king between two "robbers," the soldiers are ironically enthroning him as the true "king of the Jews," since Jesus had earlier indicated that the Jewish leaders are the real "robbers" (11:17). The two "robbers" thus represent the Jewish leaders whose true and revolutionary king is the unjustly crucified Jesus (15:27).

### d. *15:29–30* Passers-by taunt Jesus to save himself by coming down from the cross.

That those passing by "reviled" or literally "blasphemed" him while "shaking their heads" continues the portrayal of Jesus as the "suffering just one" who is scorned and despised by his accusers as they "shake their heads" at him in contempt (Pss 22:8; 109:25; Lam 2:15). Their sarcastic mockery of Jesus' apparent powerlessness furthers the profound irony presented by their crucified king. They taunt him to "save himself" by coming down from the cross in order to demonstrate his power to fulfill the boast attributed to him at his trial before the high priest (14:58), namely, that he would "destroy" the temple "sanctuary" and "rebuild it in three days." In challenging him to "save himself" by coming down from the cross, his taunters are voicing for the reader the paradoxical irony that it is precisely by remaining on the cross and losing his life that Jesus will save it. This accords with Jesus' profound pronouncement that "whoever wishes to save one's life will lose it, but whoever loses one's life for my sake and that of the gospel will save it" (8:35). By remaining on the cross and enduring the painful powerlessness of crucifixion, Jesus as the "suffering just one" will be raised from the dead by God "in three days" (8:31; 9:31; 10:34) and thus demonstrate his divine power to indeed destroy the old "sanctuary" made by hands and erect a new "sanctuary" not made by hands, the spiritual and communal "sanctuary" of authentic worship of God constituted by the followers of the risen Jesus, the "cornerstone" (12:10–11; 14:58).

### e. *15:31–32* The chief priests and scribes taunt Jesus to show he is the Christ, the King of Israel, by coming down from the cross.

The chief priests with the scribes, those Jewish leaders who took part in condemning Jesus to death for confessing that he is "the Christ, the Son of the Blessed One" (14:61–64), intensify the ridicule of the passers-by. Their jeering mockery of the crucified Jesus among themselves expresses the profoundly paradoxical irony that although Jesus "saved others, he cannot save himself." Indeed, although Jesus has "saved" others throughout the narrative by teaching, healing and exorcising, he cannot "save" himself from death because only God can and will save him by raising him after he has died (8:31, 34–38; 9:31; 10:34). As Jesus has taught and now exemplifies, all things are possible for one who has faith in the God of unlimited power (9:23; 10:27; 11:22–24). But that God will save him as he remains on the cross "to give his life as a ransom for many" (10:45; see also 14:24) means that he will "save" not only himself but "many" (= all) others in a more profound and definitive sense (15:31).

They then derisively dare Jesus to prove that he is truly "the Christ," the messiah anointed by God, and "the King" not only of the "Jews," a sociopolitical community, but of "Israel," the chosen people of God, by coming down "now" from the cross so that they may "see and believe." They want Jesus to come down "now" from the cross so that they can "see" and believe, rather than wait to "see" him in the future according to his promise that they will "see" the Son of Man in triumphant vindication and glory (14:62). Their wish to "see" him come down from the cross and save himself from death, so that they may "believe" he is their Christ and King serves as an ironic reversal for the reader, who knows that "seeing" can follow from rather than precede "believing." This was poignantly illustrated by the healing of the blind beggar, Bartimaeus (10:46–52). It was Bartimaeus' "faith" that "saved" or healed him so that he could "see" (10:52). He first "believed" in the merciful healing power of Jesus as Son of David and was thus enabled to "see" Jesus and follow him up to Jerusalem on his "way" to suffering and death. Only if the Jewish leaders (and readers) first "believe" in Jesus, will they be able to "see" that he is indeed the Christ and King of Israel with power to save himself and all others precisely because he remained on the cross and suffered the utter powerlessness of an excruciating death.

That even those who were crucified with Jesus were scornfully taunting him adds a finishing touch to the cruel mockery of Jesus, who is ironically enthroned as the true Christ and King of Israel by being crucified as the "suffering just one" despised, reviled, and mocked from all sides—by anonymous passers-by, opposing Jewish leaders, and even the robbers crucified with him (15:32).

### 2. MARK 15:21–32 AS MODEL FOR ACTION

Underlining the absence and failure of Jesus' disciples to follow and die with him, Simon of Cyrene and the two robbers, who are forced, respectively, to carry the cross and die with Jesus, serve as models calling us to freely choose to follow and persevere with Jesus on his "way" of suffering and death in order to share in his final triumph and glory.

The various taunts of the crucified Jesus as the powerless and mock-messianic king of the Jews invite us to place our faith in the God of infinite power, so that we may "see" that it is precisely and paradoxically by remaining on the cross and fully experiencing the utter loneliness, pain and powerlessness of death as the "suffering just one" of God that Jesus demonstrates that he is the true king of all, even of those who revile and crucify him, with divine power to save all people and to build us, by the power of his resurrection from the dead, into the new, communal "sanctuary" of authentic worship of God. The total trust in God that Jesus, our crucified "king," displays as the silently and innocently "suffering just one" encourages and empowers us to likewise trust totally in the boundless power of God to uphold us as we endure rejection and opposition in following Jesus' way of suffering and death.

## P. Mark 15:33–41: As Jesus Dies, the Centurion Confesses Him To Be Son of God While Women from Galilee Look On

[33]When the sixth hour had come, there was darkness over the whole land until the ninth hour. [34]And at the ninth hour Jesus called out with a loud cry, *"Eloi, Eloi, lema sabachthani?"* (Ps 22:2) which is translated, "My God, my God, why have you forsaken me?"

[35]Then some of the bystanders who heard it said, "Look, he is calling Elijah!" [36]One of them ran, filled a sponge with vinegar, put it on a reed, and gave it to him to drink, saying, "Wait, let us see if Elijah comes to take him down!"

[37]But Jesus, letting out a loud cry, expired. [38]Then the veil of the sanctuary was torn in two from top to bottom. [39]When the

centurion who stood facing him saw how he expired he said, "Truly this man was Son of God!"

⁴⁰There were also women looking on from afar, among whom were Mary Magdalene, Mary the mother of the younger James and of Joses, and Salome, ⁴¹who, when he was in Galilee, had followed him and ministered to him; and also many other women who had come up with him to Jerusalem.

### 1. MEANING OF MARK 15:33–41

#### a. *15:33–34* In darkness at the ninth hour Jesus asks why God has abandoned him.

Three hours after Jesus had been crucified (15:25) and had endured the reviling taunts of passers-by, Jewish leaders and robbers crucified with him (15:29–32), at the "sixth hour" (noon) a "darkness" came over "the whole land (earth)" and lasted until the "ninth hour" (3 p.m.). That this mysterious "darkness" occurs at midday, endures for three hours and covers the "whole land (earth)" indicates that it is an extraordinary, supernatural phenomenon brought on by God himself as a preliminary sign foreshadowing the end of the world (see 13:24). According to Amos 8:9 God himself promised to cause such a darkness on the end-time "day of the Lord": " 'On that day,' says the Lord God, 'I will make the sun go down at noon, and cover the earth with darkness in broad daylight.' " Such supernatural darkness during Jesus' crucifixion characterizes his death as a preliminary event of God's end-time with significance for the whole world. Instead of being delivered from death by God (14:35–36), the crucified Jesus, along with the whole earth, is enveloped for three hours in an ominously dreary darkness (15:33).

After suffering three hours of verbal abuse (15:25–32) and three hours of divinely caused darkness while dying on the cross, Jesus, "at the ninth hour" (3 p.m.) calls out with a "loud cry," quoting in Aramaic the first words of Psalm 22, a lament of the "suffering just one": "My God, my God, why have you forsaken me?" The reporting of Jesus' words in Aramaic along with their translation adds realism and rhetorically reinforces the great importance of his loud cry. Having endured God's silent "abandonment," symbolized by the dismal "darkness" God has caused instead of rescuing him from excruciating death at the hands of reviling accusers, Jesus begs for the reason "why" or "for what purpose" God has "forsaken" him. Although indicative of his experience of intense anguish as he dies radically alone and without divine intervention, Jesus' loud scream is not a cry of despair but the lamentful prayer of the "suffering just one," uttered with complete confidence and total trust in his God. Expressing his deep personal relationship of faith in God, Jesus addresses him twice as "my God," and with confidence in God's transcendent and sovereign plan for him calls out for God to disclose the purpose "why" he has abandoned him to death (15:34).

### b. *15:35–36* Bystanders claim Jesus is calling Elijah to rescue him.

Based upon a resemblance in sound between the Aramaic address "my God" (*Eloi*) in Jesus' loud cry and the name of the revered prophet "Elijah," some of the bystanders who heard it distort Jesus' lamentful prayer of trust in God into a plea for Elijah to rescue him, "Look, he is calling Elijah!" (15:35). In order to prolong Jesus' life, one of the bystanders offers him a drink from a sponge filled with vinegar and placed on a reed. By so doing he ironically contributes to the portrait of Jesus as the "suffering just one" whose foes gave him "vinegar to drink" (Ps 69:22). His exclamation continues the mocking taunt of the Jewish leaders, who want Jesus to come down from the cross so that they may "see and believe" that he is the Christ, the King of Israel (15:32). Although Jesus "cannot save himself" (15:31) by coming down from the cross, perhaps they will "see" and believe if God saves him by sending Elijah to take him down from the cross:

15:32 Let the Christ, the King of Israel, come down now from the cross that we may see (*idōmen*) and believe!
15:36 Wait, let us see (*idōmen*) if Elijah comes to take him down!

The attempt of the bystanders to prevent Jesus' death by twisting his lamentful prayer of trust into a mocked plea in order to "see" his rescue by Elijah illustrates their stubborn "blindness" to the divine necessity of Jesus' death as the "suffering just one." The irony for the reader is that not even Elijah can rescue Jesus, because as Jesus himself stated, "already Elijah has come and they did to him whatever they pleased, as it is written of him" (9:13). In the person of John the Baptist (1:6; 6:14–29) Elijah has already come and suffered the same fate Jesus is now suffering in accord with God's will (15:36).

### c. *15:37–39* As Jesus dies the sanctuary veil is torn and the centurion confesses him to be Son of God.

The bystanders, however, cannot prevent Jesus from dying on the cross as the "suffering just one" of God. "Letting out" and thus completing his "loud cry" of lamentful trust in God (15:34), Jesus finally "expires" on the cross (15:37). In response to Jesus' death and as a beginning to the answer of "why" God has abandoned him to death, the "veil" or curtain hanging in the temple sanctuary "was torn" by God (divine passive) in two pieces "from top to bottom," in other words, totally and irreparably destroyed from heaven downwards. This complete destruction of the sanctuary veil, symbolic of the entire temple cult, indicates the termination of the old temple sanctuary "made by hands" and thus inadequate as the place of God's presence and authentic worship, and points to the advent of the new, superior sanctuary "not made by hands." The tearing of the sanctuary veil, indicative of the entire temple's demise (13:1–2), begins to fulfill the first part of the prophecy attributed to Jesus by the false witnesses at his trial before the Sanhedrin and later used to mock his powerlessness on the cross:

> *14:58* We heard him say, "I will destroy this sanctuary made with hands and within three days I will build another not made with hands."
>
> *15:29* "Aha! You who would destroy the sanctuary and rebuild it in three days . . ."
>
> *15:38* Then the veil of the sanctuary was torn in two from top to bottom.

By his death on the cross in apparent weakness Jesus thus effects the destruction of the temple sanctuary "made by hands" and opens the way for the one "not made by hands" (15:38).

The second part of the prophecy, the building of a new temple sanctuary "not made by hands," that is, the establishment of God's communal household of prayer and authentic worship inclusive of all peoples (11:17), begins to be fulfilled with the climactic confession of the Roman centurion, representative of all the peoples to whom the gospel must be preached (13:10) and who will be included in the new, communal sanctuary of authentic worship "not made by hands." When the Roman centurion overseeing Jesus' crucifixion stood facing him and "saw" how he expired, namely, with a "loud cry" of lamentful but total trust in God (15:34, 37) as the "suffering just one," he proclaimed, "Truly this man was Son of God!"

In sharp contrast to the Jewish leaders, who taunted Jesus to come down from the cross so that they might "see" and "believe" that he is the Christ, the King of Israel (15:32), and to the bystanders who wanted to prolong his crucifixion to "see" if Elijah would come and take him down from the cross (15:36), the centurion is able to "believe" that Jesus was not only the Christ, the King of Israel but "Son of God" when he "sees" how he dies on the cross with complete confidence in God:

> 15:32 Let the Christ, the King of Israel, come down now from the cross that we may see (*idōmen*) and believe!
> 15:36 Wait, let us see (*idōmen*) if Elijah comes to take him down!
> 15:39 When the centurion who stood facing him saw (*idōn*) how he expired he said, "Truly this man was Son of God!"

Whereas Peter, the leader and spokesman of the twelve disciples, denied with cursing and swearing that he even knew "this man" Jesus, the Roman centurion functions as another substitute disciple by coming to the knowledge of the profound identity of "this man" Jesus as the human being who was truly "Son of God," when he witnesses how he dies on the cross:

> 14:71 He (Peter) began to curse and to swear, "I do not know *this man* of whom you speak."
> 15:39 The centurion . . . said, "Truly *this man* was Son of God!"

The centurion's confession that Jesus was "truly" Son of God not only confirms the truth of Jesus' own admission to the high priest that he is "the Christ, the Son of the Blessed One" (14:61–62), but reinforces and brings to a climax all of the entire gospel's previous acclamations of Jesus' profound identity as the Christ and Son of God:

> 1:1 The beginning of the gospel of Jesus *Christ, Son of God.*
> 1:11 And a voice came from the heavens, "You are my beloved *Son;* with you I am well pleased!"
> 3:11 And the unclean spirits, whenever they saw him, were falling down before him and crying out, "You are the *Son of God!*"
> 5:7 "What have you to do with me, Jesus, *Son* of the Most High *God?*"
> 8:29 Peter answered him, "You are the *Christ!*"
> 9:7 A voice came from the cloud, "This is my beloved *Son!* Listen to him!"

> *14:61* The high priest asked him and said to him, "Are you the *Christ,* the *Son* of the Blessed One?"
>
> *15:39* When the centurion who stood facing him saw how he expired he said, "Truly this man was *Son of God*!"

The shocking surprise is that the climactic confession of the entire gospel is proclaimed by a Roman centurion, a non-Jew and a non-disciple. The centurion is able to complement Peter's climactic confession that Jesus was the "Christ" (8:29) and become the first human being to acknowledge that Jesus was truly "Son of God" only because he witnessed how Jesus revealed himself to be Son of God by dying on the cross with a "loud cry" of total trust in God. The Roman centurion's confession of faith in the crucified Jesus as messianic and royal Son of God thus opens the way for the building of the new sanctuary "not made by hands," the community of authentic prayer and worship of God (15:39).

### d. *15:40–41* Women who followed Jesus in Galilee look on from afar.

To complement the witness of the Roman centurion, who stood close to Jesus and "saw" how he died, there were also "women looking on from afar." That three are specifically named—Mary Magdalene, Mary the mother of the younger James (in contrast to James the brother of John and son of Zebedee) and of Joses, and Salome—recalls the absence of the special group of three disciples—Peter, James and John—who had accompanied Jesus at critical moments and witnessed his special revelations throughout his ministry (1:16–20, 29; 3:16–17; 5:37; 9:2; 13:3). As witnesses of the revelatory death of Jesus, these three women now substitute for Peter, James and John, who have deserted Jesus along with the rest of the male disciples (15:40).

These three women, along with the many other women who came up with Jesus to Jerusalem, represent ideal disciples. Having "followed" Jesus as disciples when he was in Galilee, "ministered" or "served" him as true disciples (see 10:43–45), and accompanied him to Jerusalem (10:32–34), these women have fully followed the entire "way" of Jesus, remaining with him and witnessing his ministry in Galilee as well as his suffering and death in Jerusalem. Their presence at the crucifixion of Jesus as Jewish female disciples along with the Gentile male centurion illustrates how the new communal sanctuary "not made by hands," the community of Jesus' followers, is to be composed of all peoples—Jews and Gentiles, men and women, long-time followers and recent converts—who recognize that the mortal man Jesus is the Christ, the King of Israel and truly Son of God with power to save all others because he died on the cross as the "suffering just one" with full obedience to and total trust in God (15:41).

## 2. MARK 15:33–41 AS MODEL FOR ACTION

The death of Jesus as the "suffering just one" of God, who dies in weakness with a loud cry of lamentful but total trust in God, encourages us to overcome the rejections, ridicule, opposition, persecutions and difficulties we encounter as we follow the "way" of Jesus, by likewise dedicating our entire lives to God with complete confidence in his power to save and vindicate us in triumph. Through and with the dying Jesus we can place our entire lives at the disposal of God's salvific plan and endure our eventual and inevitable deaths as human beings not with despair in the experience of the radical loneliness of dying but with hopeful faith in God's ultimate power and plan to bring us to triumphant salvation.

The confession of the Roman centurion calls us to realize that it was precisely in and through his powerless death on the cross at the hands of his own people that Jesus revealed how he is the Christ, the King of Israel, and truly Son of God with power to destroy the inadequate temple sanctuary of inferior worship and relationship to God, and to build a new community of superior and authentic worship of God with faith in his limitless power to save all people. The exemplary witness of the Jewish women to the crucifixion of Jesus inspires us to persevere with Jesus by following and serving him and one another throughout his entire "way" of suffering and death. By imitating the Roman centurion's confession of faith in the power of the crucified Jesus and the Jewish women's persevering witness to the ministry, suffering and death of Jesus, we become part of the new and universal communal sanctuary "not made by hands," God's household of authentic worship and loving service, inclusive of all peoples and cultures of the world.

## Q. Mark 15:42–47: Pilate Grants Jesus' Body to Joseph of Arimathea Who Buries It in a Rock-Hewn Tomb

[42]When it was already evening, since it was the day of preparation, that is, the day before the sabbath, [43]Joseph of Arimathea, a distinguished member of the council, who was himself awaiting the kingdom of God, came and courageously went to Pilate and asked for the body of Jesus. [44]Pilate, however, wondered if he were already dead, and calling the centurion, he asked him if he had already died. [45]And when he learned of it from the centurion, he granted the dead body to Joseph. [46]Having bought a linen cloth, he took him down, wrapped him in the linen cloth and laid him in a tomb that had been hewn out of rock. Then he

rolled a stone against the entrance of the tomb. [47]Mary Magdalene and Mary the mother of Joses watched where he was laid.

### 1. MEANING OF MARK 15:42–47

**a. *15:42–43* Joseph of Arimathea asks Pilate for the body of Jesus.**

It was "already" evening of the momentous day of Jesus' early trial
before Pilate (15:1), of his crucifixion at the sixth hour (15:25), and of his
death cry at the ninth hour after three hours of darkness (15:33). And it
was the "day of preparation" (Friday), when work could still be done in
preparation for the day of sabbath rest (15:42).

Acting with haste, then, to bury Jesus before the sabbath, Joseph of
Arimathea comes forward and courageously asks Pilate for the body of
Jesus. It is an act of courage because Joseph is a "distinguished" member
of the "council," the Sanhedrin which had condemned Jesus to death
(14:55, 64; 15:1). In asking for the body of Jesus he risks loss of his "distinguished" status by giving proper burial to the criminal whom his own
council has condemned to an ignominious death. In the absence of disciples "from Galilee," who should be the ones to bury the body of their
master (see 6:29), Joseph "from Arimathea" functions as another substitute disciple (see 15:21, 27, 39). This Arimathean's courage in asking for
the "body" (*sōma*) of Jesus stands in sharp contrast with the cowardice of
the Galilean disciples who have betrayed, deserted and denied their master, despite having been given his "body" (*sōma*) in the form of the bread
at the Passover meal anticipating his death (14:22–25). That Joseph "was
himself awaiting the kingdom of God" makes him a sympathizer of Jesus,
whose teaching and preaching demonstrated (1:15; 4:11, 26, 30; 9:1, 47;
10:14–15, 23–25; 12:34) and whose death anticipates (14:25) the definitive arrival of God's kingdom. By requesting the body of Jesus for burial,
Joseph of Arimathea plays his role as a substitute disciple by indicating
the importance of Jesus' burial for bringing about the kingdom of
God (15:43).

**b. *15:44–45* Pilate ascertains the death of Jesus from the centurion and
grants the dead body to Joseph.**

In response to Joseph's request, Pilate, who had earlier "wondered"
about Jesus when he refused to answer the many charges brought against
him by the chief priests (15:5), now "wonders" whether Jesus is already
dead. He calls the centurion who oversaw Jesus' crucifixion to officially
verify the actual death of Jesus (15:44). The centurion continues to function as a substitute disciple as he is the one who not only climactically

confessed the crucified Jesus to be "truly Son of God" (15:39), but now gives the definitive witness that Jesus has really died. Once Pilate has received the centurion's verification, he officially "grants" the "dead body" (*ptōma*) of Jesus to Joseph, so that he can perform the task of a true disciple like the disciples of John the Baptist, who took his "dead body" (*ptōma*) for burial (6:29). This emphasis upon the reality of Jesus' death prepares for his expected resurrection after three days as the triumphant vindication over actual death (8:31; 9:31; 10:34), rather than a mere revival of one who nearly died (15:45).

**c. *15:46–47* Joseph buried the dead body of Jesus in a rock-hewn tomb and women witness it.**

That Joseph of Arimathea rather than a rescuing Elijah (15:36) "took him down" from the cross underlines Jesus' obedient willingness to completely fulfill the divine necessity that he actually undergo death as the "suffering just one" of God. After purchasing a "linen cloth" as an appropriate burial garment for the naked corpse (15:24), Joseph gives Jesus a proper and honorable burial as he "wrapped him in the linen cloth" and laid him in a genuine "tomb," one that had been hewn out of rock. He completed the official burial of Jesus by rolling a stone against the entrance of the tomb. His use of a "linen cloth" (*sindona*) to properly bury Jesus continues to illustrate how Joseph is a substitute disciple, who recalls the absence of the disciples who deserted Jesus, one of whom even left behind his "linen cloth" (*sindona*) when he abandoned Jesus in fearful flight (14:51–52). Like the disciples of John the Baptist, who "laid" the "dead body" of their master in a "tomb," Joseph acts as a true disciple when he took the "dead body" of Jesus and "laid" it in a "tomb":

> *6:29* When his disciples heard about it, they came and took his dead body (*ptōma*) and laid it in a tomb (*ethēkan auto en mnēmeiǭ*).
>
> *15:45* He (Pilate) granted the dead body (*ptōma*) to Joseph . . .
> *15:46* and he laid him in a tomb (*ethēken auton en mnēmeiǭ*).

Further complementing the centurion's confession and witness to the death of Jesus as Son of God and Joseph's role in properly burying him, Mary Magdalene and Mary the mother of Joses continue the full witness of women disciples to both the ministry and death of Jesus (15:40–41) as they "watched" where Jesus was buried. Having participated in the ministry of Jesus in Galilee, having remained with him during his crucifixion in Jerusalem, and having now witnessed the burial that underlines the reality of his death, these women disciples are uniquely qualified and prepared to witness the predicted resurrection of Jesus from the dead (15:47).

## 2. MARK 15:42–47 AS MODEL FOR ACTION

Joseph of Arimathea's courageous burial of Jesus as one expecting the kingdom of God induces us to accept the divine necessity of the death of Jesus, and the risk of our own suffering and death in following him, in order to bring about the glorious and salvific kingdom of God. We are called to realize that Jesus endured the full reality of death by truly dying and being buried, so that his resurrection signals the definitive triumph of a new and transcendent life over the apparent finality of death. Only by faithfully persevering, like the women disciples, on the full "way" of Jesus by sharing in his ministry of service as well as in his suffering and death can we become true disciples and reliable witnesses of his resurrection as the hope of our ultimate triumph over death.

## Notes

1. On the feast of Passover and Unleavened Bread, see "Jewish Feasts" in Chapter I.
2. In Mark 7:21–23 "deceit" (*dolos*) is one of the evils that "come from within and defile a person."
3. Manicardi, *Il cammino,* 133–34.
4. According to *Harper's Bible Dictionary* (p. 988), spikenard was "a scented ointment or perfume imported from the Himalayas in alabaster boxes and opened on special occasions (Song of Sol. 1:12; 4:13, 14)." According to Lane (*Mark,* 492): "The costly perfume is identified as nard, the aromatic oil extracted from a root native to India. To retain the fragrance of nard, enough ointment for one application was sealed in small alabaster flasks. The long neck of the flask had to be broken to release the aroma."
5. In Mark 6:37 "two hundred days wages" is enough to buy bread for 5000. Jewish piety called for almsgiving especially during the time of Passover, when many poor pilgrims were present; see John 13:39.
6. F. Lentzen-Deis, "Passionsbericht als Handlungsmodell? Überlegungen zu Anstössen aus der "pragmatischen" Sprachwissenschaft für die exegetischen Methoden," *Der Prozess gegen Jesus: Historische Rückfrage und theologische Deutung* (QD 112; ed. K. Kertelge; Freiburg/Basel/Wien: Herder, 1988, 216–17.

7. See "Women and Children" in Chapter I.

8. Although, strictly speaking, the first day of Passover or Unleavened Bread began with the evening Passover meal, Mark includes the slaughter of the Passover lambs in the temple on the afternoon before the meal as part of the first day of Unleavened Bread.

9. A "man" carrying a jar of water is a distinctive sign, since usually women performed this task; see R. Pesch, *Das Markusevangelium: Kommentar zu Kap. 8, 27–16, 20* (HTKNT 2/2; Freiburg/Basel/Wien: Herder, 1977) 343.

10. Mark 4:38; 5:35; 9:17, 38; 10:17, 20, 35; 12:14, 19, 32; 13:1.

11. This is the last and climactic reference to Jesus as "teacher" in the Marcan narrative. For the previous references to his "teaching," see Mark 1:21–22, 27; 2:13; 4:1–2; 6:2, 6, 34; 8:31; 9:31; 10:1; 11:17–18; 12:14, 35, 38.

12. See "Suffering Servant and Suffering Just One" in Chapter I.

13. On the concept of covenant, see J. Behm, "*diathēkē*," *TDNT* 2.132–34; J. Unterman, "Covenant," *Harper's Bible Dictionary*, 190–92.

14. Note the salvific and liberating effect of the "blood" of God's "covenant" in Zech 9:11: "As for you also, because of the blood of my covenant with you, I will set your captives free from the waterless pit."

15. Jeremias, "*polloi*," 536–45.

16. Traditionally the Passover meal concluded with the singing of the "Hallel," Pss 113–18.

17. In Mark 6:1–6 Jesus is amazed by the "lack of faith" (6:6) demonstrated by the people of his home town when they "take offense" or "are scandalized" (6:3) by him.

18. "Papa" or "daddy" might be the English equivalent.

19. S. E. Dowd, *Prayer, Power, and the Problem of Suffering: Mark 11:22–25 in the Context of Markan Theology* (SBLDS 105; Atlanta: Scholars, 1988): "The narrative up to this point has emphasized God's power and willingness to eliminate suffering no less than the necessity for Jesus' suffering and death. It is the real possibility of divine rescue at this point in the narrative that makes the scene in Gethsemane so terrible (p. 157). . . . The scene is terrible, not because Jesus must suffer, but because his suffering is the will of the God who is powerful enough to prevent it, and who has eliminated so much suffering in the narrative prior to this scene" (p. 158).

20. The command to "watch and pray" is in the second person plural, indicating that it is directed not just to Peter but to the group of disciples.

21. Note the intensification of affection in the progression from "I shall kiss" (*philesō*, 14:44) to "he affectionately kissed (*katephilēsen*) him" (14:45). M. Zerwick and M. Grosvenor (*A Grammatical Analysis of*

*the Greek New Testament* [1st vol.; Rome: Biblical Institute, 1974, 158]) suggests for *katephilēsen* the translation: "he kissed him with every show of affection."

22. In Zech 13:7 a "sword" is the weapon which "strikes" the shepherd.

23. See "High Priest" in Chapter I.

24. See "Temple" in Chapter I.

25. This sentence is placed in parentheses because it is lacking in some important manuscripts.

26. See "King" in Chapter I.

27. Crucifixion was a form of execution widely employed by the Romans as a deterrent to rebellion.

28. The "purple robe" that King Alexander has Jonathan clothed in to honor him as an official "friend" of the king (1 Macc 10:59–66) is accompanied by a "golden crown" (1 Macc 10:20).

29. The earliest and best manuscripts omit verse 28, "And the scripture was fulfilled which says, 'And he was counted among the wicked' (Isa 53:12)." It may have been inserted from Luke 22:37.

30. "Myrrh" refers to an aromatic gum grown in Arabia, Abyssinia and India with narcotic qualities. According to Proverbs 31:6, "Give strong drink to him who is perishing, and wine to those in bitter distress."

# IX

---

# Mark 16:1-8

*The Resurrection of Jesus and the Way of the Lord.*

## Mark 16:1–8: Upon Hearing That Jesus Is Risen and Is Going to Galilee, the Women Flee from the Tomb in Fear

¹When the sabbath was over, Mary Magdalcne, Mary the mother of James, and Salome bought spices so that they might go and anoint him. ²Very early on the first day of the week they came to the tomb when the sun had risen. ³And they were saying to one another, "Who will roll back the stone for us from the entrance of the tomb?" ⁴And looking up, they saw that the stone had been rolled back; it was very large. ⁵Then entering the tomb, they saw a young man sitting on the right side, clothed in a white robe, and they were utterly amazed. ⁶He said to them, "Do not be amazed! You seek Jesus of Nazareth, the crucified. He has been raised! He is not here. Behold, the place where they laid him. ⁷But go and tell his disciples and Peter, 'He is going before you to Galilee; there you will see him, as he told you.' " ⁸Then they went out and ran away from the tomb, for trembling and astonishment had come upon them. And they said nothing to anyone, for they were afraid.

### 1. MEANING OF MARK 16:1-8

a. *16:1–4* When the women come to the tomb to anoint Jesus, they see that the large stone has been rolled back.

Once the sabbath, the day of rest following the burial of Jesus (15:42), had passed, three of the named women who had witnessed the crucifixion of Jesus, Mary Magdalene, Mary the mother of James (and Joses, 15:40,

47), and Salome (15:40–41), two of whom (the two named "Mary") had also witnessed his burial (15:47), "bought" spices in order to anoint the dead body of Jesus. Their desired intention to anoint Jesus with spices they have "bought" continues their "service" to him as disciples who have followed him from Galilee (15:41) and complements Joseph of Arimathea's concern to give Jesus a true and proper burial with the linen cloth he "bought" to wrap Jesus' body (15:46). Their wish to "anoint" the body of Jesus arouses dramatic tension for the reader, as it clashes with the fact that Jesus' body has already been anointed for burial by the woman at Bethany (14:3–9). These women, then, seemingly unaware that Jesus has already been anointed, are not expecting the fulfillment of Jesus' predictions that he would rise from the dead "after three days" (8:31; 9:31; 10:34) (16:1).

The women come to Jesus' tomb "very early on the first day of the week," that is, on the third day after his death, the time of his predicted resurrection. Besides accentuating their "very early" arrival, the notice that they come "when the sun had risen" not only indicates a new situation in contrast to the three hours of total darkness preceding the death of Jesus (15:33) but symbolically hints that Jesus, too, has already "risen" (16:2).

Having witnessed that Joseph of Arimathea had "rolled a stone against the entrance of the tomb" (15:46) after burying Jesus, the women generate added suspense as they acknowledge to one another their inability to remove the stone, which was "very large" (16:4), with their rhetorical question, "Who will roll back the stone for us from the entrance of the tomb?" (16:3). The suspense builds as they "look up" and see that the large stone already "had been rolled back." This mysterious and unexpected resolution to the problem preventing their entrance into the tomb not only enables them to enter it but gives them a new reason for entering it—to discover why the stone has already been rolled back (16:4).

**b. *16:5–7* A young man announces Jesus' resurrection and tells the women to direct the disciples to Galilee to see him.**

When the women enter the tomb, an "epiphany" or more exactly an "angelophany" commences.[1] They suddenly and unexpectedly "see" a mysterious "young man," who functions as the appearing "angel" of the angelophany (see Acts 1:10; 10:30; 2 Macc 3:26, 33). He is "sitting on the right side," that is, in a position of divine power and authority (12:36; 14:62), ready to deliver a divine revelation to the women. That he is "clothed in a white robe" confirms his status as an appropriately garbed heavenly figure (see 9:3), an "angel" or messenger sent by God. In accord with the conventions of the epiphany genre the women's initial reaction to the startling appearance of the "young man" as a heavenly figure is "utter amazement" (16:5).

Actualizing the comfort-bringing formula common to the epiphany genre, the angelic young man calms and reassures the women, "Do not be amazed!" (see 6:50). He then begins the revelatory message of the angelophany by acknowledging that the women have come to the tomb seeking Jesus of Nazareth as "the crucified" one. But the young man transforms their expectation of finding Jesus as the crucified one with his marvelous message that the crucified one "has been raised!" The young man thus confirms the fulfillment of the previous predictions of Jesus himself, that three days after his suffering and death he would be raised (8:31; 9:31; 10:34). Reinforcing the divine revelation of Jesus' resurrection, the young man asserts that "he is not here" in the tomb, the realm of the dead where the women seek him. As further evidence that Jesus has been raised, the young man invites the women to observe "the place," the now empty tomb, "where," as the women themselves had earlier witnessed (15:47), "they laid him" (16:6).

Having disclosed to the women the divine revelation of Jesus' resurrection, the young man indicates the role these women, as the privileged witnesses of the angelophany, are invited to play in extending this marvelous message to the rest of the disciples. He commands them to "go" and "tell" his disciples, all of whom had abandoned him like "scattered sheep" (14:27) when he was arrested (14:50–52), and Peter, the first-called and spokesman of the disciples, who had three times denied his close relationship with Jesus (14:66–72), the message that "he is going before you to Galilee; there you will see him, as he told you." That the risen Jesus is not in the tomb but "is going before you to Galilee" confirms the fulfillment of Jesus' previous promise of leading the disciples back to communion with him in Galilee after his resurrection, "as he told you" (14:28). And whereas Jesus was earlier "going before" his followers, leading them as they were amazed and afraid, on the "way" up to Jerusalem as the place of his suffering and death (10:32), he is now "going before" his disciples to Galilee, leading them back to the place of their close communion with him before they deserted him on his "way" to suffering and death. By "going before" his disciples to Galilee, the risen Jesus thus continues to lead, accomplish and actualize the salvific "way of the Lord" (1:2–3) as announced by John the Baptist at the beginning of the gospel:

*1:2–3* "Behold, I send my messenger before you,
who will prepare your *way*.
The voice of one crying in the wilderness:

'Make ready the *way of the Lord,*
    make straight his paths!' ''

*10:32*  They were on the *way,* going up to Jerusalem, and Jesus
        was *going before* them.

*14:28*  But after I have been raised up, I will *go before* you to
        Galilee.

*16:7*   He is *going before* you to Galilee; there you will see him,
        as he told you.

That in Galilee the disciples "will see" the risen Jesus who had been crucified means that they will then be enabled to fully understand and believe in him. This is confirmed by the fact that when the centurion "saw" how Jesus died he was able to confess his faith in Jesus and understand how he was "truly Son of God" by dying on the cross (15:39). This understanding and "believing" by the centurion after he "saw" how Jesus died on the cross contrasted the mocking provocation of the bystanders (15:35–36) and Jewish leaders, who wanted to "see" him come down from the cross in order to "believe" (15:31–32). When the disciples "see" in Galilee that Jesus, who remained on the cross, has now been raised from the dead, they will be able to understand and believe that he is not only the Christ, the King of Israel (15:32) but truly Son of God. And that they "will see" the risen Jesus in Galilee anticipates and assures the eventual "seeing" by disciples and the whole world of Jesus' final return as the gloriously triumphant Son of Man (13:26; 14:62).

That the risen Jesus is going before the disciples to "Galilee" means that he is leading them back to the place where he began proclaiming the gospel of God, announcing the arrival of God's kingdom and calling for repentance and faith in the gospel (1:14–15). Galilee is where the first disciples were invited to become "fishers of people" by leaving jobs and families to follow the "way" of Jesus and proclaim the gospel (1:16–20; 10:29–30). It was throughout "all of Galilee" that Jesus preached the gospel, healed and exorcised (1:28, 39). It was from Galilee that the gospel spread to all the surrounding regions (3:7–12) so that Jesus chose twelve disciples to be with him and gave them authority to preach the gospel and heal (3:13–19; 6:7–13). It was in Galilee that Jesus began revealing to the disciples "the mystery" of the kingdom of God (4:11).

When the disciples follow Jesus back to Galilee, then, they will be able to renew their discipleship by denying themselves, taking up their cross and following Jesus, so that they may save their lives by losing them for the sake of Jesus and the gospel (8:34–38). In and from Galilee they can continue their task of preaching the gospel and healing all peoples throughout the world (13:10; 14:9), playing their part in building God's new communal household of prayer composed of and open to all peoples of the world (11:17). The "beginning of the gospel of Jesus Christ, Son of God" (1:1) and the salvific "way of the Lord" actualized by the "way" of Jesus (1:2–3) is to be continued, extended and prolonged by the disciples who follow the dynamic "way" of the risen Jesus now "going before" and leading them back to and beyond "Galilee" (16:7).

### c. *16:8* The women run away from the tomb in fear and say nothing to anyone.

In response to the role offered them by the young man in the angelophany, the women, because they are completely overcome with "trembling and astonishment" by the awesome divine revelation of Jesus' resurrection, go out of and run away from the tomb. They are so overwhelmed with "fear" at their unexpected experience of the divincly given message of the resurrection of Jesus that they "said nothing to anyone." Their silence stands in ironic contrast to the previous failures of Jesus to silence the exciting message of his authoritative teaching and healing power as well as his profound identity (1:25, 34, 44–45; 3:11–12; 7:36).

Although for the integrity of the narrative it must be presumed that the women's silence is only temporary, it brings the narrative to an open-ended conclusion. Although the reader expects that the women will eventually relay the message of the young man to the disciples and Peter and that they will follow and "see" the risen Jesus in Galilee, this is not narrated. Instead, the end of the narrative places the reader, who identifies with both the disciples and the women and who has thus been given the message of the young man, in a position of deciding whether or not to follow the risen Jesus who "goes before" and leads him/her back to and beyond the "beginning" of the gospel in Galilee. By pointing back to the beginning in Galilee, the end of the narrative invites the reader to continue, extend and prolong, with the risen Jesus always and ever "going before" and leading the "way," the disciples' task of bringing and proclaiming the gospel of Jesus Christ, Son of God (1:1) not just to Galilee but beyond it to all peoples of the world (11:17; 13:10; 14:9). Returning to Galilee where Jesus' gospel of God's kingdom could not be kept secret and silent calls for the reader to make known the marvelous message of the triumphant resurrection of Jesus which the fearful women are too amazed and astonished to utter.

This concluding scene of the narrative, then, confronts the reader anew with following the salvific "way of the Lord" as actualized by the dynamic "way" of the now risen Jesus (1:2–3). At the end of the story the reader is placed "on the way" with the risen Jesus "going before" and leading him/her back to and beyond Galilee to "see," understand, believe and experience how Jesus is the Christ, the King of Israel and Son of God, who will return in final glory as Son of Man, by following his "way" which leads through humble and loving service, suffering and death to triumphant resurrection.

## 2. MARK 16:1-8 AS MODEL FOR ACTION

The women's reaction of extreme astonishment and fearful silence at the divine revelation of Jesus' resurrection makes us realize how overwhelmingly magnificent and truly extraordinary this message is. Their silent stupor induces us to dare to utter the unutterable message of Jesus' triumph over death and to invite others to follow the risen Jesus, who is ever and always going before and leading disciples back to and beyond Galilee to "see," understand and believe that he is the Christ, the Son of God, because he is the crucified one who is now the risen one.

The exhilarating message of the young man prompts us, despite our past desertions and denials of Jesus by failing to persevere on his "way" of service, suffering and death, to renew our discipleship by following the lead of the risen Jesus, who continually calls us back to and beyond the beginning of his gospel of God's kingdom for all peoples of the world. The concluding scene of Mark's gospel reminds us that we are ever and always "on the way" to "Galilee," called to become and remain disciples of Jesus by denying ourselves, taking up our crosses and following him (8:34), bearing witness to and proclaiming his gospel to all peoples and cultures of the world (11:17; 13:10; 14:9), despite persecutions and opposition (8:38; 10:29–30; 13:9–13). By following the lead of the risen Jesus back to and beyond Galilee, we can "see," understand and discover anew how Jesus is the risen Lord of the dynamic "way" that leads through humble service and the powerlessness of suffering and death to triumphant resurrection with power to build God's new community of prayer open to all peoples (11:17; 14:58; 15:29, 38) and to finally establish the kingdom of God. As the risen Lord of the "way," Jesus thus challenges and empowers us to follow the ongoing salvific "way of the Lord" (1:2–3) that he has actualized and set in motion for us.

## Note

1. For a definition of the literary genre of "epiphany," see Mark 4:37 in Chapter IV. The sea-rescue stories in Mark 4:35–41 and 6:45–52 as well as the transfiguration of Jesus in 9:2–8 all exemplify the "epiphany" genre.

# X

# Appendix: Mark 16:9–20

## The "Longer Ending" of Mark[1]

### Mark 16:9–20: The Risen Jesus Commissions and Empowers the Eleven Disciples To Preach the Gospel to All

[9]Having risen early on the first day of the week, he appeared first to Mary Magdalene, from whom he had expelled seven demons. [10]She went and told those who had been with him, who were mourning and weeping. [11]But when they heard that he was alive and had been seen by her, they did not believe.

[12]After this he appeared in another form to two of them walking along on their way to the country. [13]They went back and told the others; but they did not believe them either.

[14]Finally he appeared to the Eleven themselves as they sat at table, and he rebuked their unbelief and hardness of heart because they had not believed those who saw him after he had been raised. [15]He said to them, "Go into the whole world and proclaim the gospel to every creature. [16]Whoever believes and is baptized will be saved; whoever does not believe will be condemned. [17]These signs will accompany those who believe: in my name they will expel demons, they will speak new languages. [18]They will pick up serpents with their hands, and if they drink any deadly thing, it will not harm them. They will lay hands on the sick, and they will recover."

[19]So then the Lord Jesus, after he spoke to them, was taken up into heaven and took his seat at the right hand of God. [20]Then going forth they proclaimed everywhere, while the Lord worked with them and confirmed the word through accompanying signs.

### 1. MEANING OF MARK 16:9–20

**a.** *16:9–11* **After Jesus appears to Mary Magdalene, she tells those who had been with him, but they do not believe.**

After Jesus had "risen" from the dead "early on the first day of the week" (16:1–2), he appeared "first" to an individual woman, Mary Magdalene (15:40, 47; 16:1). That he appeared "first" to her creates the expectation of further appearances to others. Mary Magdalene is characterized as one who had personally experienced the salvific healing power of Jesus during his ministry. Indeed, he had expelled "seven demons" from her (see Luke 8:2), indicative that she had been freed from a very intense and serious case of demonic possession. The risen Jesus thus appears to one with whom he had already been personally associated through exorcism (16:9).

Having witnessed the risen Jesus, Mary Magdalene went and reported it to "those who had been with him," that is, those disciples specially privileged "to be with" Jesus during his ministry (3:14). That they were "mourning and weeping" expresses their loss of communion with Jesus because of his death but discloses their failure to understand his predictions that he would rise from the dead and be reunited with them (8:31; 9:10, 31; 10:34; 14:28) (16:10). When they heard Mary Magdalene's report that she had "seen" him "alive," tension develops as "they did not believe" (16:11).

**b.** *16:12–13* **Jesus appears to two who tell the rest, but they do not believe.**

After his appearance to Mary Magdalene Jesus appeared "in another form," that is, as a heavenly figure (see 9:2) raised from the dead, to two of them, that is, to two of the disciples who had earlier been with him (16:10). He appeared to them as they were leaving the city and walking along toward the country (16:12). They then returned to the city and reported Jesus' appearance to the other disciples, but they did not believe them. Tension mounts as the disciples of Jesus refuse to accept not only the individual witness of the woman, Mary Magdalene, but the testimony of "two" of their own group that Jesus is risen and alive (16:13).

**c.** *16:14–18* **After appearing to the Eleven, Jesus commissions them to preach the gospel to all.**

"Finally," as the climax of his gradual progression of resurrection appearances to more and more people, Jesus appeared to the group of "Eleven" disciples themselves, the special group of the "Twelve" (3:13–

19) minus Judas, who betrayed him (3:19; 14:10–11, 21). The risen Jesus appeared to the Eleven "as they sat at table," that is, in the context of the table fellowship they had enjoyed with him before his death (2:18–20; 6:30–44; 8:1–10; 14:3–9, 22–25). As the climactic response to the increasing tension of their failure to believe in his resurrection, he sharply "rebuked" their stubborn "hardness of heart" (3:5; 6:52; 10:5) and refusal to "believe" the testimony of Mary Magdalene and the other "two" disciples, who "saw him after he had been raised" (16:14).

Now that the Eleven have seen for themselves that Jesus has indeed been raised from the dead, he commissions and authorizes them to accomplish the task of global evangelization (3:14–15; 6:12–13; 13:10; 14:9) by going into the "whole world" and proclaiming the gospel of the arrival of God's kingdom (1:14–15) through the ministry, death and resurrection of Jesus Christ, Son of God (1:1) "to every creature" (16:15). Their preaching of the gospel throughout the world is crucial for enabling all the peoples of the world to make the critical decision to participate in God's end-time salvation. Those individuals who "believe" in the good news about Jesus and are ritually "baptized" as evidence of their repentance and belief (1:4–5,15), "will be saved" by God (divine passive) from condemnation in the last judgment. Accordingly, those who fail to believe in the gospel are warned that they "will be condemned" in the final judgment of God (16:16).

Furthermore, the risen Jesus promises that certain powerful "signs" will be manifested by those who do believe in the gospel. In the "name" or by the power of Jesus they will expel demons, and thus continue the exorcistic ministry of Jesus (3:15; 6:13) by extending and effecting throughout the whole world personal experiences of Jesus' liberation and salvation from the mysterious power of evil forces. That believers "will speak new languages" promises them the ability to communicate the gospel to all the various peoples and cultures of the world (Acts 2:4, 11) (16:17). The risen Jesus assures evangelizing believers of full divine protection from the hostile powers of evil. They will be able to handle the poisonous "serpents" (see Luke 10:19; Acts 28:3–6) and drink the deadly poison they may encounter from opponents in their task of evangelization without fear of being harmed. Empowered by Jesus to expel demons, believers will also share in and extend his healing ministry by laying their hands on the sick and curing them (6:13) (16:18).

**d. *16:19–20* After Jesus is taken up to heaven, the Eleven preach everywhere with the continuing help of the Lord.**

After the risen "Lord" Jesus "spoke" to the Eleven, authoritatively commissioning and empowering them for the task of global evangelization, he "was taken up into heaven" (see 2 Kgs 2:11), the transcendent realm of God, and was "enthroned" as "Lord" with divine power as he "took his seat at the right hand of God" (see Ps 110:1; Mk 12:36; 14:62) (16:19). In obedient response to the commission of the risen Jesus, the Eleven went forth and proclaimed the gospel "everywhere," that is, to the whole world and every creature, as Jesus had commanded (16:15). From his position of divine power and authority at God's right hand the risen and ascended Lord Jesus "worked with them" in their task of global evangelization and confirmed the "word" of the gospel through the "accompanying signs" of healing power, effective communication, and protection from evil forces that Jesus had promised believers (16:17–18). With the Lord Jesus assisting them from his seat at God's right hand, then, the Eleven disciples are enabled to bring the gospel of God's kingdom to all peoples and cultures of the world (16:20).

## 2. MARK 16:9–20 AS MODEL FOR ACTION

The risen Jesus' rebuke of the Eleven disciples' failure to believe those who saw him alive after he was raised from the dead induces us, who have not personally seen the risen Jesus, to base our faith upon the reliable testimony offered us by those who first experienced his resurrection.

Identifying with the disciples, we are called to continue their task of global evangelization by bringing the gospel of the arrival of the kingdom of God through the person of Jesus Christ, Son of God, to all the various peoples and cultures of the world. The enthronement of the risen and ascended Jesus at God's right hand assures us of his continual assistance and empowerment for this mission. Equipped with the powerful "signs" of divine healing, effective communication and divine protection from the menace of evil, we are enabled to confront all individuals throughout the world with the opportunity to believe and be baptized in order to participate in God's final and definitive salvation and victory over death.

## Note

1. Although it is not part of the original Gospel of Mark, this so-called "Longer Ending" of Mark has traditionally been included as part of the canonical gospel. Composed by the second century, it represents very early and authentic Christian tradition. It is termed the "Longer Ending" to distinguish it from the "Shorter Ending" found in some manuscripts:

"But they reported briefly to Peter and those with him all that they had been told. And after this Jesus himself sent out by means of them, from east to west, the sacred and imperishable proclamation of eternal salvation." Apparently these later "endings" were attempts to supplement the surprisingly abrupt conclusion of the original Gospel of Mark.

# Bibliography

Achtemeier, P. J. *Mark.* 2d ed. Philadelphia: Fortress, 1986.

Backhaus, K. " 'Dort werdet ihr Ihn sehen' (Mk 16, 7). Die redaktionelle Schussnotiz des zweiten Evangeliums als dessen christologische Summe." *TGl* 76 (1986) 277–94.

Barta, K. A. *The Gospel of Mark.* Message of Biblical Spirituality 9. Wilmington: Glazier, 1988.

Bartelmus, R. "Mk 2, 27 und die ältesten Fassungen des Arbeitsruhegebotes im AT. Biblisch-theologische Beobachtungen zur Sabbatfrage." *BN* 41 (1988) 41–64.

Bassler, J. M. "The Parable of the Loaves." *JR* 66 (1986) 157–72.

Beavis, M. A. "The Trial before the Sanhedrin (Mark 14:53–65): Reader Response and Greco-Roman Readers." *CBQ* 49 (1987) 581–96.

———. "Women as Models of Faith in Mark." *BTB* 18 (1988) 3–9.

Bennett, W. J. "The Herodians of Mark's Gospel." *NovT* 17 (1975) 9–14.

Best, E. *Following Jesus: Discipleship in the Gospel of Mark.* JSNTSup 4. Sheffield: JSOT, 1981.

———. *Mark: The Gospel as Story.* Edinburgh: T. & T. Clark, 1983.

———. "The Gospel of Mark: Who Was the Reader?" *IBS* 11 (1989) 124–32.

Biguzzi, G. *"Io distruggerò questo tempio":* Il tempio e il giudaismo nel vangelo di Marco. Rome: Pontificia Università Urbaniana, 1987.

Bishop, J. *"Parabole* and *Parrhesia* in Mark." *Int* 40 (1986) 39–52.

Black, D. A. "The Text of Mark 6.20." *NTS* 34 (1988) 141–45.

Boers, H. "Reflections on the Gospel of Mark: A Structural Investigation." SBLASP 26 (1987) 255–67.

Boomershine, T. E. *Mark, the Storyteller: A Rhetorical-Critical Investiga-*

*tion of Mark's Passion and Resurrection Narrative.* New York: Union Theological Seminary, 1974.

———. "Mark 16:8 and the Apostolic Commission." *JBL* 100 (1981) 225–39.

———. "Peter's Denial as Polemic or Confession: The Implications of Media Criticism for Biblical Hermeneutics." *Orality, Aurality, and Biblical Narrative.* Semeia 39. Ed. L. Silberman. Decatur: Scholars, 1987, 47–68.

Boomershine, T. E. and Bartholomew, G. L. "The Narrative Technique of Mark 16:8." *JBL* 100 (1981) 213–23.

Booth, R. P. *Jesus and the Laws of Purity: Tradition History and Legal History in Mark 7.* JSNTSup 13. Sheffield: JSOT, 1986.

Bratcher, R. G. and Nida, E. A. *A Translator's Handbook on the Gospel of Mark.* Leiden: Brill, 1961.

Breytenbach, C. "Das Markusevangelium als episodische Erzählung. Mit Überlegungen zum 'Aufbau' des zweiten Evangeliums." *Der Erzähler des Evangeliums: Methodische Neuansätze in der Markus-forschung.* Ed. F. Hahn. Stuttgart: Katholisches Bibelwerk, 1985, 137–69.

Brower, K. "Elijah in the Markan Passion Narrative." *JSNT* 18 (1983) 85–101.

Brown, R. E. "The Burial of Jesus (Mark 15:42–47)." *CBQ* 50 (1988) 233–45.

Burchard, C. "Markus 15:34." *ZNW* 74 (1983) 1–11.

Caragounis, C. C. *The Son of Man: Vision and Interpretation.* WUNT 38. Tübingen: Mohr-Siebeck, 1986.

Casey, P. M. "Culture and Historicity: The Plucking of the Grain (Mark 2:23–28)." *NTS* 34 (1988) 1–23.

Caza, L. "Le relief que Marc a donné au cri de la croix." *ScEs* 39 (1987) 171–91.

Chronis, H. L. "The Torn Veil: Cultus and Christology in Mark 15:37–39." *JBL* 101 (1982) 97–114.

Collins, A. Y. "The Origin of the Designation of Jesus as 'Son of Man'." *HTR* 80 (1987) 391–407.

Cook, M. J. *Mark's Treatment of the Jewish Leaders.* NovTSup 51. Leiden: Brill, 1978.

Cosby, M. R. "Mark 14:51–52 and the Problem of Gospel Narrative." *Perspectives in Religious Studies* 11 (1984) 219–31.

Cotter, W. J. " 'For It Was Not the Season for Figs'." *CBQ* 48 (1986) 62–66.

Couffignal, R. " 'Les femmes au tombeau et le jeune homme en blanc.' Approches nouvelles de Marc, XVI, 1–8." *RevThom* 87 (1987) 642–54.

Crockett, B. R. "The Function of Mathetological Prayer in Mark." *IBS* 10 (1988) 123–39.

Culpepper, R. A. "The Passion and the Resurrection in Mark." *RevExp* 75 (1978) 583–600.

————. "Mark 10:50: Why Mention the Garment?" *JBL* 101 (1982) 131–32.

Davis, P. G. "Mark's Christological Paradox." *JSNT* 35 (1989) 3–18.

Dewey, J. *Markan Public Debate: Literary Technique, Concentric Structure, and Theology in Mark 2:1–3:6.* SBLDS 48. Chico: Scholars, 1980.

————. "Point of View and the Disciples in Mark." SBLASP 21 (1982) 97–106.

————. "Oral Methods of Structuring Narrative in Mark." *Int* 43 (1989) 32–44.

Dodd, C. H. *The Parables of the Kingdom.* New York: Charles Scribner's Sons, 1961.

Donahue, J. R. *Are You the Christ? The Trial Narrative in the Gospel of Mark.* SBLDS 10. Missoula: Scholars, 1973.

————. "Jesus as the Parable of God in the Gospel of Mark." *Int* 32 (1978) 369–86.

————. *The Theology and Setting of Discipleship in the Gospel of Mark.* Milwaukee: Marquette University, 1983.

————. *The Gospel in Parable: Metaphor, Narrative, and Theology in the Synoptic Gospels.* Philadelphia: Fortress, 1988.

————. "Mark." *Harper's Bible Commentary.* Ed. J. L. Mays. San Francisco: Harper & Row, 1988, 983–1009.

Doohan, L. *Mark: Visionary of Early Christianity.* Santa Fe, NM: Bear & Co., 1986.

Dormeyer, D. "Die Kompositionsmetapher 'Evangelium Jesu Christi, des Sohnes Gottes' Mk 1.1. Ihre Theologische und Literarische Aufgabe in der Jesus-Biographie des Markus." *NTS* 33 (1987) 452–68.

Dowd, S. E. *Prayer, Power, and the Problem of Suffering: Mark 11:22–25 in the Context of Markan Theology.* SBLDS 105. Atlanta: Scholars, 1988.

Drury, J. "Mark." *The Literary Guide to the Bible.* Ed. R. Alter and F. Kermode. Cambridge: Harvard University, 1987, 402–17.

Edwards, J. R. "Markan Sandwiches: The Significance of Interpolations in Markan Narratives." *NovT* 31 (1989) 193–216.

Ernst, J. *Das Evangelium nach Markus.* RNT. Regensburg: Pustet, 1981.

Evans, C. A. "The Function of Isaiah 6:9–10 in Mark and John." *NovT* 24 (1982) 124–38.

Fay, G. "Introduction to Incomprehension: The Literary Structure of Mark 4:1–34." *CBQ* 51 (1989) 65–81.

Feldmeier, R. *Die Krisis des Gottessohnes: Die Gethsemaneerzählung als Schlüssel der Markuspassion.* WUNT 2/21. Tübingen: Mohr-Siebeck, 1987.

Fiorenza, E. S. *In Memory of Her: A Feminist Theological Reconstruction of Christian Origins.* New York: Crossroad, 1983.

Fitzpatrick, M. "From Ritual Observance to Ethics: The Argument of Mark 7:1–23." *AusBR* 35 (1987) 22–27.

Fleddermann, H. "The Flight of a Naked Young Man (Mark 14:51–52)." *CBQ* 41 (1979) 412–18.

———. "The Discipleship Discourse (Mark 9:33–50)." *CBQ* 43 (1981) 57–75.

———. "A Warning about the Scribes (Mark 12:37b–40)." *CBQ* 44 (1982) 52–67.

———. " 'And He Wanted to Pass by Them' (Mark 6:48c)." *CBQ* 45 (1983) 389–95.

Focant, C. "L'Incompréhension des Disciples dans le deuxième Evangile." *RB* 82 (1975) 161–85.

Fowler, R. M. *Loaves and Fishes: The Function of the Feeding Stories in the Gospel of Mark.* SBLDS 54. Chico: Scholars, 1981.

———. *Let the Reader Understand: Reader-Response Criticism and the Gospel of Mark.* Minneapolis: Fortress, 1991.

———. "Who is 'the Reader' of Mark's Gospel?" SBLASP 22 (1983) 31–53.

Freyne, S. "The Disciples in Mark and the *maskilim* in Daniel. A Comparison." *JSNT* 16 (1982) 7–23.

———. *Galilee, Jesus and the Gospels: Literary Approaches and Historical Investigations.* Philadelphia: Fortress, 1988.

Funk, R. W. "Gospel of Mark: Parables and Aphorisms." *Forum* 4, 3 (1988) 124–43.

Fusco, V. *Parola e regno: La sezione delle parabole (Mc. 4, 1–34) nella prospettiva marciana.* Aloisiana 13. Brescia: Morcelliana, 1980.

———. "L'économie de la Révélation dans l'evangile de Marc." *NRT* 104 (1982) 532–54.

Garland, D. E. " 'I Am the Lord Your Healer': Mark 1:21–2:12." *RevExp* 85 (1988) 327–43.

Giesen, H. "Der Auferstandene und seine Gemeinde. Zum Inhalt und zur Funktion des ursprünglichen Markusschlusses (16, 1–8)." SUNT 12 (1987) 99–139.

———. "Dämonenaustreibungen—Erweis der Nähe der Herrschaft Gottes. Zu Mk 1,21–28." *Theologie der Gegenwart* 32 (1989) 24–37.

Gill, A. "Women Ministers in the Gospel of Mark." *AusBR* 35 (1987) 14–21.

Gnilka, J. *Das Evangelium nach Markus: (Mk 1–8, 26).* EKKNT 2/1. Zürich: Benziger/Neukirchener, 1978.

———. *Das Evangelium nach Markus: (Mk 8, 27–16, 20).* EKKNT 2/2. Zürich: Benziger/Neukirchener, 1979.

Grassi, J. A. "Abba, Father (Mark 14:36): Another Approach." *JAAR* 50 (1982) 449–58.

———. "The Secret Heroine of Mark's Drama." *BTB* 18 (1988) 10–15.

———. *The Hidden Heroes of the Gospels: Feminine Counterparts of Jesus.* Collegeville, MN: Liturgical Press, 1989.

Haacker, K. "Kaisertribut und Gottesdienst (Eine Auslegung von Markus 12, 13–17)." *TBei* 17 (1986) 285–92.

Harrington, D. J. "A Map of Books on Mark." *BTB* 15 (1985) 12–16.

———. "The Gospel According to Mark." *The New Jerome Biblical Commentary.* Ed. R. E. Brown, J. A. Fitzmyer and R. E. Murphy. Englewood Cliffs: Prentice Hall, 1990, 596–629.

Hartman, L. *Prophecy Interpreted: The Formation of Some Jewish Apocalyptic Texts and of the Eschatological Discourse Mark 13 Par.* ConBNT 1. Lund: Gleerup, 1966.

Hatton, H. A. "Unraveling the Agents and Events." *BT* 37 (1986) 417–20.

Hedrick, C. W. "What Is a Gospel? Geography, Time and Narrative Structure." *Perspectives in Religious Studies* 10 (1983) 255–68.

———. "The Role of 'Summary Statements' in the Composition of the

Gospel of Mark: A Dialog with Karl Schmidt and Norman Perrin." *NovT* 26 (1984) 289–311.

———. "Narrator and Story in the Gospel of Mark: *Hermeneia* and *Paradosis.*" *Perspectives in Religious Studies* 14 (1987) 239–58.

Heil, J. P. *Jesus Walking on the Sea: Meaning and Gospel Functions of Matt 14:22–33, Mark 6:45–52 and John 6:15b–21.* AnBib 87. Rome: Biblical Institute, 1981.

———. "Interpreting the Miracles of Jesus." *McKendree Pastoral Review* 3 (1986) 15–45.

Hengel, M. "Mc 7,3 *pygme:* Die Geschichte einer exegetischen Aporie und der Versuch ihrer Lösung." *ZNW* 60 (1969) 182–98.

———. *Studies in the Gospel of Mark.* Philadelphia: Fortress, 1985.

Hollenbach, B. "Lest They Should Turn and Be Forgiven: Irony." *BT* 34 (1983) 312–21.

Hre Kio, S. "A Prayer Framework in Mark 11." *BT* 37 (1986) 323–28.

Humphrey, H. "Jesus as Wisdom in Mark." *BTB* 19 (1989) 48–53.

Jackson, H. M. "The Death of Jesus in Mark and the Miracle from the Cross." *NTS* 33 (1987) 16–37.

Jeremias, J. *The Parables of Jesus.* New York: Charles Scribner's Sons, 1963.

Johnson, E. S. "Is Mark 15.39 the Key to Mark's Christology?" *JSNT* 31 (1987) 3–22.

Juel, D. *Messiah and Temple.* SBLDS 31. Missoula: Scholars, 1977.

Kealy, S. P. *Mark's Gospel: A History of Its Interpretation. From the Beginning until 1979.* New York: Paulist, 1982.

Kee, H. C. "The Function of Scriptural Quotations and Allusions in Mark 11–16." *Jesus und Paulus.* W. G. Kümmel Festschrift. Ed. E. E. Ellis and E. Grässer. Göttingen: Vandenhoeck & Ruprecht, 1975, 165–88.

———. *Community of the New Age: Studies in Mark's Gospel.* Philadelphia: Westminster, 1977.

———. *Miracle in the Early Christian World: A Study in Sociohistorical Method.* New Haven: Yale University, 1983.

———. *Medicine, Miracle and Magic in New Testament Times.* SNTSMS 55. Cambridge: Cambridge University, 1986.

Keegan, T. J. *Interpreting the Bible: A Popular Introduction to Biblical Hermeneutics.* Mahwah: Paulist, 1985.

Kelber, W. H. *Mark's Story of Jesus.* Philadelphia: Fortress, 1979.

———. *The Oral and the Written Gospel: The Hermeneutics of Speaking and Writing in the Synoptic Tradition, Mark, Paul, and Q.* Philadelphia: Fortress, 1983.

———. "Narrative as Interpretation and Interpretation of Narrative: Hermeneutical Reflections on the Gospels." *Orality, Aurality, and Biblical Narrative.* Semeia 39. Ed. L. Silberman. Decatur: Scholars, 1987, 107–33.

———. "Narrative and Disclosure: Mechanisms of Concealing, Revealing, and Reveiling." *Genre, Narrativity, and Theology.* Semeia 43. Ed. M. Gerhart and J. G. Williams. Atlanta: Scholars, 1988, 1–20.

Keller, J. "Jesus and the Critics: A Logico-Critical Analysis of the Marcan Confrontations." *Int* 40 (1986) 29–38.

Kermode, F. *The Genesis of Secrecy: On the Interpretation of Narrative.* Cambridge: Harvard University, 1979.

Kilgallen, J. *A Brief Commentary on the Gospel of Mark.* Mahwah: Paulist, 1989.

Kingsbury, J. D. *Conflict in Mark: Jesus, Authorities, Disciples.* Minneapolis: Fortress, 1989.

Klauck, H.-J. "Die erzählerische Rolle der Jünger im Markusevangelium. Eine narrative Analyse." *NovT* 24 (1982) 1–26.

Kort, W. A. *Story, Text, and Scripture: Literary Interests in Biblical Narrative.* University Park: Pennsylvania State University, 1988.

Körtner, H. J. "Das Fischmotiv im Speisungswunder." *ZNW* 75 (1984) 24–35.

Lane, W. L. *The Gospel According to Mark: The English Text with Introduction, Exposition and Notes.* NICNT. Grand Rapids: Eerdmans, 1974.

Lattke, M. "Salz der Freundschaft in Mk 9:50c." *ZNW* 75 (1984) 44–59.

Lee-Pollard, D. A. "Powerlessness as Power: A Key Emphasis in the Gospel of Mark." *SJT* 40 (1987) 173–88.

Lemcio, E. E. "The Intention of the Evangelist, Mark." *NTS* 32 (1986) 187–206.

Lentzen-Deis, F. *Die Taufe Jesu nach den Synoptikern: Literarkritische und gattungsgeschichtliche Untersuchungen.* Frankfurter Theologische Studien 4. Frankfurt: Knecht, 1970.

————. "The Gospel between Myth and Historicity—as Demonstrated in the Account about the Baptism of Jesus." *Tantur Yearbook* (1980–81) 165–86.

————. "Passionsbericht als Handlungsmodell? Überlegungen zu Anstössen aus der 'pragmatischen' Sprachwissenschaft für die exegetischen Methoden." *Der Prozess gegen Jesus: Historische Rückfrage und theologische Deutung.* QD 112. Ed. K. Kertelge. Freiburg/Basel/Wien: Herder, 1988, 191–232.

Lincoln, A. T. "The Promise and the Failure: Mark 16:7, 8." *JBL* 108 (1989) 283–300.

Lohfink, G. "Das Gleichnis von Sämann (Mk 4, 3–9)." *BZ* 30 (1986) 36–69.

Lohse, E. *The New Testament Environment.* Nashville: Abingdon, 1976.

Lührmann, D. *Das Markusevangelium.* HNT 3. Tübingen: Mohr-Siebeck, 1987.

————. "Die Pharisäer und die Schriftgelehrten im Markusevangelium." *ZNW* 78 (1987) 169–85.

Mack, B. L. *A Myth of Innocence: Mark and Christian Origins.* Philadelphia: Fortress, 1988.

Magness, J. L. *Sense and Absence: Structure and Suspension in the Ending of Mark's Gospel.* Atlanta: Scholars, 1986.

Malbon, E. S. "Galilee and Jerusalem: History and Literature in Marcan Interpretation." *CBQ* 44 (1982) 242–55.

————. "Fallible Followers: Women and Men in the Gospel of Mark." *The Bible and Feminist Hermeneutics.* Semeia 28. Ed. M. A. Tolbert. Chico: Scholars, 1983, 29–48.

————. "The Jesus of Mark and the Sea of Galilee." *JBL* 103 (1984) 363–77.

————. "*Tēoikia autou:* Mark 2.15 in Context." *NTS* 31 (1985) 282–92.

————. "Mark: Myth and Parable." *BTB* 16 (1986) 8–17.

————. *Narrative Space and Mythic Meaning in Mark.* San Francisco: Harper & Row, 1986.

————. "Disciples/Crowds/Whoever: Markan Characters and Readers." *NovT* 28 (1986) 104–30.

————. "The Jewish Leaders in the Gospel of Mark: A Literary Study of Marcan Characterization." *JBL* 108 (1989) 259–81.

Malina, B. J. "A Conflict Approach to Mark 7." *Forum* 4, 3 (1988) 3–30.

Manicardi, E. *Il cammino di Gesù nel Vangelo di Marco: Schema narrativo e tema cristologico.* AnBib 96. Rome: Biblical Institute, 1981.

Mann, C. S. *Mark: A New Translation with Introduction and Commentary.* AB 27. Garden City, NY: Doubleday, 1986.

Mansfield, M. R. *"Spirit and Gospel" in Mark.* Peabody, MA: Hendrickson, 1987.

Marcus, J. "Mark 4:10–12 and Marcan Epistemology." *JBL* 103 (1984) 557–74.

———. *The Mystery of the Kingdom of God.* SBLDS 90. Atlanta: Scholars, 1986.

———. "Entering into the Kingly Power of God." *JBL* 107 (1988) 663–75.

———. "Mark 14:61: 'Are You the Messiah-Son-of-God?' " *NovT* 31 (1989) 125–41.

———. "Mark 9, 11–13: 'As It Has Been Written'." *ZNW* 80 (1989) 42–63.

Marshall, C. D. *Faith as a Theme in Mark's Narrative.* SNTSMS 64. Cambridge: Cambridge University, 1989.

Matera, F. J. *The Kingship of Jesus: Composition and Theology in Mark 15.* SBLDS 66. Chico: Scholars, 1982.

———. *Passion Narratives and Gospel Theologies: Interpreting the Synoptics through Their Passion Stories.* Mahwah: Paulist, 1986.

———. *What Are They Saying About Mark?* Mahwah: Paulist, 1987.

———. "The Prologue as the Interpretative Key to Mark's Gospel." *JSNT* 34 (1988) 3–20.

———. "The Incomprehension of the Disciples and Peter's Confession (Mark 6, 14–8, 30)." *Bib* 70 (1989) 153–72.

Mauser, U. W. *Christ in the Wilderness: The Wilderness Theme in the Second Gospel and its Basis in the Biblical Tradition.* SBT 39. Naperville, IL: Allenson, 1963.

May, D. M. "Mark 3:20–35 from the Perspective of Shame/Honor." *BTB* 17 (1987) 83–87.

Mazzucco, C. "L'arresto di Gesù nel Vangelo di Marco (Mc 14, 43–52)." *RivB* 35 (1987) 257–82.

McCowen, A. *Personal Mark: An Actor's Proclamation of St. Mark's Gospel.* New York: Crossroad, 1985.

McVann, M. "Conjectures About a Guilty Bystander: The Sword Slashing in Mark 14:47." *Listening* 21 (1986) 124–37.

———. "The Passion in Mark: Transformation Ritual." *BTB* 18 (1988) 96–101.

Meyer, B. F. "The Expiation Motif in the Eucharistic Words: A Key to the History of Jesus?" *Greg* 69 (1988) 461–87.

Moo, D. J. *The Old Testament in the Gospel Passion Narratives.* Sheffield: Almond, 1983.

Moore, S. D. "Narrative Commentaries on the Bible: Context, Roots, and Prospects." *Forum* 3, 3 (1987) 29–62.

———. "Stories of Reading: Doing Gospel Criticism As/With a 'Reader'." SBLASP 27 (1988) 141–59.

Motyer, S. "The Rending of the Veil: A Markan Pentecost?" *NTS* 33 (1987) 155–57.

Munro, W. "Women Disciples in Mark?" *CBQ* 44 (1982) 225–41.

Myers, C. *Binding the Strong Man: A Political Reading of Mark's Story of Jesus.* Maryknoll, NY: Orbis, 1988.

Neyrey, J. H. "The Idea of Purity in Mark's Gospel." *Social-Scientific Criticism of the New Testament and Its Social World.* Semeia 35. Ed. J. H. Elliott. Decatur: Scholars, 1986, 91–128.

———. "A Symbolic Approach to Mark 7." *Forum* 4, 3 (1988) 63–91.

Nickelsburg, G. "The Genre and Function of the Markan Passion Narrative." *HTR* 73 (1980) 153–84.

Nineham, D. E. *Saint Mark.* Baltimore: Penguin, 1963.

O'Collins, G. "The Fearful Silence of Three Women (Mark 16:8c)." *Greg* 69 (1988) 489–503.

Ong, W. J. "Text as Interpretation: Mark and After." *Orality, Aurality, and Biblical Narrative.* Semeia 39. Ed. L. Silberman. Decatur: Scholars, 1987, 7–26.

Overman, J. A. "The God-Fearers: Some Neglected Features." *JSNT* 32 (1988) 17–26.

Parsons, M. C. " 'Allegorizing Allegory': Narrative Analysis and Parable Interpretation." *Perspectives in Religious Studies* 15 (1988) 147–64.

Patten, P. "The Form and Function of Parable in Select Apocalyptic Literature and Their Significance for Parables in the Gospel of Mark." *NTS* 29 (1983) 246–58.

Pavur, C. M. "The Grain is Ripe: Parabolic Meaning in Mark 4:26–29." *BTB* 17 (1987) 21–23.

Peabody, D. B. *Mark as Composer.* New Gospel Studies 1. Macon, GA: Mercer University, 1987.

Pesch, R. *Das Markusevangelium: Einleitung und Kommentar zu Kap. 1, 1–8, 26.* HTKNT 2/1. Freiburg/Basel/Wien: Herder, 1976.

———. *Das Markusevangelium: Kommentar zu Kap. 8, 27–16, 20.* HTKNT 2/2. Freiburg/Basel/Wien: Herder, 1977.

Petersen, N. R. " 'Point of View' in Mark's Narrative." *The Poetics of Faith: Essays Offered to Amos Niven Wilder: Part 1: Rhetoric, Eschatology, and Ethics in the New Testament.* Semeia 12. Ed. W. A. Beardslee. Missoula: Scholars, 1978, 97–121.

———. "When is the End not the End? Literary Reflections on the Ending of Mark's Narrative." *Int* 34 (1980) 151–66.

———. "The Reader in the Gospel." *Neot* 18 (1984) 38–51.

Pilch, J. J. "A Structural Functional Analysis of Mark 7." *Forum* 4, 3 (1988) 31–62.

Pimentel, P. "The 'unclean spirits' of St. Mark's Gospel." *ExpTim* 99 (1988) 173–75.

Ramaroson, L. " 'Parole-semence' ou 'Peuple-semence' dans la parabole du Semeur?" *ScEs* 40 (1988) 91–101.

Rebell, W. " 'Sein Leben verlieren' (Mark 8.35 parr.) als Strukturmoment vor- und nachösterlichen Glaubens." *NTS* 35 (1989) 202–18.

Resseguie, J. L. "Reader-Response Criticism and the Synoptic Gospels." *JAAR* 52 (1984) 307–24.

Reynolds, S. M. "*Pygme* (Mark 7,3) as 'Cupped Hand'." *JBL* 85 (1966) 87–88.

———. "A Note on Dr. Hengel's Interpretation of *pygme* in Mark 7, 3." *ZNW* 62 (1971) 295–96.

Rhoads, D. "Narrative Criticism and the Gospel of Mark." *JAAR* 50 (1982) 411–34.

Rhoads, D. and Michie, D. *Mark as Story: An Introduction to the Narrative of a Gospel.* Philadelphia: Fortress, 1982.

Robbins, V. K. *Jesus the Teacher: A Socio-Rhetorical Interpretation of Mark.* Philadelphia: Fortress, 1984.

———. "Pronouncement Stories from a Rhetorical Perspective." *Forum* 4, 2 (1988) 3–32.

Roth, W. *Hebrew Gospel: Cracking the Code of Mark.* Oak Park, IL: Meyer-Stone, 1988.

Rowley, H. H. "The Herodians in the Gospels." *JTS* 41 (1940) 14–27.

Saldarini, A. J. *Pharisees, Scribes and Sadducees in Palestinian Society: A Sociological Approach.* Wilmington: Glazier, 1988.

———. "Political and Social Roles of the Pharisees and Scribes in Galilee." SBLASP 27 (1988) 200–209.

Schenke, L. "Der Aufbau des Markusevangeliums—ein hermeneutischer Schlüssel?" *BN* 32 (1986) 54–82.

Schottroff, L. "Maria Magdalena und die Frauen am Grabe Jesu." *EvT* 42 (1982) 3–25.

Schwankl, O. "Die Sadduzäerfrage (Mk 12,18–27) und die Auferstehungserwartung Jesu." *Wissenschaft und Weisheit* 50 (1987) 81–92.

Sellew, P. "Beelzebul in Mark 3: Dialogue, Story, or Sayings Cluster?" *Forum* 4, 3 (1988) 93–108.

Selvidge, M. J. " 'And Those Who Followed Feared' (Mark 10:32)." *CBQ* 45 (1983) 396–400.

———. "Mark 5:25–34 and Leviticus 15:19–20." *JBL* 103 (1984) 619–23.

Senior, D. *The Passion of Jesus in the Gospel of Mark.* Wilmington: Glazier, 1984.

———. " 'With Swords and Clubs . . .'—The Setting of Mark's Community and His Critique of Abusive Power." *BTB* 17 (1987) 10–20.

Smith, S. H. "The Role of Jesus' Opponents in the Markan Drama." *NTS* 35 (1989) 161–82.

———. "The Literary Structure of Mark 11:1–12:40." *NovT* 31 (1989) 104–24.

Snodgrass, K. *The Parable of the Wicked Tenants: An Inquiry into Parable Interpretation.* WUNT 27. Tübingen: Mohr-Siebeck, 1983.

Söding, T. "Die Nachfolgeforderung Jesu im Markusevangelium." *TTZ* 94 (1985) 292–310.

———. "Gebet und Gebetsmahnung Jesu in Getsemani. Eine redaktionskritische Auslegung von Mk 14, 32–42." *BZ* 31 (1987) 76–100.

Standaert, B. *L'évangile selon Marc: Commentaire.* Lire la Bible 61. Paris: Les Editions du Cerf, 1983.

Stegemann, E. W. "Zur Rolle von Petrus, Jakobus und Johannes im Markusevangelium." *TZ* 42 (1986) 366–74.

Steinhauser, M. G. "The Form of the Bartimaeus Narrative (Mark 10.46–52)." *NTS* 32 (1986) 583–95.

Stenger, W. "Die Grundlegung des Evangeliums von Jesus Christus. Zur kompositionellen Struktur des Markusevangeliums." *LB* 61 (1988) 7–56.

Stevens, B. A. " 'Why "must" the Son of Man suffer?' The Divine Warrior in the Gospel of Mark." *BZ* 31 (1987) 101–10.

Stock, A. *Call to Discipleship: A Literary Study of Mark's Gospel.* GNS 1. Wilmington: Glazier, 1982.

———. *The Method and Message of Mark.* Wilmington: Glazier, 1989.

Stock, K. *Boten aus dem Mit-Ihm-Sein: Das Verhältnis zwischen Jesus und den Zwölf nach Markus.* AnBib 70. Rome: Biblical Institute, 1975.

———. "Das Bekenntnis des Centurio. Mk 15,39 im Rahmen des Markusevangeliums." *ZKT* 100 (1978) 289–301.

———. "Gliederung und Zusammenhang in Mk 11–12." *Bib* 59 (1978) 481–515.

Stuhlmann, R. "Beobachtungen und Überlegungen zu Markus 4:26–29." *NTS* 19 (1973) 153–62.

Sweetland, D. M. *Our Journey with Jesus: Discipleship according to Mark.* GNS 22. Wilmington: Glazier, 1987.

Swetnam, J. "No Sign of Jonah." *Bib* 66 (1985) 126–30.

Tannehill, R. C. *The Sword of His Mouth.* Philadelphia: Fortress, 1975.

———. "The Disciples in Mark: The Function of a Narrative Role." *JR* 57 (1977) 386–405.

———. "The Gospel of Mark as Narrative Christology." *Perspectives on Mark's Gospel.* Semeia 16. Ed. N. R. Petersen. Missoula: Scholars, 1979, 57–95.

———. "Attitudinal Shift in Synoptic Pronouncement Stories." *Orientation by Disorientation: Studies in Literary Criticism and Biblical Literary Criticism.* Ed. R. A. Spencer. Pittsburgh: Pickwick, 1980, 183–97.

———. "Tension in Synoptic Sayings and Stories." *Int* 34 (1980) 138–50.

———. "Introduction: The Pronouncement Story and its Types." *Pronouncement Stories.* Semeia 20. Ed. R. C. Tannehill. Chico: Scholars, 1981, 1–13.

———. "Varieties of Synoptic Pronouncement Stories." *Pronouncement Stories.* Semeia 20. Ed. R. C. Tannehill. Chico: Scholars, 1981, 101–19.

Theissen, G. *The Miracle Stories of the Early Christian Tradition.* Philadelphia: Fortress, 1983.

————. "Lokal- und Sozialkolorit in der Geschichte von der syrophönikischen Frau (Mk 7:24–30)." *ZNW* 75 (1984) 202–25.

Thomas, J. C. "A Reconsideration of the Ending of Mark." *JETS* 26 (1983) 407–19.

Thompson, M. R. *The Role of Disbelief in Mark: A New Approach to the Second Gospel.* Mahwah: Paulist, 1989.

Tolbert, M. A. *Sowing the Gospel: Mark's World in Literary-Rhetorical Perspective.* Minneapolis; Fortress, 1989.

Tuckett, C. M. "Mark's Concerns in the Parables Chapter (Mark 4, 1–34)." *Bib* 69 (1988) 1–26.

van Iersel, B. *Reading Mark.* Collegeville: Liturgical Press, 1988.

Via, D. O. *The Ethics of Mark's Gospel—In the Middle of Time.* Philadelphia: Fortress, 1985.

————. "Irony as Hope in Mark's Gospel: A Reply to Werner Kelber." *Genre, Narrativity, and Theology.* Semeia 43. Ed. M. Gerhart and J. G. Williams. Atlanta: Scholars, 1988, 21–27.

Viviano, B. T. "The High Priest's Servant's Ear: Mark 14:47." *RB* 96 (1989) 71–80.

von Wahlde, U. C. "Mark 9:33–50: Discipleship: The Authority That Serves." *BZ* 29 (1985) 49–67.

Vorster, W. S. "Mark: Collector, Redactor, Author, Narrator?" *Journal of Theology for Southern Africa* 31 (1980) 46–61.

————. "The Function of the Use of the Old Testament in Mark." *Neot* 14 (1981) 62–72.

————. "Meaning and Reference: The Parables of Jesus in Mark 4." *Text and Reality: Aspects of Reference in Biblical Texts.* Ed. B. C. Lategan and W. S. Vorster. Atlanta: Scholars, 1985, 27–65.

————. "Literary Reflections on Mark 13:5–37: A Narrated Speech of Jesus." *Neot* 21 (1987) 203–24.

————. "Characterization of Peter in the Gospel of Mark." *Neot* 21 (1987) 57–76.

Waetjen, H. C. *A Reordering of Power: A Socio-Political Reading of Mark's Gospel.* Minneapolis: Fortress, 1989.

Wallace, M. I. "Parsimony of Presence in Mark: Narratology, the Reader and Genre Analysis in Paul Ricoeur." *SR* 18 (1989) 201–12.

Walsh, R. G. "Tragic Dimensions in Mark." *BTB* 19 (1989) 94–99.

White, J. L. "Beware of Leavened Bread. Markan Imagery in the Last Supper." *Forum* 3, 4 (1987) 49–63.

Williams, J. G. *Gospel Against Parable: Mark's Language of Mystery.* Decatur: Almond, 1985.

Wright, A. G. "The Widow's Mites: Praise or Lament?—A Matter of Context." *CBQ* 44 (1982) 256–65.

Wright, J. "Spirit and Wilderness: The Interplay of Two Motifs within the Hebrew Bible as a Background to Mark 1:2–13." *Perspectives on Language and Text: Essays and Poems in Honor of Francis I. Andersen's Sixtieth Birthday July 28, 1985.* Ed. E. W. Conrad and E. G. Newing. Winona Lake: Eisenbrauns, 1987, 269–98.

Zmijewski, J. "Die Sohn-Gottes-Prädikation im Markusevangelium. Zur Frage einer eigenständigen markinischen Titelchristologie." SUNT 12 (1987) 5–34.

# Scripture Index

371